AF793065

The Real Living Wage

The Real Living Wage

Civil Regulation and the Employment Relationship

EDMUND HEERY
DEBORAH HANN
AND
DAVID NASH

OXFORD
UNIVERSITY PRESS

OXFORD
UNIVERSITY PRESS

Great Clarendon Street, Oxford, OX2 6DP,
United Kingdom

Oxford University Press is a department of the University of Oxford.
It furthers the University's objective of excellence in research, scholarship,
and education by publishing worldwide. Oxford is a registered trade mark of
Oxford University Press in the UK and in certain other countries

© Edmund Heery, Deborah Hann and David Nash 2023

The moral rights of the authors have been asserted

All rights reserved. No part of this publication may be reproduced, stored in
a retrieval system, or transmitted, in any form or by any means, without the
prior permission in writing of Oxford University Press, or as expressly permitted
by law, by licence or under terms agreed with the appropriate reprographics
rights organization. Enquiries concerning reproduction outside the scope of the
above should be sent to the Rights Department, Oxford University Press, at the
address above

You must not circulate this work in any other form
and you must impose this same condition on any acquirer

Published in the United States of America by Oxford University Press
198 Madison Avenue, New York, NY 10016, United States of America

British Library Cataloguing in Publication Data
Data available

Library of Congress Control Number: 2023932439

ISBN 978–0–19–883526–4

DOI: 10.1093/oso/9780198835264.001.0001

Printed and bound by
CPI Group (UK) Ltd, Croydon, CR0 4YY

Links to third party websites are provided by Oxford in good faith and
for information only. Oxford disclaims any responsibility for the materials
contained in any third party website referenced in this work.

To our families for their support and to the memory of Willy Brown, a great industrial relationist who taught us a great deal about pay and its centrality to the employment relationship

Preface

This book presents a multimethod case study of the campaign to promote the UK's Real Living Wage, a voluntary standard developed and promoted by Citizens UK, the British arm of the community organizing movement. Since 2011, an organizational offshoot of Citizens UK, the Living Wage Foundation, has accredited employers that agree to pay the Living Wage, and in this period nearly 13,000 organizations have joined the accreditation scheme. Tens of thousands of low-wage workers, found in all parts of the economy and all parts of the country, have benefitted as a result. The Living Wage scheme, we believe, is an impressive example of what can be described as 'civil regulation', the growth of employment norms, standards, and rules of behaviour created by civil society organizations, like Citizens UK.

Our research began in 2014 when we noticed that the website of the Living Wage Foundation listed all accredited Living Wage Employers and thought that identifying the characteristics of these businesses would make an excellent student dissertation. Our students proved unreceptive, and so we decided to generate a dataset of Living Wage Employers ourselves. Since then the project has grown like Topsy, identifying new themes and adding additional methods. In 2015, for instance, we began an interview programme to explore the trade union response to the Living Wage campaign, while a year later we carried out a survey of all Living Wage Employers, an exercise that we repeated in 2021. We have also conducted interviews with employers and campaigners. As this book goes to press, the research continues, and we are still maintaining our database of Living Wage Employers, observing campaign events, and adding to an extensive archive of the Living Wage campaign.

Throughout the project we have worked closely with the Living Wage Foundation, and we are extremely grateful for the support the Foundation team has given to our research, including helping to fund our 2016 and 2021 employer surveys. We have tried to reciprocate, and over the past eight years we have produced reports, briefings, and research notes for the Living Wage Foundation and its partner organizations, Cynnal Cymru in Wales and the Poverty Alliance in Scotland. We have also spoken at campaign events, presenting evidence on the benefits of the campaign for employees and employers and on the important part that public authorities and place-based campaigns can play in spreading a voluntary standard of this kind. Cardiff Business School is a member of the Citizens UK network, and in recent years our students have become involved in Living Wage campaign activity as part of their programmes of study. Today, they are highly receptive to learning about the role of business in society through the medium of the Living Wage.

Although we are active supporters of the Living Wage campaign, we feel it is important to stress that this book is not an example of scholar-activism. *The Real Living Wage* is a research monograph that seeks to present an evidence-based assessment of the Living Wage campaign, which we hope is balanced and judicious. We hope that supporters of the campaign and sceptics will both accept that the book offers a fair account. The Living Wage campaign and the civil regulation which it has produced are noteworthy developments in the UK's system of employment relations, and we believe it is important that they should be described, explained, and assessed. This book attempts to perform these tasks, presenting a sympathetic but independent overview of the Living Wage campaign.

Many people have helped us in developing our case study of the Living Wage campaign. We owe a particular debt of gratitude to those at Citizens UK and the Living Wage Foundation, who have provided data, facilitated interviews, helped in the design of surveys, invited us to meetings and campaign actions, supported our students, and answered our questions. We would particularly like to thank the following, without whom the project would not have been possible: Lynn Anderson, Mari Arthur, Katherine Chapman, Jonathan Cox, Jessica Goble, Clare Goff, Graham Griffiths, Shaheen Hasmet, Sam Hepher, Sarah Hopkins, Dan Howard, Sara Johnson, Emma Kosmin, Tess Lanning, Mara Lilley, Lola McEvoy, John Paxton, Michael Pugh, Caroline Reilly, Joe Richardson, and Alistair Rooms.

An important facet of our research has involved looking at the interface between the trade union movement and the Living Wage campaign, and we have received excellent cooperation both from the TUC and its member unions. We are especially grateful to the following for helping us develop this element of the research project: Alex Bevan, Matthew Egan, Chris Fabby, Laurie Heselden, Nick Ireland, Tony Lennon, Kevin Lucas, Kevan Nelson, Mike Payne, Paul Sellars, Peter Urwin, and Dave Watson.

Much of the information presented in the chapters that follow comes from employers, who have completed questionnaires, agreed to interviews, and provided us with background information. We are very grateful to all who have helped us in these ways. Amongst the ranks of our employer contacts, some have provided additional support, suggesting lines of inquiry and identifying other interviewees. We are particularly grateful to help of this kind that we have received from Peter Allan, Adele Cope, Laurence Hopkins, Leigh Hudson, Tim Knowles, Guy Leach, Derek Miller, Guy Stallard, Jayne Sadgrove, and Diggory Steele.

A final group of people who have supported our research are academic colleagues, both at Cardiff University and beyond. Fellow researchers have provided references, offered comments and suggestions, advised on data collection, and given us moral support. Cardiff Business School has also helped fund the research and provided tangible support for survey data collection and research travel.

We are particularly grateful to the support we have received from the following: Rachel Ashworth, Helen Blakely, Calum Carson, Martha Crawford, Rhys Davies, Steve Davies, Tony Dobbins, Alan Felstead, Leon Gooberman, Marco Hauptmeier, Calvin Jones, Katy Huxley, Jean Jenkins, Kevin Morgan, Celia Netanta, Mike Peel, Peter Prowse, and Steve Williams.

While many have helped us, the usual disclaimer applies. We are solely responsible for the book and any sins of commission or omission that it contains; any errors, infelicities, or missteps are ours alone.

August 2022

Contents

List of Figures

List of Tables

List of Abbreviations

ASHE	Annual Survey of Hours and Earnings
BECTU	Broadcasting, Entertainment, Communications, and Theatre Union
BEIS	Department for Business, Energy, and Industrial Strategy
BitC	Business in the Community
CSO	Civil Society Organization
CSR	Corporate Social Responsibility
EU	European Union
FE	Further Education
FTSE100	*The Financial Times* Stock Exchange 100 index
HMRC	Her Majesty's Revenue and Customs
HR	Human Resources
IWGB	Independent Workers' Union of Great Britain
LGBT	Lesbian, Gay, Bisexual, Trans
MIS	Minimum Income Standard
NGO	Non-Governmental Organization
NHS	National Health Service
NLW	National Living Wage
NMW	National Minimum Wage
NUPE	National Union of Public Employees
OECD	Organization of Economic Cooperation and Development
ONS	Office of National Statistics
PCS	Public and Commercial Services Union
PFI	Private Finance Initiative
RSA	Royal Society for Arts, Manufactures, and Commerce
RSP	Recognized Service Provider
QMUL	Queen Mary University of London
SEIU	Service Employees International Union
SNP	Scottish National Party
SOAS	School of Oriental and African Studies
STUC	Scottish Trades Union Congress
TUC	Trades Union Congress
UCATT	Union of Construction, Allied Trades, and Technicians (now part of UNITE)
UCU	University and College Union
UK	United Kingdom
USDAW	Union of Shop, Distributive, and Allied Workers
UVW	United Voices of the World
V&A	Victoria and Albert Museum
WTUC	Wales Trades Union Congress

Note on Terminology

The title of our book is *The Real Living Wage*. This title reflects the fact that campaigners use the prefix 'real' to differentiate the voluntary Living Wage, promoted by Citizens UK and the Living Wage Foundation, from the National Living Wage, the name given to the highest adult statutory minimum wage in the UK since 2016. The voluntary Living Wage is based on research into the expenditure needs of low-wage families, whereas the National Living Wage is set at a percentage of median hourly pay. The use of the word 'real' is intended to highlight this difference and to point to the fact that it is only the Real Living Wage that is based on an estimate of what wage employees need to enjoy a decent standard of living. Our survey of accredited organizations in 2016, moreover, revealed a strong preference for the Real Living Wage label among Living Wage Employers. In the text that follows we have often dropped the 'real' prefix and refer to the Living Wage (capitalized). Similarly, we refer to Living Wage Employers, Living Wage Places, and Living Wage Funders. The reason for dropping the prefix is simply one of brevity, but it is important to note that when capitals are used, the Living Wage refers to the Real Living Wage. Capitals are not used when we are referring to the principle or broader concept of the 'living wage' rather than the specific labour market standard promoted by Citizens UK and the Living Wage Foundation. When we mention the National Living Wage, the text always uses the full title or the abbreviation NLW.

1
Civil Regulation

Announcing the Living Wage, 2016

At a ceremony attended by more than 200 employers and campaigners at the British Library in October 2016, Sadiq Kahn, Mayor of London, announced a new rate for the London Living Wage of £9.75 per hour. Simultaneously, at equivalent events in Cardiff and in Airdrie, Carwyn Jones, then First Minister of Wales, and Nicola Sturgeon, First Minister of Scotland, announced that the out-of-London Living Wage was rising to £8.45 per hour. All three announcements were arranged by Citizens UK, the civil society organization behind the UK Living Wage campaign, acting in conjunction with its Scottish and Welsh allies, the Poverty Alliance in Scotland, and Cynnal Cymru in Wales. The announcements themselves were examples of what has been described as 'civil regulation' (Williams et al. 2011), the unilateral formulation of standards and norms of good management practice by civil society organizations that they seek to have adopted by employers. Regulation of this kind is a growing feature of the economies of many countries and has attracted the attention of researchers and commentators, some of whom are critical in their assessment and some of whom are favourable (*cf.* Freeman 2005; Wills and Linneker 2013). The purpose of this book is to provide an analysis of the Living Wage in the United Kingdom and to use this experience as a critical case both to reflect on the phenomenon of civil regulation and to intervene in the debate between its supporters and detractors. The Living Wage has been adopted in the UK by nearly 13,000 employers, covers ten per cent of the workforce, and has led to often substantial increases in pay for tens of thousands of low-wage workers. It is a striking example of the impact of civil society on the employment relationship, and in what follows we present a broad-based account of this important development.

The three announcement ceremonies in England, Scotland, and Wales followed a common format and together provide insight into the nature of the Living Wage campaign. They were called to announce the new rates of the London and UK Living Wage and emphasized both that these rates were based on independent research into the expenditure needs of low-wage families and were substantially above the statutory minimum wage, including the confusingly titled National Living Wage, a higher statutory minimum wage for workers aged 25 and over that was introduced by the UK Government earlier that year. The Citizens UK rate is often described as the Real Living Wage to differentiate it from the statutory National Living Wage, which is not based on estimates of the income needs of those on low

The Real Living Wage. Edmund Heery, Deborah Hann and David Nash, Oxford University Press.
© Edmund Heery, Deborah Hann and David Nash (2023). DOI: 10.1093/oso/9780198835264.003.0001

pay. The ceremonies also emphasized the pressing need for the Living Wage, with evidence cited at all three ceremonies of the great extent of low-pay and in-work poverty in the UK labour market. At the event in Airdrie, for instance, Peter Kelly of the Poverty Alliance stressed that 430,000 Scottish workers were receiving less than the Living Wage, an increase on the previous year, and declared: 'That's why it's more important than ever for leading employers to join the growing movement of businesses and organizations that are going further than the government minimum and making sure their employees earn enough to cover the real cost of living'.

As Kelly's comment makes clear, the 'real' Living Wage is a voluntary standard that the campaign seeks to persuade employers to adopt. Reflecting this purpose, all three ceremonies were 'business-friendly' events, hosted by recently accredited Living Wage Employers—the British Library, Cardiff City Council, and the Bell Group, a Scottish-based painting and decorating contractor—with an invited employer audience and prominent business representatives amongst the speakers. The event in London was led by Katherine Chapman, Director of the Living Wage Foundation, the business-facing division within Citizens UK which accredits organizations that adopt the Living Wage, and which promotes the standard to employers. In her remarks and in those of co-campaigners in Scotland and Wales, there was a particular stress on the 'business case' for the Living Wage and the tangible benefits that accrue to employers that adopt the standard, including improvements in recruitment, retention, and employee performance. Business speakers echoed these arguments but also stressed the inherent rightness of adopting the Living Wage. Roly Keating, Chief Executive of the British Library, declared that the decision to become a Living Wage Employer was in line with the organization's values and the desire to treat all within it with 'respect and consideration'. There was a 'moral case' for signing up to the Living Wage, he said: 'It was easy, simple, and right'.

The three ceremonies also provided insight into the nature of the Living Wage campaign and the methods used by campaigners. Citizens UK is a network of largely faith-based organizations, and representatives of religious organizations were notable amongst those attending the events and amongst the speakers. The accreditation of the British Library as a Living Wage Employer, indeed, began when two representatives of a local church asked to meet with management and raised the question of the organization signing up to the Living Wage. The ceremonies also prominently featured video and direct testimony from those affected by the Living Wage, a notable campaign technique of the community organizing movement of which Citizens UK is a part (Walls 2015). In London, a young woman from the furniture company IKEA gave testimony as to the difference the Living Wage had made to her life: it had enabled her to belatedly go on honeymoon with her partner a year after their wedding and allowed her to pay off debts accumulated before IKEA introduced the Living Wage. In a manner that reinforced the business-friendly nature of the event, she spoke of her gratitude to her employer and declared she was 'proud to work for IKEA'.

Testimony was also given at the London event by a group of Camden schoolgirls, whose parents had benefitted from the Living Wage. Children often take part in Citizens UK events, and the girls attested both to the disruptive effects of low pay on family life, requiring parents to work excessive hours, and the improvements that flowed from being paid the Living Wage. The Living Wage campaign originated in the East End of London in the early 2000s when a 'listening exercise' by the predecessor of Citizens UK, The East London Citizens Organization (TELCO), found that long hours of work and multiple jobs often imposed a major strain on family life. The campaign was launched to address this issue and to enable low-paid workers to participate more fully in both community and family life. Integral to the latter objective was a belief that stronger families enable social mobility, providing a supportive context in which youngsters from low-income families can best realize their potential. This future-orientation of the campaign was underlined at the British Library event by a senior executive from the insurance company Aviva, who stated that it was important for businesses to 'care more and leave a positive legacy ... to be a good ancestor'.

While presenting testimony is one campaign method, expressing thanks and rewarding those who support the Living Wage is another. Indeed, the two methods often merge when employees receiving the Living Wage publicly thank their employers, as at IKEA. At all three announcement ceremonies awards were given to employers and to campaigners who had made a special commitment and acted as Living Wage champions. In London, there was special acknowledgement of the part played by the accountancy firm KPMG, with an award both for the company and for one of its executives, Mike Kelly, who had been seconded to the Living Wage campaign and acted as a champion of the standard within both KPMG and the wider world of business over a period of ten years. While reinforcing good employer behaviour through awards is one aspect of the Living Wage campaign, however, another is exposing those who fail to pay the rate. The three announcement ceremonies took place in Living Wage Week, the height of the campaigning year with multiple events taking place to highlight the campaign and secure media attention. Amongst this programme of activity were events targeted at non-compliant employers. In Wales, for instance, a group of campaigners organized a whisky tasting at Penderyn distillery during Living Wage Week to expose the fact that the business did not pay the Living Wage and to call upon it, as an iconic Welsh brand, to become accredited. Shaming non-paying businesses in this way through actions that expose failure to pay the Living Wage in a manner likely to attract media attention is the other side of Living Wage campaigning.

Trade union representatives were present at all three award ceremonies, and unions are part of the coalition of forces that has promoted the Living Wage. Unions did not play a prominent part at any of the ceremonies, however, and while they have supported the Living Wage and encouraged its adoption, they are not the main initiators of the campaign. Indeed, there is a degree of ambivalence in union support for the Living Wage, and tension has arisen between Citizens UK and some within the trade union movement. The Living Wage is illustrative of a new form of industrial relations, in which civil society organizations speak on behalf of workers and seek to generate civil regulation on their behalf. The relationship between this new form and the older pattern of industrial relations, based on worker representation through trade unions and collective bargaining, is complex, characterized by both mutual reinforcement and occasional antagonism. The Living Wage provides insight into this complex relationship, in which new institutions of worker voice and employment regulation sit alongside the old.

While trade unionists did not play a prominent role at the ceremonies, politicians most certainly did. Political leaders announced the new rates for the Living Wage, and the location of the events in London, Airdrie, and Cardiff points to the importance of constitutional devolution in promoting the emergence of distinctive national and regional patterns of employment relations (Samuel and Bacon 2015). All three political leaders offered strong support for the Living Wage, which has attracted backing from all the main political parties in the UK, a fact that reflects the popularity of measures of this kind. In London, Scotland, and Wales politicians have used their devolved powers to promote the Living Wage, with a particular emphasis on using procurement to encourage its adoption by private sector suppliers (Heery et al. 2020). For this reason, winning political support for the Living Wage has been a major objective of the campaign. Campaigners have sought to use political influence to amplify the impact of the Living Wage, enlisting the support of national, regional, and local politicians to supplement direct approaches to employers. The political dimension to the Living Wage campaign is one of its most striking aspects, indicative of a fresh preparedness to use the power of the state to intervene within and shape the employment relationship; a reversal of the deregulatory thrust of much public policy over the past three decades.

The themes visible in the three announcement ceremonies are explored in the book that follows. The book examines, in turn, (1) the properties of the Living Wage as a form of voluntary, civil regulation; (2) the nature of the Living Wage campaign, the civil society organizations behind it, and the methods they have used; (3) the response to the campaign of employers, including the characteristics and motivations of employers that have signed up to the standard; (4) the response to the Living Wage of trade unions and the degree this has been characterized by cooperation or conflict; and (5) the politics of the Living Wage and its role within public policy. In addition, the book seeks to evaluate the Living Wage, assessing to what extent it has been successful in combatting low pay and the validity of the claim that there is a 'business case' for paying the Living Wage. The plan of the book is presented further and in more elaborate form below, but before then it is necessary to describe the context in which the Living Wage campaign has emerged and the extent of the problem of low pay to which it is a response.

The Problem of Low Pay

The UK labour market is characterized by extensive low pay, with large numbers of workers subsisting on wages at or slightly above the statutory minimum. There are several ways in which the scale of this problem can be measured (D'Arcy 2018). 'Core' low-pay measures the percentage of employees whose hourly rate, excluding overtime and premium payments, is below two-thirds of the median hourly rate of pay of all workers. A 'wage-floor' definition, in contrast, embraces those employees earning below, at, or one per cent above the age-appropriate minimum wage and is used to measure those on bare, subsistence rates of pay. Another option is to use a 'needs-based' definition, which includes those earning below the Real Living Wage. Estimates of the latter kind have been produced each year from 2011 by the Resolution Foundation, a research and policy organization that focuses on low-pay and in-work poverty. The estimates are derived from the ONS Annual Survey of Hours and Earnings (ASHE) and report the number of employee jobs (not employees) that are paid below either the London or the UK Living Wage, as appropriate.

Table 1.1 shows the number and percentage of employee jobs across the UK that were paid below the Living Wage for the years for which data are available. It indicates that for most of the period more than a fifth of jobs were low-paid, in

Table 1.1 Employee jobs paid below the Living Wage, 2011–2021

Year	Number of jobs (000s)	Percentage of jobs
2011	4,660	22
2012	4,787	20
2013	4,865	20
2014	5,695	22
2015	6,270	23
2016	6,160	23
2017	5,910	22
2018	6,535	24
2019	5,795	21
2020	5,847	21
2021	4,540	17

Source: Resolution Foundation, *Low Pay Britain* (multiple years); available at https://www.resolutionfoundation.org

the sense of offering a wage that is insufficient to provide the modest but decent standard of living that the Living Wage is meant to ensure. The table also indicates, however, that there has been a reduction in the number and percentage of low-paid jobs in recent years, which is probably due to the positive impact of the government's National Living Wage, the higher statutory rate for those aged 25 and over that was introduced in 2016 (Cominetti et al. 2022). Despite this amelioration, however, the table demonstrates that the UK faces a substantial and persistent problem of low pay.

The Resolution Foundation analysis also demonstrates that low pay is distributed unevenly across the UK labour market and tends to be concentrated in jobs with specific characteristics and amongst certain types of workers. Evidence to this effect is presented in Table 1.2, which shows estimates for 2020 for the number of low-paid workers performing jobs with specific characteristics, and this figure is expressed both as a percentage of workers in each category and as a percentage of all who are paid below the Living Wage. Thus, the table indicates that there is a gender dimension to the distribution of low pay, in that 3.5 million women were paid below the Living Wage in that year, twenty-five per cent of all women employees and fifty-nine per cent of all low-paid workers, while the equivalent figures for men were 2.4 million and eighteen and forty-one per cent.

Apart from sex, the table indicates that both younger and older workers are likely to be low-paid, as are those working part-time and on temporary contracts; non-standard or atypical work, the data suggest, often carries a wage penalty. It also indicates that low pay is related to occupation, with large percentages of workers in elementary, sales and customer service, and personal service occupations being paid below the Living Wage. Perhaps unsurprisingly, those in occupations that require lower levels of formal qualification are more at risk of low pay.

Another risk factor is the branch of economic activity in which a job is located. There are striking industry differences in the incidence of low pay: two thirds of workers in hospitality earn below the Living Wage and more than a third do so in retail and wholesale trade, arts and recreation, agriculture, and administrative services, which includes office cleaning and security. In contrast, in finance, public administration, and information and communications, the percentages of low-paid jobs are relatively small. A final thing to note about the relationship between low pay and economic activity is that there is a relatively high percentage of low-paid workers in both small employing organizations and in the very largest. Small organizations are particularly likely to pay low wages, but nearly a quarter of jobs in the largest employing organizations are also low-paid. Some of the largest businesses in the UK are found in retail, entertainment, hospitality, and business services, and many of these organizations contain large concentrations of low-paid employment.

The final evidence contained in Table 1.2 shows that there is a geographical aspect to the distribution of low pay, and the table demonstrates that the percentage

Table 1.2 Low pay and job characteristics, 2020

Job characteristics	Number of jobs below Real Living Wage (000s)	% in group below threshold	% all below threshold
All employees	5,847	21	100
Sex			
Women	3,478	25	59
Men	2,369	18	41
Age			
16–20	928	74	16
21–24	711	39	12
25–30	751	20	13
31–35	528	16	9
36–40	482	15	8
41–45	449	15	8
46–50	496	15	8
51–55	503	16	9
56–60	486	19	8
61–65	335	23	6
66+	176	30	3
Hours worked			
Part-time	2,987	37	51
Full-time	2,860	15	49
Contract			
Temporary/casual	636	29	11
Permanent	5,211	21	89
Occupation			
Elementary	1,606	56	27
Sales & customer service	1,073	51	18
Personal services	964	37	16
Process & machinery operatives	446	31	8
Skilled trades	506	26	9
Admin & secretarial	587	20	10
Managers & senior officials	195	6	3
Assoc professional & technical	331	8	6
Professional	139	2	2
Industry			
Hotels & restaurants	809	68	14
Wholesale & retail	1,541	39	26
Agriculture	72	37	1
Arts & recreation	197	36	3
Admin & support services	517	34	9
Other service activities	178	33	3
Health & social work	800	19	14

Continued

Table 1.2 *Continued*

Job characteristics	Number of jobs below Real Living Wage (000s)	% in group below threshold	% all below threshold
Manufacturing	495	19	8
Construction	182	17	3
Water supply & waste	29	15	0
Real estate	57	14	1
Education	470	11	8
Transport & storage	145	13	2
Professional & technical	215	11	4
Information & communications	67	6	1
Public administration	36	3	1
Finance	33	3	1
Organization size			
0–9 employees	953	37	16
10–49 employees	1,277	30	22
50–249 employees	890	24	15
250–4999 employees	1,146	20	20
5000+ employees	1,123	24	19
Nation & region			
East Midlands	467	24	8
Yorkshire & the Humber	546	24	9
North-East	234	24	4
Wales	294	24	5
South-West	561	24	10
West Midlands	540	23	9
North-West	680	23	12
East of England	542	21	9
London	828	20	14
South-East	764	18	13
Scotland	392	16	7

Source: Cominetti et al. (2021)

of low-paid jobs is significantly higher in some parts of the country than in others. In the North-East, Yorkshire, East Midlands, Wales, and the South-West, twenty-four per cent of jobs are low-paid, while in Scotland and the South-East the figure drops below twenty per cent. Indeed, it is only in these latter two regions and in London that the percentage of low-paid jobs falls below the national average. It is also important to note that there are significant intra-regional differences in the distribution of low pay, which are particularly apparent in London. While the London region has a relatively low percentage of jobs paid below the Living Wage, there are parts of London with very high percentages of low-paid employment. In outer London boroughs, such as Brent, Enfield, Harrow, Redbridge, Sutton, and

Waltham Forest, well over a third of jobs are paid below the London Living Wage. In inner London, in Camden, the City of London, Islington, Tower Hamlets, and Westminster, in contrast, between five and thirteen per cent of jobs are low-paid. In interpreting these figures, it is important to remember that the estimates refer to the location of jobs rather than workers: many affluent commuters from Harrow and Sutton will travel to high paid jobs in the City of London. Nevertheless, the figures underline the geographical aspect to the UK's problem of low pay, with concentrations of low-paid employment found within specific localities.

The evidence presented above indicates that low pay is a persistent and substantial feature of the UK labour market. But in what sense is low pay problematic and on what grounds might it be deemed undesirable? One way of answering these questions is to identify the problematic features of low-paid employment for those who experience it. The first problematic feature is that for many, low pay is a life-sentence, an enduring feature of a life-time career. To be sure, some transition through low-paid employment, using it as a temporary source of income before moving to higher-paid work. According to the Resolution Foundation, however, only about a sixth of low-paid workers make a transition of this kind, with the remainder either staying in low-paid work or cycling between jobs with higher pay and those with low pay (D'Arcy 2018; D'Arcy and Finch 2017; see also Shildrick et al. 2010). Remaining stuck in low-paid employment is more likely for women, those who are older, those in the private sector, those who work in sales and customer service, and those in elementary occupations.

A second problematic feature is that many low-paid jobs have other negative features that compound the problem of low pay: they are 'bad' jobs that have conditions that are less favourable than those found in higher-paid employment. Qualitative research by the Resolution Foundation, for example, found that while low-paid workers often enjoyed aspects of the work they did, they also noted disadvantages, particularly with regard to working time. Low-paid workers working full-time complained of the need to work long, unsociable hours to make ends meet—as we have seen similar complaints helped trigger the Living Wage campaign—while part-timers complained both of insufficient hours and of unpredictable schedules that disrupted family life (D'Arcy 2017; see also Blyton and Jenkins 2012; Clark and Colling 2018; Smith and McBride 2021). Accounts by journalists who have worked undercover in low-wage employment have identified similar problems with working time, and note also the use of intrusive management control and disrespectful treatment of low-paid employees, which at the extreme lurches into coercion and abuse (Bloodworth 2018; Toynbee 2003).

More formal, quantitative research has further examined the features of low-paid work. This research indicates that not all negative job features are associated with low pay: the low-paid are less likely to experience high levels of effort intensity than those in high paid employment (Green et al. 2015; see also Williams et al. 2020). Nevertheless, there is evidence that attests to the multiple disadvantages of low-paid employment. Low-paid work provides fewer opportunities to use skills and exercise discretion (Green et al. 2015; see also Williams et al. 2020); low-paid workers are more likely to experience unemployment and can be locked in a 'low pay, no pay' cycle (Cominetti et al. 2022; Stewart 1999); and low pay is associated with reduced access to positive employment features, such as training and fringe benefits (Sutherland 2016; see also Social Mobility Commission 2019). Moreover, a study by the Resolution Foundation of monthly salary payments into bank accounts found that the low-paid were more likely to experience 'pay volatility', including substantial reductions in month-to-month income over a period of one year (Tomlinson 2018). Other negative aspects of the employment relationship, therefore, frequently compound the disadvantage of low pay.

A third problematic feature of low pay is that it can lead to poverty. Of course, this is not always the case: many low-paid workers live in households with other sources of income that act as a shield against poverty. Nevertheless, for many others being on low pay means a difficult existence characterized by deprivation. According to the annual review published by the Joseph Rowntree Foundation, 14 million people in the UK, twenty-two per cent of the population, were living in poverty in 2019 (defined as an income below sixty per cent of the median for their family type) (Joseph Rowntree Foundation 2020). A majority of those experiencing poverty (fifty-six per cent) live in a family in which someone works, and the percentage of those working who experience poverty has risen from ten to thirteen per cent over the past twenty years. Those working part-time, in single-worker households, the disabled, members of ethnic minorities, and people employed in hospitality, agriculture, administrative support services, and retail are most likely to experience in-work poverty. It is noteworthy that the increase in the value of the statutory minimum wage and the introduction of the higher National Living Wage in 2016 have not been sufficient to reverse the growth in in-work poverty, as cuts to benefits and tax credits have wiped out any gains in income. Moreover, many low-paid workers have been adversely affected by the COVID-19 epidemic, experiencing further reduction of their incomes (Joseph Rowntree Foundation 2021).

The impact of poverty is severe and has powerful negative consequences for quality of life. Those on low pay and those in low-income households are notably more likely to report poor life satisfaction and an absence of subjective well-being (Bangham 2019; see also Marmot et al. 2020). In addition, those on low incomes are more likely to experience mental and other health problems, live in areas with high rates of mortality, experience family and relationship difficulties, lack savings, and run into debt. Low pay is a major contributing factor to these problems, interacting with changes in the benefit system, high housing costs, and rates of inflation that have reduced real incomes, to push a substantial percentage of the UK working population into poverty. For many, paid work has ceased to provide a route to a decent standard of living.

While low pay often has serious adverse consequences for those who experience it, it can also carry substantial negative consequences for the wider economy and society. Conclusions of this kind are necessarily more speculative but feature prominently in the literature on low pay. With regard to the economy, it has been argued that the large number of low-paid jobs in the United Kingdom both form a constituent part of and reinforce business strategies that focus on cost-reduction, rely upon on low levels of skill, and generate low productivity. An economy disproportionately reliant on strategies of this kind, it is argued, not only imposes costs on the working population but cannot sustain desirable rates of growth into the future (Grimshaw et al. 2008). A parallel argument has been made with regard to the social costs of low pay. As we have seen, low pay can be a source of poverty, with all its attendant deprivations and need for palliative responses. In addition, the exposure of a large percentage of the population to low pay exacerbates the more general problems of income and wealth inequality. The vast degree of inequality seen in contemporary Britain is a social ill, not simply on moral grounds but because it intensifies a series of other problems that range from increased criminality and substance abuse to lower levels of social mobility (Green et al. 2015). Low pay, therefore, exerts both direct and indirect negative influences on society.

A final adverse consequence of low pay lies within the political sphere. The rise of populist movements and the related decline of social democracy have been attributed to declining economic conditions for those in the bottom third of the labour market, particularly in the period since the global financial crisis (Crouch 2019; Zielonka 2018). Britain's own populist paroxysm, the vote in favour of Brexit, has often been interpreted in this way, as a rebellion of the 'left behind' (Goodwin and Heath 2016). We feel that this interpretation needs to be qualified: there were cultural, ideological, ethnic, generational, and geographical aspects to the Brexit vote that are not reducible to the expression of economic interests (Sobolewska and Ford 2020). Nevertheless, it is undeniable that hostility to the European Union was very strong in English and Welsh towns that had experienced deindustrialization and with labour markets characterized by low pay and precarious employment (Goodwin and Heath 2016). The malfunctioning of the labour market is seemingly a theme in the populist narrative.

Responses to Low Pay

Much UK public policy over the past two decades has been concerned with expanding or maintaining the supply of low-paid labour to the economy. Free movement of labour within the European Union served this function, particularly after the accession of East European countries in 2004, and since Brexit steps have been taken to ensure continuity of supply for industries like agriculture. The period of austerity since the global financial crisis, moreover, has seen cuts to welfare benefits and increasing conditionality of welfare payments, with the aim of forcing recipients onto the labour market and into employment (Beatty and Fothergill 2018). Reproducing low-paid work has long been a tacit if not an explicit objective of UK public policy (Grimshaw et al. 2008).

Alongside this policy, however, there have been notable attempts to try and reduce low pay and mitigate its effects, and there is widespread concern amongst policy makers to improve conditions in the lower reaches of the labour market. The most significant response since the late 1980s has been the use of transfer payments and tax credits to mitigate the effects of low pay. This policy reached its apotheosis under the Blair-Brown New Labour governments of the 2000s and continues to shape public policy. At its heart is an attempt partly to decouple income from wages, allowing the latter to be set at low rates through supply and demand and using means-tested benefits to bring income up to an acceptable level. A radical inflection of this approach, which seeks to further decouple income from wages without means testing, is the proposal for a Universal Basic Income (Martinelli 2017).

Overlaying reliance on tax credits has been the use of a statutory minimum wage, which establishes an obligatory wage floor below which pay rates ostensibly cannot fall. Again, Blair's New Labour government made the running on this front, introducing the UK's National Minimum Wage (NMW) in 1998, the first time the country had a statutory minimum that applied across all industries and occupations. Since its introduction the value of the NMW has increased, and in 2016 a higher National Living Wage (NLW) for workers aged 25 and over was introduced by the Conservative government, with the aim of fixing this new rate at two thirds of median hourly earnings (Brown 2017; Hirsch 2017). The NLW formed part of a switch in labour market policy that reduced the emphasis on tax credits and benefits, as part of a wider programme of public expenditure cuts, shifting more of the burden of dealing with low pay to employers.

While mitigating the effects of low pay through transfer payments and establishing legal minima have been the two main responses in the UK, other proposals have entered the policy-making domain. Several of these look backwards and seek to revive labour market institutions that flourished in the twentieth century. One proposal is to re-establish wages councils in low-paid industries; that is, tripartite boards composed of union and employer representatives and independent experts that could establish rates of pay above the statutory minima and shape other aspects of the employment relationship, such as training, equal opportunities, and superannuation (Brown and Wright 2018; Hughes and Dundon 2018). Another proposal that has been influential within the Labour Party is to recreate industry-level collective bargaining, which could set core terms and conditions and reduce the competitive pressure on firms to continually seek to reduce labour costs (Ewing et al. 2018). A third proposal is to use public procurement to raise wages and compel public service contractors to provide decent work. A change of this kind represents a return to a more activist model of state intervention, in which the power of purchase is used to shape employment practice directly in supplier organizations. Theorists of the 'foundational economy' are particularly strong advocates of this third approach, arguing for comprehensive 'social licensing', in which receipt of state contracts, grants, or other concessions is linked explicitly to adherence to good labour standards (Foundational Economy Collective 2018).

The Living Wage campaign is another response to the problem of low pay. However, it differs from those described above in significant ways. Its point of origin is different, emerging not from the political or legislative process or from the labour movement, but from civil society. It is the community organizing movement that has given birth to the campaign, a relatively new actor on the employment scene within the UK. Moreover, the campaign can be placed alongside other single-issue movements that seek to shape the employment relationship and which together comprise a significant wave of innovation within the employment systems of Britain and other developed economies in recent years (Dundon et al. 2020; Williams et al. 2011). Citizens UK and the Living Wage Foundation form a piece with the LGBT+ charity Stonewall, Age UK, Carers UK, the whistleblowing charity Protect, and many disability organizations, all of which have become active in seeking to shape the world of work. The campaign is also distinctive with regard to its method for dealing with low pay. It promotes private regulation of the employment relationship, seeking to persuade businesses to voluntarily become accredited as Living Wage Employers in a manner that diverges sharply from reliance on legal regulation or joint regulation through collective bargaining, which are the favoured methods of other responses. As was stated above, the Living Wage campaign is a notable example of the civil regulation of the employment relationship and, as such, can serve as a case study for analysing and evaluating this approach to labour market governance.

Civil Regulation

The concept of civil regulation emerged within the field of corporate governance and refers to attempts by NGOs and other civil society actors to exercise oversight over and influence the behaviour of business organizations (Levi-Faur 2009). It has been used particularly to analyse the activities of environmental NGOs in seeking to promote sustainable business practice by establishing codes of practice with supporting audit and accreditation regimes that aim to protect the natural environment from forestry, mining, and agriculture (Newell 2008). The concept has also been used to examine the attempt by NGOs to regulate the employment relationship, though typically with a focus on global supply chains and employment conditions in manufacturing facilities in the global south (Vogel 2010a). Studies of civil regulation have often focused on the activities of international NGOs and their attempts to develop a rule-based order that can govern the activities of multinational companies that draw resources from across the globe (Vogel 2010b). They are concerned mainly with global civil society and its efforts to promote sustainable business practice and adherence to labour standards on an international scale.

In this study, the concept of civil regulation is deployed in a rather different setting. It is used to guide the analysis of labour market regulation within a single, developed economy, and the primary authors of this regulation are country-specific civil society organizations (CSOs), such as Citizens UK and the Living Wage Foundation, which mainly confine their activities to the United Kingdom. Within this context, the term itself encompasses three distinct properties of regulation. First, civil regulation is a form of private regulation and, as such, can be distinguished from all forms of public regulation. In Vogel's terms, a defining feature of civil regulation is that its 'legitimacy, governance, and implementation are not rooted in public authority' (Vogel 2010b: 69). However, civil regulation can also be distinguished from private regulation that emanates from private actors other than CSOs. Businesses may develop their own codes of conduct to regulate the behaviour of suppliers (Tsogas 2001; Wright and Kaine 2015) and may formulate labour and other standards that are promoted broadly to the wider population of business enterprises. The National Equality Standard, promoted by management consultancy EY, is an example of the latter. Moreover, representative organizations of business may formulate rules of good practice for member companies. In the UK, Business in the Community, the Business Disability Forum, and Inclusive Employers are collective organizations of this type (Gooberman et al. 2020). For our purpose, the term 'civil regulation' is best confined to private regulation developed by CSOs and is distinguishable from private regulation emanating from other sources.

Second, civil regulation is a form of unilateral regulation. We mean by this that the substantive and procedural rules that comprise bodies of civil regulation are authored solely by CSOs, which then seek to have them adopted by employers and other actors within the labour market. CSOs may consult with those they aspire to regulate in developing their standards and, as we will see below, this has been the practice of the Living Wage Foundation, which has sought the views of a variety of stakeholders in formulating the Living Wage standard. Ultimately, however, the Foundation retains primary responsibility for the Living Wage. Unilateral regulation of this form can be contrasted with forms of private regulation that are jointly authored by a combination of types of labour market actor. A notable example of the latter is collective bargaining, in which the rules governing the employment relationship are negotiated and set out in agreements between employers and trade unions. Joint regulation of this form was the dominant method of labour market governance in the UK and many other countries for much of the twentieth century. Other forms of joint regulation may bring together a broader set of actors, including CSOs (Kuruvilla 2021). The Ethical Trading Initiative is a multi-stakeholder body of this kind that draws companies, unions, and CSOs into the formulation of labour standards for global supply chains, and there are other organizations of this broad type involved in domestic labour market regulation (Heery et al. 2017). What separates these latter initiatives from civil regulation is that they are exercises in multilateral, not unilateral, regulation.

The third and final defining feature of civil regulation is that it is voluntary: employers are not obliged or required by law to commit to the regulation promoted by CSOs but choose to do so. Civil regulation shares this voluntary property with a broad swathe of 'soft' regulation that includes codes of practice and certification schemes developed by government as well as standards advanced by other private labour market actors. It is a feature too of the UK's 'voluntarist' system of industrial relations, in which collective agreements—the products of joint regulation between unions and employers—typically are not legally binding. Instead of the compulsion which underpins hard, legal regulation, backed ultimately by the coercive power of the state, voluntary regulation relies heavily on market-based incentives to encourage compliance. This characteristic is seen most clearly in corporate codes that regulate supply chains, in which winning and retaining contracts with global brands is purportedly dependent on adherence to voluntary regulation (Locke 2013). Beyond direct contractual benefits of this kind, however, voluntary regulation is often promoted on the grounds of a 'business case'; that adherence to good labour standards or to standards of environmental stewardship will strengthen corporate reputation, attract consumers, and improve human resource management (Vogel 2010a). There is also often a more coercive side to this message that emphasizes the risks of non-compliance, which may be considerable when brands can be tarnished through association with bad labour or poor environmental practice. Campaigners for civil regulation typically exploit this risk by exposing or threatening to expose corporate malpractice as a means of leveraging compliance (Donaghey et al. 2014).

Research and Debate on Civil Regulation

Research on civil regulation and other forms of private and voluntary forms of governance has grown substantially across several academic fields in recent years, including politics, international relations, corporate strategy, international business, and employment relations. Within this body of literature, debate and inquiry have become focused on several core themes, all of which are explored for the specific case of the Living Wage in the chapters that follow. The first of these themes deals with the content of private regulation, the nature and quality of the rules that lie at its heart. In the literature on private regulation of employment relations within international supply chains, for example, researchers have observed a process of evolution in which substantive rules have become more elaborate and seemingly more robust over time (Bartley 2018). This process has been driven by repeated exposure of labour abuses within supply chains by social movement organizations, which has generated an effort by global brands to reform regulation to reduce the risk of exposure (Frenkel and Kim 2004; Locke et al. 2007; Schuessler et al. 2019). Indicators of this trend include the adoption of increasingly complex codes of practice, the development of international standards to be applied in multiple locations, overriding weaker local forms of regulation, acknowledgement that best practice must involve going beyond legal minima, and acceptance by brands of responsibility for an expanding range of operational matters across their supply chains. There seems to be an evolutionary 'logic of regulation', in which initial attempts become more substantively complex over time.

Running alongside this elaboration of substantive rules has been the elaboration of procedures for ensuring compliance. Within the international economy, third party organizations have emerged whose task it is to audit and report on regulatory compliance within supply chains, and there has been pressure to make this process more rigorous and transparent (Donaghey et al. 2014). For critics of private regulation, these procedures, even when reformed, are frequently regarded as inadequate, and the weakness of enforcement mechanisms has been identified as a key point of failure within systems of private regulation (Kuruvilla 2021). This critique is linked to a call for further reform to ensure that inspection is independent, involves worker representatives within supplier firms, and is fully transparent (O'Rourke 2006). Another, less common critique questions whether low-trust auditing regimes of this kind can ever be effective, as they generate resistance and evasion by the organizations they seek to regulate. 'Deterrence approaches' to regulation, it is suggested, merely stimulate ritualistic compliance and are best replaced by a high-trust, 'capability-building approach', in which brands support and invest in supplier businesses to help them achieve good employment standards (Locke 2013; see also Frenkel and Kim 2004).

A second theme in the literature on private regulation addresses the methods used by campaigners to promote it to business. Researchers have noted that CSOs promoting private regulation use distinctive methods and mobilize distinctive resources, particularly when compared with the methods used by trade unions. Donaghey et al. (2014) note that CSOs campaigning on labour rights have typically made use of boycotts and protests by customers, a resource located in the realm of consumption which is distinct from the positional and associational resources of workers, located in the realm of production. It is the repeated deployment of this consumer resource by CSOs, indeed, that has driven the evolution of private regulation towards more elaborate forms. For Tapia (2013), in contrast, the distinctive quality of CSOs lies in their capacity to mobilize supporters in protest against labour abuse, a capacity which she claims is often greater than that possessed by unions. The value-based orientation of CSO supporters, Tapia suggests, endows

CSOs with greater mobilizing capacity than does the more instrumentally orientated membership of trade unions. In a similar vein, Heckscher and McCarthy (2014) have argued that CSOs possess a greater ability than unions to engage in what they refer to as 'swarming', the bringing together of a diverse cross-section of individuals and groups through social media to protest on a particular issue or against a particular target.

Another line of argument about the methods used to produce private regulation has focused on the relationship between CSOs and employers. Commentators on this relationship have noted a long-term shift within international civil society away from an adversarial approach to business, focused on 'naming and shaming' companies that flout environmental and labour standards, towards cooperation with companies and business associations aimed at developing and enforcing voluntary codes. According to Vogel (2010a: 477), the willingness of CSOs 'to enter into alliances with global firms has been critical to the emergence, legitimacy, and relative effectiveness of many civil regulations'. This shift in orientation to business of many campaigning organizations, however, has generated a backlash, with critical scholars arguing that once radical CSOs have lost their edge and have become incorporated within a global political economy in which business interests have primacy (Dauvergne and Lebaron 2014). While commentators who have compared CSOs to trade unions have often stressed the greater capacity of the former to mobilize protest, therefore, those who focus on the CSO relationship with employers have pointed to the diminution of that capacity as new ways of dealing with business have come to the fore.

The next theme in the literature addresses the response of employers to private regulation. An initial response noted by researchers is to resist attempts to regulate business activity, often by refusing to accept responsibility for working conditions in supplier businesses (Locke et al. 2007). Private regulation frequently seeks to extend the obligations of business to encompass standards that stretch beyond legal minima and include operations across supply chains, within formally separate but dependent supplier companies. These attempts to stretch responsibility have often been resisted, at least when the question of compliance with private regulation is initially broached.

After a phase of resistance, however, many companies have accepted private regulation, and the latter is now a ubiquitous and, in many respects, taken-for-granted feature of the environment in which multinational enterprises operate. How has this situation come about and why have businesses accepted private, voluntary regulation? One explanation found within the literature perceives acceptance as a defensive move, intended to forestall more exacting, compulsory regulation by the state (Kinderman 2012; Schuessler et al. 2019). This argument implies that businesses will be particularly receptive to private regulation at points in time and in jurisdictions where political pressure for public regulation is rising or intense. Another explanation also emphasizes defensiveness but in the sense of protecting brand value and other assets from the charge of corporate irresponsibility from campaigners. Businesses may accept private regulation to reduce reputational risk and to shore up the value of assets, a response that may be particularly likely amongst customer-facing enterprises or those with visible brands and vulnerable reputations (Frenkel and Kim 2004; Vogel 2010a). A third explanation identifies business opportunities within private regulation. Commitment to the latter, it is argued, may enhance brand value, secure access to key markets or sources of finance, and generate a range of beneficial side effects, including building a positive employer brand. According to this view, companies that are most receptive to private regulation will be those that can secure competitive advantage from doing so: a positive reputation gained from an active CSR policy, for instance, may be an asset for companies engaged in the 'war for talent', seeking to recruit young or highly educated employees (Bhattarchaya et al. 2008; Meister and Willyerd 2010). A fourth explanation also emphasizes economic calculation but identifies the limited cost for many businesses of complying with private regulation. Where regulations are weak or poorly enforced, or when organizations are largely compliant prior to being certified, then it may be relatively costless for them to sign up (Hoque 2003; Richards 2001). On this view, it may be enterprises with a strong, prior reputation in the field of HRM, or which are highly profitable, or which possess substantial management resources that are most likely to accept private regulation.

A final reason why employing organizations might accept private regulation is normative. Businesses may be receptive to regulation because it accords with organizational values and mission, quite independently of any reputational or other gains that might accrue (Werner 2021b). Critical writers often assume that corporate decision-making is deeply cynical, but this may not always be the case and there may be scope for values-based decision-making within many organizations (Casey et al. 2021; Jackson et al. 2018). If this is true, then one might expect compliance with private regulation to be found in certain types of business; perhaps firms with a paternalistic management style, or with a strong culture, marked by the values of founding entrepreneurs, or with a well-resourced CSR function whose task is to give effect to the enterprise's ethical commitments. One might also expect compliance amongst public sector organizations, adhering to the 'good employer' tradition, or from not-for-profit organizations, which are themselves committed to a social justice objective. Moreover, even if one is right to be sceptical about the motives of business decision-makers, the widespread issuing of pledges to manage responsibly or sustainably can serve as a commitment trap, requiring action despite the fact that underlying commitments may be shallow or bogus.

The fourth theme in the literature on private regulation examines its relationship with traditional, union-based industrial relations. The default approach to labour market regulation in western developed economies for much of the twentieth century rested upon trade union representation of workers and was conducted through collective bargaining. The rise of private and voluntary forms of regulation represents a break with this traditional system, and researchers have begun to examine how these different approaches to labour market regulation impact upon one another. One line of argument has identified conflict and tension, and has suggested that the articulation of worker interests through civil society organizations and the spread of private regulation pose a threat to the union-based system. In work on private regulation of international supply chains, for instance, it is sometimes suggested that an effect is to forestall unionization and crowd out more traditional, more effective means of regulating the employment relationship (Compa 2001; Kuruvilla 2021). Two main formulations of this 'replacement thesis' can be identified in the literature on private regulation. On the one hand, there is a structural version of the argument, which explains the emergence of civil society organizations and their transformative impact on employment in terms of deep-seated changes in economy and society that have generated new social movements while eroding the 'old', class-based movement of organized labour (Heckscher and McCarthy 2014; Piore and Safford 2006). On the other hand, there is an actor-centred explanation that stresses the part played by employers and governments in sponsoring private regulation deliberately to undermine trade unionism (Jackson et al. 2018). Whatever the explanation, advocates of the replacement thesis identify the potential for conflict both in the relationship between private regulation and collective bargaining and between civil society organizations and trade unions.

There is another line of argument, however, which identifies broad scope for cooperation in the relationship between civil society and trade unions. Advocates of what can be labelled the 'reinforcement thesis' argue that private voluntary regulation and regulation through collective bargaining can complement one another, and that trade unions and civil society organizations can form effective alliances. Research on union-community coalitions has emerged as a prominent theme within the literature on union revitalization, with contributors identifying different types of coalition and the conditions that allow them to be formed and to thrive (Frege et al. 2004; Mayer 2009; Tattersall 2018). Work on international supply chains has explored similar themes, examining the connections between global campaigns on labour standards and processes of union formation in emerging economies (O'Rourke 2006). Researchers have also examined how voluntary codes can stimulate collective bargaining through clauses on freedom of association and similar provisions (Kuruvilla 2021). In this vein of work, it is argued that there can be mutuality of interests between civil society organizations and trade unions, with the former providing mobilizing capacity and support to trade unions seeking to organize workers and the latter providing scrutiny and enforcement of voluntary codes through workplace representatives (Donaghey et al. 2014; Harvey et al. 2017).

The fifth theme in the literature examines how private regulation interacts with the public sphere. A common interpretation of this interaction is that private regulation serves as a functional alternative to regulation by the state, providing guides to behaviour and a degree of protection for the environment, workers, and communities where public authority is absent or deficient. There are different versions of this argument. It has been suggested that private regulation is particularly apparent on an international scale because of the limited capacity of intergovernmental institutions to regulate the global economy; that there is a functional requirement for private regulation in many emerging economies because weak states lack the ability to regulate their economies; and that private regulation may be appropriate for dealing with emergent issues that have yet to be addressed by public authorities (Jackson et al. 2018; Vogel 2010a). All these arguments effectively echo the replacement thesis, found in the literature on private regulation and trade unions: they all suggest that private regulation can, and maybe should, replace regulation through public authorities.

While there is empirical support for arguments of this kind, an alternative position has emerged which views the relationship between private and public regulation in more positive terms. Again, this position is expressed through a variety of arguments. One such argument points to the role of states in sponsoring civil society organizations and the private regulation to which they give rise. In the UK, for instance, government was actively involved in the formation of Business in the Community (BitC), the main business membership organization that promotes corporate social responsibility, and actively encouraged BitC to develop employment standards, such as those within its gender equality programme, Opportunity Now (Kinderman 2012; Marinetto 1999; Richards 2001). Governments have also sponsored organizations involved in the promotion of international labour standards: in the UK the Blair Government helped establish the Ethical Trading Initiative and in the USA the Clinton administration created the Fair Labor Association (Bartley 2018; Vogel 2010b). Another argument corresponds to the trade union reinforcement thesis and claims that states provide valuable backing to private regulation, making it more effective. Research on the regulation of labour standards within international supply chains suggests that codes of conduct are more effective when public policy is more supportive both in the home country in which brands are located and in host countries where manufacturing operations are based (Locke et al. 2007; Locke et al. 2013; Schuessler et al. 2019). A final argument claims that private and public forms of regulation can complement one another, joining together in a 'smart mix' of different regulatory forms. According to Kinderman (2016), promotion of a 'smart mix' has become the dominant policy prescription in global governance circles and is exemplified by the European Union's non-financial reporting directive, adopted in 2014. This directive requires European businesses to report on the social, environmental, and human rights impacts of their activities but confers wide discretion to choose exactly how this will be done, thereby combining elements of hard law with private regulation.

Most discussion of the state's interaction with private regulation is concerned with the state's role as a legislator or regulator. However, other forms of state intervention in the economy may also have relevance to this question. States are major employers, and there is a long tradition of employers in the public realm adopting norms of good practice both because of their intrinsic worth and to serve as a model for the private sector (Winchester and Bach 1995). States are also major purchasers of goods and services, and, as we have seen, there is renewed emphasis in policy discussion on the active use of public procurement to secure social and community benefits (Barnard 2017). Neither of these levers, employment or procurement, feature significantly in the literature on private regulation, but both can potentially be used to promote the latter. Public sector employers may incorporate private regulation within their traditional conception of the 'good employer', and they may similarly make compliance with ostensibly voluntary standards a condition for the award of public contracts. It is not just as legislators and regulators, but as employers and as purchasers, that public authorities may interact with private voluntary regulation.

The final theme in the literature on private, voluntary regulation addresses its effectiveness in promoting good labour standards. Much of the research literature is deeply sceptical about this point and has questioned whether private regulation is effective in improving employment conditions for workers. Thus, recent studies of the private regulation of global supply chains report that there are few discernible positive effects even when conditions seemingly are most propitious (Kuruvilla 2021; Lebaron et al. 2022). Findings of this type have also been reported for soft regulation of domestic labour markets: studies of the UK Government's Positive About Disabled People standard and of the Athena Swan standard for gender equality in higher education report that conforming employers were no more likely than their non-conforming peers to report positive outcomes (Gregory-Smith 2018; Hoque et al. 2014). Several reasons have been adduced to explain findings of this kind. With regard to the private regulation of international supply chains, it has been claimed that the underlying purpose of initiatives of this type is to influence consumer perceptions of business rather than to address genuinely the problem of poor labour standards; that voluntary regulation is intrinsically weak and that the auditing and reporting mechanisms that surround private regulations are often ineffectual; that the supplier businesses targeted by regulation possess the resources to frustrate attempts to shape their behaviour; and that the business model of many western brands relies upon low-cost production and of itself undermines attempts to upgrade labour standards (Anner 2019; Kuruvilla 2021).

While this critique is potent, not all research is bleak in its assessment of private regulation, and the literature contains a second position that makes a, albeit guarded, defence. This defence notes that while there are limits to private regulation, it is not without effect, and there is evidence of corporate codes of conduct and associated initiatives exerting a positive impact on employment practice within international supply chains. The work of Locke and his colleagues exemplifies this second position. Locke has noted major weaknesses of private regulation, including the tendency for initiatives to dissipate over time and for supplier factories to cycle in and out of compliance with code requirements. But he also notes that private regulation has led to some tangible improvements, particularly with regard to health and safety, and that initiatives can have a greater positive effect when certain conditions are met. He identifies among the latter reliance upon relational rather than spot contracting with suppliers, use of a 'capability-building approach' to promote good practice, the presence of local civil society organizations and trade unions that can monitor the implementation of codes, and a supportive public policy context characterized by respect for the rule of law (Locke 2013; see also Distelhorst et al. 2017; Frenkel and Kim 2004; Kuruvilla 2021; Locke et al. 2007; Locke et al. 2013). Findings of this kind, moreover, have been reproduced in studies of private regulation within developed economies: recent research on the efforts of UK-based retailers and oil companies to regulate labour standards in their supply chains has identified a number of positive impacts (Heery et al. 2017; Wright and Brown 2013). There is a range of perspectives on the effectiveness of private regulation, therefore, though it must be noted that this range encompasses relatively few statements of outright support. The range of academic opinion is limited, extending from outright sceptics about private regulation who favour alternative, harder approaches to raising labour standards, to guarded supporters whose defence of private regulation often starts from acceptance that other, more effective methods are unavailable.

The literature on the effects of private regulation has also dealt with consequences for employers. There is perhaps less concern with this set of outcomes, at least amongst those examining the regulation of international supply chains, but the issue has been addressed and several positions adopted. The first position is broadly positive, identifying a series of benefits for employing organizations from the adoption of private regulation. It has been variously suggested that compliance with voluntary codes of labour standards can enhance corporate reputation and reduce reputational risk; serve as a tool for marketing products to ethical consumers; stimulate the upgrading of production processes, allowing supplier firms to switch to high-value added lines; and advance the financial and commercial interests of the business, facilitating access to investment or to contracts conditional upon conformance to ethical standards (Joint Ethical Trading Initiatives 2015; Vogel 2010b). A second, less positive position can also be detected within the research literature, however. It was noted above that concern has repeatedly been expressed about the capacity of private regulation to upgrade employment practice within supply chains. The apparent reason for this is that compliance is costly, directly raising labour costs, potentially inhibiting the flexibility of just-in-time supply systems, and embroiling both brands and suppliers in a bureaucratic process of recording and reporting (Locke 2013). While it may be regrettable, this position holds that resistance to private regulation may nevertheless be economically rational. A third position can also be identified, though in this case the clearest argument is found beyond the literature on private regulation in the broader discussion of the 'business case' for progressive management. The latter encompasses an extensive literature on the impact on employing organizations of equality and diversity programmes. Much of this literature demonstrates positive business effects, but this is not always the case. In a number of studies positive effects for minority workers have been identified alongside consequences for employers that are broadly neutral, neither positive nor negative (e.g. Forth and Rincon-Aznar 2008). It may be that this third position also holds for much private regulation: that schemes produce benefits for employees at minimal cost to business but without generating a powerful thrust to business performance. In combination, these three positions in the literature suggest that the impact of private regulation on business may be variable and contingent upon circumstance, potentially performance-enhancing, performance-inhibiting, or performance-neutral.

Plan of the Book

In the chapters that follow, each of the themes in the literature on private and civil regulation are explored using the specific case of the Real Living Wage. The research literature on private regulation provides a frame for the presentation of our case study of the Living Wage, guiding the analysis and providing research questions that are answered using our case study evidence. In addition, our research is used to reflect upon wider themes in the literature on private regulation, adding to the latter and contributing to the debate on voluntary forms of governance. In time-honoured fashion, our research on the Living Wage is both guided by and used to engage with a wider set of arguments.

The theme that guides Chapter 2 is concerned with the content of private regulation. The chapter analyses the substantive content of the Living Wage standard, describing it as a form of payment for need, reviewing the process through which it is determined, and listing the obligations that it imposes on employers, including the crucial requirement to pay the Living Wage to the employees of contractors as well as direct employees. The chapter also explains why the Living Wage is an exemplary form of civil regulation and considers the degree to which it conforms to various tests of robustness of the latter that have been identified in the wider literature. The chapter concludes by examining the evolution of the Living Wage standard and the launch by campaigners of additional, supplementary standards. The Living Wage, it is shown, has displayed an evolutionary 'logic of regulation', and the chapter examines how and why this has occurred.

The theme that guides Chapter 3 is that of the methods used by civil society organizations to promote private regulation. The chapter begins by introducing the civil society organizations responsible for the Living Wage, Citizens UK, and its offshoot, the Living Wage Foundation. These organizations have often acted through partnerships with other CSOs, such as the Poverty Alliance and Cynnal Cymru, which have promoted the Living Wage in Scotland and Wales respectively, and the chapter also describes the broad network of organizations that have become associated with the campaign. Having introduced the institutions, the chapter then goes on to examine methods, looking in turn at three issues. The first is that of the distinctiveness of campaign methods, which is explored through the concept of 'community organizing', and the manner in which the campaign techniques associated with the latter have been deployed to advance the Living Wage. The second issue is that of partnering with business and the manner and extent to which Living Wage campaigners have developed a 'business case' for the Living Wage and sought to draw employers towards the standard through an appeal to their enlightened self-interest. The final theme addresses campaign relationships and the ways in which campaigners have sought to build support for the Living Wage within civil society and amongst trade unions and public authorities.

In Chapter 4, employers take centre stage, and the frame is provided by literature on business responses to civil regulation. The first part of the chapter deals with the characteristics of Living Wage Employers, identifying the attributes and economic and geographical location of organizations that have signed up to accreditation. The next part of the chapter examines employer motives for adopting the Living Wage, examining the extent to which instrumental motives and a desire to secure business advantage have been paramount or whether 'expressive' motives and a desire to support the campaign have been at the fore. This section also considers the extent to which institutional pressures, such as exposure to Living Wage campaigners or trade unions, have driven accreditation. The chapter concludes by examining employer resistance to the Living Wage and identifies the motivations and conditions that have led some to reject the standard. An important conclusion here is that employer responses to the Living Wage are spread broadly along a continuum, with fiercely resistant organizations at one end and employers that have gone beyond the formal requirements of the Living Wage standard at the other.

Chapter 5 switches attention to trade unions and examines the part the traditional labour movement has played within the Living Wage campaign. Three broad types of union response to the campaign are identified. In the first place, unions have cooperated with the campaign by becoming accredited as employers themselves, affiliating to Citizens UK and providing backing to attempts to persuade employers to adopt the Living Wage. In some cases, this cooperation has approximated to the kind of union-community coalition identified in the literature on union revitalization (Tattersall 2018). In the second place, unions have resisted the campaign, formulating a critique of its methods, refusing cooperation, and developing alternative living wage standards, such as the £10.00 living wage that unions have persuaded the Labour Party to adopt. The final response we label 'appropriation', in which unions have adopted the Living Wage and promoted it independently of the Living Wage campaign, using their traditional repertoire of strikes and collective bargaining. This response is perhaps the most significant, and we argue that unions have played an important part in diffusing the Living Wage in the unionized segment of the UK economy.

In Chapter 6, the focus is the Living Wage and public authorities. It is argued in the chapter that adoption of the Living Wage is a good indicator of a continuing 'good employer' commitment amongst public sector organizations. The latter are shown to be more likely to adopt the Living Wage than employers in the private sector, and the analysis also identifies which branches of public service are most likely to seek accreditation. Part of this analysis focuses on local government and identifies the importance of the 'political contingency' (Ferner 1988) in explaining which public sector organizations are especially likely to adopt the Living Wage. Regional and local authorities under the control of social democratic parties, it is demonstrated, have a much greater propensity to accredit. The remainder of the chapter looks at the steps that public authorities have taken to diffuse the Living Wage in their areas of jurisdiction. Promotion of the Living Wage has often formed part of a broader commitment to 'inclusive growth' (Lee 2018) and has embraced a wide set of initiatives, including tying the Living Wage to procurement and business funding. Public authorities, it is shown, have often acted as 'anchor institutions' (Guinan and O'Neill 2020), encouraging the adoption of the Living Wage amongst other local employers. This supportive role played by public authorities casts doubt on the functional argument outlined above, that civil regulation thrives where the state is absent and there are failures of public governance.

In Chapter 7 the concern is with the impact of the Living Wage. The first part of the chapter addresses the common argument that voluntary regulation is ineffectual and has failed to raise labour standards (Kuruvilla 2021). We present original data on the coverage of the Living Wage, the number and types of workers that have benefitted, and the scale of the redistributive impact of the standard. Our evidence shows that a substantial number of low-wage workers have benefitted from the Living Wage, frequently receiving substantial pay increases, indicating that voluntary regulation can produce a positive, redistributive effect. We also note that there are limits to this effect, however, and suggest that even when relatively successful, private regulation suffers from a problem of limited scale. In the second part of the chapter the focus turns to employers, and we consider the degree to which the Living Wage has generated positive effects for business. The evidence indicates that the Living Wage has produced effects of this kind, but again there is a question of scale. Almost universally employers that have committed to the Living Wage believe that it has benefitted their organizations, but for the most part reported effects have been modest. The Living Wage appears in the evidence as a benign but not a transformative measure when viewed from the perspective of most employers. Chapter 7 concludes by examining some of the wider impacts of the Living Wage. A central objective here is to test another critical argument: that civil regulation can erode other, more effective ways of regulating employment, such as collective bargaining and employment law (Compa 2001; Kinderman 2016). In neither case is this argument shown to be valid. Civil regulation, in the form of the Living Wage, can coexist with other forms of regulation in a 'smart mix', in which different forms of regulation are layered upon one another.

In Chapter 8, the main findings of the study are summarized, and we draw some broader conclusions about the significance of our Living Wage case study for the study of employment relations. One set of conclusions relates to the significance of civil regulation and the civil society organizations that promote it. We conclude that the latter are important 'new actors' (Heery et al. 2012) in the system of employments relations, and that civil regulation has become an important feature of the multiform system of regulation that now governs the employment relationship. Nevertheless, there are limits to the reach and impact of civil regulation, and we believe it will continue to play a largely supplementary role within complex, developed economies characterized by multiple institutions of labour market regulation. Civil regulation, we conclude, can add to but is unlikely to replace regulation of the labour market through its more established relatives, employment law and collective bargaining. Another set of conclusions concerns employers. We suggest that the acceptance of the Living Wage by large numbers of employers in the UK is indicative of new wave of paternalism in management strategy. We sketch out the characteristics of this 'neo-paternalism' and contrast it with the classical form of paternalism that emerged in the nineteenth and early twentieth centuries. Much contemporary academic writing on employer behaviour propounds an 'immiseration' thesis, in which 'unruly' employers seek to escape from regulation and impose new forms of degraded and precarious employment on the workforce (Streeck 2009). The case study of the Living Wage, we believe, provides a partial correction to this orthodox account. Our third set of conclusions draws out the implications of the Living Wage case for the analysis of trade unions. Here, we make use of the concept of union 'resilience' (Moore et al. 2019), understood as the continuing ability of the trade union movement to adapt to new issues, such as the Living Wage, and incorporate them within its established repertoire of action. This response differs notably, we believe, from those advocated in the prescriptive literature on trade union revitalization, which emphasize the development of a new repertoire, often focused on coalition-building with other social movements. Our final set of conclusions relates to the role of government in employment relations. Here, we argue that the positive response of many public authorities to the Living Wage is indicative of the revival of a more activist conception of the state's role within the labour market, which breaks with the neoliberal orthodoxy of the past four decades. We also argue that state intervention in the employment relationship, in the form of support for the Living Wage, flows from and is part of a broader current of economic development policy. Central to the latter are notions of 'inclusive growth' and 'community wealth building'. Promotion of the Living Wage, we argue, has become a signature policy for public authorities influenced by this new paradigm of economic development (Lupton et al. 2019).

Researching the Living Wage

In exploring the themes set out above, we draw upon an extensive research project into the Real Living Wage that was developed between 2014 and 2022. This project followed a mixed-method design that brought together a range of quantitative and qualitative research techniques that allowed both for the 'triangulation' of research findings and for the exploration of multiple issues. In combination, the different methods have generated a case study of the Living Wage in the UK that encompasses different facets of the scheme, and which has allowed us to consider the latter 'in the round': it has allowed us to examine the origin and form of the Living Wage, the nature of the campaign to promote it, the involvement and response of different labour market actors, and its impact and effects. Civil regulation is an increasingly significant phenomenon both within the global economy and in the domestic economies of many Western democracies. Our research has been designed to use the case of the Living Wage to reflect upon this broader development.

The methods that have been used to develop the case study of the Living Wage are as follows:-

1. *Employer database*: at the core of the project has been the development of a database of all accredited Living Wage Employers (LWEs), including those that have lapsed and dropped out of the scheme. This dataset contains information on all 12,728 employers who joined the scheme between May 2011, when it was launched, and May 2022. For most of these employers we have assembled data on their structural characteristics (e.g. size, sector, industry, age, location), aspects of management policy, such as adherence to a social justice mission, and the impact of the Living Wage (i.e. the number and types of worker that have received pay increases through the scheme and the value of such increases). These data have partly been provided to us by the Living Wage Foundation and partly they have come from Companies House and other sources of official data, and from employers' own websites. An important feature of the dataset is that for each employer we have the five-digit industry code and the local authority in which the organization is located, which has allowed us to systematically compare LWEs

with general patterns in the economy using official data that are collected on an industry or geographical basis. For example, these data have allowed us to establish whether LWEs are found disproportionately in low-paying industries or localities, in parts of the economy with a high union presence or with a high proportion of women employees, or in areas with Labour or nationalist-controlled political authorities. The data have also allowed us to examine whether accredited employers tend to be found where Citizens UK has an active local chapter that campaigns for the Living Wage. In addition to the core employer dataset, we have also generated an additional dataset that makes use of the employer profiles. This dataset records the number and characteristics of LWEs in all local authorities of Great Britain, 407 regional and local authorities in total (i.e. Northern Ireland is not included). It has permitted fuller analysis of the geographical distribution of the Living Wage and has been of particular benefit in exploring the impact of local political support on the pattern of accreditation.

2. *Surveys of employers*: the second component of the project comprised two population surveys of LWEs carried out in 2016 and 2021. Both surveys were completed by the named contact of the Living Wage Foundation and covered a broad range of questions relating to employer responses to the Living Wage. The questionnaires contained items on employer motives for introducing the Living Wage, associated changes in business practice that accompanied the decision, the role of trade unions, the impact on contractors, and the effects of the scheme on a broad range of business operations. In addition, the surveys collected further information on the characteristics of employees who had benefitted from the Living Wage, including evidence on occupational characteristics. Both surveys included a qualitative component, which allowed respondents to write down their reflections on the Living Wage, and information of this kind from the 2016 survey is used in Chapter 4. The quantitative data that are presented, however, come solely from the 2021 survey. This survey was sent to all 6,993 employers who were accredited at the time, 1,532 of whom responded (twenty-two per cent). Respondents to the survey were broadly representative of the survey population. Evidence from the 2021 employer survey provides the core of Chapters 4 and 7, which consider employer reasons for seeking accreditation and the impact of the scheme respectively. The evidence also features in the chapter on trade unions and the Living Wage.
3. *Interviews*: the third component of the research was an extensive interview programme with those directly involved with the Living Wage. Interviews began in 2014, and over seven years more than one hundred semi-structured interviews were conducted, most of which were recorded and transcribed for systematic analysis. Three groups of participants were included in this interview programme. The first group were trade union officers and representatives. Interviews were carried out with thirty-four trade union

representatives from nine unions, including BECTU, GMB, UNISON, UNITE, and USDAW. Several interviews were also carried out with representatives of the TUC. The union interviews focused on union policy on the Living Wage, relationships with Citizens UK and the Living Wage Foundation, and the extent and nature of union campaigning on the Living Wage. The second group to be interviewed were employers and representatives of employers' organizations. A total of thirty-seven interviews were carried out with managers from a broad cross section of accredited employers, ranging from large corporates to small, family businesses and including public sector and not-for-profit organizations. These interviews have provided an important check on the data gathered from the survey of employers on employer motives for introducing the Living Wage and have also permitted a more detailed examination of how the standard has been implemented, and what consequences have arisen. The final group to be interviewed were Living Wage campaigners, including employees of Citizens UK and the Living Wage Foundation, and officers of partner organizations, such as the Poverty Alliance and ShareAction. A total of twenty-seven interviews were conducted with Living Wage campaigners. These interviews had a particular focus on campaign strategy and methods, allowing us to generate a full account of the latter in Chapter 3. The content of the campaigner interviews was broad, however, and the material has informed all chapters of the book.

4. *Observation*: a fourth method that has been used is the systematic observation of Living Wage campaign events and meetings. We have attended more than ninety events of this kind and have written detailed reports on open, public events. The latter notably include a series of public accountability assemblies, organized by Citizens UK in different parts of the country, which have had as their express purpose securing the commitment of political leaders to the Living Wage. The team has also attended events to announce the uprating of the Living Wage in Wales and in London—an example is provided by the vignette at the start of this chapter—meetings of campaigners, and consultation meetings to review the Living Wage. The information gathered through observation has informed all sections of the book but has been particularly valuable in writing Chapter 3 on the Living Wage campaign.
5. *Documentary research*: the final method that has been used in the research is the collection and analysis of documents on the Living Wage. An important source of this material has been the Living Wage Foundation, which has commissioned a series of detailed reports on the design and operation of the Living Wage, which provide the underpinning for our chapter on the content of the Living Wage standard. Another important source has been the websites of news organizations, trade unions, local and regional government, and employers, which have provided information on policy responses to the Living Wage and details of individual campaigns. We have relied upon and quoted from these accounts throughout the book, but they

have been particularly helpful in developing our analysis of trade union responses to the Living Wage, the actions of public authorities, and the nature of campaigning activity.

Case study research using multiple methods has long been a central feature of the academic field of employment relations (Brown and Wright 1994). The strength of work in this tradition is that it has provided a rich description of the world of work that has considered case study organizations in a rounded fashion. We believe that our case study of the Living Wage sits squarely within this tradition, providing a full, multifaceted account of the scheme that draws upon a unique set of original evidence. In the past, however, case study research within the employment field has primarily focused on individual workplaces and employing organizations and has dealt with a traditional range of issues, such as trade unionism, collective bargaining, work organization, and workplace conflict. Our case study represents a double break with work of this kind. Although fully within the employment relations tradition, it comprises a case study of a form of civil regulation rather than with an organization as such, and it is concerned with a new form of employment relations that sometimes sits uneasily with the old. Our aim has been to provide a traditional account of a new departure within the British employment scene. It is to the presentation of that account that we now turn.

2
The Real Living Wage

Introduction

This chapter addresses the first of the themes identified above, dealing with the content of civil regulation. In what follows the Real Living Wage is described and analysed, with a detailed examination of both the substantive content of the standard and of the procedural rules that guide how it operates. This account is developed over four sections. In the first we examine the Living Wage as a form of pay determination, the central principle of which is payment for need. The purpose of the Living Wage is to provide employees with a decent standard of living, and the elevation of this principle of need contrasts with more orthodox approaches to remuneration, which emphasize payment on the basis of skills or job demands, or aim to match the product and labour market context the employer is facing. In the second section we demonstrate that the Living Wage can be rightly classified as a form of civil regulation. We analyse the scheme and show that it is a form of private regulation that depends on the voluntary compliance of employers, and which has been developed unilaterally by civil society. In the third section, we apply tests of robustness of private regulation that have been developed by researchers concerned primarily with codes of international labour standards. In this section we consider the extent to which the UK's Living Wage goes beyond legally required minimum standards, whether it embodies international normative standards, the degree to which it has been designed to facilitate worker participation, and the rigour of the procedures that have been put in place to ensure effective implementation and employer compliance. We also examine the extent to which the Living Wage has been characterized by a 'capability approach' to regulation, in which the campaign has worked actively with member employers to increase their ability to implement the Living Wage successfully. Finally, we consider the evolution of the Living Wage and show that the scheme has become more elaborate with time, with supplementary standards and forms of accreditation being created that seek to reinforce the initial core standard. We analyse and seek to explain this process of elaboration and question whether it follows the evolutionary logic of regulation seen in other systems of private governance.

The Real Living Wage. Edmund Heery, Deborah Hann and David Nash, Oxford University Press.
© Edmund Heery, Deborah Hann and David Nash (2023). DOI: 10.1093/oso/9780198835264.003.0002

Payment for Need

The principle of pay determination underlying the Real Living Wage is that of payment for need. The Living Wage is set at a rate that is designed to ensure that full-time employees can sustain a frugal but decent standard of living for themselves and their families. Importantly, the rate is not conceived of as a subsistence wage and is meant to allow expenditure on leisure and personal development as well as on the 'necessaries' of life, such as food, accommodation, utilities, transport, and childcare. In this way the Living Wage embodies the notion of inclusion and seeks to permit the full participation of those on low incomes in the life of society in a way that a minimum, subsistence wage does not. This notion of inclusion encompasses payment of a wage that is sufficient to avoid overwork, in the form of long hours or multiple employment, to enable full participation of those receiving the Living Wage in family and community life. It also encompasses support for social mobility. The Living Wage is intended to ensure that children do not grow up in households that are deprived and, as has been noted, the calculation of the rate includes costs associated with personal development, such as provision of a home computer to help with homework. These features of the Living Wage mean that it is congruent with the 'capability' approach to economic development articulated by Amartya Sen, Martha Nussbaum, and others (Carr et al. 2016; Werner 2016). This approach declares that the object of development, and of public policy, should be to promote the 'substantive freedom' or 'functional capability' of human subjects. Arguably the Living Wage, with its emphasis on payment for need, seeks precisely to further objectives of this kind.

Another normative concept that is congruent with the Living Wage is the statement that 'labour is not a commodity', articulated by the International Labour Organization in the Declaration of Philadelphia (Lee 1994). It is congruent precisely because the Living Wage seeks to prioritize the principle of worker need in wage determination ahead of market forces or other principles that prioritize the interests of employers. The standard recognizes that workers have distinct interests and a legitimate expectation that these interests will be recognized within the system of employment through the provision of decent work that sustains a good quality of life. It rests on the conviction that the function of the wage is to serve the needs of employees as much as it is to allow employers to resource their organizations through the recruitment, retention, and motivation of the commodity of labour. The Declaration of Philadelphia also implies that employees should be treated with dignity and respect in the course of their employment and, again, this belief is congruent with the Living Wage. In the publicity released by the Living Wage Foundation, and at public events, it is common for those receiving the Living Wage to describe it in normative terms: to state that being paid the Living Wage has made them feel respected and valued by their employer (see also Werner 2021a).

How widespread these feelings are it is not possible to say, but they suggest that the standard may carry a positive symbolic meaning for employees, quite apart from any material benefits that they may receive. It recognizes their worth as members of the organization in which they are employed, in the way that payment at the legal minimum does not.

The notion of payment for need, like the Living Wage itself, is not a new principle of pay determination but one with a long history. In the past, the belief that the wage should be set at a level that met the needs of wage-earners was typically highly gendered. For much of the nineteenth and twentieth centuries, for example, trade unions and many social reformers pursued the objective of the 'family wage', a rate of pay sufficient to support a male breadwinner and a dependent, non-working wife and children (Land 1980). Moreover, there is evidence that a perceived male need for higher pay continues to shape wage outcomes in the labour market in the form of the 'fatherhood wage premium', a higher rate of pay that applies to men with parenting responsibilities (Fuller and Prince Cooke 2018). The Living Wage has attempted to break with gendered conceptions of employee need of this kind. It does so by basing the calculation of employee need not on the requirements of a single family-type—the male breadwinner family—but on a range of domestic arrangements. As is explained more fully below, the rate calculated is derived from an average of the expenditure needs of different types of households—single person, couples, and households with and without children. There is no attempt to prop up a single type of household, characterized by the presence of a male-breadwinner, or to privilege male wage-earners. Indeed, living wage campaigners in the UK and in other countries have often advocated the standard on the basis that it will primarily benefit low-waged, working women (Figart et al. 2002; Living Wage Foundation 2017b).

The principle of payment for need is only one of several that shape the operation of the labour market, and which determine employee earnings. Other principles include: (1) paying the person, in which pay is based on the skills, qualifications, and competencies that employees bring to the job role. Seniority based payments and separate rates of pay for younger workers are based on this principle because they assume that performance is largely a function of experience; (2) paying the job, in which pay is based on the demands of the job role, which in larger organizations may be determined through a formal job evaluation process; (3) payment for performance, where earnings are linked to measures of job output, which can encompass units of production, productivity, sales, or profit; and (4) payment according to context, where earnings are determined with reference to the labour or product market conditions that the employer is facing. Examples of context-based forms of payment include the rate for the job set through supply and demand in the labour market, affordability, which links pay to the financial performance of the firm, and arrangements such as indexation, which link earnings within the organization to movements in pay in the wider labour market. The statutory NLW, with its goal of pegging the minimum wage to median earnings, is an example of this latter type of arrangement.

The central feature of the Living Wage is that payment for need takes precedence over these other principles of payment for those on low incomes. In the specialist literature on employee remuneration, the principle of payment for need is largely neglected, but with the advent of the Living Wage movement it has assumed a central place in the management of remuneration in thousands of organizations, partly displacing other principles that have been the focus of much greater attention. Moreover, payment for need has not only taken precedence over other principles; it can inhibit, or indeed contradict, their application in organizations where the Living Wage is applied. For example, adoption of the Living Wage can disrupt pay structures founded on the principle of paying the job by raising the pay of those at the base of the structure and compressing differentials. One consequence of this can be a reduced capacity to recruit employees into team-leader or supervisory positions when the pay advantage of occupying a role of this kind has been diminished. The Living Wage can also inhibit the use of payment for performance: by raising base pay it can diminish the proportion of total reward available for bonuses and other, non-guaranteed performance payments, rendering their incentive power less effective. Finally, the introduction of the Living Wage can contradict a market-based pay strategy, in which rates are determined through supply and demand. Employers operating in the health service, for example, informed us that the Living Wage had increased pay for those in less-skilled occupations such as cleaners, security staff, and van-drivers, for which there was a plentiful supply of labour, but had no impact on the supply of professional and semi-professional workers, such as nurses, where there was a major shortage. The scheme effectively allocated wage costs to those parts of the pay structure where there was an absence of market pressure and away from those where pressures of this kind were strongly apparent.

Partly in recognition of tensions of this kind, the Living Wage has been designed to allow some accommodation with other principles of pay determination. Accredited employers are under no obligation to pay the Living Wage to those under 18 or to apprentices, an accommodation with the principle of paying the person with its assumption that younger or less qualified employees are less productive. There is also an accommodation with the principle of affordability, a central component of the belief that pay should be matched to context. This accommodation takes the form of a limit on the annual percentage increase in the Living Wage, which is restricted to three percentage points once the annual increase in inflation has been taken into account (D'Arcy and Finch 2019). The intention of this provision is to shield employers from an excessively costly increase in the Living Wage in any single year, regardless of the rate determined through the process of calculating employee need. In this specific instance, the principle of payment according to context effectively overrides payment for need.

Calculating the Living Wage

The estimation of worker needs, on which the Living Wage is based, is taken from the Minimum Income Standard (MIS), first developed by researchers at Loughborough University in 2008 and updated and maintained since (Davis et al. 2020; Hirsch 2017; Hirsch and Valdez-Martinez 2017). The MIS employs a focus-group methodology to identify the minimum requirements of those living in different types of low-income household, including those with a single person, couples without children, and singles and couples with varying numbers of children at different ages. Separate focus groups are used for estimating requirements in London and the rest of the UK. The focus groups are drawn from the type of family whose needs they assess but are socioeconomically and demographically diverse and are encouraged to form a consensus, as the purpose is to formulate a standard that can attract general, public support. Budget items, identified by the focus groups that are incorporated into the standard, include: food, moderate alcohol consumption (but not tobacco), clothing, utility bills, council tax, household goods and services, personal goods and services, social and cultural participation such as holidays and days out, travel costs including motoring outside London, childcare, and rent. Focus groups continue to meet to reassess expenditure needs, and the basket of items included within the standard changes over time. For example, the cost of a DVD player has recently been removed and replaced with that of a TV subscription service, and payment into a workplace pension scheme has been included. Once the expenditure needs have been identified, researchers estimate the costs of paying for each item and use this information to calculate the MIS for each family type. The standard consists of the minimum weekly income that is required to meet the expenditure needs that have been identified, taking account of tax levels and thresholds and the likely benefits to which families are entitled. They are adjusted annually to factor in the rate of inflation.

The UK and London Living Wage rates are derived from these annual MIS estimates. Each year a weighted average of the MIS for seventeen different family types is produced for London and the remainder of the UK, and the Living Wage is the hourly rate of pay that a full-time worker, employed for 37.5 hours, would have to be paid to secure an income equal to the appropriate weighted average (Cominetti 2020). The averaging process means that the Living Wage will generate an income above the MIS for workers in some family types and below for others, but the value of having single rather than multiple rates is felt to outweigh this unevenness of outcomes. Once the rates have been calculated they are submitted to the Living Wage Commission for approval and are then announced in Living Wage Week in November, with accredited employers then having six months to implement the new rates.

The MIS has formed the basis of the UK Living Wage since the launch of the Foundation's accreditation scheme in 2011. The London Living Wage, however, was initially calculated using a different method that did not rely on focus groups or involve members of the public in its formulation. The use of two different methods within a single campaign was judged to be unsustainable, and in 2016 the MIS method was extended to London (D'Arcy and Finch 2019). At the same time, the Resolution Foundation assumed responsibility for calculating both Living Wage rates. Since that point there has been further refinement of the methodology, but the link to the MIS and to substantial underpinning research to identify the income requirements of those in low-income households have remained constant. This link provides a solid empirical foundation for the Living Wage and is an important source of its legitimacy.

Hourly Base Rate

The Living Wage is an annual hourly rate of pay intended to cover living costs and provide a full-time worker with a decent standard of living. In 2022, the UK-wide rate stood at £9.90 an hour and the London rate at £11.05. The Living Wage Foundation does not calculate an annual Living Wage salary because the contractual hours of work of salaried employees can vary quite substantially. For illustrative purposes, however, it does produce an estimate of an annual salary for an employee contracted to work 37.5 hours per week for 52 weeks per year. In 2022 a Living Wage salary for a worker with these hours would be £21,548 in London and £19,305 elsewhere in the UK.

Another important point about the wage is that it captures a basic rate of pay and does not include premium payments, supplements, bonuses, tips, and employee benefits. It is legitimate for accredited Living Wage Employers to include guaranteed additional payments when calculating the wages of employees entitled to the Living Wage, such as a time away from home allowance or an inner-city weighting. But the Living Wage Foundation makes it clear that non-cash benefits, payments which are deferred such as pension contributions, and non-guaranteed supplements such as productivity or sales bonuses cannot be included. The exclusion of payments and benefits of this kind has been a source of dissension amongst some employers, leading them to remain aloof from the scheme. This dissension connects to a broader theme in management writing on pay and reward. It is sometimes suggested in the latter that the focus of policy should be on 'total compensation' and that labour costs should be calculated on the basis of the complete reward package, including all supplements to the base wage or salary (Lawler III 1990). The Living Wage campaign has explicitly rejected calculations of this kind. Instead, it has focused on base pay; that component of remuneration that is most stable, not at risk through being tied to business fluctuations or measures of performance, and which is paid on a weekly or monthly basis to enable employees to sustain their living standards. This rejection of contingency and preference for stability reflects the basic purpose of the Living Wage: it is a form of payment that is intended, above all, to serve employee need.

The Living Wage as Civil Regulation

In the previous chapter it was stated that the Living Wage is a form of civil regulation, and the purpose of this section is to substantiate this claim. Civil regulation, it has been argued, is distinguished by three characteristics: it is a form of private regulation that is distinct from regulation by public authorities; it is a voluntary form of regulation to which employers can choose to commit and which is supported by accreditation and economic incentives; and it relies upon unilateral regulation, in which civil society organizations formulate the rules of labour market governance that they then seek to have accepted by other actors. All these characteristics of civil regulation are readily apparent in the case of the Living Wage.

Private Regulation

In the UK, the Real Living Wage is a purely private initiative, developed and applied by the Living Wage Foundation in conjunction with its various allies. There is no legal underpinning for the standard, other than the legal contract employers sign with the Foundation when they agree to become accredited Living Wage Employers. The standard is not obligatory, and it is not enforced by law, unlike the various age-related statutory minimum wages that apply within the UK. Moreover, there is no intention on the part of campaigners to endow the Living Wage with statutory force by having it transcribed into employment law. The current private status of the standard is not viewed as a staging post to later legal enactment, and for some campaigners at least there is intrinsic value in maintaining the voluntary nature of the Living Wage. The aim is to promote a responsible form of capitalism, in which employers accept their responsibility to protect the well-being of employees and act with 'virtue' to secure this end. Such a purpose accords with the concept of active citizenship that underpins the community organizing movement, from which the Living Wage originates, and seeks to transpose the persona of the active, virtuous citizen to employers. Significantly, the campaign has been described by the Living Wage Foundation as a 'movement' of employers.

While the UK Living Wage has retained its private character, the campaign has nevertheless attempted to shape public policy. As will be shown in later chapters, a great deal of campaign effort has been invested in trying to secure political support for the Living Wage and in shaping the behaviour of public authorities. Much of this effort has been directed at local authorities and city regions, and at the devolved national governments of Scotland and Wales; that is, below the level of

UK government where legislative power on employment matters is concentrated. At local, regional, and national levels public authorities have been regarded by campaigners as 'anchor institutions', which may not have the capacity to legislate on wages, but which do possess other levers that can be used to promote the Living Wage within their areas of jurisdiction. The campaign has sought to make use of these levers, enlisting the power of public authorities as employers, purchasers, and funders to help diffuse the Living Wage (Heery et al. 2020).

Voluntary Regulation

The Living Wage is a form of voluntary regulation, a standard that employers can choose to adopt. If they do choose to adopt the Living Wage, then they can be formally accredited by the Living Wage Foundation for doing so. Accreditation, certification, and other forms of badging are a common feature of voluntary regulation and can provide a means of signalling to employees, customers, investors, and clients what are the values of the organization, what standards it seeks to uphold, and how it behaves (Dineen and Allen 2016; Gregory-Smith 2018; Hoque 2003). They provide a visible symbol to a range of internal and external stakeholders of how the organization aspires to act. Once accredited, Living Wage Employers can use the Living Wage logo on their websites, letterhead, email addresses, and in other forms of communication. The Living Wage Foundation encourages visible display of accreditation of this kind and in its own communication strategy repeatedly celebrates the commitment of individual employers to the Living Wage. This celebration also encompasses a set of awards for exemplary Living Wage Employers, presented at an annual ceremony. Positive reinforcement of employer accreditation in this way is another common feature of systems of voluntary regulation (Bowkett et al. 2017; Demougin et al. 2021).

In return for accreditation, employers enter into a number of obligations. They sign a license with the Living Wage Foundation, which commits them to specific commitments as follows:

- Payment of the Living Wage to all directly employed staff, regardless of the hours they work or their level of seniority, from the point of accreditation.
- Ensuring that the Living Wage is paid to the employees of contractors working on the employers' premises for at least two hours a day and for a period of eight consecutive weeks. Payment of the Living Wage to the employees of contractors can be phased in following accreditation, allowing employees to be moved onto the new rate of pay at the point at which service contracts are renegotiated. Where there is phased implementation of the Living Wage in this manner, the employer must formulate a time-limited plan for its introduction, which is reviewed jointly with the Living Wage Foundation.

- Ensuring that self-employed workers are paid the Living Wage, provided that they work on the employer's premises for two hours a day for a period of eight weeks.
- Payment of the Living Wage to all direct and eligible indirect workers who are aged 18 and over, including students and those who may be living at home with parents.
- Payment of the higher, London Living Wage to all direct and indirect employees whose workplace is located in one of the boroughs that comprise Greater London.
- Raising the pay of those receiving the Living Wage to the new annual rate within six months of its announcement in the first week of November (in 2022, the new rate was announced early, in September, with employers having the option to introduce it at that point to help employees with the cost-of-living crisis).
- Payment of an annual subscription to the Living Wage Foundation, which starts at £60 per year for organizations with fewer than ten employees and rises to a maximum of £3,000 for larger employers.

It can be noted that these commitments do not require payment of the Living Wage to those aged below 18 or those working as apprentices, though many employers do extend payment to these groups. They also do not require payment of the Living Wage to volunteers, to those working outside the UK, or to the employees of contractors who provide intermittent services to the employer, such as those making deliveries or carrying out short-term maintenance. Some Living Wage Employers, however, do encourage all suppliers to adopt the standard, and some of the large multinational companies that are accredited have sought to extend the principle of the Living Wage across their entire range of operations.

As with other voluntary standards, the Living Wage Foundation has endeavoured to reinforce the commitments made by employers through a system of economic incentives. The latter are discussed more fully in the next chapter, but it is worth noting the main elements of this endeavour here. First, the Foundation has commissioned, published, and publicized research which shows that employers can benefit from paying the Living Wage, using this evidence to argue that there is a 'business case' for accreditation (Barford et al. 2022; Coulson and Bonner 2015; Heery et al. 2017; Hughes et al. 2016; Werner and Lim 2016; Wills and Kakpo et al. 2009). Second, the Foundation has encouraged institutions that support its objectives to provide direct, tangible incentives for employers to adopt the Living Wage. Public authorities embedding the standard within their procurement policies is one example of incentive provision of this kind. Third, there has been an attempt to create a Living Wage consumer brand, using the Living Wage logo and a communication and marketing strategy to encourage consumers to 'buy Living Wage'.

Unilateral Regulation

The final characteristic of civil regulation is that it is formulated unilaterally within civil society. The standards and rules of which it is comprised are created by civil society organizations, which then seek to have these regulations adopted by other economic, social, and political actors. In the case of the Living Wage this act of unilateral creation is the prime responsibility of the Living Wage Foundation, which is responsible for developing the standard, calculating and announcing the annual rate, and promoting it to employers. The Foundation also has oversight of and responsibility for the system of employer accreditation. In carrying out these responsibilities, the Living Wage Foundation works with several partners, which are themselves civil society organizations. The Foundation contracts with the Resolution Foundation to calculate the UK and London Living Wage rates; the Poverty Alliance and Cynnal Cymru share responsibility for accrediting employers in Scotland and Wales; and ShareAction, the campaigning body for ethical investment, promotes the Living Wage to large companies listed on the Stock Exchange. The Living Wage Foundation itself, moreover, is funded by a further set of civil society organizations, which exist to promote action against poverty, including the People's Health Trust, the Joseph Rowntree Foundation, and Comic Relief. It is from this network of civil society organizations, with the Living Wage Foundation at its centre, that the Living Wage originates.

This pattern of unilateral regulation contrasts with other arrangements for regulating the base of the labour market. Since 1997, for instance, the UK's statutory minimum wage has been set through the Low Pay Commission (LPC). The latter is an advisory body established by the UK government to recommend the level of the National Minimum Wage. Since 2016, the LPC has also been charged with monitoring and evaluating the National Living Wage and with recommending annual increases in the latter that will allow it to reach two-thirds of median hourly earnings by 2024. The critical difference between the LPC and the Living Wage Foundation is not just that the former is a statutory body whose advice can be transcribed into law, but that it is a multistakeholder organization that embodies the principle of social partnership (Metcalf 1999). The LPC has a tripartite composition, which includes representatives of the trade unions (nominated by the TUC), representatives of business, and independent experts—academics with expertise in labour economics and industrial relations. As such, the LPC can be said to be engaged in a process of multilateral regulation, encompassing several distinct interests, which contrasts with the unilateral regulation of the Living Wage Foundation.

The contrast between multilateral and unilateral regulation, however, is not as stark as it might first appear. While the Living Wage Foundation has ultimate responsibility for the Living Wage, it has consulted widely on aspects of the scheme, including with trade union and business representatives. This commitment to consultation with those the Foundation aspires to regulate has found institutional expression. The Foundation has an advisory board, with a membership comprised of executives from accredited organizations, faith leaders, representatives of partners, campaigning organizations, and a representative of the TUC. In addition, in 2016 the Living Wage Commission was established (Howard 2022). The initial brief for this body was to oversee the merging of the London and UK-wide Living Wage schemes, but it has been retained as an oversight body that formally approves the Living Wage rates each year and offers guidance on the development of the campaign, including refinement of the method of calculation. The Commission has a multistakeholder composition, drawn from leaders of accredited organizations, trade unions, faith groups, civil society, and academic experts. It is modelled on the LPC. The setting up of the Commission represents a softening over time of the unilateral character of the Living Wage, an attempt to widen consultation and draw a broad set of affected interests into the governance of the scheme.

Tests of Robustness

In this section we apply some of the tests of robustness developed by students of private regulation to the case of the Living Wage. Five tests are considered in all. We examine the content of the Living Wage standard to establish: (1) the extent it exceeds the legal requirements of the statutory minimum wage; (2) whether it is based on principles set out in international treaties and by international government agencies; (3) the degree to which the formal content of the scheme provides an opportunity for worker representatives to take part in its application; (4) whether the procedures that govern the scheme contain robust provision for external scrutiny of employer compliance with the standard; and (5) whether the operation of the scheme embodies a 'capability approach' in which the campaign works cooperatively with employers to actively support them in their implementation of the Living Wage.

Beyond the Legal Minimum

When American sports footwear and clothing brand Nike first began to regulate its global supply chain, it said that it would ensure that all its supplier factories were fully compliant with local health and safety and labour legislation (Locke et al. 2007). Since then, under continuing pressure from human rights campaigners, Nike has strengthened its position and proclaimed a commitment to standards that exceed legal requirements. For example, since 1998 it has insisted that air quality in supplier factories must meet the standards set by the US Occupational

Safety and Health administration, overriding those set by local legislatures. It has also insisted on lower age limits for employees that exceed many national minimum age laws. Developments of this kind are commonplace in the field of private regulation, with employers signing up to standards that go beyond legal minima and embrace norms of best practice (Tsogas 2001).

This aspiration to exceed legal minima is also apparent in the case of the Living Wage. The campaign emerged from dissatisfaction with the low rate at which the NMW had been set in the late 1990s, and ever since it has had as its core objective the promotion of a wage that exceeds the statutory legal minimum. The Living Wage standard goes beyond the law in three main ways. First, it provides an hourly rate of pay that is higher than the various age-related minima that are required by law. Second, eligibility rules are more inclusive, with the full rate being paid to all aged 18 and over compared with the current 23 years age limit for the National Living Wage. Third, the standard encompasses indirect workers, employed by contractors, and in this way reaches beyond the legal obligations of the direct employer.

Table 2.1 shows the current age-specific statutory minimum wage rates in the UK and compares them with the current UK-wide and London Living Wage rates. It shows that the latter are higher than the former; that they extend beyond the legal minima. Thus, the UK-wide Living Wage is four per cent higher than the National Living Wage and is much higher again than the lower statutory rates for younger adults aged 18 and over. The gaps between the London Living Wage and the statutory minima are wider: in the case of workers aged between 18 and 20 there is a positive differential of more than 62 per cent. The only point in the table where the advantage breaks down is with regard to junior workers and those on apprenticeships: the Living Wage sets only an adult wage rate and, as we have seen, does not encompass those on training contracts. Despite these exclusions, it is clear from

Table 2.1 UK and London Living Wage as a percentage of age-specific statutory minimum wage rates, 2022

Age-bands	Age-specific minimum rates[1]		UK Living Wage		London Living Wage	
	£	%	£	%	£	%
23 +	9.50	100	9.90	104.2	11.05	116.3
21–22	9.18	100	9.90	107.8	11.05	120.4
18–20	6.83	100	9.90	144.9	11.05	161.8
16–17	4.81	100	n/a	100	n/a	100
Apprentices	4.81	100	n/a	100	n/a	100

1. Rates in force from 1 April 2022; note that when first introduced the National Living Wage was payable to those aged 25 and over but subsequently the age limit has dropped to 23 and will fall further to 21 by 2024.

the table that young workers are especially likely to have been beneficiaries of the Living Wage, and the same is true of those working in London. For a young worker employed for 37.5 hours a week outside London who moved from the statutory minimum to the Living Wage, there would be a weekly increase of pay of £115.13, worth £5,986.50 over the course year. For an equivalent young worker in London, the weekly increase would be £158.25 and the annual gain £8,229.00. These are very substantial increases, capable of changing the experience of working life for those who receive them.

Table 2.2 illustrates how the relationship between the Living Wage and the statutory minimum wage has changed over time. It shows that over the past decade two trends have been apparent. In the period of austerity after the global financial crisis, the gap between the statutory minimum and both the London and UK-wide Living Wage increased, reaching a maximum for the latter of twenty-three per cent in 2015/2016. Since then, the gap has closed, dropping below ten per cent for the UK-wide rate in 2020/2021. A major cause of this narrowing has been the introduction of the NLW and the Government's policy of increasing the

Table 2.2 The gap between the statutory minimum wage and the Living Wage over time, 2003–2022

Year	Statutory minimum[1]	London Living Wage		UK Living Wage	
		£	% Difference	£	% Difference
2003/4	4.50	6.40	42.2	-	
2004/5	4.85	6.50	34.0	-	
2005/6	5.05	6.70	32.7	-	
2006/7	5.35	7.05	31.8	-	
2007/8	5.52	7.20	30.4	-	
2008/9	5.73	7.45	30.0	-	
2009/10	5.80	7.60	31.0	-	
2010/11	5.93	7.85	32.4	-	
2011/12	6.08	8.30	36.5	7.20	18.4
2012/13	6.19	8.55	38.1	7.45	20.4
2013/14	6.31	8.80	39.5	7.65	21.2
2014/15	6.50	9.15	40.8	7.85	20.8
2015/16	6.70	9.40	40.3	8.25	23.1
2016/17	7.20	9.75	35.4	8.45	17.4
2017/18	7.50	10.20	36.0	8.75	16.7
2018/19	7.83	10.55	34.7	9.00	14.9
2019/20	8.21	10.75	30.9	9.30	13.3
2020/21	8.72	10.85	24.4	9.50	8.9
2021/22	8.91	11.05	24.0	9.90	11.1

Source: Living Wage Foundation.
1. The highest age-related statutory minimum wage, e.g. the NLW, after 2016

value of the latter in pursuit of the target of two-thirds of median hourly earnings (Cominetti et al. 2022). If this downward trend continues much further, however, the distinctive claim of the Living Wage to support a standard of living that is substantially above that which can be afforded on the NLW will be compromised.

Global Standards

A second test of the robustness of private regulation is whether the latter incorporates global standards. The latter might consist either of broad principles, such as the core commitments to end child labour, forced labour, and discrimination on the grounds of race and sex adumbrated by the International Labour Organization (ILO), or of more detailed regulations dealing with specific features of the employment relationship, such as wages, working time, or health and safety. It is common for global prescriptions of this kind to be embedded in systems of private regulation developed by either global brands or international NGOs (Donaghey et al. 2014; Tsogas 2001). There are a variety reasons for doing so. Adherence to global standards can raise the legitimacy of private codes, override weaker country-specific regulation, and can enhance the efficiency of regulation by ensuring that common principles and rules are adhered to across a supply chain or within a particular industry. The efficiency gains of standardized regulation of this kind can accrue to both regulators and to those who are regulated. The former gain from applying a single set of regulations across their span of operations, while the latter gain when codes associated with different brands have common features and provisions. The multiplicity of private schemes of regulation to which individual supplier companies may be subject has been identified as a major problem in the research literature on corporate codes (Kuruvilla 2021; Locke 2013). Standardizing codes, such that they incorporate accepted global standards, is one way of dealing with this problem.

The principle that workers should receive a living wage is proclaimed in a number of international conventions and declarations, including the United Nations Declaration of Human Rights of 1948 and the Council of Europe's European Charter of 1961. The ILO has also declared support for this principle, most recently in its 2008 Declaration on Social Justice for a Fair Globalization (Anker 2011; see also Zimmer 2019). However, the ILO has not produced a convention on the living wage (as opposed to the minimum wage), and there is no accepted international definition of the living wage or an accepted methodology for its calculation. As a result of this absence, there is no reference to international standards in the formulation of the UK Living Wage, and the latter does not enshrine international principles or detailed regulation. It is a regulatory standard that has been developed, *de novo*, within the UK.

Despite the home-grown quality of the UK Living Wage standard, it has emerged from an international movement to promote a standard of this kind. The UK Living Wage campaign in certain respects represents a transfer of the American campaign to Britain, via the community organizing movement which established a London offshoot, The East London Communities Organization (TELCO), in 1996. It was TELCO that initiated the Living Wage campaign. Subsequently, links have been developed with living wage campaigners in other countries, including Canada, Hong Kong, India, New Zealand/Aoetearoa, and South Africa, and since 2015 the Foundation has developed a Global Living Wage Initiative (Living Wage Foundation 2021a). The latter has produced a set of Living Wage core principles to guide international campaigning, which largely embody the existing features of the UK Living Wage standard (see Figure 2.1). The Initiative has also promoted the Living Wage as a means of furthering the UN's Sustainable Development Goals and published case studies of campaigns in different parts of the globe to promote mutual learning (Living Wage Foundation 2017b; 2021a).

The purpose of the Global Living Wage Initiative is to develop a unifying international standard, in part to secure the efficiency benefits of standardization outlined above. The question of standardization has also been an important consideration for the Living Wage campaign within the UK. In the UK, like the USA, the Living Wage campaign began as a local initiative. The first campaign began in the East End of London in 2001 and was followed by similar initiatives in other British cities, such as Glasgow, Brighton, Lincoln, and Oxford. As we have seen, a division also emerged between the method used to calculate the UK Living Wage rate, which was based on the MIS, and the method used to determine the London Living Wage. This latter division is now closed, and the other local

1. A Living Wage should be calculated by reference to the income an individual needs to earn in order to live a decent life (where basic standards of living are met) and to participate fully in society
2. The Living Wage for any country and location should be set by reference to local living standards and needs
3. The Living Wage should be set in a transparent way, independent of control or manipulation by government, employers or other parties
4. A Living Wage should be sufficient to pay for a locally agreed basket of goods, which is likely to include food, housing, utilities, transport, a degree of leisure and potentially education, health insurance, childcare, servicing debt and savings. A Living Wage is likely to include support for family members as needed in the local context
5. A Living Wage should be paid to all employees over a locally agreed minimum working age
6. A Living Wage should be paid voluntarily by employers

Figure 2.1 The principles of the Global Living Wage
Source: Living Wage Foundation (2015)

living wage rates and systems of accreditation have largely been absorbed within the UK-wide campaign, coordinated by the Living Wage Foundation. It is common for campaigners to refer to the Scottish or Welsh Living Wage, or to the Glasgow, Birmingham, or Greater Manchester Living Wage, but this is essentially rebadging of the national standard to facilitate local identification with the campaign. There is still some variation: Oxford City Council promotes its own Living Wage, which is higher than the Living Wage Foundation's UK rate, reflecting high living costs in the city, and the Brighton Living Wage operates a separate system of accreditation for employers. The primary development though has been one of standardization across the UK, with the Living Wage Foundation rates and methods of accreditation being adopted in all parts of the country. The reason for this largely stems from the needs of large employers, who in consultation with the Foundation made it clear that they wanted a single rate to apply across the UK outside of London which could be readily incorporated into their nationwide pay structures. Standardization was primarily a response to the needs of those being regulated.

Employee Participation

A third test of robustness developed by some commentators is whether systems of private regulation are supportive of freedom of association and give scope for employees and their representatives to take part in their development and implementation (Kuruvilla 2021; Tsogas 2001). Debate over this issue has been particularly marked in the wake of the Rana Plaza disaster in Bangladesh in 2013. The response to the disaster followed two courses. On the one hand, there was the development of the Accord for Fire and Building Safety in Bangladesh, while on the other there was the formation of the Alliance for Bangladesh Worker Safety (Donaghey and Reinecke 2018). The most striking difference between these two international attempts to improve health and safety in the Bangladeshi garment sector is that the Accord gives a central place to trade unions—Donaghey and Reinecke characterize the Accord as an experiment in 'labour-driven governance'—while the Alliance offered no role to trade unions and was developed primarily by American brands with a reputation for anti-unionism. Significantly, the Accord continues to operate while the Alliance was discontinued in 2018.

To what extent has the emphasis on union representation and participation seen in the Accord been reproduced within the Living Wage? The first thing to note is that unions form part of the membership of Citizens UK, have taken part in the Living Wage campaign, and are represented on the Advisory Board of the Living Wage Foundation and the Living Wage Commission. Trade unions have therefore participated in the governance of the Living Wage and have been given opportunities to influence the standard and its operation. Trade unions have also incorporated the Living Wage in their own collective bargaining and campaigning activity, independently of the 'official' Living Wage campaign. It remains though that the Living Wage standard provides no formal role for the trade unions or other worker representatives in the process of accreditation and implementation of the Living Wage, including within organizations in which trade unions are recognized by the employer. The advice issued to employers by the Living Wage Foundation urges them to communicate effectively with employees about the Living Wage, but the latter is not tied to a formal requirement for worker participation or agreement. The Living Wage standard in this respect corresponds most closely to the Bangladesh Alliance rather than the Accord. Like the Alliance it rests on unitary assumptions, seeks to persuade employers that raising labour standards is in their own interest as well as in the interest of employees, and identifies management, not worker representatives, as the key agent of change.

Monitoring and Enforcement

Systems of regulation require supporting arrangements to secure compliance, which typically include monitoring and enforcement. Arrangements of this kind have been widely discussed in the literature on international private regulation, and several common features have been identified. The latter include: the collection of HR and other records from supplier businesses to gauge the level of compliance with codes and standards; the use of independent, third party monitors to collect and review these data; interviewing employees about working conditions and setting up of disclosure procedures through which auditors can be alerted to contravention of standards; the rating of companies in terms of their level of compliance with private codes through numerical scores or ordinal scales; and provision for non-compliant businesses to be excluded from supply chains if there is a repeated record of failure (Locke et al. 2007). The presence of robust, independent arrangements of this kind are conventionally regarded as essential for the effective regulation of labour standards within global value chains, though there is also a critique on the grounds that top-down, low-trust systems of monitoring simply generate minimal compliance, evasion, and manipulation of records (Locke 2013).

Most of these arrangements are not applied in the case of the Living Wage. There is no collection of payroll or other data to check that the Living Wage is being paid by accredited employers and no use of independent auditors to visit the latter and interview their employees. Employers are asked to provide information to the Living Wage Foundation at the point of accreditation on the number and type of employees receiving a pay increase and since 2018 have been asked to supply these figures on an annual basis. The purpose of collecting this information, however, is to estimate the positive impact of the Living Wage and not to monitor compliance. Living Wage Employers are not rated in terms of their level of compliance as the standard is conceived of in binary terms, but, as has been explained, it is possible for employers to phase in the payment of the Living Wage to indirect employees, and when this occurs a plan is agreed with the Foundation and employers asked to report on progress in extending the Living Wage to these workers. There is provision in the license agreement that the Living Wage Foundation makes with employers for accreditation to be terminated if an employer fails to apply the Living Wage. This provision is rarely used, but on occasion campaigners have taken action against employers that have failed to honour their agreement. For example, the Poverty Alliance related the case of a public sector organization in Scotland which informed them that they had rolled over an existing contract with a supplier rather than change it to allow payment of the Living Wage, as had previously been agreed, because of financial pressures. The Alliance told the employer that this was not acceptable and, on being informed that accreditation was being suspended, the employer relented and negotiated a new service contract with its supplier that resulted in a pay increase for 200 workers. It must be stressed again, however, that episodes of this kind are infrequent. It is much more common for employers who find that they are not able to conform with their license agreement either to withdraw from the scheme or to simply allow their membership to lapse leading to their exclusion from the list of accredited organizations. Exit rather than expulsion is the way in which a failure to comply is usually dealt with.

One element of the international compliance package that does operate in the case of the Living Wage is a whistleblowing procedure. There is provision for an employee of an accredited organization to initiate what is known as an Employee Concerns Enquiry through the Foundation's website if they believe that they are not being paid the Living Wage. Campaign workers informed us that this procedure is only rarely invoked, most complaints come from employees working for non-accredited organizations or whose jobs are outside the scheme, and that when genuine underpayment is identified this is usually due to error and is corrected by apologetic employers. In a very small number of cases, however, complaints have led to employers being excluded from accreditation.

The question of monitoring compliance not only arises in the relationship between the Foundation and accredited Living Wage Employers. It is also relevant to the relationship between accredited organizations and contractors whose employees are eligible for the Living Wage. Our interviews with employers suggested that the latter generally do not take steps to monitor whether contractors are paying the Living Wage. In the same way in which the Living Wage Foundation trusts Living Wage Employers to honour their commitment to pay the Living Wage, so accredited organizations trust their suppliers to do the same. For example, a remuneration manager at a university likened the Living Wage clause in contracts with suppliers to a clause requiring that they operate a safe system of work. Like the safety clause, it is taken on trust that the commitment to pay the Living Wage will be honoured without intrusive checking. In another case, the HR manager of a UK-wide educational charity explained that it was not possible to check whether suppliers were paying the Living Wage across a range of contracts operating in different parts of the country. He did say, however, that these contracts were lucrative to suppliers and that risking their loss by failing to honour the Living Wage clause was unlikely. Underpinning this faith in contractors to implement the Living Wage is the fact that in most cases the cost of doing so is absorbed by the client: seventy-one per cent of employers responding to our 2021 survey who used contractors reported that they had absorbed the cost of pay increases. Subsidizing the cost of raising standards in this way arguably distinguishes the domestic form of private regulation produced by the Living Wage Foundation from that found in international supply chains. In the latter, it has been noted, 'predatory pricing' designed to concentrate value in global brands can work against attempts to upgrade standards (Anner 2019; Barrientos et al. 2019).

The Living Wage emerges from the monitoring and enforcement test as a relatively soft form of private regulation, a feature that has been identified as a flaw by more sceptical observers (Johnson et al. 2019). It is debatable, though, whether this is a major source of weakness. As has been noted, empirical studies of seemingly robust systems to enforce compliance with private regulation indicate that they can be ineffective: the light touch applied by the Living Wage Foundation may be just as likely to secure compliance without imposing substantial monitoring costs. It is also important to note that the structural position occupied by Living Wage Employers with regard to the Foundation is not equivalent to that occupied by supplier companies with regard to global brands applying corporate codes of conduct. Living Wage Employers are not in a position of economic dependence on the Foundation and have chosen voluntarily to become accredited. Given this situation, there is seemingly less need for monitoring. In addition, supplier companies to Living Wage Employers are often shielded from the economic cost of paying higher wages and therefore have a reduced incentive to try and avoid compliance. The type of domestic regulation developed by the Living Wage campaign is arguably less requiring of extensive monitoring and enforcement procedures than are the international forms of regulation developed within global value chains.

Capability Approach

A capability approach to private regulation is one that seeks to help those being regulated meet standards. In the field of international private regulation, such an approach can involve brands providing management, training, and other resources to their suppliers as well as attempts to upgrade production systems and thereby raise productivity so that higher labour standards can be more readily afforded. Underpinning efforts of this kind is often a form of 'relational contracting', in which brands develop a long-term relationship with suppliers founded on cooperation and mutual adjustment (Distelhorst et al. 2017).

Some of these elements are found in the relationship between the Living Wage Foundation and its member employers, and to a degree they have become more pronounced over time. The Foundation seeks to obtain an open-ended commitment to paying the Living Wage from accredited employers and celebrates and tries to reinforce this commitment during Living Wage Week, through its social media activity, and in its direct communication with accredited organizations. The Foundation refers to its campaign as a 'movement' of employers and continually endeavours to reproduce employer support. It strives to develop a long-term relationship with its member-employers that is not purely transactional.

More recently, the Living Wage Foundation has added a fee-based consultancy service to its repertoire. The Living Work Consultancy takes the form of either open or bespoke training and is aimed at organizations that are considering adopting the Living Wage. The training covers identifying an organization-specific business case for the Living Wage, enlisting the support of stakeholders, overcoming internal barriers, and developing a plan for implementation. The programme seeks explicitly to link the introduction of the Living Wage to other areas of HRM to promote a broad 'good work agenda', precisely in the manner suggested by advocates of a capability approach. The Foundation's publicity refers to securing a 'win-win for everyone: employees who have more meaningful jobs and employers who increase their organization's productivity'.

It remains though that the vast majority of accredited Living Wage Employers do not make use of this service, and our interviews with employers suggested that they had only limited contact with the Foundation once they had become accredited. The impression was also gathered that, for many, Living Wage accreditation was a relatively discrete change, which had not stimulated a wider review of HR practice. Some organizations have been prompted to revise pay and grading structures to accommodate the Living Wage, and some have redesigned jobs and introduced associated training, but in most cases change of this kind has not occurred: more than three-quarters of employers responding to our survey said that they had absorbed 'the cost of the Living Wage without making significant changes to working practices'.

In this regard, the Living Wage campaign not only falls short of the most ambitious forms of capability approach but also differs from the domestic regulation promoted by some of its CSO peers. Organizations like Stonewall, the Business Disability Forum, and the Equality Challenge Unit operate what can be termed an 'account-management' form of private regulation, in which their staff work closely with member-clients to develop a business plan to implement standards, review progress, and provide feedback and an overall rating, and then repeat the cycle on annual basis (Demougin et al. 2021). The Living Wage Foundation reviews plans to extend the Living Wage to employees of contractors where this is relevant but in other respects is not involved in this kind of ongoing intervention. This is partly because of the nature of the Living Wage standard: a discrete change to rates of pay which differs from the charters, covering multiple issues, promoted by other CSOs. Partly too, it flows from logistical considerations. The Living Wage has many more supporting companies than these other schemes of private regulation, including many small organizations paying only a modest accreditation fee. Stonewall, the Business Disability Forum, and the Equality Challenge Unit, in contrast, recruit amongst large corporates and public service organizations and charge substantial fees that fund the account-management model. There is arguably less need for a capability approach to regulation given the nature of the Living Wage standard, therefore, but also limited capacity on the part of the Foundation itself to develop this kind of ongoing supportive relationship for the bulk of its member-employers.

Evolution of the Living Wage

In accounts of international private regulation, it is possible to identify an evolutionary logic of regulation. Within this logic, relatively modest initial attempts give way to the adoption of more rigorous standards and more exacting regimes of enforcement as the initial measures are exposed as largely ineffectual (Locke et al. 2007). Successive exposés of poor work conditions by human rights campaigners push brands to develop more elaborate systems of regulation for their supply chains. Underpinning this evolution is the central interest of global corporations in protecting their brands and in reducing the risks to which they are exposed. It is the institutional interest of corporations in managing and reducing risk that drives the elaboration of private regulation.

There are echoes of this process in the Living Wage campaign. In 2019, the Living Wage Foundation launched a Living Hours standard to sit alongside the Living Wage. The new standard seeks to secure minimum and more predictable hours for low-wage employees and can be seen partly as a response to criticism that a higher hourly wage represents only a limited improvement to employees working short hours or on zero-hours contracts. Other supplementary standards that have been developed by the Foundation, however, do not possess this kind of rationale. The Foundation has created a Recognized Service Provider standard for supplier companies, a Living Wage Funder standard for grant-making organizations, and has initiated a Living Wage Places scheme under which city-regions, cities, towns, boroughs, and even buildings can secure recognition for promoting the Living Wage (Howard 2022). What unites these supplementary standards is that they create new mechanisms for spreading the Living Wage and are designed to maintain the momentum of the campaign. Attack from critics for earlier failure has not been a significant driving force. Rather, it is entrepreneurial activity amongst campaigners, identifying fresh opportunities to promote the Living Wage, which has led to the evolution of additional standards. To the extent that there is an institutional interest underpinning this development, it is the interest of the Living Wage Foundation itself, seeking to elaborate its regulatory role, grow its own organization, and secure its future.

Recognized Living Wage Service Providers

The first supplementary standard introduced by the campaign was that for Recognized Service Providers (RSPs), which was created in 2012 for business service firms that give an undertaking to support and promote the Living Wage. Businesses that have signed up to the standard include some of the UK's premier facilities management companies, such as Compass, ISS, Mitie, OCS, and Sodexo, as well as many smaller cleaning, security, and other contract businesses. By May 2022, there were 174 RSPs, employing a total of 319,480 workers. The standard itself contains two main requirements. In the first place, accredited providers are required to pay the Living Wage to their own, permanent workforce located at head office, in precisely the same way that accredited Living Wage Employers are required to do. In the second place, providers are required to include a tender based on paying the Living Wage, alongside a tender based on market rates, whenever they bid for work with clients. Provided the client accepts the higher-cost tender then all employees working on this contract must be paid the Living Wage. This second provision embodies the assumptions that it is the responsibility of client businesses to ensure that employees working for contractors are paid the Living Wage and that clients, not contractors, will fund the higher rate of pay.

The standard also contains several reporting requirements. At the point of accreditation, service providers are asked to report the total number of employees working on contracts with client firms who are paid the Living Wage. On each anniversary of accreditation, providers are asked to report an updated figure to enable the Living Wage Foundation to track progress over time and identify whether inclusion in the scheme is leading to a growth in Living Wage coverage for the contract workforce. The RSPs accredited in 2022 reported that 138,311 employees were being paid the Living Wage at the point they joined the scheme and that this figure had subsequently risen to 173,377, a substantial increase of twenty-five per cent.

The Service Provider standard has a double rationale. On the one hand, it seeks to ensure that there is a substantial group of business service contractors which are available to Living Wage Employers and which are familiar with and supportive of the Living Wage standard. For this reason, all RSPs are listed on the Living Wage Foundation website and many are included in the *Living Wage Foundation Business Directory*. On the other hand, RSPs are meant to act as ambassadors for the Living Wage, bringing the standard to the attention of clients through the tendering process. The evidence just presented indicates a degree of success in this regard. Underpinning both rationales is the more fundamental belief that commercial relationships between businesses can serve as a vector for diffusing good labour standards.

A final thing to note about the RSP standard is that it explicitly rejects the argument that the Living Wage campaign should oppose outsourcing and strive to have contract jobs brought back in-house. What are sometimes described as 'indie unions', for instance, have campaigned both for the Living Wage and for the 'in-housing' of outsourced cleaning, catering, portering, and security services at universities and other public service organizations in London (Peró 2019; Shenker 2019). Through the RSP accreditation, the Living Wage campaign has effectively rejected this kind of linkage. The objective of the campaign is to secure the regulation of outsourcing through the application of the Living Wage standard, not its abolition (Heery et al. 2022).

Living Wage Funders

The Living Wage Funder standard also seeks to use business-to-business relationships to spread the Living Wage. The standard was introduced in 2018 with the explicit aim of tackling low pay in the charity sector, where it was estimated a third of jobs were paid below the Living Wage (Living Wage Foundation 2017a). Those that have committed to the standard include some of the UK's major funders of charitable activity (e.g. Comic Relief and the National Lottery Community Fund), charitable foundations established by businesses (e.g. Aviva, Coutts, KPMG, Lloyd's Bank, and Nationwide), specialist funders of particular types of charity (e.g. The People's Health Trust, Jerwood Arts, and Youth Music), and local authorities that fund charitable activity, including the London Boroughs of Brent, Croydon, Islington, Lambeth, and Southwark.

The standard has three main elements. First, Funders must themselves become accredited as Living Wage Employers, ensuring that the Living Wage is paid to their direct workforce and to any contract employees working on their premises. Second, Funders are required to ensure that any posts they fund in charities are funded at the Living Wage, 'where possible'. To this end, in their guidance on making grant applications, Funders are asked to make it clear that applying charities should base costs on paying 'at least the Real Living Wage'. Third, while it is not a requirement that charities receiving funds must themselves become accredited employers, funding bodies are encouraged to promote accreditation to those they fund. This encouragement can take the form of sharing details about accreditation in regular communication with grantees, including a question about accreditation in grant monitoring, and funding the annual cost of accreditation for grant-holders. In addition to these three core requirements, Living Wage Funders are also asked to report on the number and value of the grants they provide to charities and the extent of take-up of the Living Wage amongst third-sector organizations receiving funding. While the Service Provider standard seeks to diffuse the Living Wage along purchaser-provider connections, therefore, the Funder standard targets the financing of activity in the not-for-profit sector, seeking to disseminate the Living Wage through connections between grant-makers and grant-holders.

Living Wage Places

The idea of accrediting places where there are concentrations of Living Wage Employers emerged quite early in the campaign. It was only in 2019, however, that the Living Wage Places accreditation was launched, largely as a consequence of developments in Scotland. In the mid-2010s, Scottish local authorities in Dundee, Perth and Kinross, and Fife launched Fairness Commissions to inquire into poverty, inequality, and social exclusion, and these led to calls for the creation of Living Wage cities and towns. In response, the Poverty Alliance commissioned a report into the feasibility of a place-based form of accreditation, and the positive recommendations from this exercise led to the development of the Living Wage Places scheme (Rocket Science 2017). The latter was launched in 2019, with Dundee being recognized as the first Living Wage City and Glenrothes in Fife becoming the first Living Wage Town.

The Living Wage Places scheme seeks to include places on a variety of scales, with provision for the accreditation of Living Wage buildings, zones, neighbourhoods, boroughs, towns, cities, and regions. The basis of accreditation varies in accordance with the scale of the place being accredited (Living Wage Foundation 2019b). For buildings and for zones, there is a straightforward standard-based form of accreditation, in which all employers located in a building or zone must individually be accredited as Living Wage Employers for the place-based accreditation to apply. In the case of a Living Wage Building, therefore, all the businesses leasing space in a multi-occupier facility must pay the Living Wage. International House in Brixton, a property owned by Lambeth Council and occupied by a mix of social enterprises and creative businesses, was the first building to be accredited on this basis. Cardiff University's Social Science Research Park (SBARC), which hosts several independent research organizations, is the first Living Wage Building in Wales. Living Wage Zones are on a larger scale, comprising 'managed campuses, development sites, and industrial parks', in which all businesses pay the Living Wage. The announcement of the first Living Wage Zones was delayed by the onset of COVID-19, but it is hoped that the first sites in London will be accredited as the economy recovers from the pandemic, including the Queen Elizabeth Olympic Park in East London.

For places on a larger scale, the basis of accreditation differs and is process-based, requiring evidence of local commitment and activity to promote the Living Wage. The central component of this process-based system is a requirement to create a Living Wage Action Group, drawn from local employers, which will develop a three-year Action Plan for growing Living Wage accreditation amongst employers in the area. Other requirements are as follows: (1) the Action Group must include the local authority, major private sector businesses, a representative of the not-for-profit sector, a representative of small business, and a business network such as the local Chamber of Commerce; (2) there is also a requirement to include 'anchor institutions' in the membership of the Action Group and to prioritize the recruitment of organizations of this type through the Action Plan. Anchor institutions are large employers with a local supply chain, which are strongly identified with the local area. They can include utility companies, transport hubs and providers, universities and colleges, cultural organizations such as theatres and museums, and sports teams and venues. They can also include long-established private businesses that exemplify a particular place: in Dundee, DC Thomson, the publisher of *Beano* and *Dandy*, is one such business and has been a strong supporter of the Living Wage City initiative; (3) the first task of the Action Group is to assemble baseline data of the extent of Living Wage take-up in the area and the extent and pattern of low pay. It is assumed that only places which already have a substantial number of Living Wage Employers, and which are therefore credible candidates to become Living Wage regions, cities, boroughs, or towns, will be accredited; (4) the three-year Action Plan should be derived from the baseline analysis and set ambitious but achievable targets, which are reviewed on an annual basis. Targets must cover the number of Living Wage Employers, the number of employees covered by the Living Wage, and the number of workers benefitting directly through a pay increase. It is also common to identify particular local priorities, which may include targeting low-wage industries or particular areas within a city or town: the Dundee Action Group has prioritized employers in the city's new Waterfront development, while the Action Group in Cardiff has targeted the 'southern arc' of the city, where low incomes are concentrated; (5) finally, the Action Plan must also be congruent with the broader approach of the Living Wage campaign, with its 'business-friendly' orientation and its commitment to involving employers in campaign activities and the recruitment of their peers. Provided these requirements are adhered to, the Action Plan is approved by the Living Wage Foundation and the Action Group signs a group license to enable it to use the 'Making Living Wage Places' branding. In return, the Foundation and its Scottish and Welsh partners provide support, including organizers to recruit local employers and a communications strategy to celebrate and publicize the initiative.

The main rationale for the Living Wage Places scheme is a desire to use the 'place ripple effect' (Living Wage Foundation 2019b) to expand Living Wage coverage and impact. Living Wage Employers tend to be clustered in specific localities and 'anchor institutions', like local authorities can seemingly play an important role in creating clusters of this kind. The aim of the accreditation is to foster self-generating groups of Living Wage Employers in a given place, in time creating a situation within local economies where it is expected that responsible businesses will pay the Living Wage. In addition to this policy rationale there is also an institutional rationale behind the scheme. It was explained that the Places accreditation had been developed partly for 'defensive' reasons; 'to manage the risk of stakeholders self-identifying as Living Wage places and damaging the brand'. In other words, the Poverty Alliance and Living Wage Foundation wanted an accreditation scheme to ensure that local campaigns correctly and fully applied the Living Wage standard. There is flexibility in the Living Wage Places scheme, with places able to develop their own, tailored Action Plan, but the common requirements outlined above are meant also to provide a degree of cross-UK standardization.

Two other contextual factors also shaped the Living Wage Places scheme. First, there was an attempt to learn from other forms of place-based accreditations, such as Fairtrade Towns, the Purple Flag for successful night-time destinations, and Social Enterprise Places. The initial Scottish report produced for the Poverty Alliance included a review of such schemes and incorporated elements drawn from other initiatives in its recommendations (Rocket Science 2017). From Fairtrade Towns, the Living Wage Places accreditation has taken the requirement for local authority involvement and the creation of a steering or action group formed from local businesses. There is a mimetic quality to the Living Wage Places scheme, therefore, as there is to other features of the campaign, with a deliberate attempt to learn from other systems of private regulation.

The other contextual factor comes from the public policy world. The Living Wage Places scheme is informed by the concept of 'inclusive growth' (Living Wage Foundation 2019b). The latter has gained currency in the field of economic development in recent years and identifies a key role for local and regional government in promoting economic activity that is socially inclusive, including the creation of decent jobs with fair wages (Beatty et al. 2016; SCRIG 2018). There is a pronounced localism in the notion of 'inclusive growth', with key parts allocated to local anchor-institutions and to non-conventional businesses, such as social enterprises, mutuals, and cooperatives, which often are defined by attachment to place. Place-based Living Wage schemes, with their attempt to enlist civic patriotism to the cause of lifting employees out of poverty pay, fit neatly with this policy agenda. In Dundee, the Living Wage City initiative is intended to ensure that the benefits of the city's new industries in leisure, culture, and professional services, found at the Waterfront development and grouped around the iconic V&A Scottish Design Museum, are extended to those in low-wage employment.

Living Hours

While the Service Provider, Funder, and Places schemes recognize those who champion the Living Wage, the Living Hours accreditation creates a new substantive standard for working time that sits alongside that for pay. The scheme is an important step in a process of 'diversification', launched by the Living Wage Foundation, which over time may add other accreditations such as Living Pensions. The Living Hours scheme was launched formally by the Foundation in October 2020, with Aviva and Standard Life Aberdeen announced as the first accredited organizations. Other large firms have subsequently joined the scheme, and it is hoped that it will attract several hundred existing members of the Living Wage network to the new standard going forwards. There has also been discussion of developing a 'places' version of the standard, with accreditation for Living Hours cities and towns.

The Living Hours standard has three main components (Living Wage Foundation 2019a). First, there is a requirement to give four weeks' notice of rosters and shifts, with full guaranteed payment to employees if shifts are cancelled. The purpose of this provision is to make working time, and therefore earnings, more predictable and to allow employees to integrate their earning cycle with the payment of utility, rent, and other bills. Second, contracts of employment should reflect the actual hours worked and should be reviewed on a regular basis and altered if it is found that usual hours exceed contracted hours. The purpose in this case is to remove uncertainty over hours and earnings and to provide protection from victimization for employees on variable hours who raise legitimate concerns about their work. Third, there should be a guaranteed minimum of sixteen hours work per week for all employees unless they specifically ask for a shorter-hour contract through a formal process. The objectives of this component are to raise incomes by increasing hours worked and to tackle the problem of under-employment, of employees working fewer hours than they want or need, while also maintaining flexibility for those workers who do want shorter hours. The sixteen-hours provision also complements aspects of the UK's welfare regime; for example, parents need to be working at least sixteen hours per week to qualify for childcare vouchers. Importantly, and just like the Living Wage standard, Living Hours applies to indirect as well as direct employees and obligates large employers to assume responsibility for working time arrangements within their supply chain.

The development of the Living Hours standard shares several features both with the broader Living Wage campaign and with civil regulation developed by other organizations. One feature shared with other pieces of civil regulation is the grounding of the campaign in research evidence (Heery, Abbott, and Williams

2012). An empirical case has been made for the Living Hours standard, which attests to the insecure condition of many low-wage workers and the deleterious effects of insecurity on family life, community participation, and mental and physical health (Living Wage Foundation 2019a). In making this case, the Foundation drew upon research published by the Joseph Rowntree Foundation and Citizens Advice and commissioned its own study from the New Economics Foundation. An additional source of evidence, however, arose from the community organizing tradition. Citizens UK conducted a 'listening exercise' through its local chapters, which contacted more than 700 low-wage workers and fed their experiences of insecure work and their ideas about how it could be tackled into the final recommendations. More recently, this work has been reinforced by a commissioned survey of workers' experience of precarious work arrangements carried out in 2021 (Richardson 2021; 2022). Other elements of the process have included consultation with stakeholders, including labour market experts, employers, and trade unions, the creation of a representative steering group to oversee implementation, and the formulation of a 'business case' to persuade employers that they too could gain from greater working time security for their employees. The objective of this consultative process was to 'base the standard on consensus between employers, employees, and civil society', from the belief that this would build legitimacy and ensure that the standard was both 'meaningful and feasible' (Living Wage Foundation 2019a: 16).

The development of the Living Hours standard was also shaped by contextual factors. One of these was developments in public policy. Just as the Living Wage Places scheme was informed by the concept of 'inclusive growth', so was the Living Hours standard influenced by the heightened policy interest in precarious work which followed the publication of the Taylor Review of Modern Working Practices (Taylor et al. 2017). One campaigner expressed the view that the Foundation had to develop a position on short and variable hours in the wake of the review's publication. Another contextual factor was the change in UK government policy towards the NLW and the announcement first made in 2019 that the statutory minimum would increase to two-thirds of median hourly earnings by 2024, with workers aged 21 and over being phased onto the full adult rate (HM Treasury 2020). This change, as we have seen, has eroded the differential between the Living Wage and the NLW rate, thereby providing an incentive for the Foundation to develop new schemes of accreditation. The diversification strategy, of which Living Hours is the standard bearer, emanates to a degree from this institutional interest. Finally, the development of the Living Hours standard has been demand-driven, not just in the sense that there is a policy need to address precarious work, but also in the sense that employers have expressed a desire for a standard of this kind. Our 2021 survey of employers indicated that nearly half would 'definitely' or 'probably' sign up to Living Hours in the future. This backing from employer-supporters has been informed not by a perception that the original Living Wage standard was failing, but rather from a perception of its success and a desire to reproduce that success in the area of working time. The Living Wage has served as a model for Living Hours; it has not been seen as a flawed initiative requiring remedial action.

Conclusion

The purpose of this chapter has been to provide an analysis of the Living Wage standard, to identify its defining characteristics as a piece of employment regulation. Four main conclusions have emerged from this analysis. First, the Living Wage is a method of pay determination that foregrounds employee need and prioritizes this principle over other factors that might determine pay, such as performance, skill, or business context. In prioritizing employee need in this way, the Living Wage poses a challenge to orthodox thinking about pay in the field of human resource management. In the latter, pay and other elements of reward management are typically regarded as instruments of business strategy that can be used to mould employee behaviour and drive forwards the business interests of employers (Lawler III 1990). The Living Wage challenges thinking of this kind because it focuses on the distinct interest of employees in receiving a wage that allows a decent standard of living, relegating employer interests in pay determination to a secondary position. The Living Wage campaign is not hostile to business, and the business benefits of the Living Wage standard are often promoted by campaigners, but the central message of the campaign is nevertheless that 'fair pay' should take precedence over 'strategic pay' in the process of wage determination.

Second, the Living Wage is a form of civil regulation and exhibits all the properties of regulation of this kind that were outlined in the previous chapter. Thus, the Living Wage is a form of private regulation, separate from legislated minima; it is voluntary, such that employers choose and are not obligated to apply the standard and economic and other incentives have been put in place to try and influence employer choice; it has emerged from civil society and the international community organizing movement; and the civil society organizations with responsibility for the standard, the Living Wage Foundation and its partners, have developed the standard unilaterally, albeit following consultation with various stakeholders. Civil regulation is a growing feature of the labour markets of the UK and other developed economies, and the Living Wage is a striking example of this trend (Williams et al. 2011).

A third characteristic of the Living Wage is that it is a relatively soft form of regulation. In seeking to raise pay, the standard goes beyond legal minima but in other regards it does not fare well in tests of robustness that have emerged from the literature on international private regulation. The Living Wage does not embody international standards, though there have been attempts to establish a standard of this kind based on the UK's experience. The Living Wage also does not explicitly promote worker participation in the application of the standard and is accompanied neither by an independent system of compliance monitoring nor by an extensive effort to build employer capability to comply. For some, these characteristics are weaknesses, but we suggest that the voluntary nature of the Living Wage and the fact that employers are expected to fund higher wages within their supply-chain render these features rather less problematic than might be thought. The Living Wage is a soft form of regulation but, as we will show in Chapter 7, it has proved effective, both in attracting employers and in raising wages for a substantial number of low-paid employees.

Finally, the Living Wage is an evolving body of regulation, with supplementary standards and schemes of accreditation being added over time. One purpose of these supplementary standards is to develop new mechanisms for spreading the Living Wage by enlisting the support of service providers, funders of charities, and place-based action groups. Another purpose has been diversification, seeking to reproduce the success of the Living Wage through the Living Hours standard and possibly other additional schemes that will be launched in the future. What is notable about this evolution is that it has not been driven by failure and the repeated exposure of the shortcomings of private regulation by social justice activists, as has been the case with international corporate codes. Several factors have driven the evolution of the Living Wage standard, but one important feature has been the entrepreneurial character of the campaign itself. The Living Wage Foundation and its partners have striven to maintain campaign momentum and seek out new regulatory opportunities, and it is this effort that has driven the evolution of the Living Wage. In the next chapter, this campaign effort is considered directly as we examine campaign strategy and methods.

3
The Campaign for the Real Living Wage

Introduction

The focus of this chapter is on the organizations that have developed the Real Living Wage and the methods that they have employed to promote it. While the previous chapter considered the content of civil regulation therefore, this chapter considers the civil society organizations which disseminate regulation of this kind. In the first section we examine Citizens UK and the Living Wage Foundation, the connected organizations responsible for the Living Wage campaign. Both can be classified as social movement organizations, formal organizations that have emerged from and seek to advance the contemporary movement for economic justice (Tarrow 1998). In other respects, however, Citizens UK and the Foundation differ. The former is a meta-organization that coordinates an extensive network of affiliated organizations committed to community organizing, while the latter is a 'professional movement organization' (McCarthy and Zald 1973) with the specific purpose of recruiting employers to the Living Wage standard. As we will see, the structure, workforce, and methods of both organizations diverge from one another, reflecting these basic differences in character and purpose.

The second section provides an overview of campaign strategy, identifying key developments including the targeting of specific groups of employers, diversification to encompass Living Hours and potentially other employment issues, and the response to COVID-19. A feature that emerges strongly from this analysis, we believe, is the entrepreneurial nature of the campaign and the launching of successive initiatives to maintain its momentum. The campaign, decidedly, has been led by 'social movement entrepreneurs' (McCarthy and Zald 1973). In the third section, the focus switches to campaign methods and the ways in which campaigners have tried to pressure or encourage employers to adopt the Living Wage standard. A notable difference is again identified here between Citizens UK and the Living Wage Foundation, with the former drawing directly upon American broad-based community organizing practice while the latter has relied upon methods that are employer-supporting, which develop a 'business case' rationale for Living Wage accreditation, and which are shared with other organizations that seek to encourage responsible business. The section considers how these different campaign methods interrelate with one another, identifying both synergy and a degree of tension.

The Real Living Wage. Edmund Heery, Deborah Hann and David Nash, Oxford University Press.
© Edmund Heery, Deborah Hann and David Nash (2023). DOI: 10.1093/oso/9780198835264.003.0003

The final section of the chapter examines campaign relationships, looking at how Citizens UK and the Living Wage Foundation have sought to involve other institutions in the campaign. One such relationship is that with other civil society organizations, and we show that campaigners have worked jointly with a broad range of partner institutions. Citizens UK and the Living Wage Foundation, we demonstrate, occupy central positions in an ecosystem of economic justice organizations, which habitually network, contract, and ally with one another. Another type of partner is trade unions, which are present both within Citizens UK's formal network and the looser network of partners enlisted by the Living Wage Foundation. We examine the reasons for, extent, and nature of campaign attempts to involve trade unions and also identify points of tension. The final relationship examined is that with public authorities, and we look at why and how Living Wage campaigners have attempted to enlist the support of the UK Government, the devolved governments of Scotland and Wales, and regional and local authorities. Although the Living Wage is a private form of regulation, winning the support of those in positions of public authority has often been a central objective of Living Wage campaigners.

Living Wage Organizations

The origins of Citizens UK date back to 1989 when the Community Organizing Foundation was established as a British outpost of the American community organizing movement (Wills 2016). The Community Organizing Foundation transitioned into The East London Communities Organization (TELCO) in 1996, which in turn evolved into London Citizens and then Citizens UK as the reach of the organization extended beyond the capital. The defining purpose of Citizens UK is that it seeks to build power in disadvantaged communities, recruiting member organizations and training their 'leaders' in the practice of community organizing (Walls 2015). The techniques which comprise the latter are then deployed within campaigns at a variety of scales, encompassing the entire UK in some cases but being confined to local issues in others. Since 2001, the campaign for the Real Living Wage has been one of the organization's core projects.

Reflecting its community organizing mission, Citizens UK is divided up into local chapters, each of which has its own membership of affiliated organizations. By late 2021, Citizens UK had founded seventeen chapters, covering much of England and Wales: Scotland and Northern Ireland are not yet part of the Citizens network, though they have been included in the Living Wage campaign. The Citizens' network has therefore grown substantially from its London base, and seems likely to spread further in the immediate future. Chapters themselves can operate at a variety of scales, including cities (e.g. Birmingham Citizens, Brighton and Hove Citizens, Nottingham Citizens), counties (e.g. Essex Citizens,

Somerset Citizens), city-regions (e.g. Greater Manchester Citizens, Thames Valley Citizens, Tyne and Wear Citizens), and in one case an entire country: Citizens Cymru-Wales. Within some chapters there are also formally designated alliances that operate at a smaller scale. Thus, Essex Citizens comprises a longstanding alliance in Colchester and two newer groupings in Chelmsford and Southend, while Thames Valley Citizens includes alliances in Milton Keynes, Oxford, and Reading. This pattern is also seen in London, where TELCO, North London Citizens, and South London Citizens encompass alliances operating at the level of individual London boroughs (e.g. Brent Citizens, Newham Citizens, Southwark Citizens). A major consideration influencing the geographical scope of chapters is to position the latter as interlocuters with political authorities. Greater Manchester Citizens was established in the wake of the decision to create a directly elected Metro Mayor for the City Region, and its scale of operations encompasses the ten boroughs of Greater Manchester, matching the remit of the Mayoral office. In Wales, a similar consideration underpinned the decision to operate at a country-wide scale; to endow Citizens Cymru-Wales with the representative authority to engage with Welsh Government.

Citizens UK is a 'meta-organization' (Berkowitz and Dumez 2016); its membership does not consist of individuals but of organizations, though many of the latter are representative bodies with their own individual membership. Table 3.1 shows the characteristics of Citizens' organizational membership. It is clear from the table that Citizens UK is a faith-dominated organization, reflecting the character of its American parent, the Industrial Areas Foundation (Osterman 2006). Just under half of affiliated bodies are faith organizations, and many of the educational and community bodies that have joined the network also have a faith identity. Most of the main religions are represented in the faith membership of Citizens UK—Christianity, Islam, Judaism, and Sikhism—as are separate denominations within these faiths. Christian affiliates, for example, include Anglican, Catholic, Baptist, Methodist, and Quaker organizations, as well as the Salvation Army. The organizations themselves range from individual congregations—churches, chapels,

Table 3.1 Characteristics of Citizens UK member organizations, 2021

Type of organization	Number	Per cent
Faith organizations	231	47.0
Educational institutions	131	26.7
Community and campaigning organizations	110	22.4
Trade unions	19	3.9
Total	**491**	**100**

Source: Citizens UK website: https://www.citizensuk.org/local_chapters.

mosques, synagogues—to higher level religious organizations. The latter include several Anglican and Roman Catholic dioceses, and these have often functioned as 'strategic partners', providing additional funding and support to local chapters. The centrality of faith organizations in the Citizens' network indicates that religious belief continues to provide an important source of social mobilization (Jamoul and Wills 2008; Wills and Datta et al. 2009).

The second main group of member organizations are educational institutions, encompassing universities, university departments, student unions, sixth form colleges, secondary schools, and primary schools. Universities have also often functioned as strategic partners within the network, providing core support. Cardiff University has acted in this capacity in Wales, and the Head of Cardiff Business School chairs the Living Wage for Wales Leadership team, a body that coordinates the campaign in Wales, and sits on the Living Wage Commission. Cardiff Business School students have also taken part in the Living Wage campaign, devising 'actions' for non-paying employers to encourage them to enter a dialogue with Citizens about accreditation. School students, including those at primary school, have also been involved in activity of this kind. One of the highlights of the research project was seeing the staff and students from St Anthony's Roman Catholic primary school in Newham perform their Living Wage song, 'Realize, Wake Up, Pay Up', before MPs at the Houses of Parliament. A primary purpose of educational organizations belonging to the network is to encourage participation of this kind. Citizens UK has campaigned for a reduction of the voting age to 16, conducts registration drives amongst young voters, and is keen to induct young people into the practice of active citizenship through involvement in its network.

The third group of members are community organizations, which include local associations and action groups, ethnic organizations, local branches of large NGOs, such as Oxfam, and service-providing organizations, such as health centres. Often these organizations have a faith component, but they are also often defined by their location within poor communities, either as service-providing bodies or in terms of their membership. Their presence in the network underlines Citizens' commitment to acting on a local scale through community participation (Wills 2012). The fourth and smallest group of member organizations are trade unions. Not only do unions make up a small proportion of the membership; they are also concentrated in a minority of chapters. Only three chapters reported trade union membership in late 2021—Birmingham, Nottingham, and Greater Manchester—and union membership is concentrated overwhelmingly in the latter, where UNISON North-West is a strategic partner and sixteen UNISON branches are chapter members. The only other participating unions are RCN and UCU, which are members of the Nottingham chapter. In other parts of the country, most notably London, unions have been active participants in the network in the past. Union branches in health and local government were central members of TELCO, involved in the first years of Living Wage campaigning (Littman et al.

2010; Wills 2009). The Citizens' network has found it difficult to sustain union participation over time, however, reflecting the rather difficult relationship that has sometimes arisen between the two movements.

The job of coordinating the Citizens UK network, developing leaders, and supporting campaigns is performed by a small professional staff of community organizers. The latter are based at Citizens' head office in the East End of London and in local offices where there are active chapters. There are about thirty staff in total, all of whom are trained community organizers. The workforce is relatively young and diverse, and while some come from faith backgrounds this is not uniformly the case. Most had a history of student and community activism prior to joining Citizens, and they display a very high level of engagement in the work they perform. They share the attributes of others in social justice jobs (Rooks 2004; Simms et al. 2013). Interestingly, when asked why they were working for Citizens UK several stated that they were attracted to the organization because it was effective: it had used community organizing to win substantial improvements for poor communities, including payment of the Living Wage, in a manner that organizations they had worked for in the past had failed to do.

Living Wage Foundation

The Living Wage Foundation was established by Citizens UK in 2011 and remains tied to its parent: in formal terms the Foundation is a 'project team' within Citizens. From its inception, however, the Foundation was intended to operate at arm's length from Citizens UK, in part to avoid the success of the Living Wage campaign swamping Citizens' other activities. To this end, the Living Wage Foundation has its own director and management team, its own strategy and business plan, its own branding and media, and until recently was housed in separate offices. From its website it is not immediately obvious that it is part of Citizens UK.

The distinctiveness of the Foundation is further reflected in aspects of its organizational structure, which depart from those of Citizens. The Foundation is organized on a primarily functional basis, contrasting with the geographical, chapter-based structure of its parent. The workforce is divided into three teams: an operational team of Programme Managers is responsible for promoting the Living Wage to employers, oversees accreditation, and provides information and support to employers; a communications team maintains the organization's website and very active social media presence and is responsible for press and publicity; and a business development team is responsible for the diversification of the accreditation scheme, the Global Living Wage project, special projects, and consultancy. The presence of the latter attests to the entrepreneurial nature of the organization. As the organization is small—about thirty-five employees at the end of 2021—the boundaries between these teams are fluid, and at key points, such as Living

Wage Week in November, the entire workforce will combine to work on the same project.

Another distinctive feature of the Foundation concerns its relationship with its member organizations, the employers, with whom it signs a licence agreement and who fund its operations. To a degree, the Foundation seeks to reproduce active participation in the Living Wage campaign amongst its employer members in the way that Citizens UK encourages activism within its chapters. The Foundation often refers to its members as a 'movement of employers' and relies upon 'principal partners', employers that act as champions of the Living Wage and which correspond to the 'strategic partners' within Citizens UK chapters. Moreover, underpinning the Foundation's entire project is a conviction that virtuous employers can and should behave as corporate *citizens*, adopting good employment standards. It remains though that most accredited employers have a passive relationship with the Foundation, limited to fulfilling the terms of their licence and paying an annual subscription; they are not the active participants of a campaigning organization like the community organizations within Citizens UK.

While the Foundation is not primarily an activist organization, it does seek to involve member-employers and other stakeholders in its governance. Like many other civil society organizations, the Living Wage Foundation makes use of stakeholder consultation within its process of decision-making (Heery et al. 2012). Member employers are consulted directly through surveys and other information-gathering exercises, and the Foundation has established consultative bodies through which employers and other stakeholders can participate. There is an Advisory Board made up of representatives of leading employers, anti-poverty and social justice organizations, and the Foundation's Welsh and Scottish partners that act as a sounding board for policy making and which may also advise on the accreditation of individual employers when cases raise broader questions of principle. Members of the board lead task groups focused on specific industries or issues that draw a further set of stakeholder representatives into decision-making. There are also specialist bodies that bring together Living Wage Funders and Recognized Service Providers and exercise oversight of these supplementary systems of accreditation. Finally, there is the Living Wage Commission, which is chaired by a leading employer representative, oversees the calculation of the Living Wage, and considers how the standard should be adapted to take account of developments in public policy.

A final distinctive feature of the Foundation concerns its workforce. The latter share many of the characteristics of their counterparts within Citizens. They are relatively young, including some in their first main career job, the majority are women, they are ethnically diverse, and they are highly educated. The Foundation's workforce, however, are not trained community organizers. Most have done some training in community organizing, but their skill set was described as different to that of those supporting the Citizens' network. They were said to typically have project management, relational management, and business engagement skills and experience, and while some have backgrounds in social activism and work in other social justice organizations others have come from more conventional employment in retail, fashion, university administration, and consultancy. What does unite the Foundation workforce with that of their Citizens peers, however, is a high level of engagement and commitment to work. A member of management, with prior experience of the public sector, said that they were the 'most highly motivated and engaged team' she had ever managed: 'They believe in the mission'.

Campaign Strategy

The Living Wage campaign was launched by TELCO in the East End of London in 2001. Amongst the first employers to be targeted were large financial and professional service firms at Canary Wharf and local authorities and NHS Trusts (Littman et al. 2010; Wills and Linneker 2012). In the intervening period the campaign has expanded massively to encompass the entire country and all major fields of economic activity. Key milestones in this process of growth have included the development and then merging of methodologies for calculating both the London and UK Living Wage rates, the creation of the Living Wage Foundation and the launching of the accreditation scheme, the introduction of supplementary standards for service providers, funders, and Living Wage places, and the emergence of distinctive campaigns in Scotland and Wales, which in the former case has received substantial support from Scottish Government (Heery et al. 2020; Howard 2022).

The campaign has also faced major challenges in this period. The introduction of the National Living Wage in 2016 not only appropriated the language of the campaign, but also raised the prospect of the statutory minimum, increasing first to sixty per cent and then to two-thirds of median hourly earnings, which would bring it very close to the Real Living Wage rate by the mid-2020s. The possibility of this convergence has been an important consideration in the launching of Living Hours, an attempt to diversify the 'offer' that the campaign makes to employers. Another severe challenge has been the COVID-19 pandemic, which potentially could have seriously impacted levels of Living Wage accreditation as businesses faltered or decided that higher rates of pay could no longer be afforded. In bringing the low rates of pay of 'key workers' to public attention, however, the crisis also provided a potential opportunity for Living Wage campaigners. In what follows, we do not present a narrative account of the campaign, but rather identify some of its key features, particularly in the period since the launching of the accreditation scheme in 2011. We end by considering how the campaign has been affected by COVID-19 and how campaigners have responded.

A criticism of living wage campaigns in the USA is that they lack scale and are confined to local initiatives in particular cities (Freeman 2005). One of the striking features of the Living Wage campaign in the UK, however, has been its scaling-up; originating in the East End of London, it has grown to first cover the entire capital before spreading through England, Scotland, Wales, and Northern Ireland. The Global Living Wage, moreover, is an attempt to diffuse the principles that underpin the standard on an international scale. One of the reasons for the Living Wage Foundation's appetite for partnering with other organizations, in Scotland, Wales, and beyond, is to provide geographical reach to the campaign, allowing for scaling-up of this kind. Another aspect of scaling-up has been the development of a single methodology for calculating the Living Wage and the formulation of a single UK rate that applies in all parts of the country except London. The development of this national standard has led to some tension with local living wage schemes, which continue to operate in some parts of the country. Local campaigns may promote their own living wage, above or below the Foundation rate, and even when they adopt the latter may apply their own principles of accreditation. The Foundation has often reached a *modus vivendi* with local campaigns, but its objective of establishing an integrated, UK-wide standard inevitably conflicts to a degree with local ventures of this kind.

Another defining feature of the campaign has been its reliance upon expertise, seen most explicitly in the extensive commissioning of research to provide evidential support for its claims and objectives. As we have seen, the Living Wage standard is based on research into the income needs of low-income families, and this foundation in independent research endows it with legitimacy. Other pieces of research have identified a pressing need for the Living Wage, revealing the scale of low pay and in-work poverty across the UK and in particular sectors, such as charities, shown that uplifting wages can provide a major boost to low-income communities, and provided evidence of benefits to business (Coulson and Bonner 2015; Jensen and Wills 2013; KPMG 2015; Living Wage Foundation 2017a; Living Wage Foundation 2018; Wills and Kakpo et al. 2009). Our own research has contributed to this effort (Heery et al. 2017). Research of this kind is often used by civil society organizations to legitimate their activities and provide a basis for political influence (Heery et al. 2012). Furnishing an evidence-base for policy is a central element of the 'politics of expertise' in which the Foundation and many other civil society organizations are engaged (Hilton et al. 2013).

A third, defining feature of the campaign is that it is planned in a deliberate and formal way. The Living Wage Foundation has a rolling three-year strategy, which identifies priorities, sets targets, identifies performance indicators, and reviews success. Central to this process of strategy is targeting, the selection of specific sectors, industries, and types of employers for campaigning activity. Groups of employers that have been targeted for campaigning activity include: large corporates that are members of the FTSE100; Premier League football clubs; local authorities; universities; government agencies and organizations in receipt of UK or national government funding; the banking, legal, and tech industries; and low-wage industries such as hospitality, retail, and social care. Through the Living Wage Places scheme, campaigners have also targeted leading employers in particular localities, including transport hubs and providers, utility companies, NHS Trusts and Boards, further education colleges, and cultural and entertainment organizations, such as museums, galleries, and theatres. In many cases this targeting has been guided by the setting of formal, time-limited recruitment targets.

The selection of employer targets has been driven by several considerations. One consideration is the likely receptiveness of employers to the campaign: campaigners spoke to us of targeting 'low-hanging fruit' that could be brought within the scheme with relatively limited campaigning effort. Receptiveness can be a function of congruence between the objectives of the campaign and the purpose and mission of employers targeted. Local authorities have proved receptive, for instance, because signing up to the Living Wage accords with their own priorities of 'community wealth-building' or 'inclusive growth' (Guinan and O'Neill 2020; Lupton et al. 2019). Receptiveness can also be a function of the ease with which employers can comply with the Living Wage standard: employers in tech, financial, and professional services have proved receptive in part because these are high wage industries and the cost of introducing the Living Wage is relatively low.

A second principle that has guided targeting and which has been stressed particularly since 2015 is the need to maximize the impact of the campaign, measured in terms of the number of low-wage workers receiving a pay increase. This principle has led to the targeting of employers in low-wage industries, such as cleaning, security, retail, adult social care, childcare, and hospitality. These are industries characterized by low pay, where the need for the Living Wage is most acute. For this very reason, however, employers are less receptive to the campaign and successes can be hard won. The targeting of low-wage industries, therefore, has been tempered with a degree of realism, in which effort directed at more demanding targets is balanced with that directed at industries where employers are more receptive. Impact can be delivered not just by targeting low-wage industries, but also by targeting large employers. Local government and higher education are not defined by low pay in the way that hospitality is, but they are characterized by the presence of very large employers, with hundreds of low-paid support workers providing cleaning, catering, and security alongside higher-paid administrators and professionals. Local authorities and universities have also been targeted through the Living Wage Places scheme because they can function as 'anchor institutions', promoting the Living Wage along their supply chains and within their locality. Employers of this type have been selected as targets because they can generate indirect impact, spreading the Living Wage to other employers by virtue of their size, purchasing power, and influence.

Another principle of selection has been social justice. The initial focus of the campaign on City firms based at Canary Wharf, the continuing focus on the

FTSE100, and the targeting of Premier League clubs have been motivated by the egregious inequality in these institutions, with cleaners, catering staff, and match-day attendants working for minimum wage, while executives and professional footballers are paid astronomical salaries. They have been targeted in the words of one campaign worker, 'because there's a huge injustice'. Major corporates and football teams have also been targeted to build campaign momentum. A trade union official complained to us that the campaign was too concerned with collecting 'scalps', that is, recruiting high-profile employers. There is an element of truth in this, in that the campaign has deliberately targeted businesses whose signing up is noteworthy and likely to attract media attention and who potentially might serve as a model for other employers. A final issue that has influenced targeting is the presence of allies or partners who can help the campaign persuade employers to accredit. The tech industry has been targeted, for example, partly because techUK, the employers' organization, is itself a Living Wage Employer and has worked with the Foundation to promote the Living Wage to its member-businesses. Public authorities have also often acted as campaign supporters in this way (see Chapter 6). In Wales, universities have been 'a core campaign target', and the sector is now fully accredited, an achievement that was facilitated by downward pressure from Welsh Government, the sector's principal funder, which complemented the upward pressure from campaigners.

A feature of campaign strategy that has become more pronounced over time is diversification, the launching of supplementary standards and systems of accreditation in addition to the Living Wage described in the previous chapter. Diversification has been followed for a variety of reasons. One reason is the recognition that 'low pay isn't the only thing affecting low-wage workers' and that there are other sources of in-work poverty, such as short and unpredictable hours, which can be addressed through additional systems of accreditation (Richardson 2021; 2022). Campaigners working for the Foundation stressed that it has an 'in-work poverty mission' and that pursuing this central purpose implies the development of additional standards to supplement the Living Wage. Another reason is that both Citizens UK and the Foundation have been encouraged by stakeholders to diversify. Listening exercises carried out by Citizens through its member organizations have identified a range of employment problems experienced by those living in poor communities, while the Foundation has been encouraged by member-employers to diversify its activities. Both sources of encouragement were pivotal to the development of the Living Hours scheme. Diversification has also been pursued to keep the Foundation 'relevant' and secure its future. Additional schemes of accreditation and new consultancy services can potentially generate a fresh stream of income to maintain the campaign, a consideration that has become acute with the possibility of the NLW reaching parity with the Foundation's core Living Wage standard. There are institutional as well as social justice reasons for the strategy of diversification.

COVID-19

The accreditation scheme for Living Wage Employers was launched in 2011 as the UK was beginning to recover from the great financial crisis of 2008. As it approached its tenth anniversary, the scheme was hit by an even sharper collapse of economic activity brought on by the outbreak of COVID-19. Since March 2020, the UK has experienced successive waves of coronavirus, the worst public health crisis of the last hundred years, which in turn have delivered a seismic shock to the economy. As the pandemic has abated, economic activity has recovered but remains depressed, as bottlenecks in distribution, labour and commodity shortages, and rising inflation have exerted negative effects. The adverse impact of Brexit, moreover, has interacted with the effects of the pandemic to generate uniquely difficult economic circumstances.

How has this combination of shocks affected the Living Wage campaign? To a perhaps surprising degree, the campaign weathered the coronavirus pandemic successfully. The onset of COVID-19 led to an increase in the number of employers dropping out of accreditation: in the eighteen months between March 2020 and August 2021, 698 employers left the scheme compared with 482 employers in the equivalent period before the crisis broke. This loss of accredited employers, however, was more than compensated by an increase in recruitment, with 2,887 employers joining the scheme during the pandemic compared with 2,269 in the preceding period. Recruitment was particularly strong over the summer of 2021, when more than 200 employers joined per month, suggesting that demand for accreditation built up during the pandemic, providing a boost to recruitment as the recovery got underway. Moreover, the employers recruited during the pandemic included major businesses (e.g. BP, Network Rail, Visa Europe, Talk Talk, Tate & Lyle, Severn Trent, and Zurich Insurance) and public service organizations, including the Northern Ireland Executive and a series of local authorities, NHS Trusts, and universities. A total of ninety-eight employers with 500 or more employees were accredited during the first eighteen months of the pandemic, which directly employed nearly 427,000 people and reported 28,270 workers had received a Living Wage pay increase.

The onset of the pandemic also led to an adjustment to campaign strategy. One response was to allow a small number of employers to delay implementing the 2019–2020 increase in the Living Wage, though on the condition that they cease to badge themselves as Living Wage Employers until the rate was adopted. It was also agreed that a small number of businesses could extend the period for bringing outsourced workers onto the Living Wage rate. The vast majority of Living Wage Employers, however, neither sought nor were granted extensions of this kind. In a key demonstration that the campaign would continue to operate as normal despite COVID-19, new UK and London Living Wage rates were announced in both 2020 and 2021.

Another response was to shift targeting, de-prioritizing recruitment in parts of the economy adversely affected by COVID-19, such as leisure and hospitality, and putting more emphasis on sectors that experienced limited negative effects. The main priority target identified during the crisis was social care. In April 2020, Citizens UK and the Living Wage Foundation launched a Living Wage for Social Care campaign, with the aim of securing funding from central government for the Living Wage to be paid to all social care employees, a sum estimated to be in the region of £1.5bn (Gardiner and Hussein 2015). Running alongside this political objective, was a push to accredit individual social care employers and a renewed effort to persuade local authorities to adopt the Living Wage. In the summer of 2021, the Foundation issued a toolkit for providers and local authority commissioners of social care, which provided practical guidance on how they could support the Living Wage (Living Wage Foundation 2021b). The background to this campaign was the upwelling of public support for care workers, symbolized by the Clap-for-Carers on Thursday evenings in the early stages of the pandemic. The coronavirus crisis was identified by campaigners as providing an opportunity to make a breakthrough in a core industry, characterized by low-wage employment. In developing the campaign, Citizens UK made use of worker testimony, actions at care homes, and a variety of techniques to exert pressure on politicians. It is to an analysis of this campaigning repertoire that we now turn.

Campaign Methods

The Living Wage campaign is distinctive in that it has relied upon two sets of methods to encourage employers to adopt the Living Wage. On the one hand, community organizing has been deployed by Citizens UK to pressure employers into adopting the Living Wage, while on the other the Foundation has used methods common to the promotion of responsible business to persuade employers to voluntarily implement the standard. These separate repertoires were repeatedly described to us as the 'carrot and the stick'; complementary approaches that could be used to spread the Living Wage amongst employers. In what follows, we consider each set of methods in turn, before turning to the relationship between them. It is important to note at the outset, however, that the different approaches have not been deployed with the same frequency. In our 2021 survey of Living Wage Employers, only six per cent reported that responding 'to Living Wage campaigners from outside the organisation encouraging you to pay the Living Wage' was a major reason for becoming accredited. Most employers have been recruited to the Living Wage through the system established by the Living Wage Foundation, with only a minority of usually larger employers becoming the target of community organizing.

Community Organizing

The techniques used by Citizens UK to promote the Living Wage have been developed and refined by the American community organizing movement over decades and are set out in manuals such as Saul Alinsky's *Rules for Radicals* (1972). These techniques have been applied directly to the British context and give the Living Wage campaign activity developed by Citizens UK a distinctive character. Campaigns directed at individual employers have recurrent features, with the same techniques applied to multiple cases. There is a standardized, repetitive quality to campaign activity, which although it contains elements of spontaneity and active participation by supporters, is also carefully planned and managed. It takes the form of the application of a canon of good practice, articulated through a specialist vocabulary, by those trained in community organizing. In what follows, we identify the main techniques that form this canon and describe how they have been used to promote the Living Wage. Not all the techniques we describe feature in all campaigns, but they have all been used repeatedly and together compose Citizens UK's campaigning repertoire.

Listening campaigns. The Living Wage campaign originated in a 'listening campaign' carried out by TELCO in the East End of London in 2000, and the origins of subsequent campaigns to secure the Living Wage from individual employers have often lain in the same technique. A campaign of this kind involves trained 'leaders' from Citizens UK affiliates holding 'one-to-ones' with members of their community to identify the challenges they face and the changes that they would like to see to improve their lives. Through listening of this kind, ordinary people, including those in low-wage employment, are encouraged to 'tell their stories'. The leaders collecting these stories may themselves be in low-wage employment, but this is not necessarily the case: the listening exercise that preceded the successful campaign for the Living Wage at Manchester University targeted cleaners and other low-wage employees but was conducted by students trained by Greater Manchester Citizens. The primary purpose of a listening campaign is to identify campaign priorities. Tyne and Wear Citizens, for example, initiated a listening campaign after its inauguration, which led to the identification of three priorities: hate crime, mental health, and the Living Wage. In addition to strategy development, however, listening can serve other ends. The one-to-one conversations are a means of collecting 'testimony', which can be used in a subsequent Living Wage campaign and can also serve to identify workplace 'leaders'. Listening can be more than just a form of consultation; it can be a form of organizing.

Power analysis. Another technique that can be used in the early stages of a Living Wage campaign is power analysis, a method developed by the American campaigner Jane McAlevey (2016). A power analysis involves plotting the position of potential allies and opponents of the Living Wage on two axes. On the first, groups and organizations are positioned in terms of their degree of support, while on the other position is determined by the power of groups to affect the outcome. A power analysis can inform campaigning in two main ways. On the one hand, it can lead to attempts to build up the power of those who already support the Living Wage through organizing activity and the development of alliances. On the other hand, it can lead to an attempt to influence powerful opponents to persuade them to alter their position. A power analysis of this kind lay at the heart of the Living Wage for Social Care campaign and prompted attempts by Citizens UK chapters to form new alliances, partnering with care homes and in some cases seeking to involve trade unions in campaign activity. It also led to the identification of the Conservative Party as the principal powerholder with the capacity to determine the outcome of the campaign and a concerted effort to influence Conservative politicians, to push them towards support. To this end, backbench Conservative MPs who might support the campaign were identified, as were Conservative leaders of local authorities responsible for commissioning social care. The aim was to persuade these politicians to support the campaign through virtual delegations and listening to the testimony of care-workers, and then use their influence to exert pressure on the Conservative Government.

Developing Leaders. A mantra of community organizing is that organizers should not do things for people that they can do themselves. Accordingly, a central component of campaigns is identifying and developing 'leaders' who can participate in campaigns, cultivate support, and act as spokespeople. The language of 'empowerment' is often used to describe this process, as it can involve those with no experience of civic participation acquiring the capacity to shape their communities. A Citizens UK Organizer told us he first became interested in community organizing when he saw a cleaner address a large meeting at his university calling for the Living Wage. The person, he said, 'was just like my Mum', also a cleaner, and stated that 'I had never seen anyone like my Mum in public life before'. As this case indicates, leaders drawn into Living Wage campaigns are often themselves low-wage workers seeking to be paid the Living Wage. A cleaner named Olawele was central to the campaign to secure the Living Wage at London Stadium, home of West Ham United, and then played a key part in spreading the campaign to London City Airport by approaching cleaners there. Olawele has continued to campaign for the Living Wage through Newham Citizens, has spoken to MPs at the Houses of Parliament, and addressed an assembly of 1,500 people to mark the second anniversary of Sadiq Kahn's election as London Mayor. During an emotional speech Olawele waved his pay slip to celebrate being paid the new rate of pay: 'Sadiq Kahn gave him a hug ... It was a touching moment'.

While the leaders of Living Wage campaigns may be drawn from the low-paid themselves, this is not exclusively the case and attempts to secure the Living Wage can involve activists from a broad range of backgrounds. At universities, members of staff and students have often played a leading role: at Cardiff University two social science lecturers played a key part, involving students in a listening campaign amongst University cleaners which included recording video testimony of life on low pay. In another Welsh campaign, at Cardiff Airport, the leadership group included an airport baggage checker but also local Methodists, a person from a local foodbank, and the secretary of the UNISON branch at the local council. At the UK level, a large network of leaders was created for the Living Wage for Social Care campaign, which included those working in social care but also academics, teachers, faith leaders, members of community groups, and trade union representatives. The rationale for this broad base of participants derives from the fact that Citizens UK seeks to represent local *communities*. Low wages create harm within these communities, and therefore a multiplicity of local groups, extending beyond the directly affected workforce, have an interest in campaigning for a Living Wage. As a senior member of Citizens UK put it, 'the origin, legitimacy, and mandate' of campaigns, and of those who lead them, come from place-based institutions.

Testimony. The main way in which ordinary workers become involved in Living Wage campaigns led by Citizens is by giving 'testimony'. In this testimony people on low pay speak about their own experiences and either relate the deprivations to which low pay gives rise or describe how their lives could be improved through higher pay. In all cases testimony is personal, and it is often emotionally charged. One piece of 'poignant testimony' collected in the North East described how a person had to walk a long distance to work because she could not afford bus fares. Stories of this kind, it was said, often 'resonate with whoever the power-people are' because they have little direct knowledge of the conditions under which poor people live their lives. Testimony can be delivered in a range of contexts and through different media. The websites of Citizens UK and the Living Wage Foundation contain video clips and quotations from workers' testimony, and these are also circulated via social media and have occasionally featured in the mass media. Testimony can also be delivered in person at public meetings and assemblies, meetings with employers and politicians, and with fellow-campaigners. During the Living Wage for Social Care campaign, care workers took part in Care Conversations on Facebook, relaying their experiences to thousands of participants. Care workers and other providers of testimony received training to help them engage in this activity, and Citizens UK has amplified the reach and impact of their stories through its media strategy—as with other aspects of campaigning, the process of gathering and diffusing testimony is deliberate and managed. The impact is often substantial, persuading people to support the campaign and shaming those in positions of power to respond. As a trade union member of Greater Manchester Citizens expressed it, 'Putting the workers in a room with politicians is very powerful'.

Actions. Testimony is one way of pressuring employers into adopting the Living Wage; organizing campaign 'actions' is another. When an employer is selected for campaign activity the first approach of Citizens is to ask for a meeting to negotiate the introduction of the Living Wage. In some cases an approach of this kind is sufficient, and the employer agrees to meet. A community organizer from Tyne and Wear Citizens said that an approach to Virgin Money elicited a response of this sort: organizers envisaged an extended campaign with 'actions on the streets of Newcastle' but this proved unnecessary. In cases where employers are unresponsive, however, actions are used as a means of exerting pressure; their purpose is to elicit a reaction from those who are powerful. Actions can assume a wide variety of forms but typically they are of short duration, involve small numbers of leaders and supporters, are themed, often possess elements of street-theatre, and are tailored for media attention. Invariably those involved identify strengths and weaknesses and lessons to be learnt immediately after the action comes to an end. Examples of actions from South Wales that we have been told about or observed include: (1) a one-hour picket-line with chanting outside the offices of the Welsh Rugby Union, which ended with an out-sized letter inviting its Chief Executive to a meeting being handed to security staff; (2) a whisky-tasting outside Penderyn Distillery, coupled with a request for a meeting to discuss Living Wage accreditation; (3) a 'jammy dodger' action outside Cardiff Airport, during which biscuits were handed out to passers-by to highlight the fact that the Managing Director had 'dodged' a scheduled meeting to discuss the Living Wage; (4) groups of students from Cardiff Business School dressed as Santa and his elves presenting hampers of Living Wage produce to BBC Wales and other public service organizations in Cardiff, again with a request for a meeting to discuss the Living Wage. Often, employers are informed about actions before they take place so that they can change tack and avoid possible embarrassment. A scheduled action outside the Welsh Millennium Centre on the opening night of *Tiger Bay: The Musical*—'set in the early 1900s where extreme poverty meets supreme wealth and coal is king'—designed to highlight the contradiction between the show's theme and the fact that the centre did not pay the Living Wage, had precisely this effect.

Actions of this type are intended to publicly shame employers by pointing out their failure to act as they should. Occasionally actions go further and may disrupt an employer's business, albeit temporarily and in a non-confrontational way. An early example is an action targeted against HSBC in 2001, when campaigners flooded the bank's busiest branch in central London and disrupted its activity at lunchtime by asking for a huge volume of small change to be counted and changed into notes, while at other service points activists queued to inquire about opening an account. On this occasion, police were called but the action ended peaceably. In another disruptive action in 2007, activists from London Citizens briefly occupied the Turbine Hall at Tate Modern during the Shibboleth exhibition—a large crack in the Turbine Hall floor symbolizing the gap between rich and poor—to highlight the gallery's failure to pay the Living Wage. A community leader in the North East explained that while actions of this kind are designed to pressure employers, they strive to do so 'nicely and politely', and the ultimate aim always is 'to build a relationship' with the targeted employer. As such, the actions organized by Citizens UK contrast sharply with the more militant approach to Living Wage campaigning of indie unions, like IWGB and UVW, which similarly includes street theatre but combines it with strike action and is typically much more adversarial (Shenker 2019).

A form of action that featured prominently during the Living Wage for Social Care campaign, and which emphasizes the faith component of the Citizens' network, is a care home blessing. Blessings are conducted by local priests or bishops, typically at a care home with which a Citizens chapter has partnered. As well as prayer and a short religious ceremony outside the care home, which can involve Citizens' members standing in a ring around the building, gifts are usually presented to staff and residents, the Citizens UK logo and rainbow insignia are visible, and the event is filmed for social media. The purpose of this kind of action is to emphasize the general case for the Living Wage in social care rather than to pressure an individual care employer. The blessings, moreover, were episodes within a broader campaign, which encompassed other, more conventional pressure-group tactics. The latter included an e-petition, requests for supporters to write to their MPs and to local councillors, and the release of a charter, which set out good care and employment standards for both providers and commissioners of care. Use of actions is a hallmark of community organizing, but they are often combined with other methods.

Negotiations. The purpose of actions is to bring employers (or politicians) to the negotiating table; they have an instrumental as well as an expressive purpose and are not simply a form of protest. Community organizers from Citizens often quote American politician Elizabeth Warren to reinforce this point: 'If you don't have a seat at the table, then you are probably on the menu'. The aborted picket line at the opening night of *Tiger Bay* led to a phone call from the Millennium Centre's management in which a first meeting to discuss the Living Wage was arranged, and this was its objective. This emphasis on using direct action to establish a negotiating relationship is another feature of Citizens UK which differentiates it from indie unions, which have tended to eschew collective bargaining and established forms of union recognition (Peró 2019). A feature that is shared with indie unions, however, is a desire to involve 'leaders' directly in meetings with employers (Shenker 2019). Workers who have participated in the campaign, as well as representatives of community organizations, typically attend negotiations to introduce the Living Wage, alongside professional community organizers and representatives from the Living Wage Foundation. Even schoolchildren have been involved on occasion. If the initial meetings are successful, then the task of processing accreditation will be left to the Foundation, but it is believed to be essential for campaign activists to be involved in the early stages. The purpose of involving activists in this way is not to avoid a sell-out by professional negotiators—as it often is in the union world—but to provide development to community leaders. By taking part in meetings with senior managers and politicians, ordinary people can gain confidence and realize the power they have through community organizing.

Thanking. The final stage in a Citizens Living Wage campaign is to provide recognition and express gratitude to employers who have adopted the standard, often in an informal, personalized manner. A small e-cigarette retailer in South Wales was thanked with a cake baked by community activists; on another occasion, we witnessed a rather embarrassed HR director having a garland placed round her neck by contract cleaning staff who had been moved on to the Living Wage. Often testimony is used to express thanks to employers, particularly at public events during Living Wage Week. It is usual to feature low-paid workers who attest to the difference the Living Wage has made to their lives and express gratitude to their employers (see Chapter 1). The purpose of thanking in this way is to cement the commitment that employers have made, reinforcing the decision to adopt the Living Wage through an act of recognition. Some from the trade union movement to whom we spoke, however, expressed disquiet, saying that offering thanks in this way smacked of deference. On this view, decent employment conditions are an entitlement, something to be expected, not something for which thanks need be given.

Responsible Business

A rather different approach to spreading the Living Wage is used by the Living Wage Foundation. A Senior Programme Manager said of the Foundation that it is 'not really a campaigning body' and identified internal firewalls that separate its work from that of Citizens: for example, the Foundation's Living Wage logo does not feature, and its staff do not take part in, actions organized by Citizens. Moreover, while the Foundation makes use of some community organizing techniques it also has additional influences, and its methods resemble those of other organizations that seek to encourage responsible business. Thus, Living Wage Week is modelled on the Fairtrade Foundation's Fairtrade Fortnight and, as we have seen, the Living Wage Places scheme is influenced by the Fairtrade Towns programme (Rocket Science 2017). The Foundation's repertoire is shared with organizations such as Stonewall, Business in the Community, the Business Disability Forum, and the Employers' Network for Equality and Inclusion, which similarly rely upon fee-based accreditation or membership schemes, employer champions, and award ceremonies to promote civil regulation (Bowkett et al. 2017; Demougin et al. 2021; Williams et al. 2011). The defining feature of the Living Wage Foundation is that it is a 'business-friendly' or 'business-facing' organization, and it is this aspect of its mission that leads its staff not to participate in the actions organized by Citizens. Instead of exerting pressure at street level, the methods used by the Foundation seek to elicit the voluntary implementation of the Living Wage by its business supporters.

Rationale. An important part of this effort to attract business is furnishing a rationale for the Living Wage. Central to this rationale is the 'business case', a set of instrumental arguments that paying the Living Wage confers competitive and other benefits on accredited organizations. Thus, the Foundation's website has a page on why the Living Wage is 'Good for Business', which opens with a finding from our research that ninety-three per cent of Living Wage Employers report that the scheme has benefitted their business (https://www.livingwage.org.uk/good-for-business). Other pages contain case studies of accredited organizations, in which senior managers attest to the positive effects of the Living Wage. A quotation from IKEA reports that:

> Introducing the Living Wage is not only the right thing to do for our co-workers; it also makes good business sense. This is a long-term investment in our people based on our values and our belief that a team with good compensation and working conditions is in, a position to provide a great experience to our customers.

Much of the research commissioned or supported by the Foundation has been directed at validating claims of this kind, providing evidence that paying the Living Wage improves the performance of accredited employers (Heery et al. 2017). It must be emphasized, however, that the rationale for the Living Wage is not confined to the business case. The Foundation's website also contains a page on how the Living Wage is 'Good for Society' (https://www.livingwage.org.uk/good-for-society), which features testimony from employees who have received the Living Wage talking about the positive impact on their lives. In the last five years of the campaign there has been a heightened concern to show that the campaign is impactful and to track both the number of workers benefitting and the value of the wage on average and in aggregate. The Foundation effectively makes an 'ethical or social justice case' (Dickens 1994: 16) as well as a business case for civil regulation and appeals to employers not just on instrumental terms but in terms of business citizenship.

Incentives. To sharpen the business case the Foundation has developed secondary incentives to encourage employers to accredit. Indeed, the accreditation scheme itself is designed as an incentive, with licenced employers entitled to display the logo and report that they are accredited when advertising jobs, seeking funding, submitting a tender, and inviting investment. As we saw in the previous chapter, the supplementary standards introduced by the Foundation—the Service Provider, Funder, and Living Wage Places schemes—are intended to reinforce these incentives. Other incentives have also been put in place. The Foundation produces a 'business to business' guide to Living Wage Employers and has also experimented with attempts to establish a Living Wage consumer brand, equivalent to Fairtrade. It publishes an annual *Living Wage Christmas Gift Guide*, and the Foundation's website contains an interactive map, which allows consumers to identify Living Wage businesses in their local area (https://www.livingwage.org.uk/living-wage-map). In addition to providing incentives, the Foundation has attempted to reduce the costs of accreditation. The annual membership fee is low, particularly for small businesses and not-for-profit organizations, a factor which partly explains high membership levels amongst these groups. Membership fees for larger organizations were increased substantially in 2016, to allow the Foundation to expand its range of activities, but they are still relatively low compared to the fees charged by other organizations promoting similar schemes. The Foundation has also tried to keep the administrative costs associated with accreditation to a minimum. For smaller organizations application is through a web-portal and is almost fully automated, while for larger organizations which may have extensive contracts with suppliers, the Foundation provides consultancy support to help them through the process. The absence of intrusive monitoring of member-employers, noted above, is partly to make the scheme as non-burdensome as possible.

Communications. Communicating the rationale for the Living Wage to employers and relaying information about incentives are the subject of a sophisticated communications strategy. The Foundation employs public relations professionals, and media work lies at the core of its activity. The latter encompasses an attractive website, an active social media presence across all main platforms, and close contacts with mainstream media in press, radio, and television. The Foundation is good at obtaining Living Wage coverage. Its Twitter feed exemplifies the different elements of the Foundation's media strategy. It variously highlights research on in-work poverty and makes the case for the Living Wage, articulates the business-case, promotes consumer products from Living Wage Employers, features worker-testimony, and celebrates the accreditation of individual businesses. During the early stages of the coronavirus pandemic the feed highlighted community action by accredited organizations, such as the repurposing of distilleries to produce hand gel. While the Twitter feed is aimed at a general audience, the media team also produces tailored communications. There are toolkits on the website for investors, local authorities, social care providers, and retailers, and regular briefings on the campaign are produced for politicians. The Foundation's media work is interwoven with a programme of events, at the heart of which is Living Wage Week every November. During Living Wage Week, the new rates for the London and UK-Living Wage are announced, usually by senior politicians, with a programme of supporting events to promote the Living Wage and reach out to employers. Other highlights in the Foundation's campaigning year include the annual Living Wage Awards and a Parliamentary Reception. In between these large set-pieces there are scores of media appearances and presentations at business breakfasts, workshops, conventions, research launches, and public meetings. Until 2020 this work was carried out in-person by the Foundation's geographically mobile workforce, though during the pandemic it assumed a virtual form. Whatever the format, publicity has provided the oxygen of the campaign.

Recruitment. The Foundation recruits employers to the Living Wage in two main ways. The first method is reactive, in which the Foundation responds to expressions of interest from employers via its website: 'There is a steady stream that comes to us'. This method has grown in importance over time and is the way in which most small and medium-sized employers are recruited. 'Brand recognition' plays a key part in sustaining reactive recruitment of this kind, and much of it depends on the Foundation's active media strategy. Employers learn about the Living Wage through social media, news coverage, presentations to business audiences, Foundation stalls at conventions, and the like, and it is contact of this kind that prompts many to become accredited (see also Carson 2022). There is always a peak in employer inquiries around Living Wage Week. The second method is proactive recruitment, in which the Foundation actively seeks to persuade organizations to adopt the Living Wage. This method tends to be used for larger employers and for strategic targets, within specific industries and where there is a Living Wage Places initiative. Selecting employers for proactive recruitment may be informed by a 'power-structure analysis' of the kind described above, and all Foundation Programme Managers are now trained in this technique. The approach to employers may take the form of a cold-call. This was the case with Everton Football Club, where analysis identified the clear alignment of the club's community programme with the Living Wage, which led to a formal approach to the chief executive and subsequent accreditation. In many cases, however, proactive recruitment depends on introductions from existing members of the Foundation's employer network, who make an initial approach or smooth the path for programme managers. Andy Burnham's office was reported to have helped with the accreditation of councils in Greater Manchester, while in the legal profession HR managers in accredited firms helped with introductions to their counterparts in those that were yet to sign up. The need to key in to existing business networks and relationships when engaged in recruitment was stressed repeatedly in our interviews with Foundation staff. Other businesses, rather than outside campaigners, were identified as the most persuasive advocates of the Living Wage for a business audience.

In larger organizations accreditation can be an extended process: consumer products business Reckitt Benckiser began to meet with the Foundation in 2017, but it was not until January 2020 that its accreditation was completed. Accreditation is especially likely to be prolonged when it encompasses employees of subcontractors. Managers from a number of large organizations reported that identifying and renegotiating supplier contracts in order to meet the terms of accreditation was demanding: Heathrow Airport said that they had revised seventy-nine primary supply contracts. In some cases there may be a degree of negotiation over which precise jobs are covered by the licence agreement, which can also involve referral to the Foundation's advisory board for approval. Examples include local authorities which have been allowed to delay the extension of the Living Wage to outsourced social care, and other public service organizations which have been allowed to delay payment of the Living Wage to contract employees on long-term PFI contracts. In addition to negotiation over the precise terms of the licence, in complex cases the Foundation may provide advice to organizations going through the process of accreditation. Help of this kind can include the review of contracts with suppliers and can also involve helping specialist managers build a case for the Living Wage to be taken to the main board. The Foundation's consultancy service has grown out of work of this type.

Retention. The Foundation also has methods in place to retain employers in membership, a form of after-sales service. There are regular bulletins to keep accredited organizations informed about the campaign, together with invitations to take part in Living Wage Week and other events over the course of the campaigning year. There is a deliberate attempt to instil 'a sense of being part of a network' and foster a sense of identification with the campaign. Employers are consulted about campaign developments, such as diversification, and provided with opportunities to participate to build this sense of identification. More prosaically, the Foundation has developed a 'hand-over pack' to be used when the named contact in an accredited organization leaves their post and operates a procedure to persuade employers that allow their accreditation to lapse to rejoin.

Champions: Another way in which the Foundation seeks to develop a sense of movement is by developing employer champions, which provide active support and serve as 'ambassadors'. The most visible way in which this is done is through the Principal Partner scheme. Principal Partners include major employers, such as Aviva, KPMG, Linklaters, Nationwide, and QMUL, as well as anti-poverty organizations, such as the Joseph Rowntree Foundation, Oxfam, and Trust for London. They provide resources to the Foundation, including executive time, chair boards, committees, and meetings, and act as an inner core, a sounding board on policy for the Foundation's leadership. Beyond this core a much wider body of employers provides support to the Foundation. They host meetings, give presentations, publicize the Living Wage, recruit their peers, participate in events, and serve on industry forums, leadership groups, and steering bodies for Living Wage City initiatives.

An example of the work of employer champions can be seen in Dundee. A core participant in the group promoting Dundee as a Living Wage City is the Dundee and Angus Chamber of Commerce. The chamber was persuaded to support the campaign after hearing about the positive experience of another champion, utility firm SSE, and has since actively promoted the Living Wage to its member firms. Promotion has included press and media appearances, featuring the Living

Wage in member-bulletins, and organizing recruitment events, including a 'bring-a-friend' Living Wage workshop for existing and potential accreditees, which attracted more than fifty local businesses. Another active, local firm, which is also a member of the steering group, is Thornton's Investment Management. In addition to the steering group, the company participates in a network of local HR managers and has used this vehicle to spread knowledge of the Living Wage and persuade other employers to join. A third business champion in Dundee is the publisher DC Thomson, which has arranged media coverage of Living Wage Scotland and whose Managing Director has been a highly visible advocate.

While employer champions play an essential part in the Foundation's work, it was emphasized to us that not all businesses wish to offer this level of support. For some employers, it was said, 'It's a matter of just get the marque', of becoming accredited to secure a position on tender lists and the like. For others, though, there is a desire to be more actively engaged, particularly when accreditation has grown from a set of values or mission. Where this desire is apparent the Foundation engages in 'relationship-building', offering opportunities for managers within these firms to be more fully involved. This process was described to us as akin to the development of community leaders by Citizens UK: it can start with 'one-to-ones' and include managers giving testimony about why they committed to the Living Wage. This parallel should perhaps not be overdrawn, however. Reliance upon and cultivation of business champions is characteristic of a broad range of organizations promoting civil regulation and is not unique to those which practice community organizing.

Recognition. The final method in the Foundation's repertoire is to recognize the commitment and achievements of its employer supporters. The annual award ceremonies held by the Living Wage Foundation and Living Wage Scotland are the most visible way in which the contribution of employers is recognized. The Foundation's 2019 Living Wage Champions event was held at London's Guildhall, hosted by personal finance expert Martin Lewis, and sponsored by Aviva, Heathrow Airport, and the City of London Corporation. A range of awards were given to place and industry champions, campaigns and campaigners, businesses that had overcome challenges to become accredited, and businesses that had gone beyond the Living Wage to tackle other causes of in-work poverty. There was also an award nominated by employees. Winners were chosen from shortlists by panels of experts. The purpose of this kind of ceremony is partly to obtain publicity but also to reinforce the commitment of employers through a public act of celebration. Indeed, recognition of this kind is ongoing and is not confined to formal events. On a daily basis, employers who have signed up to the Living Wage are featured on the Foundation's social media, typically with a photo of staff holding a Living Wage plaque and a statement thanking them for their support. As with other elements of the Foundation's repertoire, recognition of employers in this way is ubiquitous amongst civil society organizations promoting private regulation

(Heery and Williams 2020). Recognizing and reinforcing employer support is an essential component of the regulatory regime such organizations create.

Relationship between Methods

Although the methods used by Citizens UK and the Living Wage Foundation are distinct, they are compatible. On the one hand, they can be applied sequentially, such that a campaign initiated by Citizens reaches its conclusion in the accreditation of the employer by the Foundation. On the other hand, the methods can substitute for one another, with Citizens replacing the Foundation when the latter's efforts prove unsuccessful and vice versa. An example of the first pattern can be seen at Heathrow Airport, where West London Citizens launched a campaign to secure the Living Wage with the support of local faith groups and by identifying leaders amongst airport cleaners. Five years later Heathrow Airport became an accredited Living Wage Employer and has since been an active proponent of the standard within the business community. Prior to the disruption caused by COVID-19, the airport established a people network made up of managers from businesses operating on the Heathrow campus, but which are not part of its direct supply-chain, with the intention of spreading the Living Wage to all businesses operating on the site. An example of the second pattern can be seen in a Premier League football club, which rebuffed all approaches from Citizens UK but was happy to negotiate the introduction of the Living Wage for its match-day support staff with the Foundation. In another example of substitution, attempts by the Foundation to coax a utility company to accredit failed to achieve a breakthrough until Citizens informed the employer that they were going to hold an action with the theme of 'Don't let them flush away low pay', which led to the opening of negotiations and accreditation.

Despite compatibility, there is a degree of tension in the methods used by Citizens and the Foundation. This tension occasionally found expression in mutual criticism. Staff in the Foundation grumbled to us about Citizens UK actions stiffening employer resistance, making it harder to secure accreditation, while a community organizer, no longer working for Citizens, cast doubt on the entire model of accreditation used by the Foundation, suggesting that gains won without community mobilization are vulnerable to reversal: 'When the [internal] champion goes, it disappears'. Underlying this mutual criticism is a recognition that the methods of the Foundation involve some dilution of the principle of community organizing. Thus, a person involved in the Dundee Living Wage City campaign characterized it as follows: 'To be honest, this is nae a bottom-up culture ... It's top-down; it's a social justice, enabling culture'. Another interviewee noted that the approach of the Foundation did not conform to 'the principle of never do for people what they can do for themselves'; rather it involved 'hiring a bunch of people with the right expertise to accredit employers'. A third interviewee, with experience of the campaign almost from its inception, said that he had been surprised by the level of support for the campaign that had emerged amongst employers: 'I had no idea of the potential to harness the support of employers'. It was from recognition of this potential that the creation of the Foundation and the accreditation system had grown. These developments have led to less overall reliance on the methods of community organizing within the campaign over time and the emergence of a new set of methods, which emphasize cooperation with business and resemble those of other CSOs that seek to promote corporate responsibility (Bunyan 2016). These newer methods have proved effective at spreading the Living Wage standard, but sometimes they sit awkwardly with the older approach, rooted in community organizing.

Campaign Relationships

It was stated above that one of the aims of power analysis is to identify allies who can help spread the Living Wage amongst employers. In this section we examine the relationships Living Wage campaigners have developed with three groups that have been identified as allies in this way: civil society organizations, trade unions, and public authorities such as devolved, regional, and local government. For each of these groups we identify precisely with whom alliances have been forged, the motivations which underpin alliances, and the form they have taken. We also identify the limitations to the relationships between Citizens UK and the Living Wage Foundation and their allies and the occasional tensions which have emerged. Alliance-building has been a defining feature of the Living Wage campaign, but it has been selective in its choice of allies, variable in form and motive, and has run up against several constraints.

Civil Society

The Living Wage campaign is a product of civil society, and campaigners have often looked to other civil society organizations for help and support. Most of these partners share the social justice and anti-poverty mission of the Living Wage campaign and, in this regard, are natural allies. They include the accreditation partners in Scotland and Wales, the Poverty Alliance and Cynnal Cymru, ShareAction, the organization which mobilizes investor power to promote social and environmental justice, anti-poverty organizations like Oxfam, the People's Health Trust, Trust for London, and the Joseph Rowntree Foundation, and the Resolution Foundation, the think-tank which focuses on labour market issues affecting the lower paid and which calculates the Real Living Wage rates. In many cases, the Living Wage

Foundation has a contractual relationship with bodies of this kind, commissioning activities or receiving grants from its CSO partners. Additionally, however, representatives of these bodies participate in the governance of the Foundation and contribute directly to its activities. They are also recurrent partners, working with the Foundation on a succession of projects and providing ongoing support and publicity. As has been explained, the Foundation's civil society partners add to the reach of the campaign and by providing a range of resources, including expertise and funding, they supplement the limited capacities of the Foundation itself. An important function of coalition-building is to bring resources to organizations which have only limited capacity to pursue objectives on their own, and Living Wage alliances with other civil society organizations have precisely this purpose (Frege et al. 2004).

One of the main ways in which civil society partners contribute to the campaign is by directly recruiting employers. In Scotland, the Poverty Alliance runs Living Wage Scotland, the Scottish programme to promote the Living Wage and accredit employers. It assumed this role in 2014, and since its inception Living Wage Scotland has been funded by the Scottish Government, allowing the appointment of a small team of Living Wage organizers. The Poverty Alliance is another meta-organization, with a membership of more than 350 public sector bodies, anti-poverty organizations, trade unions, charities, and religious institutions. It is a well-established presence in Scottish public policy, and the Living Wage campaign has been able to draw upon this organizational capital, providing it with access to networks and decision-makers. Cynnal Cymru has performed a similar role in Wales since 2016. Cynnal Cymru is a sustainability charity, initially set up by Welsh Government, which promotes sustainable business practice to organizations in Wales. Like the Poverty Alliance it has a membership network, which includes major employers from the private and not-for-profit sectors, and which serves as a channel for publicizing the Living Wage. Cynnal Cymru is less well-resourced than its Scottish counterpart, though in 2022 it received government funding for the appointment of a Living Wage organizer. Living Wage Scotland and Cynnal Cymru reproduce the approach to campaigning of the Living Wage Foundation. They are business-facing organizations and do not become involved in the kinds of campaign run by Citizens UK.

Another business-facing organization that is involved in Living Wage campaigning is ShareAction. ShareAction is a specialist campaigning body, which targets large, listed companies in the UK and which exists to 'make investment a source for good', seeking to persuade investors to use their leverage to encourage businesses to adopt socially just and environmentally responsible policies. For several years, ShareAction has worked closely with the Living Wage Foundation to encourage members of the FTSE100 to become accredited Living Wage Employers. One avenue for pursuing this objective is the organization's network of 'collaborative investors', a group of about thirty institutional investors which encourage the businesses in which they invest to adopt the Living Wage. An established practice of the group is to write to the chief executives of listed companies asking them to consider accreditation and making a business case for the Living Wage. The latter often highlights the 'reputational risks' associated with failing to act ethically. A toolkit with advice for investors on how they can encourage their investee companies to adopt the Living Wage was jointly released by the Living Wage Foundation and ShareAction in 2020 (Living Wage Foundation 2020).

A second avenue is to run public campaigns that target individual businesses and pressure them to adopt the Living Wage. These campaigns can include social media activity and actions outside corporate premises, but their culmination is invariably an intervention at the annual shareholder's meeting at which questions are asked about the business's reward policy and a proposal is put forward about Living Wage accreditation. Proposals of this kind are typically submitted by members of ShareAction's AGM Army, trained volunteers who own shares in the target company, and they may be accompanied by testimony from low-wage employees. Although there is an element of 'naming-and-shaming' about interventions of this kind—a campaign targeting house-builder Persimmon exploited widespread coverage of the very high remuneration package awarded to its chief executive—the tone of campaigning was described to us as 'non-aggressive' and aimed always at 'sparking a dialogue'. The object is to secure a meeting with the company's senior management at which an introduction can be made to the Living Wage Foundation, which can then take over and progress accreditation. In many cases this type of approach has proved effective, and by May 2022, fifty-two of the FTSE100, including Persimmon, were accredited Living Wage Employers.

While working with civil society allies is central to the method of Citizens UK and the Living Wage Foundation, there are limits to their appetite for joint working. Living Wage campaigners have sought actively to recruit allies, drawing other civil society organizations behind their campaign, but there is little interest in supporting other campaigns initiated by other campaigners, even when these call for payment of the Living Wage. As we have seen, local Living Wage campaigns have been viewed as problematic, potentially compromising the national Living Wage 'brand', and there is a preference to rely upon chapters of Citizens UK for local campaign support rather than work with non-affiliated outsiders. There is an element of 'vanguardism' in the orientation of the Living Wage campaign to civil society, in which support is sought from other organizations but tends not to be offered reciprocally (Frege et al. 2004).

Trade Unions

Trade unions are another type of ally which has provided backing to the Living Wage campaign, though not as closely or as persistently as have CSOs. The Living Wage Foundation's contact with the trade union movement is primarily through the Trades Union Congress (TUC). The General Secretary of the TUC sits on the Living Wage Commission, and there is an additional representative on the Foundation's Advisory Board. TUC regional organizations have also contributed to the campaign. The Wales TUC is represented on the Living Wage for Wales leadership team and the steering group for the Cardiff Living Wage City project, and the South-West TUC is centrally involved in the Living Wage City initiative in Bristol. In the absence of a Bristol chapter, the South-West TUC was described to us as the 'Citizens UK proxy in Bristol, in the South-West. Essentially, they're like the campaigning body'. A similar set of relationships exists in Scotland where the Scottish TUC is represented on the governing body of the Poverty Alliance, while UNISON is represented on the leadership team of Living Wage Scotland. There is no union representation on the steering group of the Dundee Living Wage City campaign, however, reflecting the unevenness of union participation.

Another way in which unions have allied with the Living Wage campaign is by affiliating to Citizens UK chapters and contributing to local campaign activity. The participants in this case are typically local union branches and regional bodies, with UNISON being the main contributor. As was noted above, UNISON is a major participant in Greater Manchester Citizens and in the past was centrally involved in Living Wage campaigning in London, though formal union involvement in the capital has now ended. Other unions have been involved in Citizens, but on a much more limited basis. While formal union participation in Citizens UK is uneven, there is wider involvement of local unions in individual Living Wage campaigns targeting individual employers. Branches of UCU have often supported attempts to promote the Living Wage in universities, and FDA has backed a campaign to secure the Living Wage for cleaners in Whitehall. Unions were also involved in the Living Wage for Social Care campaign during the pandemic, with UNISON again taking the lead role.

Like CSOs, trade unions have contributed directly to the recruitment of employers to the Living Wage. The South West TUC, for instance, worked with the Mayor of Bristol to contact 150 leading Bristol employers, together with union representatives, to ask them to become accredited. But union allies have also provided other benefits to the campaign. Particularly important is the legitimacy that unions can confer on the Living Wage standard. Unions are significant institutional actors within the labour market and their backing for the scheme is important in generating support and smoothing away opposition. It is for this reason that unions occupy positions within the governance structures of the Living Wage Foundation, Poverty Alliance, and Living Wage Places schemes, and why they have been consulted about campaign strategy. A Foundation manager described the role of the unions in the creation of Living Hours as 'kicking the tyres on the standard', bringing their expertise to bear on its substantive content and ensuring it is acceptable to a union constituency.

Another way in which alliances with unions support the campaign is by providing access to unionized workplaces and workers. The Living Wage campaign has been developed beyond the workplace, within civil society, and one consequence is that it can find it difficult to contact low-wage workers. Unions can facilitate contact of this kind and it is notable that many of the care-workers who have given testimony in the Social Care campaign are members of UNISON. In addition to providing access, unions can reinforce the Living Wage post-accreditation. It was explained that they can provide scrutiny, ensuring employers 'stick by their commitment' to pay the Living Wage, and can address associated issues such as short or unpredictable hours that reinforce low pay. Several community organizers observed that workers affected by the Living Wage need ongoing representation at the workplace through a trade union; as one said, 'Nothing beats having a union on the ground'. There was recognition, therefore, of the potential complementarity of a single-issue campaign, developed on the terrain of civil society and trade union action at the workplace (Heery et al. 2012).

While there was acknowledgement that union allies could help reinforce the Living Wage campaign, there was recognition, and often frustration, that they sometimes failed to do so. A senior organizer with Citizens UK said that while unions had participated in the network, their involvement was typically not sustained. A variety of reasons were adduced for this rather limited commitment to the campaign. Unions, it was said, typically did not conceive of themselves as place-based institutions and were remote from the local, community-based action that formed the basis of most Citizens' activity. Relatedly, the focus of their activists was on workplace matters, or union politics, or factional competition in the Labour Party and, in some parts of the country, such as Wales, close connections with the governing party reduced the perceived need for joint working with civil society organizations (cf. Hauptmeier and Turner 2007). Others observed that there was little interest displayed by unions in the admittedly challenging task of organizing low-paid workers in precarious employment, and that in some cases unions had 'circled the wagons' with employers to frustrate Living Wage campaigns and defend collective agreements that enshrined lower rates of pay. One Community Organizer said she had tried to interest unions in the recruitment of cleaners involved in a Living Wage campaign but had experienced hostility when she made contact. The same organizer asked us if there were British equivalents to American worker-centres that might take on the role of organizing workers in accredited employers, and there has been occasional discussion amongst campaigners about creating a membership body, a kind of proto-union to provide ongoing support to low-wage workers covered by the Living Wage. These discussions have never borne fruition, but they point to the limitations of the policy of allying with unions: while some in the union movement have provided strong support, this response has been far from uniform and occasionally unions have been indifferent and sometimes hostile to the campaign (cf. Holgate 2009).

Public Authorities

The final group with which Living Wage campaigners have tried to cultivate alliances are politicians and the public authorities that they lead. Citizens UK, including the Living Wage Foundation, the Poverty Alliance, and Cynnal Cymru are registered charities and so are forbidden from engaging directly in party politics. It is legitimate for these organizations to seek to influence political decision-making, however, albeit within a tight set of legal constraints, and all have been active in trying to do so (Abbott and Williams 2014). Seeking the support of public authorities and political leaders has been a core feature of the Living Wage campaign.

The main way in which Citizens UK has sought to win political support is through public meetings known as citizens' or accountability assemblies. The latter are another established method of North American community organizing, which has been transferred intact to the UK (Walls 2015). Accountability assemblies are public meetings at which Citizens UK attempts to secure the commitment of politicians to its substantive programme, including support for the Living Wage, together with an undertaking to work with Citizens in the process of implementation. Assemblies are most frequently held prior to elections, though they may also be organized to celebrate progress and secure renewed commitment during a period of elected office, as with the event to mark the first two years of Sadiq Kahn's term as London Mayor, mentioned above. The politicians targeted through assemblies may be standing in UK general elections, elections for devolved national governments, in city and city-region mayoral elections, or local authority elections. At whatever level of the political system the assembly is pitched, however, they tend to assume a standard format and are tightly planned, scripted events. In some cases, such as the elections for London Mayor, the audience, made up of members of Citizens UK affiliated organizations, can be in the thousands.

Common elements of accountability assemblies include: a roll-call of the Citizens UK affiliated organizations attending the meeting; the introduction and election by a public show of hands of the diverse group of leaders who will conduct the meeting and quiz politicians (professional community organizers plan and produce the script for the meeting but play no public part); elements of performance including tableaux, processions, and musical performances, all of which frequently involve schoolchildren; provision of testimony either in person or through video, including testimony from low-wage workers about the Living Wage; and the offering of thanks to politicians and to employers that are present for the prior action they have taken to support the campaign. At the centre of the event there is a hustings at which politicians from all the main parties standing in the election are asked to present their own agenda and then respond to the 'asks' put forward by Citizens, including those relating to the Living Wage. The leaders often engage in 'pinning', trying to get the politicians to make explicit and specific commitments to the proposals put forwards, rather than offering vague assurances. Specific proposals to which politicians have been asked to commit at meetings that we have attended include using advertising space on London buses and in tube stations to publicize the Living Wage, personally announcing the new rates in Living Wage Week, ensuring that all employers in receipt of public investment develop a Living Wage plan, and agreeing to organize a 'social care summit', at which proposals would be developed for spreading the Living Wage in adult social care in Wales. While the audience can clap and show approval when politicians are speaking at assemblies, booing and barracking are not allowed. The assemblies are orderly, and in all cases include a request for politicians to 'work with us' and agree to a meeting with a group of Citizens' leaders to implement what has been agreed.

In many cases assemblies are successful in winning support from politicians from across the spectrum to offer backing to the Living Wage campaign: successive Labour and Conservative candidates for London Mayor have backed the Living Wage, as have the leaders of the Conservative, Labour, Liberal, and nationalist parties in Wales. Follow-up meetings have been held and action plans developed, which have included steps to promote the Living Wage. A particular priority for the Foundation has been developing relations with elected metro mayors, and they have worked closely with the mayoral offices in London, Greater Manchester, and other English city-regions. A Foundation programme manager described to us why it is important to forge a positive relationship with metro mayors:

> They have a big public presence in the regions; they're well-known figures and if they are talking about something, it will be on the agenda of local authorities and businesses. And I think that's the main reason that we need to get them on board ... They don't really have that much sort of, you know political power in terms of policy and legislation but their convening power and influencing power is quite strong. So, if we can get them on board, get them talking about the Living Wage and accreditations, then we'll see growth come naturally from that.

As well as a general capacity to shape the policy agenda in the regions, metro mayors are also associated with a specific initiative that is of direct relevance to the Foundation. First in London and Greater Manchester and then in Liverpool and the North East, metro mayors have launched employment charters that seek to encourage local employers to adopt good standards, including the Living Wage. Living Wage campaigners have endorsed these charters and tried to make their Living Wage commitment as strong as possible; they are a vehicle through which the soft power of elected office can extend the reach of the campaign.

The Foundation has also sought to build positive relationships with local authorities, most strikingly through the Living Wage Places scheme. As we have seen, the latter seeks to develop place-based campaigns, which spread the Living Wage through buildings, zones, boroughs, towns, and cities. Invariably, local authorities have lain at the heart of these initiatives, and they have relied on the backing of local politicians and the expertise of council officers to make them effective. The places scheme depends upon local authorities acting as 'anchor institutions', a concept that has arrived with another American import, the movement for 'community wealth-building' (Guinan and O'Neill 2020). By using their purchasing, funding, taxing, convening, and influencing powers, local authorities can encourage other employers in their districts to adopt the Living Wage, and it is because they can potentially perform this anchoring role that local authorities have been identified as attractive allies by campaigners.

Another location at which the Foundation has built relationships with political leaders is the Houses of Parliament. As was noted above, the Foundation organizes an annual parliamentary reception, attended by scores of politicians, and has also developed links with individual parliamentarians from a range of parties. Members of the All-Parliamentary Group on Poverty, such as Kevin Hollinrake (Conservative) and Neil Gray (SNP) have been strong supporters, as are several Labour MPs. These political supporters can make representations on behalf of the Foundation in parliament, both within their parties and back in their own constituencies. The Labour MP Catherine West, for example, raised the issue of paying the Living Wage to contract cleaning staff at Boris Johnson's first-ever Prime Minister's questions in 2019, eliciting a favourable response, while another Labour MP, Stephen Timms, helped broker a meeting between the Foundation and Tate & Lyle, based in his East London constituency, which resulted in the latter becoming accredited. Like metro mayors, members of parliament have considerable influencing power and the Foundation has endeavoured to tap into their networks and use this power to spread accreditation.

While the Living Wage campaign has tried to secure political support from across the spectrum, politicians from some parties have proved more receptive than others. The devolved national governments of Scotland and Wales, led respectively by the SNP and the Labour Party, local councils controlled by the same two parties, and Labour metro mayors, such as Sadiq Kahn and Andy Burnham, have provided stronger support for the Living Wage than have the Conservative-controlled UK Government and Conservative regional and local authorities (see Chapter 6). This pattern of response is problematic because the entrenched position of the Conservatives in UK national and much of local government serves as a brake on the spread of the Living Wage (Heery et al. 2020). For this reason, the campaign has been particularly assiduous at developing contacts with Conservative politicians and appreciative of those who have lent support. It is also for this reason that the Living Wage for Social Care campaign has prioritized building relations with Conservative MPs and council leaders, hoping through this route to secure Government backing for payment of the Living Wage in social care. The Living Wage campaign successfully won the support of Boris Johnson when he was London Mayor; it tried to repeat that success when he was Prime Minister.

Conclusion

In this chapter we have profiled the linked organizations behind the Living Wage campaign, Citizens UK, and the Living Wage Foundation, examined their strategy and the methods they use to promote the Living Wage, and reviewed their relationships with other civil society organizations, trade unions, and public authorities. To conclude, we want to relate the findings presented above to the wider literature on civil regulation, introduced in Chapter 1. One current in this literature has argued that civil society organizations tend to rely on distinctive methods, particularly when compared with trade unions. Thus it has been variously argued that CSOs often mobilize consumer interests to promote civil regulation, using consumer boycotts and protests to compel brands to adopt good environmental or employment standards (Donaghey et al. 2014); that CSOs have greater mobilizing capacity than trade unions because of their social justice mission and so can rely to a much greater degree on pressure tactics to secure their objectives (Tapia 2013); and that CSOs have developed new, less structured methods, such as 'swarming', in which loosely coupled groups and networks come together suddenly to exert intense pressure on a target company or public authority through social media before dispersing equally rapidly (Heckscher and McCarthy 2014). To what extent are these claims about the distinctiveness of civil society methods borne out by the case of the Living Wage campaign?

The straightforward answer for all three versions, is 'not very much'. As we have seen, Living Wage campaigners have tried to develop a Living Wage consumer brand and add consumer preference to the list of economic incentives that can encourage employers to adopt the Living Wage. But this has not been the defining feature of the campaign. Moreover, there has been no use of consumer pressure against recalcitrant employers, and groups other than consumers, such as investors and public authorities, have occupied a more central position in the strategic thinking of campaigners. The claim that CSOs occupy the realm of consumption while trade unions occupy production we believe is too simplistic and underestimates the range of interests that organizations like Citizens UK and the Living Wage Foundation can mobilize to pursue their objectives.

The same judgement is warranted in the case of the claim that the values-led quality of social justice campaigns like that for the Living Wage endows them with a high mobilizing capacity and an ability to draw low-wage workers into protest action against employers. As the preceding account demonstrates, however, most campaigning activity does not involve the use of pressure tactics, and the Foundation and its allies have been able to rely upon employer self-referral and peer-to-peer recruitment to maintain the flow of accreditation. Moreover, when activists have been mobilized in campaigns against resistant employers they have often come from place-based organizations beyond the workplace. In some campaigns, low-wage workers themselves have been key leaders, mobilizing their colleagues and initiating actions, but often this has not been the case. The involvement of the low-paid in many situations has been confined to the giving of 'one or two testimonies', a powerful form of action but one that does not require a high level of mobilization.

The methods used by Living Wage campaigners also do not conform to the image of fluid, loosely coupled, and ephemeral protest expressed by the concept of 'swarming'. The community organizing movement emerged during the high period of American modernism in the mid-twentieth century, and it bears the stamp of its time of origin. Campaigning activity is planned, scripted, conducted through the sharply delimited roles of 'organizer' and 'leader', articulated through a specialized vocabulary, reviewed and assessed, and overwhelmingly goal-orientated. There is more than a pinch of scientific management in the community organizing mix, which lies at the polar opposite to the spontaneity and expressive quality of some other social movements. Campaigning for the Living Wage is also a long-term activity; the campaign itself has reached its twentieth anniversary, and attempts to accredit individual organizations can themselves take years, with successive attempts being launched when conditions are favourable. There are distinctive features to the Living Wage campaign, seen in the application by Citizens UK of a particular campaigning repertoire developed over decades by the American community organizing movement, but these features separate the campaign from other social movements rather than lead it to approximate to a common civil society type.

Another current in the literature on civil regulation has identified increased reliance amongst advocates on business support (Vogel 2010a). This claim is confirmed by the evidence set out above, which shows that there has been a primary reliance on 'business-friendly' methods amongst Living Wage campaigners, at least since the launch of the accreditation scheme in 2011. Both the Foundation and its partners have sought to persuade employers that signing up to the Living Wage is not only right in itself but also in their own economic interest, and they have relied on a portfolio of techniques including toolkits, case-studies, business champions, award schemes, and business-targeting events and publicity, in the manner of other organizations that seek to encourage responsible business. In its orientation to business, the Foundation conforms to a common pattern amongst business-facing campaigns (Heery and Williams 2020). Indeed, this orientation is also visible in the efforts to promote the Living Wage of Citizens UK. While the latter makes use of 'actions' to exert pressure on business, typically these do not disrupt business activity but are designed to embarrass and highlight failings of corporate conduct. The actions themselves often employ whimsical themes and are deliberately non-threatening, designed to elicit a constructive response and the opening of negotiations. The Living Wage campaign is distinctive in having two facets to its campaigning activity—'the carrot and the stick'—but both are designed to forge a cooperative relationship with business partners.

In the academic literature on civil society there is a developed theme on union-community coalitions, which foregrounds the relationship between civil society and the labour movement (Heery 2019). Much of this literature identifies scope for a fruitful alliance between trade unions and new employment actors, in which the workplace presence of the former provides a means to diffuse and enforce standards promoted by the latter. As we have seen, many Living Wage campaigners see trade unions in precisely these terms, as potential allies who can provide access to low-wage workers, encourage employers to adopt the Living Wage, monitor business compliance, and secure additional improvements for low-wage workers. There is also recognition that unions play an important part in legitimizing the Living Wage standard. Despite these elements of fruitful joint-working, however, the relationship between Citizens UK, the Foundation, and trade unions has not always been good. There is an uneven and occasionally fraught quality to the relationship between the two sides, which is not captured by the positive literature on union-community alliances. What stands out from the findings on the Living Wage campaign's relationships with other organizations is not the link to trade unions but the much stronger and much broader set of connections to other civil society organizations. Both Citizens UK and the Foundation work closely with other civil society partners, and the latter bring a range of expertise and other resources to the campaign. Indeed, the core activity of the campaign—recruiting employers to the Living Wage standard—is often devolved to partner organizations. It is the ubiquity of alliances within the realm of civil society that stands out prominently from the research, rather than coalition across the boundary with the labour movement.

A final theme in the literature on civil regulation concerns its capacity to act as a functional alternative to public policy and to statutory regulation (Vogel 2010a). Here, again, the findings from the study do not support the dominant argument within the literature. It is true that the Living Wage has compensated for the failure of the statutory minimum wage to eradicate in-work poverty, but campaigners have worked closely with public authorities and the spread of the Living Wage standard has often been dependent on public policy. The accountability assemblies organized by Citizens UK and the Living Wage Places scheme, and the attempts to cultivate support from the devolved national governments of Scotland and Wales and the English metro mayors all point in this direction. In helping spread the Living Wage standard, political leaders and public authorities have often made use of statutory powers; for example, the statutory right of devolved national governments to insist that the issue of fair work, including payment of the Living Wage, should be considered in public procurement (Heery et al. 2020). But public authorities have not been asked to legislate for a Living Wage in the way that

American campaigners have done. Winning political support has been central to the Living Wage campaign, but its aim has been to ensure that the purchasing, funding, fiscal, convening, and influencing power of the state be brought to bear in support of the Living Wage. Forging a positive relationship with branches of the state has been a pivotal feature of the Living Wage campaign, but this effort has not focused on the state's role as legislator.

4
Employers and the Real Living Wage

Introduction

We turn now from the campaign to promote the Real Living Wage to the response of employers. Forms of civil regulation, like the Living Wage, are dependent for their success on employers who must apply the standard within their organizations if it is to shape the pattern of employment relations. They occupy a key mediating position between civil regulation and the employees who it is designed to benefit. Accordingly, in this chapter we examine employer reaction to the Living Wage, looking in turn at three key issues: first, which types of employers have adopted the Living Wage; second, why they have done so and what are the key motivations that lead employers to become accredited; and third, what has led some employers to resist the Living Wage campaign and decline to become accredited. Examining these questions relies on a different primary source of evidence in each case. Our evidence on the characteristics of accredited employers comes from the dataset of Living Wage Employers and Service Providers, evidence on motives for accreditation is taken principally from our 2021 employer survey, while information on reasons for opposing the scheme comes largely from qualitative evidence: interviews and observation. To conclude the chapter we describe the full range of employer responses to the Living Wage, stretching from opposition to enthusiastic support, and reflect upon what this variable pattern of response can tell us about employer behaviour.

Characteristics of Accredited Employers

The purpose of this section is to produce a descriptive map of Living Wage accreditation. In what follows we identify the characteristics of Living Wage Employers and locate where they are found in the UK economy. A secondary purpose, however, is to use our evidence to test arguments drawn from wider debate on civil regulation, focusing on the following four claims:

1. In the literature on international civil regulation it is suggested that responsiveness to campaigns like that for the Living Wage is most pronounced amongst private sector businesses in consumer-facing industries, which

The Real Living Wage. Edmund Heery, Deborah Hann and David Nash, Oxford University Press.
© Edmund Heery, Deborah Hann and David Nash (2023). DOI: 10.1093/oso/9780198835264.003.0004

have strong brands that are vulnerable to tarnishing through activist pressure (Bartley 2018; Donaghey et al. 2014). Following this argument, one would expect to see high adoption of the Living Wage in the kinds of organization which have embraced international codes of good business practice; that is, by large private sector enterprises in retail, clothing, sporting goods, and consumer electronics.

2. In the literature advocating civil regulation, in contrast, the emphasis is on the adoption of programmes in parts of the economy where they are most needed, where problems such as in-work poverty are most acute. Advocates of the Living Wage have often made arguments of this kind, presenting the campaign as an effective and targeted anti-poverty measure for low-wage workers (Wills and Linneker 2013). They have also argued that it is an effective response to the downward pressure on pay and employment conditions exerted through outsourcing (Wills 2009). If this logic is followed, then one would expect higher rates of accreditation in low-paying industries, low-paying regions, and in parts of the economy affected by outsourcing.
3. The obverse of this needs-based argument is that the sign-up to civil regulation will be highest amongst organizations that are already largely compliant, and which will incur limited additional cost by doing so (Hoque 2003). According to this argument, Living Wage accreditation will follow the line of least resistance, with higher levels of accreditation in high-paying industries and amongst businesses located in high-paying regions, where prevailing wages in low-paying jobs are close to or exceed the Living Wage.
4. The final argument is that adherence to civil regulation will be stronger where institutions are present that encourage businesses to comply (Harvey et al. 2017; Locke et al. 2013). Accordingly, we consider whether accreditation is more prevalent in parts of the economy where public authorities are supportive, where there is a relatively high trade union presence, and where local campaigners maintain an active presence, either through a Citizens UK chapter or a Living Wage Places initiative.

Table 4.1 shows a breakdown of the number and percentage of all Living Wage Employers and Service Providers accredited since 2011 by a variety of business characteristics. The latter encompass organizational size, main sector of activity, principal industry division, whether the business operates in a low-wage industry, or an industry characterized by outsourcing, the main nation or region of the UK in which the business has its prime location, and whether or not it is headquartered in one of the country's 'core cities'. As well as showing the number and percentage of accredited organizations, the table also provides a breakdown for all UK businesses. The latter data are taken from the Business Population estimates for 2021 and provide a point of comparison, showing the extent to which the characteristics of Living Wage Employers conform to or diverge from those of the general population of employers. In what follows, we consider each of these business characteristics in sequence, establishing the relevance of the findings to the arguments just outlined as we proceed.

Organization Size

International systems of voluntary regulation are primarily targeted at large, global firms with supply chains that stretch from emerging economies in the Global South to developed economies in the Global North. The data in Table 4.1, showing the size distribution of accredited employers, indicates that the impact of the Living Wage campaign has departed, at least partially, from this pattern. Accreditation has not been confined to large organizations, and the campaign has elicited a positive response from many small and medium-sized employers. Ninety per cent of organizations accredited since 2011 have fewer than 250 employees, and more than a third are micro-businesses with a headcount of less than ten. The preponderance of small employers amongst the ranks of accredited organizations reflects the low cost of accreditation, the openness of the campaign to a broad range of employers, and perhaps the relative ease with which small firms can implement the standard.

Although most Living Wage Employers are small organizations, Table 4.1 also indicates that the campaign has had considerable success in attracting large businesses. Since 2011, 751 organizations with 500 or more employees have adopted the Living Wage. These include some of the largest employing organizations in the UK: there are 253 accredited employers with 3,000 or more employees and sixty-two with more than 10,000. Comparison of the size distribution of accredited organizations with that for the UK economy at large, moreover, indicates that larger employers are proportionally over-represented amongst those who are accredited.

While the campaign has been successful in attracting large organizations into membership, it is notable that these typically are not the large retail, clothing, or electronics brands that feature in the literature on private regulation. For example, of the ninety-nine companies that have joined the Ethical Trading Initiative only five (Burberry, Marshalls, Seasalt, Transport for London, Union Hand-Roasted) are accredited Living Wage Employers, while a sixth (Oliver Bonas) was accredited but has now lapsed. Not one of the twenty-nine UK-based brands that are signatories to the Accord on Fire and Building Safety in Bangladesh have adopted the Living Wage in their home base. IKEA is the only major global retailer that has become an accredited Living Wage Employer. The large private sector organizations that have become accredited tend to be located in banking and financial services (e.g. Lloyds Bank, Barclays, RBS, HSBC, Aviva, Santander), professional services (e.g. Arup, Deloitte, EY, KPMG, PwC), manufacturing (e.g. Astrazeneca,

Table 4.1 Characteristics of Living Wage Employers

	Accredited Employers[1]		UK Business Population[2]	
	N	%	N	%
Organization size				
Below 10 employees	4,462	35.1	1,066,155	79.3
10–49	4,948	38.9	225,845	16.8
50–249	2,122	16.7	41,275	3.1
250–499	432	3.4	5,075	0.4
500+ employees	751	5.9	5,440	0.4
Sector				
Private sector	8,490	66.7	1,281,640	95.3
Not-for-profit sector	3,820	30.0	53,720	4.1
Public sector	418	3.3	7,995	0.6
Industry division				
Agriculture, forestry, and fishing	52	0.4	50,212	3.5
Mining and quarrying	13	0.1		
Electricity and gas	60	0.5	8,845	0.6
Water supply and waste management	100	0.8		
Manufacturing	894	7.0	88,560	6.3
Construction	730	5.7	181,850	12.9
Wholesale and retail trade	936	7.4	241,151	17.0
Transport and storage	165	1.3	54,346	3.8
Accommodation and food services	588	4.6	140,652	9.9
Information and communication	1,120	8.8	81,159	5.7
Finance and insurance	379	3.0	24,270	1.7
Real estate	381	3.0	47,604	3.4
Professional, scientific, and technical activities	1,640	12.9	193,520	13.7
Administrative and support services	1,413	11.1	129,056	9.1
Public administration, and defence	300	2.4	n/a	n/a
Education	945	7.4	20.579	1.5
Health and social work	1,751	13.8	59,674	4.2
Arts, entertainment, and recreation	469	3.7	26,704	1.9
Other services	791	6.2	67,332	4.8
Low-pay and outsourcing				
Retail[3]	588	4.6	183,160	12.9
Residential social care[4]	236	1.9	7,730	0.5
Hospitality[5]	589	4.6	140,652	9.9
Cleaning[6]	401	3.2	17,210	1.2
Event catering and food services[7]	107	0.8	10,700	0.8
Private security[8]	202	1.6	5,414	0.4
Combined facilities support services[9]	80	0.6	5,275	0.4
Landscape services[10]	52	0.4	10,995	0.8
Home care[11]	375	2.9	4,090	0.3
Nations and regions				
Wales	488	3.8	55,580	3.9
Scotland	3,240	25.5	95,089	6.7

Continued

Table 4.1 *Continued*

	Accredited Employers[1]		UK Business Population[2]	
	N	%	N	%
Northern Ireland	56	0.4	36,617	2.6
England	8,944	70.3	1,229,440	86.8
London	3,442	27.0	246,259	17.4
East Midlands	395	3.1	100,668	7.1
West Midlands	482	3.8	119,456	8.4
East of England	619	4.9	139,642	9.9
North East	259	2.0	41,198	2.9
North West	1,095	8.6	142,093	10.0
South East	1,185	9.3	209,178	14.8
South West	871	6.8	124,820	8.8
Yorkshire & Humberside	596	4.7	104,616	7.4
Cities				
Core cities[12]	6,760	53.1	930,605	35.8
Other cities[13]	1,795	14.1	548,830	21.1
Non-city[14]	4,173	32.8	1,116,885	43.0
Total	12,728	100	1,414,498	100

1. Includes all Living Wage Employers and Living Wage Service Providers that have accredited since 2011, i.e. lapsed employers are included.
2. Data are taken primarily from the UK Business Population Estimates 2021, produced by BEIS and for organization size and sector refer to employing organizations with at least two employees; estimates for industry divisions, low-paying and outsourcing industries, and nations and regions refer to private sector businesses with employees. The business estimates for core cities refer to all registered businesses, including businesses without employees, and are taken from NOMIS: Official Labour Market Statistics, https://www.nomisweb.co.uk/.
3. Retail encompasses SIC Divisions 45 and 47, plus Class 7722 and Group 952.
4. Residential care comprises Division 87 plus Class 86,102.
5. Hospitality embraces Section I—accommodation and food services.
6. Cleaning comprises Group 812 and Class 9601.
7. Event catering and food services comprise SIC Classes 56210 and 56290.
8. Private security includes businesses engaged in security and investigation activities, Classes 80100, 80200, and 80300.
9. Combined services include businesses operating 'combined facilities support services' (Class 81100) and businesses providing 'combined office administrative service activities' (Class 82110) and 'photocopying and other office support activities' (Class 82190).
10. SIC Class 81300, 'landscape service activities'.
11. SIC Class 88100, 'other social work activities without accommodation for the elderly and disabled', which includes the provision of home care.
12. Great Britain's twelve 'core cities' are Birmingham, Bristol, Cardiff, Edinburgh, Glasgow, Leeds, Liverpool, London, Manchester, Newcastle, Nottingham, and Sheffield.
13. The remaining fifty cities in Great Britain, identified by the Centre for Cities. These cities include large conurbations, such as Leicester, Brighton, and Bournemouth as well as smaller cities, such as Burnley, Crawley, and Dundee. Note that in the Centre for Cities classification, an individual city may comprise two or more local authority districts. Manchester, for example, includes Bolton, Bury, Oldham, Rochdale, Salford, Stockport, Tameside, and Trafford, as well the City of Manchester itself. The grouping of data in the table makes use of these more encompassing definitions of city boundaries.
14. All other localities in the UK, including smaller towns; i.e. the category is not confined to strictly rural locations.

BAE Systems, GSK, Nestlé, Reckitt Benckiser, Unilever), and energy and utilities (e.g. BP, Centrica, SSE, EDF Energy, National Grid, Ovo Energy). There is also a cluster of large facilities management businesses, including Capita, Compass, ISS, Mitie, OCS, and Sodexo, most of which are accredited as service providers. Apart from the latter, what is distinctive about these clusters is that they tend to be found in relatively high wage industries, where the cost implications of adopting the Living Wage are comparatively limited; a pattern that is further explored below.

A final distinguishing feature of large, accredited employers, which again separates them from organizations featured in the literature on private voluntary regulation, is that many are not private businesses. They include large public sector organizations, such as the Northern Ireland, Scottish, and Welsh Governments, many local authorities, NHS Trusts and Boards, and several police forces; providers of public services, such as universities; and not-for-profit organizations. While only five company-members of the Ethical Trading Initiative are accredited Living Wage Employers, ten NGO-members are, including CAFOD, Christian Aid, Oxfam, Save the Children, and Fairtrade. Organizations campaigning against global poverty, on this evidence, are more likely to respond positively to the Living Wage than the global retail and clothing brands that they target in their campaigns.

Sector

Further evidence on the sectoral distribution of the Living Wage is shown in Table 4.1, which indicates that the standard has spread across all main sectors of the economy, with the largest concentration in the private sector. Comparison with the UK-wide distribution across sectors, however, shows that private sector businesses are disproportionately under-represented, while not-for-profit and public sector employers are over-represented. The most striking finding in the table is the very high level of accreditation amongst not-for-profit organizations, which constitute nearly a third of Living Wage Employers despite making up only a small percentage of UK employing organizations. The Living Wage has emerged from civil society, and it is within civil society that it has met its strongest positive response—a pattern that is not anticipated in the established literature on private regulation.

The likely explanation for this strong level of support from civil society is that many not-for-profit organizations share the objectives of the Living Wage campaign and have backed the latter because its aims are congruent with their own. There is an elective affinity between these organizations and Citizens UK, which has made them receptive to accreditation. This can be seen most clearly perhaps in the accreditation of faith organizations. Citizens UK is a faith-dominated network, and faith organizations have proved to be strong backers of the Living Wage.

Religious bodies make up nine per cent of accredited not-for-profit organizations and include dioceses, cathedrals, churches, the Methodist Council, and the Religious Society of Friends and many of its Quaker Meeting Houses, evangelical congregations, synagogues, and mosques. They also include religious charities, schools, and colleges from a variety of faiths and denominations.

The affinity can also be seen in the accreditation of many anti-poverty and social justice organizations. More than 1,600 accredited not-for-profit organizations (forty-four per cent) have an explicit anti-poverty or social justice mission akin to that of Citizens UK. These organizations include many prominent campaigning organizations, such as Amnesty International, Care International UK, Joseph Rowntree Foundation, One Parent Families Scotland, Shelter, and WaterAid. They also include many smaller organizations addressing specific issues. These include foodbanks, women's refuges, migrants' rights organizations, and charities providing development and other support to the long-term unemployed, ex-offenders, the homeless, and victims of alcohol and substance abuse. We discuss the motives for employers adopting the Living Wage more fully below, but it seems likely that many organizations of this type have become accredited to express solidarity with the campaign. Becoming a Living Wage Employer for these organizations has an expressive purpose, reflective of their core mission.

Another group of not-for-profit organizations that have been receptive to the Living Wage are social enterprises, businesses that operate on a commercial basis but to pursue social objectives rather than profit. Several organizations which represent and support social enterprises have become accredited employers, including Social Enterprise UK, Social Enterprise Scotland, the Social Enterprise Academy, and the Social Enterprise Mark, an accrediting body for businesses of this type. Many of the members of these organizations have also become accredited. One type of social enterprise that is strongly represented amongst accredited not-for-profit organizations are credit unions. The Association of British Credit Unions, the trade body, is an accredited Living Wage Employer, as are fifty-two individual credit unions—nineteen per cent of the total number operating in the UK. Once again, this is evidence of organizations that define their purpose in terms of social and community benefit proving to be particularly receptive to the Living Wage.

Industry

The next section of Table 4.1 provides information on the distribution of Living Wage Employers and service providers across the nineteen main industry divisions in the UK economy, though with the UK-wide comparative evidence in this case taken solely from the private sector. The evidence demonstrates, firstly, that accreditation is broadly spread and found within all divisions. However, although there is a broad spread there is also concentration in particular industry groups, with nearly forty per cent of accredited employers found in just three divisions: professional services, administrative and support services, and human health and social work. Comparison of the industry distribution of Living Wage Employers with that for private sector business across the economy, moreover, reveals a group of industries where there has been a markedly positive response to the Living Wage. Once again, human health and social work is included, as are education and other services. In all three, accreditation is concentrated within not-for-profit organizations including many faith organizations and organizations with a social justice mission. Other industries with a relatively high level of accreditation include mining and utilities, finance, and information and communications, all of which have relatively few low-paid workers (Cominetti et al. 2019). The table also reveals those industry divisions where there has been a disproportionately poor response to the Living Wage campaign. Agriculture, construction, wholesale and retail trade, transport and storage, and accommodation and food service are industries in which there are few Living Wage Employers relative to their size within the UK economy. Three of these industries—agriculture, trade, and accommodation and food service—are among the lowest paying in the UK.

Figure 4.1 provides further information on the distribution of accredited employers across low- and high-wage industries. It presents a histogram of the number of Living Wage Employers in industries (measured at the 4-digit SIC level) whose hourly median pay was greater or less than the national median figure of £14.05 in 2021. The figure shows that a narrow majority (fifty-two per cent) of accredited organizations are found in industries with rates of pay above the national median and that a substantial minority are found in the highest paying industries: sixteen per cent of accredited employers operate in industries with an hourly rate of pay at least £5.00 higher than the national median. The overall distribution shows a weak positive skew, however, and the distribution diverges to only a modest degree from normality. Many employers from industries with low rates of pay have clearly joined the scheme, alongside their high-paying counterparts. The distribution in Figure 4.1 shows that the Living Wage campaign has recruited a broad set of employers from across the economy and that while those in high-paying industries form a majority, they are not overwhelmingly dominant. There is only weak support for the third argument outlined above, that accreditation will follow the path of least resistance and be concentrated largely in industries with higher rates of pay.

Further examination of the pattern of Living Wage take-up within industries, however, reveals a more complex picture. Table 4.1 shows the pattern of Living Wage accreditation across broad industry divisions, but within these divisions there are significant points of concentration, where a sizeable number of employers in a particular branch have adopted the Living Wage. There are Living Wage hotspots within most broad industry divisions. In manufacturing, one such cluster

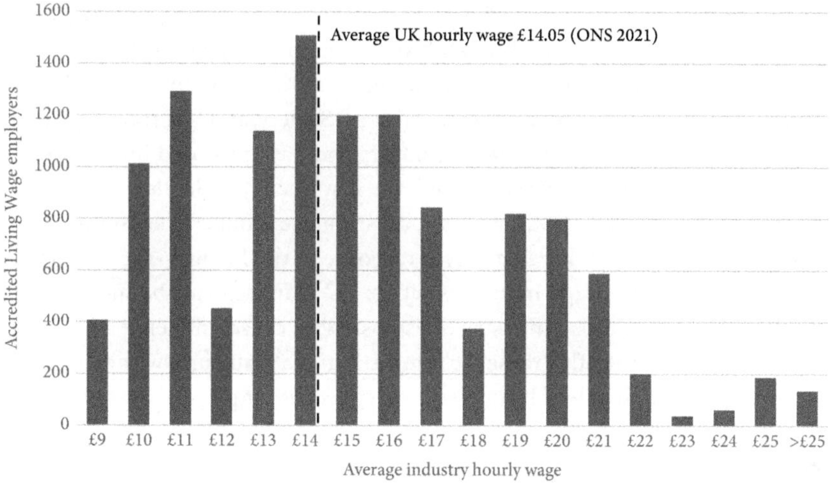

Figure 4.1 Distribution of accredited employers by average industry wage

Notes: Based on data from 12,252 accredited Living Wage Employers and Recognized Service Providers; skewness 0.623; Kolmogorov-Smirnoff test for departure from normality D (12,252) = 0.065, $p < 0.001$.

is found amongst craft brewers, where Brewdog, the national brewing and bar chain, is accredited, as are many local breweries. There has been talk amongst campaigners of holding a Living Wage beer festival. Universities form another cluster in education, where ninety-two institutions have become accredited, including the Universities of Oxford and Cambridge and several of their constituent colleges. In professional services, the law stands out as a main centre of accreditation. More than 175 law firms have become accredited Living Wage Employers, including most of the leading corporate law firms, while a further thirty barristers' chambers have also joined. Another emerging cluster can be seen in arts and entertainment, where six Premier League football teams (Brighton and Hove Albion, Chelsea, Crystal Palace, Everton, Liverpool, West Ham United) have adopted the Living Wage, alongside clubs from lower tiers of professional football (Prowse and Dobbins 2022).

In some cases, these clusters have emerged because their employers are part of the high-wage economy: universities are relatively high payers within education, while the same is true of corporate law firms within professional services. Institutional forces, however, have also helped generate these clusters. Some of these institutions have exerted pressure from below: Living Wage campaigners have targeted law firms and professional football clubs, supplemented in the case of universities with pressure from local trade union branches and student unions. Others have emerged from amongst the ranks of employers themselves, and within some clusters leading employers and employers' organizations have provided additional impetus to accreditation. In brewing, Brewdog has been a strong advocate of the Living Wage, while leading law firm Linklaters, Everton Football Club, and QMUL are formally recognized Living Wage champions. In the legal profession, The Law Society, The Law Society of Scotland, Leeds Law Society, and Liverpool Law Society are all accredited Living Wage Employers and have provided information to members about the Living Wage. Indeed, the Law Society of Scotland requires its members to pay the rate to trainee solicitors. The economic structure of industries has therefore shaped the employer response to the Living Wage, facilitating accreditation in high wage industries where the standard can be more readily afforded. But within broad industry divisions, other causal influences are apparent, and it is noteworthy that these include institutional structures within the ranks of employers, including lead businesses and collective employers' organizations.

Low-Paying and Outsourcing Industries

Figure 4.1 shows that there has been considerable success in spreading the Living Wage in industries characterized by low pay. Nearly 6,000 accredited employers are found in industries with an hourly median rate of pay below the national figure, and nearly a quarter of all employers are found in industries with an hourly rate £3.00 or more below. Moreover, there is also evidence that employers in low-paying industries have become more likely to join the scheme over time. Almost half of accredited employers in industries with rates of pay below the median have joined within the past three years.

Further information on the Living Wage in low-wage and outsourcing industries, together with comparative data from the Business Population Estimates, is shown in Table 4.1. The first four industries for which data are shown—retail, residential care, hospitality, and cleaning—have been identified by the Low Pay Commission as the lowest paying in the UK, each with forty per cent or more of jobs characterized by low pay (ONS 2015). Two of these industries, residential care and cleaning, are also distinguished by involvement in outsourcing: much of residential care is provided through contracts with local authorities and most cleaning firms provide services to corporate clients. The table also includes figures for other industries that provide outsourced support services: catering, security, combined facilities support, landscaping, and home care, much of which is also delivered through local government contracts.

Some of the earliest Living Wage actions were targeted at workers in these industries, and a central component of the 'needs-based' argument, outlined above, is that the campaign can be effective in attracting employers in low-wage and outsourcing industries (Alberti et al. 2013; Wills 2009). The findings in the table are mixed when viewed from the needs-based perspective. The two largest industries included, retail and hospitality, have disproportionately low levels of Living

Wage accreditation: in combination these industries account for twenty-three per cent of UK businesses but only nine per cent of Living Wage Employers. These figures attest to the severity of the challenge of persuading employers in low-wage industries to commit to a voluntary wage standard. The findings for outsourcing industries, however, are rather different and altogether more positive. Cleaning and residential care make up five per cent of Living Wage Employers despite making up less than two per cent of UK business, and the other outsourcing industries listed in the table show a similar pattern. All except landscaping have a level of Living Wage accreditation that is higher than or equivalent to their representation in the UK business population. It is important to recognize that a significant minority of accredited employers in outsourcing industries have signed up to the weaker service provider standard, but even taking this into account the success of the scheme in recruiting employers in these industries is quite striking.

What explains the divergence in accreditation between outsourcing and other low-wage industries? The literature on international civil regulation emphasizes consumer pressure and the greater responsiveness of employers in consumer-facing markets (Donaghey et al. 2014). This claim is not borne out by the experience of the Living Wage. Adoption of the standard has been more frequent in relatively 'invisible' industries that provide support services to the public sector and to corporate clients. It is likely that encouragement from these clients has helped diffuse the Living Wage in outsourcing industries, an issue that is explored further below. It is not exposure to consumers that drives adoption of civil regulation, the evidence suggests, but insertion into the supply chains of powerful clients. The procurement, sustainability, and public engagement policies of the latter have seemingly been more influential than the preferences of consumers.

Nations and Regions

Just as the Living Wage has spread across all sectors and industries within the UK economy, so it has spread across all nations and regions. There are Living Wage Employers in all parts of the country, stretching from the Highlands in the north of Scotland to the south coast of England and from Norfolk in the east to Ceredigion on the western edge of Wales. The standard has also crossed the Irish Sea to establish a bridgehead in Northern Ireland.

While the Living Wage is broadly spread, it is also concentrated, and Table 4.1 shows that there are two main geographical foci, Scotland and London, both of which have more than 3,000 accredited employers. London has the largest concentration, which reflects the fact that the Living Wage campaign began there, and it is the main historical base of Citizens UK. In addition, public authorities in London have actively promoted the Living Wage. Successive London mayors—Ken Livingstone, Boris Johnson, and Sadiq Kahn—have been strong advocates of the standard, as have individual London Boroughs, which have encouraged local organizations to become accredited. The structure of London's economy has also favoured accreditation. Many professional service firms are based in London, and many of the largest employing organizations that have become accredited, such as banks and insurance companies, are headquartered there.

Scotland has also benefitted from the support of public authorities. The Scottish Government has been a very strong advocate of the Living Wage, actively promoting accreditation across all sectors of the Scottish economy. The methods used by the Scottish Government are examined fully in Chapter 6, but it can be noted here they have included direct investment in the Living Wage campaign, providing funding to the Poverty Alliance to hire organizers. The positive part played by the Poverty Alliance itself is another factor accounting for the high level of accreditation in Scotland. As we have seen, the Alliance is a well-established network of anti-poverty organizations, strongly embedded in Scottish public life, which has been able to reproduce the campaigning impulse of London Citizens north of the border.

London and Scotland are the only two parts of the UK where the percentage of Living Wage Employers exceeds the percentage of all employers. Accreditation is disproportionately high in these two locations. In Northern Ireland and in the other English regions, in contrast, accreditation is disproportionately low, falling below what one might expect given the national distribution of economic activity. One possible explanation for the latter is that Citizens UK's campaigning network is patchy outside of London and exerts less pressure on employers and on public authorities to adopt the Living Wage. The one partial exception to this pattern is Wales, where the level of accreditation is almost proportionate to the number of businesses operating within the economy. In Wales, as in Scotland, there has been government support for the Living Wage, there is an active campaigning organization, Citizens Cymru-Wales, and, since 2016, Cynnal Cymru has played the part of the Poverty Alliance, accrediting Welsh employers. While the degree of success of the campaign in Wales falls short of that in Scotland, it nevertheless exceeds that of the English regions and suggests, together with Scottish experience, that political devolution has proved favourable to the Living Wage (Heery et al. 2020). More generally, the seeming influence of both political support and campaigning pressure in accounting for the greater responsiveness of employers in London, Scotland, and Wales offers support for the fourth, institutional explanation of civil regulation outlined above.

Core Cities

What is the geographical distribution of the Living Wage within the nations and regions of the UK? Table 4.1 shows the distribution of Living Wage accreditation across the UK's urban and non-urban locations and shows that there is a striking concentration of accredited employers in cities. Almost seventy per cent of accredited organizations are found in city locations, as defined by the Centre for Cities (https://www.centreforcities.org), and more than half are found in the country's twelve core cities. The latter include London, which on its own accounts for twenty-eight per cent of Living Wage accreditation, with more than 3,586 employers[1]. Other core cities with major concentrations of Living Wage Employers are Glasgow with 792, Edinburgh with 642, and Manchester with 521. This concentration in core cities partly reflects the concentration of business activity in these places, but the table indicates that even when this factor is taken into account, there are a disproportionate number of Living Wage Employers within cities. Moreover, the pattern continues to be seen in the remaining eleven core cities when London is removed: core cities other than London host twenty-five per cent of accredited employers but only fourteen per cent of businesses.

The UK's large cities have major concentrations of deprivation, and campaigners have argued that there is an urgent need for the Living Wage to address high levels of in-work poverty, particularly amongst migrant and minority populations in the 'global city' (Holgate and Wills 2007). The evidence suggests that this need is being met, but large cities are also characterized by relatively high-paid employment, and the urban bias in Living Wage accreditation could also indicate accreditation following the path of least resistance. Figure 4.2 explores this issue further and presents a distribution of accredited employers by the median hourly rate of pay in the local authority districts in which they are headquartered. It is apparent from the figure that most Living Wage Employers are found in parts of the country where median pay is above the national figure: fifty-eight per cent of accredited organizations are based in local authorities with median hourly pay above £14.05 an hour, and fifteen per cent are found in parts of the country where median hourly pay is £5.00 or more above the national median rate. Figure 4.2 provides further evidence that the Living Wage has tended to spread more readily in the UK's high wage economy. Once again, however, it is important to enter a qualification. The campaign has recruited employers right across the country, including in local authority districts with relatively low rates of pay: 5,338 accredited employers (forty-two per cent) are based in parts of the country where the median rate of pay is less than £14.05 an hour. Moreover, recruitment in these parts of the country has proceeded at a faster rate in recent years. Since 2018, 3,147 employers have signed up to the Living Wage in relatively low-wage parts of the country, fifty-nine per cent of all employers found in low-wage districts.

While the geographical distribution of accreditation partly reflects the distribution of low-paid jobs, it also reflects political influences. One such influence is the nature of political control in local authority districts. Accredited employers are disproportionately concentrated in areas where the council is controlled either by the Labour Party or by the Scottish or Welsh nationalist parties. Just

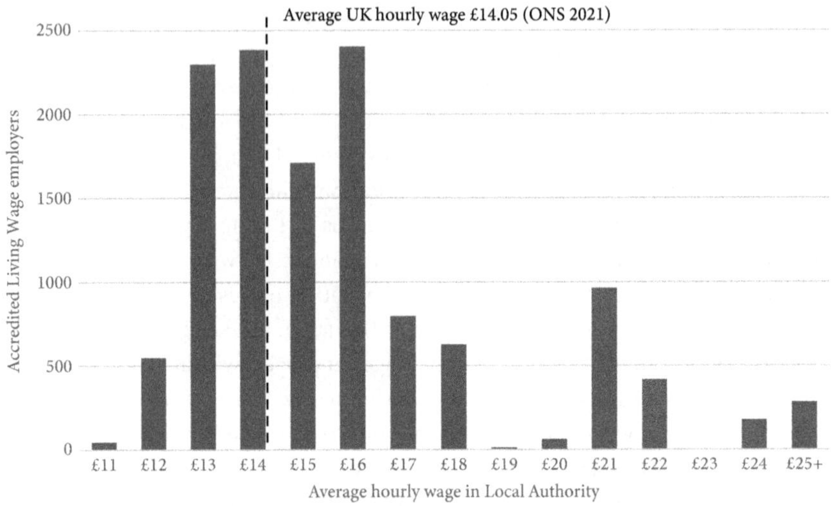

Figure 4.2 Distribution of accredited employers by average local authority wage

Notes: Based on data from 12,725 accredited Living Wage Employers and Service Providers; skewness 1.957; Kolmogorov-Smirnoff test for departure from normality D (12,725) = 0.184, $p < 0.001$.

over a third of councils in Great Britain are controlled by these 'social democratic' parties, but they account for sixty-nine per cent of Living Wage Employers. This association is explored more fully in Chapter 6, but it provides *prima facie* evidence both that local politics influences employer take-up of the Living Wage and that left-of-centre parties are most likely to encourage its adoption.

Another line of political division that has seemingly shaped adoption of the Living Wage is that between 'leave' and 'remain' (Sobolewska and Ford 2020). Living Wage accreditation is concentrated in parts of the country that voted to remain in the EU in the 2016 Brexit referendum, while leave-voting areas have relatively few Living Wage Employers. Thus, districts that voted to remain have seventy per cent of accredited employers, while the twenty-four local authorities where the remain vote was strongest, with sixty-five per cent or more voting to stay in the EU, have more than 4,300 accredited organizations (33.9 per cent). The forty-three strongest leave-voting districts, in contrast, where the leave vote was above sixty-five per cent, have only 339 accredited employers, 2.7 per cent of the total.

Remain voting is a largely urban phenomenon concentrated, especially in England and Wales, in large cities (Sobolewska and Ford 2020). In the latter there is a reinforcing set of conditions comprising relatively few low-wage jobs, left-of-centre political control, and remain voting, which seemingly support Living Wage accreditation. Even outside the large cities, however, Living Wage accreditation is associated with opposition to Brexit. Across the smaller cities of England and Wales, thirty-four per cent of Living Wage Employers are found in the nine smaller cities that voted remain. These cities include Brighton (ninety-five employers), Cambridge (sixty-six), Norwich (seventy), Oxford (sixty-three), Reading (fifty-three), and York (seventy). In contrast, leave-voting cities such as Barnsley, Burnley, Doncaster, Gloucester, Mansfield, Stoke, Sunderland, Wakefield, and Worthing have fewer than twenty each. A similar pattern can be seen in non-urban districts. There were fewer than thirty-five non-city districts that voted remain in England and Wales, but amongst those that did there are concentrations of Living Wage accreditation. Bath and North-East Somerset holds fifty Living Wage Employers, while Harrogate, Mendip, South Cambridgeshire, South Hams, South Oxfordshire, St Albans, Warwick, and Winchester have twenty or more. Non-urban districts with a strong leave vote, in contrast, tend to have relatively few accredited employers: Ashfield, Bolsover, Boston, East Lindsey, Fenland, Great Yarmouth, Hartlepool, Hyndburn, South Holland, and North-East Lincolnshire each have fewer than five.

The Brexit vote has been characterized by some as a revolt of the 'left behind' (Clarke et al. 2017), and organizations like the Centre for Towns have identified urgent needs to tackle poverty and promote growth in the post-industrial towns and declining coastal resorts that voted leave (Centre for Towns 2017). The UK Government's Levelling Up initiative purports to address these problems (HM Government 2022). Our evidence suggests that the Living Wage campaign has not intersected strongly with this agenda. Living Wage Employers are found in leave-voting areas, but there is a bias in accreditation towards large cities and relatively affluent districts. This pattern is also seen in the USA, where cities adopting local living wage laws tend to be relatively affluent and characterized by socially liberal, progressive politics (Swarts and Vasi 2011). In both countries, support for the living wage is most pronounced in university towns and other urban settings, with a highly educated, socially liberal population. Brighton, Cambridge, Norwich, and Oxford fit this pattern, as do several smaller locations where support for the Living Wage has been strong, such as Lewes in East Sussex, Winchester in Hampshire, Totnes in Devon, and Frome in Somerset. It may be that a considerable proportion of employers in this type of location themselves have progressive or liberal attitudes, which leads, in turn, to a relatively high level of accreditation. In highly urban settings, in socially liberal small towns, and in exurban rural districts, the values of employers may incline them to the message of business citizenship articulated by the Living Wage campaign.

Union Presence

A possible, important institutional influence on the spread of the Living Wage could be trade unions. Researchers examining the spread of the Living Wage in local government have identified the positive part played by public sector trade unions, while in the USA unions have been identified as key participants in coalitions that have pressed city authorities into adopting living wage ordinances (Johnson 2017; Levin-Waldman 2005; Prowse and Fells 2016a). In the wider literature on private regulation, moreover, unions have been observed to occupy an important mediating position, encouraging employers to adopt labour standards and providing scrutiny to ensure that they are adhered to (Bird et al. 2019; Jackson et al. 2018). However, there is a contrary view to this positive assessment of the role of trade unionism in encouraging employers to adopt voluntary regulation. Freeman (2005) has suggested that in the USA the precondition for the emergence of the living wage movement has been union retreat from much of the economy, while observers of the campaign in the UK have noted a degree of union opposition to the Living Wage (Holgate 2009; Wills 2009). In Swarts and Vasi's (2011) quantitative analysis of which US cities implement living wage laws, it was found that there was no statistical association with union density.

Figure 4.3 provides a means of choosing between these competing positions. It presents a histogram of accredited employers broken down by a composite measure of union presence. The latter is the mean of union density in the sector, industry, and district in which the employer is principally located. As can be seen, the distribution is positively skewed, with most accredited employers found in parts of the economy with a low union presence. Diffusion of the Living Wage amongst employers, on this evidence, has not been heavily dependent on the institutional presence of trade unions, and the standard has clearly flourished

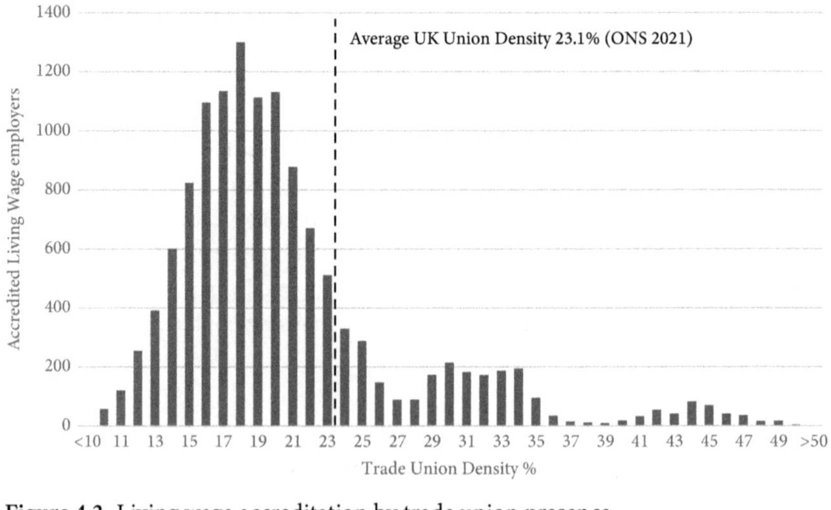

Figure 4.3 Living wage accreditation by trade union presence

Notes: Based on data from 12,720 accredited Living Wage Employers and Recognized Service Providers; skewness = 1.662; Kolmogorov-Smirnoff test for departure from normality D (12,720) = 0.158, p < 0.001.

in Britain's extensive, non-union economy. With regard to the latter point, moreover, it can be noted that many Living Wage Employers are small businesses, which typically have very low rates of unionization. It can also be noted that many are recently established enterprises—thirty per cent were incorporated in the last ten years—whereas trade union presence tends to be concentrated in mature industries and long-established employing organizations. The Living Wage has reached parts of the economy from which unions are largely absent.

While adoption of the Living Wage is heavily skewed towards parts of the economy with a limited union presence, it has also occurred within union heartlands, and about a tenth of accredited employers are found in parts of the economy where density is well above the national figure. Examples of employers falling into this category include local authorities, utility companies, and branches of the National Health Service. Trade union presence and civil regulation are clearly not incompatible and, as we will see in the next chapter, in some parts of the economy unions have played an important role in encouraging employers to adopt the Living Wage. It remains though that in most cases unions appear not to have performed this role and that in the UK, as in the USA, union presence has not been a critical institutional factor underpinning the spread of the Living Wage.

Living Wage Campaigners

A second institutional factor that might encourage employers to adopt the Living Wage is the presence of Living Wage campaigners. Where there is a local chapter of Citizens UK then there might be stronger encouragement for employers to implement the Living Wage, though not all chapters have prioritized the Living Wage to an equal degree. Another indicator of local campaigning pressure is the existence of a Living Wage Places initiative, a local campaign to create a Living Wage City, Town, or Borough, which has been accredited by the Living Wage Foundation. At present there are only a few initiatives of this kind, distributed across England, Scotland, and Wales, but clearly they represent a concerted effort to spread the Living Wage in a local area. A third manifestation of campaigning pressure are the independent attempts to promote the Living Wage in particular cities. The Brighton and Hove Living Wage Campaign and the Living Wage Campaign developed by Greater Manchester Poverty Action, described in the previous chapter, are examples of this kind of initiative.

Table 4.2 presents a frequency distribution of Living Wage accreditation in England and Wales by the presence of a local chapter of Citizens UK: Scotland and Northern Ireland are excluded because the Citizens' network has not yet been extended to these parts of the UK. Chapters are sorted into three categories, depending on their date of foundation: those established before the system of Living Wage accreditation, those set up in the first five years of the scheme's life,

Table 4.2 Living Wage accreditation in England and Wales by the presence of a Citizens UK chapter

Chapter date of foundation	Accredited employers[1]			Registered businesses[2]	
	Districts[3]	Employers	%	Number	%
1996–2011	14	2,013	21.3	260,735	10.4
2012–2016	22	2,095	22.2	322,345	12.9
2017–2022[4]	25	788	8.4	204,855	8.2
All chapters	61	4,896	51.9	787,935	31.6
Districts without a chapter	301	4,536	48.1	1,708,890	68.4

1. Includes all Living Wage Employers and Living Wage Service Providers that have been accredited in England and Wales since 2011, i.e. lapsed employers are included. N = 9,432.
2. All registered businesses grouped by local authority districts, taken from NOMIS: Official Labour Market Statistics, https://www.nomisweb.co.uk/.
3. The number of local authority districts in which Citizens UK chapters are found; for example, Greater Manchester Citizens, founded in 2016, covers all ten local authority districts that comprise Greater Manchester. For Wales, the only districts that have been included are those with an active Citizens Cymru-Wales presence in early 2021; i.e. Cardiff, Merthyr Tydfil, Rhondda-Cynon-Taf, Pembrokeshire, and Ceredigion.
4. These figures include Bristol City Council. There is no Citizens UK chapter in Bristol, but there is an active Living Wage City campaign, and the city has been included because of the latter. All other cities with Living Wage Places initiatives in England and Wales (Cardiff, Greater Manchester, Salford, and Southwark) also have Citizens UK chapters and so are included in the estimates.

and more recent chapters, including those in Preston, Peterborough, and Oxford, which are still in the process of formation. As with other tables, comparative data for the number of registered businesses are also provided, to assess whether accreditation is disproportionately concentrated in parts of the country where Citizens UK has an active presence.

The results in the table provide strong *prima facie* evidence that the presence of Living Wage campaigners is an important institutional feature of local labour markets that has encouraged employers to adopt the standard. More than half of accredited organizations are found in local authority districts with a Citizens UK chapter, but these districts have fewer than a third of registered businesses. The table also shows an association between the rate of Living Wage accreditation and the date of foundation of chapters. Longer-established chapters that are likely to be better resourced and which have been able to sustain campaigning over time generally have higher levels of accreditation. Caution must be exercised in interpreting the results in Table 4.2: they show an association, not direct cause, and it may be that both Living Wage campaigners and receptive employers are likely to be found in the same parts of the country, such as core cities and places with a 'progressive' political culture. Nevertheless, the results are quite striking and suggest that the presence of campaigners has been an influence on the spread of the Living Wage; one that has been more significant than the presence of trade unions.

Table 4.2 does not present separate estimates of Living Wage accreditation for places with an independent campaign or that have been accredited under the Living Wage Places scheme. The reasons for this are that there are relatively few places in each category and in all but one case these places also have active chapters of Citizens UK. The exception is Bristol, which is an accredited Living Wage City, but which does not yet have a Citizens' chapter. Accreditation data for Bristol have been included in the table in recognition of the fact that Living Wage campaigners have had an institutional presence in the city since the launch of the Living Wage City in 2019. These data indicate that the initiative has been successful in spreading the standard in Bristol—a total of 191 employers have been accredited—and there are also high levels of accreditation in other Living Wage Places: Cardiff (186), Salford (100), and Southwark (299). The Living Wage Places scheme has proved similarly successful in Scotland. Dundee, the first Living Wage City, has recorded 127 Living Wage Employers since 2011; Glenrothes, the first Living Wage Town, has recorded twenty-two; while Edinburgh, which launched its Living Wage City initiative in 2021, has more than 600. Once again, this evidence suggests that the presence of campaigners has increased the receptiveness of employers to the Living Wage.

Employer Motives for Adopting the Living Wage

It is possible to infer employers' motives for adopting the Living Wage from their characteristics, but our study also collected information directly on the reasons why organizations had become accredited. Our primary source for this information is the 2021 employer survey, though the question of motives was also explored through our interviews with managers from accredited organizations. The first objective of our analysis was to establish whether employers were motivated by an 'expressive rationale', the degree to which accreditation stemmed from attachment to a set of values or a particular mission that could be expressed through the Living Wage. Studies of the adoption of the Living Wage in individual organizations have shown that a motivation of this kind is often paramount, and our purpose was to use the population survey to see if evidence of this kind has a general validity (Carson 2022; Prowse and Dobbins 2022; Werner 2021b, 2022). Our second objective was to test the validity of the 'business case' argument and to establish the extent and precise nature of the 'instrumental rationale' for adopting the Living Wage amongst employers. This analysis tested for what might be thought of as a 'positive' instrumental rationale, a belief amongst employers that the Living Wage could enhance business performance, but it also tested for two other instrumental motives. One of these is a 'defensive' instrumentalism, introducing the Living Wage to avoid risk, such as harm to the organization's reputation. The other is a 'negative' instrumentalism, the idea that the Living Wage is an attractive accreditation for those who are already largely compliant and who will therefore incur limited additional cost. The final objective was to test for an 'institutional rationale' and gauge whether signing up for the Living Wage emerged from pressure exerted by institutional actors external to the organization, including trade unions and campaigning organizations.

Employer replies to our survey questions on the reasons for adopting the Living Wage are presented in Figure 4.4 The figure includes responses to twenty-three items and indicates that all have been identified as reasons for accreditation by at least some employers. Moreover, most employers have given multiple reasons for implementing the Living Wage, often spread across the different types of rationale identified above. Becoming a Living Wage Employer, it seems, has often been a complex decision, influenced by several considerations, some of which relate to hoped-for instrumental benefits and some of which relate to the intrinsic

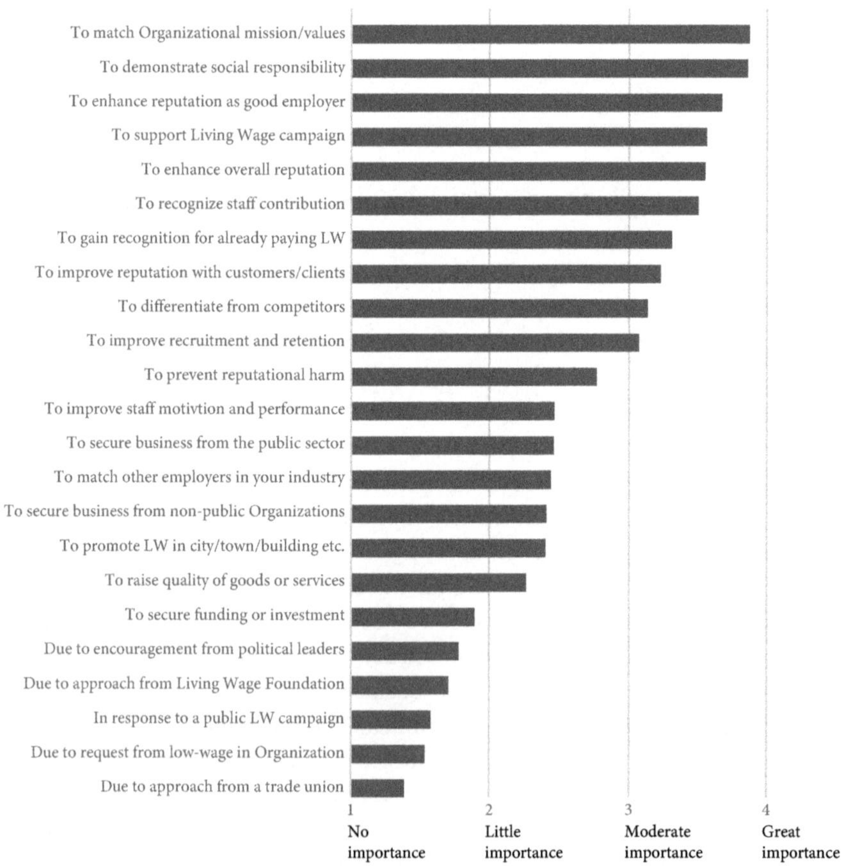

Figure 4.4 Motives for organizations seeking Living Wage accreditation

Notes: Based on 1,462–1,521 responses to 2021 survey of Living Wage Employers.

value of the standard. Despite this complexity, however, it is clear that responses form a hierarchy and that some reasons for adopting the Living Wage have more importance than others.

Expressive Motives

The most frequently cited reasons for becoming a Living Wage Employer are to demonstrate responsibility and to act in accordance with the organization's mission and values. A large percentage of employers also report that they became accredited to support the Living Wage campaign. On this evidence, an expressive rationale has been fundamental to the spread of the Living Wage, providing support for the belief of business ethicists that employing organizations can and should engage in morally responsible behaviour (Werner and Lim 2017).

Perhaps the most obvious expressive rationale is a desire to be a good employer, providing conditions of employment that match the needs of employees. Many of the explanations of accreditation we gathered through our qualitative research were couched in these terms:

> The primary reason was a sense of fairness which is at the core of the business's ethics ... 'it felt like the right thing to do'. [Engineering consultancy]
>
> As owner of the business, it has always been my goal to ensure that my employees work to live, not live to work. They should be happy and fulfilled and should most definitely be valued. All of my employees were already being paid the Living Wage! [Construction company]
>
> The organization believes strongly that people should be paid a fair day's pay for a fair day's work and that it must be enough to live on. [Carers' organization]
>
> We became a Living Wage Employer not because of some imperative to show our ethical credentials to the outside world, but because it is morally right that everyone in the organization should earn a decent wage. [Internet retailer]

The qualitative research also revealed that in many cases Living Wage accreditation has been accompanied by the adoption of other progressive employment practices. An owner-managed pet food manufacturer in West Wales with about 150 employees, for example, introduced a flexi-time system and an additional eight-days holiday at about the time it became accredited, and has a community-engagement team which involves employees in a range of community activities, including mentoring of out-of-work youngsters. Another family-owned business, a medium-sized construction company in Cardiff, has won awards for health and safety, developed an anti-slavery initiative for its supply chain, offers secure, long-term employment in a casualized industry, and operates a community volunteering scheme. In another organization, a social enterprise providing green-recycling services in Manchester, the basic purpose of the organization was described as 'to provide employment to those who otherwise would struggle to find it, like people with learning difficulties and victims of modern slavery'. Living Wage accreditation in this case sat alongside a commitment to offering secure and full-time employment of the kind its workforce would not typically be able to access, and to providing structured development to enable employees to move on and find a position in the wider job market.

In all three of these organizations, there was evidence of the organization 'satisficing', eschewing opportunities for growth or profit maximization in order to maintain employment and other practices to which owners were committed (see also Werner 2021b). The HR manager at the pet-food company stated that 'The aim of the game is not, and I know this sounds quite controversial in a way, but the aim of the game is not to make money', while her counterpart at the recycling business made the same point: 'We're not just here to make money. We're here to provide employment for these guys'. The Managing Director of the construction company explained that the firm had declined opportunities to expand beyond its present scale because to do so would dilute family control and threaten preferred methods of doing business. These three organizations were mission-driven, and it was this characteristic that both led them to and facilitated adoption of the Living Wage.

Seeking to be a responsible employer can arise from a broader set of values, and Figure 4.4 indicates that a desire to act in accordance with organizational values or mission is another major reason for adopting the Living Wage. The statements collected from employers often attested to this type of motivation:

> As a credit union we believe in ethical financial services, and it follows that we also believe in ethical employment practice. [Credit union]
>
> The Religious Society of Friends has a fundamental belief in equality and has always paid above the Living Wage to all its employees. [Faith organization]
>
> As a third sector organization, operating in a caring environment, we felt it our duty to be a Living Wage Employer. [Mental health charity]

These statements underline the point made above that many faith and social justice organizations have joined the Living Wage scheme because to do so is expressive of their fundamental purpose. In some cases, this purpose is coloured with political radicalism: the HR manager of the green recycling company mentioned above said that 'All of our directors are social activists' and that payment of the Living Wage stemmed from its nature as a 'left-leaning organization' committed to social justice. In other cases, purpose was defined in terms of strong community engagement, exemplified by the pet-food manufacturer, the largest employer in its small Welsh town for whom paying the Living Wage was part of a broader programme of investment in its local community (see also Prowse and Dobbins 2022). Both of these organizations, moreover, have a strong commitment to environmental sustainability, and in many cases accreditation is associated with an orientation of this kind. The ranks of Living Wage Employers include zero-waste shops, wholefood stores, organic catering businesses, green-energy firms, environmental consultants, and environmental charities. The Soil Association, Friends of the Earth, and Sustrans are accredited organizations. For these employers, a commitment to environmental sustainability has led to a corresponding commitment to social and economic sustainability, which in turn is expressed through Living Wage accreditation.

While the connection between organizational mission and Living Wage support is most visible in not-for-profit organizations, it is not confined to organizations of this type. In public services, accreditation has often stemmed from a traditional 'good employer' commitment (see Chapter 6), while in large corporates it has often emerged from formal commitments to responsible business or sustainability. Amongst large, private sector accredited employers, 254 (sixty-one per cent) report a formal commitment to corporate responsibility that encompasses employment issues on their website. Scepticism is often expressed about these commitments and many non-accredited businesses, which make extensive use of low-wage labour, also make declarations of this type (Rhodes 2022). If businesses do declare an intention to act responsibly, however, they can enter a commitment trap and feel compelled to take practical steps that evidence the commitments they have made. Becoming a Living Wage Employer is one way of evidencing a commitment to responsible business.

A final expressive motivation for accreditation is to provide tangible support to the Living Wage campaign. A majority of accredited employers report that this has been one of their principal reasons for joining the scheme, and our qualitative evidence supplied plentiful illustrations:

> We were already paying above the Living Wage. We joined to signify our commitment to the cause and to try and influence others to commit to the Living Wage Foundation. [Primary healthcare provider]
>
> It hasn't made a significant difference to us as all our employees already earned more than the Living Wage. We just had to make adjustments for cleaners. For us it was more a case of setting an example and showing support. [Publisher]
>
> We already pay staff the Living Wage. We joined the scheme to show support and encourage other employers to join. [Trade association]

For many employers support for the campaign has extended beyond accreditation to encompass participation in campaigning activity. Nearly eighty per cent of respondents to the 2021 survey reported that they displayed the Living Wage logo in their premises and on their website and referenced the standard in their social media. Substantial minorities have gone further and become involved in attempts to recruit fellow employers; for example, providing information to 'other employers considering accreditation' (twenty-five per cent) or taking part in events during Living Wage Week (sixteen per cent). It was reported in the previous chapter that peer recruitment has been an important means of building accreditation amongst employers, and these findings provide additional evidence that this is the case.

Instrumental Motives

Perhaps the most important thing to note about the instrumental motives reported in Figure 4.4 is that they are not the most frequently cited reasons for adopting the Living Wage. The expressive rationale, on this evidence, trumps instrumental motivation and while many employers identify potential benefits in Living Wage accreditation a greater number report that they signed up because to do so demonstrated social responsibility and expressed organizational values (see also Carson 2022). It was noted above that the 'business case' is often advanced to explain employer support for good employment standards, but the evidence shows that a rationale of this kind may not be the principal consideration behind employer decision-making. It has also been noted that Living Wage campaigners themselves often give priority to business case arguments when seeking to recruit employers. The evidence in the figure suggests that there may be a partial mismatch between this orientation in the campaign and the influences on business decision-makers, for whom 'doing the right thing' often has greater salience (see also Werner 2021b).

The second thing to note about instrumental motives in the figure is that they assume several forms but that a desire to secure reputational benefits is at the fore. Among the most frequently cited reasons for becoming accredited are to develop a reputation as a good employer, enhance overall corporate reputation, improve relations with clients, and differentiate the organization from others in the same industry or performing the same activity. A branch of Age UK in the South East of England, for instance, remarked that accreditation is 'Generally of benefit, especially when positioning the organization against competitors in the same field', while an independent coffee chain reported that 'We had great PR as a result of signing up to the London Living Wage as the Mayor came to our café to launch the recent increase in the LLW. Very useful to us as an organization and a great boost for our staff at the café!' A desire to secure reputational benefits from the Living Wage in some cases can arise from a carefully considered attempt to build a positive employer or consumer-brand. We spoke to a sustainability manager from a large manufacturing business who described accreditation in these terms, as part of an attempt to position the firm in the graduate labour market as an attractive and responsible employer. In many cases, though, a desire to obtain reputational benefits is not as thought-through as this, but rather takes the form of a generalized hope that accreditation will improve the standing of the organization in the eyes of those with whom it deals.

The next most commonly given positive reason for becoming accredited was to obtain HR benefits. Large percentages of employers reported that they hoped the Living Wage would improve recruitment and retention and raise motivation and performance. Interestingly, and as we have just noted, these hoped-for benefits were to come not just from employees directly affected by the Living Wage, but from the higher-paid, especially graduate entrants. A small consultancy, for instance, reported that 'We were already paying the Living Wage, but we thought it would be nice to have the accreditation to support tender applications and to attract junior Uni leavers'. After giving a talk about the Living Wage to undergraduate students at the University of Birmingham, one of them told us she had had a summer job operating the Twitter feed for graduate recruitment for a FTSE100 business, which frequently included references to the company's status as an accredited Living Wage Employer. According to the survey, two-thirds of accredited employers included reference to the Living Wage in the recruitment material they sent out to potential employees.

While a desire to secure HR benefits is widely reported, it is notable that using the Living Wage to recognize employees' existing contribution is the most common motivation and that more ambitious objectives, such as raising product quality, are the least. Increasing pay, whether through statutory means or through union bargaining, has often been advocated as a way of shocking organizations into radical changes that boost performance. The data in the table suggest that, on occasion, Living Wage accreditation has been viewed in this manner and has been introduced to effect substantial change in HR practice and outcomes. In rather more cases, though, the Living Wage has not been regarded as an instrument of transformative change. Rather, paying the rate has been viewed as a way of signalling to employees that they are valued and are already making a significant contribution to organizational success. The motive has been to recognize, not stimulate, good performance. As a small parish council expressed it:

> We were looking to recognize that our basic-skilled jobs were being done by people who were carrying out their duties in such a way that was above and beyond the call of duty and we wanted to reward their professionalism and dedication. Becoming a Living Wage Employer gave the council a recognized benchmark, sending a clear message to staff that they are valued and appreciated.

Beyond HR, businesses might introduce the Living Wage to secure other positive benefits, such as access to funding and winning contracts. Securing tangible business benefits has been an important reason for accreditation for some employers. For example, a public relations agency described their accreditation, grudgingly, as being 'the requirement of a large client ... We already paid our staff at above the

Living Wage, so the impact was minimal on the organization other than obtaining unnecessary accreditation'. The identity of the client is unknown in this case, but it is probable that organizations seeking contracts or grants from the public sector have most likely experienced pressures of this kind. The survey evidence indicates that a desire to obtain tangible benefits from Living Wage accreditation has been widespread—seventy per cent of organizations report that the hope of winning contracts played at least some part in their decision—but that this type of consideration has been less important than gaining reputational or HR benefits. Only a minority of employers report that securing wider business gains was pivotal to their decision to adopt the Living Wage, suggesting that often this motivation has been present but not decisive and has operated alongside others. A provider of primary healthcare in the North West, for instance, said that they notified public sector clients that they were a Living Wage Employer when bidding for contracts, but that 'wasn't the driver' for becoming accredited. The organization is a social enterprise, owned by its employees, and one of its main objectives is to provide good quality, well-paid employment. It had become accredited principally to raise the pay of the call centre operators, receptionists, and mini-bus drivers who provide its services: 'It was a values-based decision: as part of valuing our staff we pay the Living Wage'.

Another set of instrumental motivations reported in Figure 4.4 are primarily defensive: becoming accredited to prevent harm to the organization's reputation, match the behaviour of competitors, or respond to an external campaign. The value of civil regulation for businesses has often been described in these terms, as a means of managing risk, and the survey indicates that this type of consideration has often motivated adoption of the Living Wage (Jackson et al. 2018). It is important to recognize that this defensive motivation for accreditation is not just found amongst large corporate employers of the kind that feature in the literature on private regulation but is also present amongst many public sector and not-for-profit organizations. The latter have often become accredited to avoid the charge of hypocrisy: many are advocates of the Living Wage and other anti-poverty measures, and so it is important to demonstrate adherence to good standards if their advocacy is to remain credible. On several occasions at Citizens UK meetings we have heard organizers appeal to members to become accredited Living Wage Employers for precisely this reason. While a defensive instrumentalism has been important in leading employers to accreditation, the evidence from the survey suggests it has been less significant than either positive instrumentalism or expressive motivation. Avoiding harm, on this evidence, is a factor that leads organizations to comply with civil regulation, but it is by no means the sole or primary rationale.

A final instrumental reason for becoming accredited is to obtain recognition of the fact that the organization was already paying the Living Wage. 'Negative' instrumentalism of this kind was reported by a high percentage of surveyed employers: more than half reported that it was of 'great importance' in their decision to become accredited. Employers reporting motivation of this kind were also likely to report that they had sought accreditation for defensive reasons, such as to reduce harm to the organization's reputation, and to obtain wider business benefits, such as winning contracts. There is evidence here of 'box-ticking', of organizations signing up to the Living Wage because it is relatively costless to do so and in the hope of securing business advantages. In at least some organizations, however, a more complex set of motivations was at play. An HR manager from a large media company, when asked why they had signed up to the Living Wage, responded, 'Why wouldn't you?'. The cost to her organization was limited, but for this very reason non-instrumental motivations—a desire to support the campaign—could influence the decision. Others made a similar point, emphasizing that although accreditation required only minor adjustments to their own organization, they wanted to promote the Living Wage because it corresponded with the organization's mission:

> We pay well above the Living Wage. We joined and changed our cleaners but otherwise nothing for us has altered internally. For us, it is about supporting our work with children. Over-worked and under-paid parents are not good for children [Catholic children's charity].

> We were already paying all employees above the Living Wage but felt it was very important to join and support the campaign [Citizens Advice Bureau].

In other cases, employers had introduced the Living Wage and obtained accreditation afterwards to reinforce the original decision. A migrants' rights charity, for example, had introduced the Living Wage for childcare workers, drawn from the communities it served and in accordance with its aim of finding good quality employment for migrants, and then became accredited some considerable time later. Seeking recognition for already paying the Living Wage could therefore arise for several reasons, and while 'negative instrumentalism' has sometimes been at the fore, on many occasions the decision has also been shaped by an expressive rationale.

Institutional Motives

By institutional motives we mean the adoption of the Living Wage because of pressure or encouragement to do so from formal institutions beyond the organization, such as the Living Wage campaign, trade unions, or political authorities. The evidence in Figure 4.4 suggests that motives of this kind have been secondary in leading employers to Living Wage accreditation and of much less significance than instrumental or expressive motives. Fewer than ten per cent of employers report that encouragement from political leaders, accrediting organizations, external campaigners, or trade unions have been of 'great importance' in the decision to become accredited, and a majority deny that these institutions have exercised any influence. An identical pattern is seen for the item on pressure from low-paid employees seeking to be paid the Living Wage. It is perhaps particularly noteworthy that encouragement from a trade union is the least frequently reported of these institutional influences on accreditation and, indeed, even amongst employers that recognize unions only thirteen per cent reported that the union was of 'great importance' in persuading them to seek accreditation. This set of findings reinforces the message of the previous chapter on campaign strategy by showing that most employers have seemingly found their way to accreditation without being subject to community mobilization or workforce pressure (see also Carson 2022).

The one partial exception to this pattern is found in the relatively high proportion of employers who report that they have adopted the Living Wage to support an attempt to promote the standard in their 'city, town, borough, building or area'. About two-thirds of employers report that a consideration of this kind has played some part in their becoming accredited, and a quarter say that it has been of 'great importance'. This evidence provides further support for the belief that the Living Wage Places scheme has proved successful at boosting employer support and indicates that many employers are responsive to place-based initiatives that allow them to act in concert with other local organizations.

Resistance to Accreditation

In 2020 during the pandemic, senior staff from the Living Wage Foundation were invited to a virtual conference with the chief executive of a major food retailer. The Foundation had highlighted the part played by supermarket employees in maintaining an essential service to the public during lockdown and had also highlighted the profitability of food retailers, which had been spared the sharp downturn in business experienced by most other retailers. Hoping for the best the Foundation staff attended the meeting, only to be told by the CEO that his senior team had considered the question of Living Wage accreditation and decided that they would not be joining the scheme and that further meetings would be pointless. This episode is unusual, because contact was initiated by the company, but resistance to accreditation is not. The Foundation has had repeated contact with other food retailers who have similarly decided not to accredit, and the rejection of overtures by employers is part and parcel of the campaign. Even when employers do accredit, this may occur after prolonged attempts at persuasion, which gradually whittle away senior management resistance. As has been noted previously, campaigns to recruit major employers can be drawn out affairs, some of which end in success, but others run into the sands and are either abandoned or placed on the backburner until conditions change. Employer resistance is integral to the Living Wage.

Resistance to Living Wage accreditation is perhaps to be expected. According to Baccaro and Howell (2017: 20), a defining feature of the current era of neo-liberalism has been the search for 'increased employer discretion in personnel and labour market strategies'. Encompassed within this search have been attempts to secure 'discretion in wage determination', defined as 'the extent to which individual employers can adapt wage rates to the individual circumstances and ability-to-pay of their firms and use wage differentials to recruit, motivate, and retain key employees'. Pursuing discretion of this kind implies hostility to all forms of regulation that restrict employer decision-making, and for Baccaro and Howell, and others, employer attempts to escape from regulation are a defining feature of contemporary employment relations. Escape can be effected by disregarding, manipulating, or minimally complying with prevailing employment regulation, reallocating work to categories of worker who lack regulatory protection, using 'regulatory arbitrage' whereby jobs are located in the least exacting regulatory regime, and by pressing political authorities to adopt policies of deregulation (Benassi and Kornelakis 2021; Doellgast, Bidwell, and Colvin 2021; Doellgast et al. 2021; Grimshaw et al. 2019). In Streeck's (2009: 241) terms, the behaviour of capitalists is 'fundamentally unruly ... relentlessly whacking away at social rules'. If this argument is valid, then one would expect employer resistance to Living Wage to be absolute and widespread and to be motivated by a desire to defend management prerogative from external regulation. In what follows, our qualitative evidence is used to establish if this is in fact the case: that employers have resisted the Living Wage and have done so to maximize discretion.

Our interviews indicated that resistance to Living Wage accreditation was often motivated by a desire of employers to retain flexibility in the management of pay in the manner suggested by the escape-thesis. However, this motivation has not precluded employers from paying the Living Wage, at least to direct employees. Our own employer, Cardiff University, initially responded to campaigners by declaring it would ensure staff were paid the Living Wage but that it would not become accredited, and many other organizations have responded in this way. When the Living Wage has been introduced into unionized organizations this pattern of substantive commitment while retaining procedural flexibility has often been apparent, mainly because of the preferences of employers. A union officer explained that:

> A lot of companies don't want the accreditation because they do not want a third party determining their wage rates. They'd much rather do it by negotiation so that if there is something that happened, you know, if the sales fall through the floor or something like that, they're not tied to that. [BECTU National Officer]

Employers have declined to become accredited, therefore, because they are anxious about entering into a long-term and public commitment to pay the Living Wage, but this insistence on flexibility has not prevented employers applying the Living Wage standard within their organizations.

Another possible reason for employer resistance lies in the requirement to extend the Living Wage to employees of contractors. Employers have invested in 'contingent work arrangements' precisely to avoid the obligations of the standard employment relationship, and therefore one might expect sharp opposition to regulation that seeks to nullify the benefits employers get from outsourcing (Benassi and Kornelakis 2021). There are certainly cases of this kind. A professional football team, for example, refused to consider accreditation, which would have required it to fund the Living Wage for outsourced match-day attendants, and denied that it had any responsibility for terms of employment within its supplier businesses. In other cases, though, opposition is more qualified. In Wales, local authorities have refrained from accreditation because of the cost of extending the Living Wage to outsourced social care employees. There is general belief across the sector, however, that these workers deserve a pay increase, and following the Welsh Government's decision to fund the Living Wage in adult social care in 2021 an increasing number of local authorities may seek accreditation. Other organizations have resisted accreditation not because of the financial cost of extending the Living Wage to outsourced employees but because of the transaction costs involved in identifying, renegotiating, and monitoring service contracts which would be affected. A large utility company, for instance, delayed its accreditation for this reason until the CEO decided that the principle of paying the Living Wage should override other considerations.

The purpose of escaping from regulation is often to reduce labour costs, and a third reason for resisting the Living Wage is simply that the cost of compliance is excessive or cannot be afforded. We have shown that the rate of accreditation tends to be lower in industries characterized by low-wage employment, and it can be inferred from this that cost considerations often underly employer resistance. The qualitative evidence yielded several examples. A social care provider in West Wales, with a strong record of good employment practice, became accredited but was unable to sustain its commitment because the Living Wage simply could not be afforded on the local authority care contracts upon which it depended. Another small employer, running a cleaning company in London, made a similar complaint, saying that she might have to abandon the commercial side of her business because clients would not pay a premium fee to fund the Living Wage. At a larger scale, we were told by a consultant working with the Living Wage Foundation to spread the standard amongst FTSE100 companies that a business he had contacted had considered accreditation but then demurred because it estimated the cost would be in the region of £80M per year. In at least some of these cases a desire to pay the Living Wage has been hindered by financial constraints beyond the employer's control. In other cases, though, employers have decided not to pay the Living Wage based on a belief that employees do not need to be paid at that rate. A large educational charity, for example, withdrew from accreditation because of resistance from head teachers, who felt it was unnecessarily costly to pay the Living Wage to 18-year-old school students, living with their parents, who were employed as swimming pool attendants over the summer holidays. Another employer, a national arts organization, had negotiated the introduction of the Living Wage with BECTU for most of its low-paid employees but had excluded directly employed restaurant staff who supplemented basic earnings with tips. The Living Wage standard is founded on an assumption of pressing employee need for higher pay, but at least some employers do not accept this premiss and this has led to resistance to its adoption.

An aspect of employer discretion identified by Baccaro and Howell is the ability to develop a system of reward management that is tailored to the specific requirements of a business, and another reason for resisting accreditation was the potential disruption to existing pay arrangements. A leading financial services company, for instance, has had extensive discussions with the Foundation about accreditation, which have so far failed to bear fruit because its performance-related pay scheme does not guarantee a minimum level of pay equivalent to the Living Wage. Large retailers have engaged in similarly fruitless discussions, which have foundered on their desire to include annual profit-sharing payments and the value of employee discount schemes in the calculation of the Living Wage. Other organizations, which have agreed to pay the Living Wage, stated to us that increasing pay for the lower-paid was socially beneficial but did not tackle the labour market problems they were facing, which took the form of labour shortages amongst professional and technical occupations. In these cases, meeting social obligations won out, but it is likely that other employers have made the reverse decision, choosing to allocate scarce resources to shortage occupations rather than investing in higher wages for the lower-paid. Employer discretion may be valued, according to Baccaro and Howell, because it allows businesses to respond rapidly to labour market problems, and for those who are not experiencing difficulty in recruiting to low-wage jobs, this may lead to the rejection of the Living Wage.

Our qualitative evidence on employer resistance to the Living Wage is neither extensive nor representative, and we are not able to pronounce with certainty on how frequently the reasons that we have just described are used to reject the Living Wage or which are most important. Nevertheless, two conclusions can safely be drawn from the evidence. First, employer resistance to the Living Wage has been motivated by the kinds of concern identified by advocates of the escape-thesis. Thus, employers have refrained from accreditation to avoid conceding long-term influence over pay-management to an external organization, displayed a particular concern about the requirement to pay the Living Wage to employees of contractors, also displayed concern about the impact of the standard on labour costs, and have rejected accreditation to preserve existing pay practices and respond flexibly to labour market signals. Secondly, however, employer resistance to the Living Wage has not been absolute, and often employers have sought to accommodate the campaign, applying some elements of the standard while rejecting others. On this evidence, employers do not appear as 'unruly' as advocates of the thesis have claimed. Some employers have been adamant in their rejection of civil regulation, but others have been more receptive and willing to surrender a degree of discretion. There has been a range in employer resistance to the Living Wage that embraces both outright rejection and partial acceptance.

Continuum of Employer Responses to the Living Wage

This continuum of employer responses to the Living Wage also extends beyond simple acceptance. As was noted above, a substantial minority of employers have not just adopted the Living Wage but have become active participants in the campaign, promoting the standard to their peers. Others have signed up to additional standards, such as Living Hours and the Living Wage Funder scheme, and our survey evidence indicates that there is substantial interest amongst accredited employers in further additions, dealing with pensions and the like. The survey also indicated that many employers have made payments to employees that are not required by the terms of their licence agreement with the Living Wage Foundation. A third of accredited employers report that they have increased the pay of higher graded employees to maintain differentials, while sixty per cent state that they have paid the Living Wage to casual workers, not covered by the formal terms of the scheme. Many also report paying the Living Wage to apprentices and to interns, who are not covered by Living Wage accreditation requirements.

There has been a range of responses to the campaign amongst employers, therefore, that form a continuum, stretching from outright rejection, through compliance, to positive acceptance and endorsement. This continuum is shown in Table 4.3, which breaks down the range of employer responses into five broad categories as follows:

Non-compliance: In this response, employers pay both direct and indirect employees below the Living Wage and refuse to consider accreditation. In some cases, the lowest wage rate may be adjusted upwards to narrow the differential with the Living Wage, and this may form part of a medium-term process of adjustment that eventually leads to compliance. In other cases, employees may use bonuses and employee benefit schemes to ensure that 'total remuneration', when expressed as an hourly rate, is above the Living Wage while base rates remain below.

Partial compliance: This response is characterized by employer embrace of the Living Wage standard such that minimum rates of pay are set at the level of the Living Wage for at least some employees. Payment of the rate, however, may be confined to 'deserving' employees, such as adult workers with responsibility for maintaining a household or without access to pay supplements, such as tips. Another common arrangement is for the Living Wage to be guaranteed for direct employees, but not extended to indirect workers employed by contractors. A final arrangement is where both direct and indirect workers are paid the Living Wage, but the employer eschews formal accreditation, thereby retaining the ability to reduce pay-rates in the future if business conditions change.

Minimal compliance: With this response the Living Wage standard is fully implemented, with both direct and indirect employees guaranteed the rate and the employer being formally accredited. However, in cases of minimal compliance support for the Living Wage has little or no cost-implication for the employer, either because the organization was already fully compliant prior to seeking accreditation or because cuts have been made to the workforce, working time, or other elements of remuneration to fund payment of the Living Wage. As we will see in Chapter 7, clawing back the cost of the Living Wage is not common, but it has been a feature of the employer response within a small minority of accredited organizations.

Full compliance: Where there is full compliance, employers implement the standard and increase the pay of employees, incurring an increase in labour costs. In a small minority of cases the increase in pay may take the form of a Living Wage supplement, an addition to the hourly base rate which may not count as pensionable income or for the calculation of overtime and shift premia. More usually, however, the increase takes the form of an increase in base pay, with the attribute of permanence that this implies.

Beyond compliance: In this response, employers are accredited and guarantee the Living Wage to direct and indirect employees but take additional steps to combat in-work poverty that are not formally required by the terms of their accreditation. One type of additional step is to pay the Living Wage to employees who fall outside the formal terms of the accreditation, such as apprentices or casual or agency workers who are employed for fewer than eight weeks and two hours per day. Another step is to sign up to Living Hours or to other additional forms of accreditation, such as the Living Wage Funder scheme. A final way in which employers can go beyond compliance is to participate actively in the Living Wage campaign, seeking to recruit other employers to the standard. As we have seen, there is an active minority of Living Wage Employers which promote the scheme in this way, acting as Living Wage champions.

An important conclusion that can be drawn from this continuum of response concerns the escape-thesis advanced by Baccaro and Howell, Streeck, and others. Like earlier commentators on employer behaviour who have identified an impulse towards deskilling, surveillance, or precarity, these writers identify a single, encompassing purpose that is driving the recomposition of the employment relationship. The continuum of employer responses set out in Table 4.3, however, suggests that employer responses to regulation do not follow a single course and that 'unruliness' is not as marked as the thesis contends. There has been variation in the employer response to the Living Wage that includes rejection of external regulation and a desire to retain discretion, but which also embraces partial and

Table 4.3 Continuum of employer responses to the Living Wage

	Employer response to the Living Wage campaign
Non-compliance	Rejection of Living Wage standard: direct and indirect employees continue to be paid below the Living Wage
	Rejection of the Living Wage standard but acceptance of it as a reference point: lowest rate of pay of direct workers is adjusted to move closer to the Living Wage rate
	Rejection of the Living Wage standard but use of employee discount scheme or performance bonus to ensure that the 'total remuneration' of direct workers is at or above the Living Wage
Partial compliance	Payment of the Living Wage to a proportion of direct employees but rejection of the standard for 'non-deserving' direct employees and indirect workers
	Payment of the Living Wage to direct employees but not to employees of contractors
	Payment of the Living Wage to both direct and eligible indirect employees but refusal to accredit in order to retain employer discretion
Minimal compliance	Accreditation as a Living Wage Employer in recognition of the fact that the rate is already paid to all eligible employees; no increase in labour costs
	Accreditation as a Living Wage Employer leading to increases in wages for employees that are clawed back through cuts to hours, benefits, or other aspects of remuneration
Full compliance	Accreditation as a Living Wage Employer leading to increases in wages for employees that take the form of a supplement to base rates that is not pensionable and which does not feed through into the calculation of premium payments such as overtime
	Accreditation as a Living Wage Employer leading to increases in wages for eligible employees that takes the form of a consolidated increase in base rates and which is incorporated within a formal pay structure
Beyond compliance	Accreditation as a Living Wage Employer with the extension of the Living Wage to employees who are not strictly eligible: e.g. payment of the Living Wage to those on training contracts or to indirect employees working for fewer than eight weeks and two hours per day
	Accreditation as a Living Wage Employer and acceptance of additional Foundation standards, such as Living Hours
	Accreditation as a Living Wage Employer and active participation in the Living Wage campaign to promote the standard to other employing organizations

full compliance and a preparedness to go beyond the formal requirements of the Living Wage standard. The Living Wage is a voluntary scheme, and all employers retain the freedom to exit if they wish; the obligatory property of civil regulation is inherently less than that of statutory regulation or joint regulation through collective bargaining. It remains though that adopting the Living Wage involves accepting external regulation and surrendering an element of employer discretion over the management of pay. Contrary to the escape-thesis, many employers are ready and willing to accept these conditions.

Conclusion

The purpose of this chapter has been threefold: to identify the characteristics of Living Wage Employers, establish employer motives for becoming accredited, and identify the nature of employer resistance to the Living Wage campaign. The principal findings from our review are as follows:

1. The characteristics of accredited Living Wage Employers differ from those of the large, consumer-facing businesses identified in the literature on international private regulation. Living Wage Employers are drawn from a much broader pool and include many small and medium-sized enterprises and public sector and not-for-profit organizations. Moreover, those large, private-sector organizations that are accredited tend to provide business-services and do not include the retail and consumer-brands that have participated in global schemes, like the Ethical Trading Initiative. The evidence suggests that arguments about the kinds of employer that are receptive to private regulation, that have validity when applied to international forms of the latter, are less applicable to the case of domestic private regulation.
2. Living Wage accreditation is biased towards high-paying industries and high-paying parts of the country, supporting the argument that voluntary regulation tends to be accepted by employers who can more readily comply and for whom costs are limited. This argument needs to be qualified, however; the degree of bias is not strong, and there is counter evidence which supports the belief that the Living Wage has been adopted by employers where it can have most impact. While there is a bias in accreditation towards high-paying parts of the economy, there are nevertheless large numbers of accredited employers where pay is low, and in low-wage industries affected by outsourcing, such as cleaning, security, and social care, accreditation is disproportionately prevalent. The number of Living Wage Employers in these industries is also growing at a faster rate than in the rest of the economy, reflecting the efforts of campaigners to spread the standard where it can have most impact.
3. Most Living Wage Employers are found in the UK's extensive non-union economy, and the distribution of accreditation does not reflect that of union presence. The latter is often identified as a causal variable, associated with a broad range of labour market phenomena (Bryson and Forth 2011; Metcalf et al. 2001), but seemingly does not underpin employer compliance

with civil regulation, at least in the case of the Living Wage. An institutional variable which does seem to shape employer compliance is the presence of Living Wage campaigners. Civil regulation, the employer dataset indicates, is adhered to most readily where civil society is organized and provides an active, campaigning presence within local communities.

4. Two other institutions that have shaped employer responses to the Living Wage are employers' organizations and public authorities. The former have often been neglected by students of contemporary employment relations (Gooberman et al. 2018), but acting alongside individual employer champions they have played an important part in spreading the Living Wage in certain industries. Public authorities, such as the devolved governments of Scotland and Wales and regional and local authorities, have also helped spread the standard. The influence of public authorities, however, follows the lines of enduring and more recent political division. Accreditation is more prevalent where national, regional, and local government are controlled by social democratic parties, committed to redistribution, and in core cities and university towns where there was strong support for remaining in the EU.
5. Employer motives for adopting the Living Wage are complex, often driven by a variety of overlapping considerations. The strongest motivations reported in our survey of employers, however, are expressive: the desire to act in accordance with organizational values, provide support to the Living Wage campaign, and behave as a good employer. Academic commentators are often cynical about motives of this kind, regarding them as superficial, at odds with employer behaviour, and designed to distract from the realities of the latter in the manner of greenwashing (LeBaron et al. 2022; Rhodes 2022). It remains though that both ours and other research (Arrowsmith et al. 2022; Carson 2022; Prowse and Dobbins 2022; Werner 2021b, 2022) indicates that this kind of expressive rationale has been central to the adoption of the Living Wage.
6. Much of the literature on civil regulation emphasizes the 'business case' and advances the argument that there is an instrumental rationale for implementing standards like the Living Wage. Our survey evidence shows that business case considerations have influenced the decision to become accredited, though they are cited less frequently than expressive motives. The prime instrumental motive for adopting the Living Wage is to enhance the reputation of the employing organization, with the pursuit of HR or commercial benefits seemingly carrying less weight. Across the range of instrumental reasons for adopting the Living Wage it is those which are least calculable that are most frequently said to lie behind the decision to accredit. There is support, therefore, for the argument that the business case underpins employer acceptance of civil regulation, but this kind of rationale is often

not primary and often assumes a relatively soft form, in which hoped-for benefits are relatively intangible.

7. The weakest type of motive for adopting the Living Wage are those associated with institutional pressures. Only a minority of employers report that encouragement from Living Wage campaigners, politicians, trade unions, or their own employees has led to them becoming accredited. In most cases, employers report that they have found their own way to the Living Wage without being pressured by outside forces. The only partial exception to this pattern is that many employers report that they have been influenced by a place-based campaign, encouraging employers in a particular town, city, or district to adopt the Living Wage. This finding attests to the effectiveness of the Foundation's Living Wage Places scheme, but it also provides support for other place-based attempts to raise labour standards, promoted by advocates of 'community wealth-building' and 'inclusive growth' (Guinan and O'Neill 2020; Lupton et al. 2019).
8. Employers have resisted the Living Wage, and many of the reasons for opposing accreditation collected through our qualitative work conform to the 'exit-thesis', found in theoretical accounts of employer responses to regulation. Employers have resisted the Living Wage to avoid surrendering management prerogative to an outside body, to continue reaping the benefits of precarious forms of work, to retain discretion over the design of reward systems, and to minimize labour costs. What is notable about employer opposition, however, is that it is often qualified, with even resistant employers prepared to accept some elements of external regulation. We encountered few cases of absolute, diehard resistance of the kind suggested by the notion of the 'unruly' employer.
9. While employer resistance to the Living Wage stretches along a continuum, so does employer acceptance. Our survey evidence indicates that a minority of accredited employers have gone beyond the requirements of their licence agreement with the Living Wage Foundation, extending the standard to employees who can legitimately be excluded, supporting other anti-poverty measures, and actively promoting the Living Wage to fellow-employers. There is a broad range of employer responses to civil regulation that encompasses outright rejection at one extreme and active support at the other. Employers are not subject towards an overriding instinct towards 'unruliness'; many, in fact, are receptive to external regulation, accepting both that it is desirable in itself and that it can contribute positively to business performance.

The escape-thesis is an example of a common type of argument found within critical studies of the employment relationship, in which it is claimed that there is a deep-seated and encompassing trend towards the degradation of work (Heery

2016). Our research on employer responses to the Living Wage suggests that trends of this kind are not as encompassing as is often suggested. Thousands of employers, spread across all major industries and all regions of the UK, have responded positively to the Living Wage, acceded voluntarily to external regulation of their pay arrangements, and incurred higher labour costs as a consequence. How might this willingness to accept the Living Wage be interpreted? One clue can be found in the types of business described above, which have been particularly strong supporters of the Living Wage: the pet-food manufacturer in West Wales, the construction company in South Wales, and the recycling social enterprise in Manchester. These seem to us to be quintessentially paternalist employers, rooted in place with active programmes of community engagement, prepared to absorb higher costs to behave responsibly, and willing to provide employment conditions that are relatively benign, and which protect their employees. This kind of impulse, we believe, is quite common and is exemplified by the voluntary adoption of the Living Wage standard by UK employers. The spread of the Living Wage, and of other, similar voluntary standards, is arguably indicative of the revival of paternalism within the UK economy. We will return to this theme in our Conclusion, where we identify the defining characteristics of contemporary paternalism and the features that differentiate it from the classical paternalism of the late nineteenth and early twentieth centuries. The Living Wage, we argue, is an expression of neo-paternalism, a development that is largely absent from established accounts of change in the employment relationship, which tend to emphasize the degradation of work and the immiseration of workers.

Notes

1. The Centre for Cities' definition of London includes all London Boroughs and several outlying districts, such as Epping Forest, Watford, Dartford, and Epsom and Ewell, which although administratively separate form part of the greater London economy. For this reason, the estimate of Living Wage accreditation in London here is greater than that given above, which is confined to London Boroughs.

5
Trade Unions and the Real Living Wage

Introduction

In Chapter 3 we examined the manner and extent to which the Living Wage campaign has involved trade unions in its activities. In this chapter we turn the perspective around and consider the response of trade unions to the campaign. In an earlier piece one of us noted that the relationship between trade unions and civil society organizations can fall into one of three patterns: cooperation, conflict, and indifference, the latter meaning that unions act independently of CSOs, in separate spheres, and that the two institutions rarely come into contact with one another (Heery, Williams, and Abbott 2012). In what follows we show that the union reaction to the Living Wage encapsulates all three of these patterns. Unions have supported the campaign and worked cooperatively with Citizens UK and its allies to spread the Living Wage standard, but there has also been a degree of conflict, and some in the union movement have reacted negatively to the campaign and refused cooperation. In a third response, unions have appropriated the Living Wage standard and incorporated it within their own campaigning and bargaining activity, with minimal reference to the 'official' Living Wage campaign. This chapter describes and accounts for each of these responses.

A major theme in the literature on union revitalization in recent years has been that of union-community coalitions, dealing with the scope for joint work between trade unions and other social movements and the conditions that allow cross-movement cooperation to thrive (Heery 2019; Holgate 2015a; Tattersall 2018). According to Gumbrell-McCormick and Hyman (2013), the development of 'coalitional power' is one of the primary methods that unions can employ to revitalize their fortunes. Our purpose in reviewing the union response to the Living Wage is to test arguments of this kind and contribute to the wider literature on union-community coalitions. As we will see, the complex response to the Living Wage provides some support for the belief that revitalization can be achieved through coalition with civil society partners, but much of the evidence does not point in this direction. Unions have often responded positively to the Living Wage campaign and have made extensive use of the Living Wage standard in their ongoing work of bargaining, campaigning, and organizing, but with some notable exceptions they have not formed a close working relationship with other Living Wage campaigners. The kind of 'deep' coalition between unions and civil

The Real Living Wage. Edmund Heery, Deborah Hann and David Nash, Oxford University Press.
© Edmund Heery, Deborah Hann and David Nash (2023). DOI: 10.1093/oso/9780198835264.003.0005

society, advocated by theorists of union revitalization, has not been characteristic of the union response to the Living Wage.

Cooperation

As we have seen, the Living Wage campaign has sought to develop cooperation with trade unions both by encouraging unions to affiliate to local chapters of Citizens UK and by including union representatives in the Living Wage Foundation's system of stakeholder governance. In this section we examine union involvement in the campaign in greater detail, looking in turn at weak and strong forms of union participation. The weak method of participation is through union accreditation as Living Wage Employers, a tangible way of showing support for the campaign but one that requires little active involvement to spread the standard amongst employers. The strong method is through union affiliation to Citizens UK, and the involvement in local activity to promote the Living Wage that this requires. Our main focus here is on the involvement of UNISON in Greater Manchester Citizens and the attempts made by the union, alongside community allies, to spread the Living Wage in social care.

Accreditation

Table 5.1 lists the trade unions, union confederations, and union branches which have provided support to the Living Wage by becoming accredited employers. Both the TUC and STUC are accredited Living Wage Employers, while twenty-four individual unions have been accredited in the period since 2011. The latter mainly include unions affiliated to the TUC, thirty-seven per cent of whose membership are currently Living Wage Employers. These accredited unions include small specialist and large conglomerate unions, unions of professional employees and unions of manual workers, public sector and private sector unions, and unions with both left-wing and more moderate profiles. The table also lists sixteen trade union branches which have become accredited, all but one of which are branches of UNISON. This finding underscores the fact that support for the principle of the Living Wage and for the campaign are most pronounced within UNISON. This support stems from the union's long commitment to addressing the issue of low pay, which originated in its predecessor union, NUPE, and which was instrumental in turning first the TUC and then the Labour Party in favour of a statutory minimum wage (Morris 2000):

> I mean, low pay has always been an issue for UNISON and its predecessor unions, particularly NUPE. So low pay and the majority of our members, part-time low-paid women, you know, that's where the bulk of our membership is ... So low pay has always been a real part of the union's core aims to tackle. [UNISON Regional Organizer]

Table 5.1 Trade unions and trade union branches accredited as Living Wage Employers

Trade unions and union confederations	Trade union branches
1. Accord*	1. Communication Workers' Union ALGUS Branch
2. Advance*	2. UNISON Birmingham
3. ASLEF*	3. UNISON City of Stoke-on-Trent Branch#
4. Association of Teachers & Lecturers*#	4. UNISON Coventry City Branch
5. British Dietetic Association (BDA)*	5. UNISON Dudley General Branch#
6. British Medical Association (BMA)	6. UNISON Fife Branch
7. Chartered Society of Physiotherapy*	7. UNISON North Devon Health Branch#
8. College of Podiatry*	8. UNISON North Somerset Branch
9. Communication Workers' Union (CWU)*	9. UNISON Sandwell General Branch
10. Community*	10. UNISON Shropshire General Branch
11. FDA*	11. UNISON Solihull Local Government Branch
12. GMB*	12. UNISON Staffordshire Branch
13. Musicians' Union*	13. UNISON Warwickshire County Branch#
14. National Association of Schoolmasters Union of Women Teachers (NASUWT)*	14. UNISON West Midlands Community Branch
15. Nationwide Group Staff Union*	15. UNISON Wolverhampton Branch
16. Prospect*	16. UNISON Worcestershire Branch
17. Royal College of Midwives (RCM)*	
18. Royal College of Nursing (RCN)	
19. Scottish Artists Union	
20. Scottish Trades Union Congress (STUC)	
21. Society and College of Radiographers*	
22. Society of Authors	
23. Trades Union Congress (TUC)*	
24. Union of Shop, Distributive & Allied Workers (USDAW)*	
25. UNISON*	
26. University and College Union (UCU)*	

Lapsed accreditation; * TUC member or affiliate

The reasons why unions have become accredited Living Wage Employers are the same that motivate other social justice organizations to do so. Becoming an accredited employer is a way of demonstrating support for the Living Wage campaign, it serves to manage risk by reducing the chance of unions being exposed for paying low wages, and it confers legitimacy, enabling unions to call on other employers to pay the Living Wage without facing a charge of hypocrisy: 'We could not exhort others unless we did it ourselves' [TUC National official]. The desire to support the campaign and the principle of the Living Wage, we believe, is the most important of these motivations. Action of this kind, in which unions provide financial backing and moral support to good causes, is an established feature of union behaviour. It can be seen in union membership of Amnesty International and of other charitable and campaigning organizations (Heery 2010). Becoming a Living Wage Employer should be regarded as a declaration of support of this kind, a tangible action but one that typically has only limited consequences for the quotidian task of representing union members in dealings with employers and government.

Affiliation

A much stronger form of cooperation is affiliation to a local chapter of Citizens UK, with the commitment to active campaigning for the Living Wage that this implies. As we have seen, affiliation is confined to few unions and only a fraction of the Citizens' network, but when it occurs unions can become major participants in the Living Wage campaign. This was the case in London in the early years when branches of UNISON played an important part in securing the Living Wage for outsourced employees at hospitals in the East End (Littman et al. 2010; Wills 2009). Today it is best exemplified by UNISON's participation in Greater Manchester Citizens. It was reported above that UNISON North-West is a 'strategic partner' of Greater Manchester Citizens, and that a large proportion of local branches have affiliated to the network. This formal connection has provided a gateway to union participation in Living Wage campaigning. UNISON North-West has worked with other members of the Citizens' network to promote the Living Wage in social care, is a founder-member of the campaign to make Greater Manchester a Living Wage City-Region, and has been an active contributor to the Living Wage for Social Care campaign. The co-convenor of Greater Manchester Citizens is a UNISON Organizer.

The literature on union-community alliances has identified the significant part played by 'bridge-builders' in forging arrangements of this kind (Rose 2000; Voss and Sherman 2000). Bridge-builders are activists within the labour movement who also have experience of working for social movement allies and who can bring the two types of organization, with their sometimes markedly different cultures, together. To a degree, the link between UNISON and Greater Manchester Citizens relies upon activists of this kind. One of the union officers centrally involved in developing the relationship with Citizens first became active in Living Wage campaigning as a student, helping to win the Living Wage for low-paid staff at Manchester University in a Citizens-led campaign. Others in the union, including key lay activists, have undertaken community organizing training provided by Citizens. The presence of activists who straddle the union-community organizing divide, however, is not the only condition that has supported the coalition.

UNISON North-West's affiliation to Greater Manchester Citizens emerged from its organizing strategy, which originally was developed quite independently. In the period preceding its affiliation, the region had assembled a team of twenty-eight organizers to ensure members transferred their subscriptions to direct debit in the face of proposed legislation that threatened to end payroll deduction of union dues. When the legislation was not enacted, it was decided to redeploy the team to a sustained organizing drive in residential social care, intended to 'establish the union as a strong presence' in the industry over a ten-year period. It is this organizing drive that led the union to forge its partnership with Citizens. The leadership of the regional union had been influenced by the 'organizing turn' of the early 2000s and prioritized investment in organizing, particularly amongst low-wage workers (Heery 2015). Each year, UNISON North-West holds an Organizing Convention attended by hundreds of activists. It was this commitment to organizing which primed the regional union for its affiliation to Greater Manchester Citizens.

Another strand in the literature on union-community alliances emphasizes complementarity; the idea that each party can gain from the unique properties and resources the other brings to the relationship (Frege et al. 2004; Tattersall 2018). This claim found unambiguous support in the evidence from Greater Manchester. From the union side, the relationship with Citizens yielded several benefits. One such benefit is access to those employed in social care, the target of the union's organizing campaign and many of whom are members of parishes and mosques within the Citizens' network. Another benefit is Citizens' ability to mobilize community support for the union's campaign, action that could assume a variety of forms and take place at a variety of scales. A key event that demonstrated the mobilizing capacity of Greater Manchester Citizens was the accountability assembly prior to the metro mayor election of 2017, which was attended by more than 1,000 community leaders including representatives from affiliated branches of UNISON. At the assembly, Andy Burnham committed the Greater Manchester Combined Authority to becoming an accredited Living Wage Employer and to taking action to promote the Living Wage across the city-region. At a smaller scale, Greater Manchester Citizens has organized actions outside care homes to highlight the problem of low pay and other poor employment conditions in the sector. These actions have brought together faith and community leaders, alongside union activists, and have assumed the non-adversarial form typical of Citizens: at the end of one action home-baked cakes were handed to the managers, staff, and residents—'not like a union rally' [UNISON Regional Organizer].

Another way in which Citizens has mobilized support for the union was seen in a partially successful attempt to secure the Living Wage in MHA, the UK's largest charity provider of residential care with historic links to the Methodist Church. In this case, Greater Manchester Citizens organized a petition, and local Methodist congregations submitted motions to the Methodist Conference and wrote letters to MHA, while a Methodist representative on the charity's board raised the issue directly with the organization's management. In response, MHA agreed to pay the Living Wage to direct employees, though it declined to become accredited as a Living Wage Employer. As the MHA case indicates, a further resource that Citizens has brought to its relationship with UNISON is its ability to confer legitimacy on the union's campaign. It was reported that politicians were more receptive to the union message that social care be funded at a level which allowed the Living Wage to be paid when it was delivered by faith and community leaders. In political meetings, it was said, 'there is a different atmosphere with an imam, a vicar. It's less adversarial' [UNISON Regional Organizer], and this was vital in a campaign that depended on local authorities using their leverage over care providers to secure payment of the Living Wage.

While cooperation with Greater Manchester Citizens conferred benefits on UNISON and helped promote its organizing activity, there were also reciprocal gains that flowed to Citizens from its relationship with the union. UNISON helped fund the initial effort to establish Greater Manchester Citizens, and its financial contribution and the contribution of its officials and activists continue to sustain the network. Another resource that UNISON has brought to the relationship arises from its workplace presence and its ability to monitor the implementation of the Living Wage in unionized organizations. For example, the union discovered that contract employees at one of the universities in the region had failed to receive the annual Living Wage uplift and was able to ensure that this failure was corrected, while its pitch for support from local authorities stresses its ability to check that increased funding for residential care actually results in payment of the Living Wage to care workers. UNISON's political influence through the Labour Party has also been of benefit to Citizens. The union has worked closely with Andy Burnham's office to develop a Good Employment Charter for Greater Manchester, which commits signatory employers to paying the Living Wage, and the region has encouraged Labour-controlled local authorities both to become accredited employers and to adopt UNISON's Ethical Care Charter, which contains a commitment to fund the Living Wage in domiciliary care.

A third theme in the literature on union-community coalitions identifies the potential for unions to learn from their civil society partners and adopt their methods (Holgate 2015a; Tapia 2013). Union revitalization, the argument goes, can be achieved by recreating unions as social movement organizations, and this implies learning from organizations that are effective at mobilizing supporters in campaigns for social justice. As we have seen, UNISON North-West has tried to learn from Citizens, sending some of its activists and officials on community organizing training. It has also commissioned a community organizer from its sister union in the United States, the SEIU, to provide additional training. In both sets of training there has been a focus on introducing union activists to the core techniques of community organizing; relational organizing through one-to-ones, power analysis, power building through alliances, and the use of actions to develop leaders. The union has also made use of worker-testimony in its social care campaign, though it emphasized the risks of a technique that can expose activists to victimization. To a degree, therefore, UNISON has engaged in cross-movement learning, seeking to apply the techniques of community organizing to its own activity. It would be wrong to exaggerate the extent of this transfer, however. Much of UNISON's effort to organize social care workers and to promote the Living Wage relies upon its established methods and existing expertise. Learning from Citizens, moreover, has reinforced an existing commitment to organizing within the region and amounts to an incremental adjustment to strategy rather than a fundamental change of course.

By 2019, UNISON North-West's social care campaign had recruited 4,500 new union members, identified and trained a network of workplace leaders, and secured six new recognition agreements. It had also registered indirect successes, such as the payment of the Living Wage at MHA. In 2020, further advances were recorded, with local authorities, such as Salford, negotiating pay increases for social care employees and agreeing to protect the pay of those isolating because of COVID-19. The alliance with Greater Manchester Citizens was believed by those leading the campaign to have contributed substantially to these achievements. It has arisen because both the union and the community and faith groups which form the remainder of the Citizens network shared the priority of tackling low pay: promoting the Living Wage was one of the core objectives of Greater Manchester Citizens declared at its founding assembly. It was this shared purpose that allowed the relationship with the union to be forged and to flourish. The interests of the labour movement and of civil society, in this case, coincided.

Non-Affiliated Unions

Affiliation has provided a gateway to Living Wage campaigning in the North West, but non-affiliated unions have also contributed to the campaign, albeit typically not in the sustained way seen in Greater Manchester. Local union branches have supported attempts by Citizens UK to persuade employers to adopt the Living Wage, participating in joint actions and exerting combined pressure to encourage accreditation. Localized cooperation of this kind has been seen in a range of industries, though it has perhaps been most apparent in higher education, where university unions have provided considerable backing for the Living Wage campaign.

The UCU, the union for professional staff in universities, has been the most active participant in the campaign to spread the Living Wage in higher education. One branch of UCU, at the University of Nottingham, is affiliated to Citizens UK and has tried, so far unsuccessfully, to get the University to accredit: its members joined with students and community activists in 2017 in a 'clean-in', a public cleaning of the Vice-Chancellor's building to show solidarity with low-wage workers denied the Living Wage. Other branches are not affiliated but have taken part in similar campaigns. The UCU branch was involved in the first successful university campaign at QMUL in 2008, and shortly afterwards its counterpart at the University of East London registered a similar victory (Lopes and Hall 2015; Wills 2009). More recently, the UCU branch at the University of Leeds has worked with Leeds Citizens, taking part in picketing, organizing a petition, and joining in delegations to meet the University's senior management; as yet without success. At Swansea University, it was UNISON that supported the campaign, playing a part in a drawn out but ultimately successful campaign to secure accreditation, which included a union representative addressing an accountability assembly for Y Senedd election of 2016 and meeting the First Minister as part of a Citizens Cymru-Wales delegation. Finally, in 2019 at the University of Bath, joint action by UCU, UNITE, and UNISON, together with students, pressured the University to not only rescind an earlier decision to stop paying the Living Wage, but to also agree to become an accredited Living Wage Employer. In this campaign, more traditional methods featured alongside picketing, petitioning, and social media campaigning, with UNISON organizing a strike ballot to force the employer's hand.

A notable feature of most of these university campaigns, which also applies in other industries, is that the unions involved were not directly representative of the low-paid workers who were the focus of campaigning activity. The latter frequently were not unionized, delivering outsourced services through cleaning and other companies without union recognition, while the unions pressing for the Living Wage to be paid represented professional, administrative, and other relatively well-paid groups. Union involvement in these campaigns often followed a social justice, rather than a representative logic, and in this regard the unions involved resembled their campaign allies, drawn from Citizens UK and faith and community groups. All these participants were united in acting on behalf of a vulnerable and exploited group that lay beyond their own membership.

Another feature of campaigns to secure the Living Wage in universities is that in a proportion of cases there was no union involvement. Thus, Cardiff University became accredited as a Living Wage Employer in 2014 following a campaign launched by Citizens Cymru-Wales, which involved students and members of the academic staff. Many of the latter were members of UCU, but neither the UCU nor the UNISON branch at the University participated formally in the campaign. The unions were consulted by management over the decision to introduce the Living Wage but were not architects of the original decision. The same is true of Liverpool John Moores University, where the employer decided to introduce the Living Wage without any campaign pressure from students, unions, or external Living Wage campaigners. Relationships with the unions at the University were described as good, but introducing the Living Wage was an employer-led decision, with unions informed and consulted *post hoc*, at the point of implementation.

The absence of unions from Living Wage campaigns and their rather marginal involvement in the process of implementation is not confined to universities, but has been seen in other industries where unions are present (Heery et al. 2018). It seems that active involvement of trade unions alongside campaigners to secure the Living Wage is a minority trend and that the heavy investment of UNISON North-West in the Living Wage campaign is unusual. Unions frequently have not actively pressed for accreditation and have not developed the kind of 'deep' coalition with Living Wage campaigners of the kind that is celebrated in the literature on union revitalization. Cooperation with civil society organizations is but one minority element in the union response to the Living Wage; other responses, characterized by conflict and indifference, have also been apparent.

Conflict

Some in the trade union movement have reacted negatively to the spread of the Living Wage, and there has been a degree of conflict between campaigners and trade union representatives. In this section, we describe and seek to explain this conflict, dealing first with the critique of the Living Wage within the trade union movement and then with the actions that some trade unionists have taken to counter the campaign.

Critique

Trade union criticism of the Living Wage campaign has targeted three of its elements, focusing respectively on the content of the standard, the characteristics of Citizens UK, and the methods used by campaigners. Critique of the standard has assumed several forms, but common to all is a claim that a single employment standard provides only a limited and flawed basis for action to improve the condition of low-paid workers. One claim of this kind, for example, suggests that the Living Wage is insufficient as a response to in-work poverty because many employees work short or irregular hours: 'You talk to real people about getting them another 50p an hour and they say, "Yeah, I'll have that but what I really want is more hours or I want regular hours"' [TUC regional official]. Another claim of this type is that the Living Wage standard artificially separates pay from other substantive elements of the employment relationship. Union representatives from low-wage industries, with negotiated rates below the Living Wage, defended these agreements in terms of additional elements that had been secured that materially improved the terms of employment:

> The living wage hourly rate ethos doesn't fit with our bargaining in terms of the deals we've secured going forward ... We've focused really, really clearly over the

> last number of years on raising the bottom scales, looking after young workers, looking after maternity and paternity pay, our female members, flexibility, short time contracts. And really if your microscope is just right down on the hourly rate, it doesn't fit with the bargaining we do. [USDAW national official]

A third form of this argument is that the Living Wage standard elevates substantive over procedural regulation, emphasizing the payment to workers of a particular rate while neglecting the issue of worker participation in the determination of rates of pay. Trade unionists in Wales, for instance, have argued that a fair rate of pay does not equate to any given hourly-rate but is 'that which union members agree with their employer'. In this formulation the priority attached to substantive over procedural regulation in the Living Wage standard is effectively reversed.

A second line of criticism has focused on Citizens UK, with trade unionists pointing to what they believe are negative features of the organization. One target here is the method of decision-making in Citizens UK, described as falling short of the democratic norm found within unions. Citizens UK was described as being controlled firmly by its professional organizers, with only a veneer of democratic control: on more than one occasion trade unionists commented on reliance upon a show-of-hands to confirm the agenda at Citizens' assemblies, affording minimum scope for dialogue or dissent. Perhaps the main target, however, was the faith-based nature of the Citizens' network. There were complaints of pious 'do-gooders' interfering in the world of work, the rightful sphere of trade unionists, doubts about allying with religious organizations committed to positions on reproductive rights, gender, and sexuality which opposed those of the mainstream trade union movement, and a concern that the Living Wage campaign served to legitimate conservative figures—priests and imams—within migrant communities. A union branch official who was himself religious and an active participant in Citizens reported that hostility to the latter's faith component was pronounced amongst his secular union counterparts.

Union criticism of the methods used by Living Wage campaigners also assumes several forms. A regional TUC official said that Citizens was 'not always a great partner', citing both the organization's eagerness to secure the credit for 'wins' achieved through the efforts of trade unions and its unwillingness to cede a share of control of campaign strategy to its ostensible allies. The same official expressed concern that reliance on worker testimony could expose employees to victimization, while others expressed the view that the use of testimony to declare gratitude to employers for paying the Living Wage was demeaning to those involved. Perhaps the main union criticism of campaign methods, however, concerned the 'interference' of Citizens UK in workplaces where unions were recognized. There were complaints of campaigners appealing directly to employers over the heads of elected union representatives, campaign actions disrupting collective bargaining, and of ignorance of campaigners about collective bargaining, in which multiple issues are subject to negotiation and trade-offs are necessary to secure agreement. There were also complaints that the campaign could legitimate the actions of bad employers or bolster the position of anti-union, Conservative politicians (Holgate 2009).

It is important to recognize that not all trade unionists shared this critical assessment of the campaign, and some, in fact, provided a rebuttal. A UNISON official said, 'You leave your differences at the door', when working with faith organizations and that cooperation to secure the Living Wage required no endorsement of conservative social policies inimical to those adopted by unions. Another UNISON organizer remarked that the essence of community organizing was to work through network partners, like trade unions, relying on them to do the hard work that resulted in campaign wins; its very *modus operandi* was indirect—'Whose badge is on it [a successful outcome] doesn't matter'. A TUC official made a different point about union complaints of interference in collective bargaining, observing that criticism of this kind was in part defensive, arising from embarrassment that unions had failed to secure rates of pay above the Living Wage for their members. Not all within the union movement, therefore, subscribed to the critique of Citizens UK and its methods and, as we have seen, criticism exists alongside cooperation. Nevertheless, union criticism of the campaign is widespread and is an important strand in the trade union response to the Living Wage.

Opposition

Trade union criticism of Citizens UK has motivated attempts to frustrate the Living Wage campaign. One method of opposition has simply been to decline support. This response emerged quite early on when initial support for the campaign from UNISON branches in East London was overridden by opposition from the union's regional leadership. A striking example of this opposition was the failure of the union to back the campaign to secure the Living Wage at QMUL, the first university to adopt the standard (Wills 2009). In another case, an attempt to secure the Living Wage at a regional airport, without involving recognized unions, led to a withdrawal of union involvement from local campaigning. The limited membership of union branches of local chapters of Citizens UK suggests that passive resistance to the campaign amongst trade unionists may be quite widespread.

Another method of opposition has been to launch alternative initiatives that compete with the Living Wage. The most striking example of a competing initiative has been the £10.00 Living Wage, which was adopted initially by the Bakers' Union before being taken up by larger unions, the TUC, and the Labour Party. The Labour Party fought the 2019 election on a commitment to introduce a statutory minimum wage of £10.00 an hour for all workers aged 16 and over. The TUC has continued to call for the legal minimum wage to be raised to £10.00 and individual unions have included the rate in pay demands. During the pandemic, Labour Unions, the umbrella body for unions affiliated to the Labour Party, organized a virtual rally calling for the £10.00 rate for key workers, an event very similar to those arranged by Citizens UK, while in February 2021 the Labour Party itself called for all workers in the care sector to be paid a minimum of £10.00 an hour. We encountered some scepticism about the £10.00 campaign and its efficacy in leading to pay increases for low-wage workers: 'It's in everyone's conference policy', one union official remarked, implying it had not spread far beyond the conference floor. Nevertheless, the £10.00 campaign has appropriated the language of the living wage and is a union-specific initiative to raise pay at the base of the labour market that is clearly separate from and a potential rival to the Living Wage standard. Indeed, support for a higher, £15.00 an hour standard emerged within some trade unions and the left of the Labour Party in late 2021.

Why have unions criticized the Living Wage and acted either to frustrate the campaign or compete with it? An answer given by one union organizer is that the Living Wage campaign and trade unions occupy a 'similar space' and that this institutional overlap has generated rivalry. It was said above that a shared interest in tackling low pay has facilitated cooperation between the two movements, but sharing this common goal can also lead to friction, particularly as both parties are seeking to advance it by forging direct relations with employers, in one case based on collective bargaining and in the other through accreditation. An USDAW official said to us that she was happy to support the Living Wage campaign when it targeted non-union companies but felt that its role was problematic when extended to firms with union recognition. At the heart of statements like this is both a recognition of institutional rivalry and a claim that union voice should take precedence over other attempts to raise wages through dealing directly with employers. Many of the criticisms articulated above serve to delegitimate Citizens UK and the Living Wage Foundation and question their authority to speak on behalf of working people. They also serve to delegitimate their role as potential union allies. The obverse of this criticism is a belief that unions can and should serve as the single channel of workforce representation. An organizer who had been involved in the Living Wage campaign in both Canada and the United Kingdom remarked that Canadian unions were 'much more relational' than their British counterparts, less suspicious of outsiders and more prepared to work with other movements. Research evidence of the relatively limited appetite of UK unions for joint working can be found in Holgate's (2015a) three-country study of union-community alliances. While difficulties are reported in the relationship between unions and community organizers in Australia and the USA, there was least evidence of successful joint working in the UK. The strong commitment of UK trade unions to the single channel seemingly predisposes many union representatives to perceive the Living Wage campaign in terms of 'interference'; a potential threat.

Appropriation

The third union response has been to appropriate the Living Wage; that is to adopt the standard and seek to ensure the rate is paid to union members but without involving Living Wage campaigners. In this response the activities of trade unions and of campaigners to promote the Living Wage remain largely separate, thereby approximating to the concept of 'indifference' outlined above. Appropriation itself has assumed several forms, each of which is described below. Unions have sought to include the Living Wage in the process of collective bargaining at both multi-employer and single employer levels, establishing the Living Wage as the base rate within negotiated pay structures. They have also incorporated the standard in their own campaigning activity, promoting the Living Wage within specific industries or regions often through the medium of fair employment charters that include the Living Wage as one of their elements. Finally, new indie unions have made use of the standard in their campaigns to organize migrant and other workers in precarious employment and have used militant tactics to compel employers to adopt the Living Wage. All these methods have registered considerable success. Trade union appropriation of the Living Wage has been an important way of diffusing the standard beyond the ranks of accredited employers, helping to create a 'shadow' Living Wage that covers a substantial portion of the unionized economy.

Bargaining

The first method of appropriation has been to incorporate the Living Wage in collective bargaining. In some cases, this incorporation has occurred at the multi-employer level, with unions negotiating the inclusion of the Living Wage in industry agreements. Examples of agreements of this kind include those for: Scottish local government, NHS Scotland, Scottish voluntary sector housing, both Scottish and Welsh further education, and UK higher education. In other cases, such as English and Welsh local government, English further education, and NHS England, the lowest negotiated pay rate has matched the Living Wage in some years but not others, while in industries such as theatre and cooperative retail unions have raised the issue of the Living Wage without securing an agreement. In most cases, industry settlements of this kind take the form of framework agreements, which require further negotiation at individual employer level including negotiation over the implementation of the Living Wage. Particularly innovative examples of this kind of framework agreement are those negotiated by UNISON, with organizations representing Catholic, Church of England, and cooperative schools. These agreements urge member schools to adopt the Living Wage—for example by saying it conforms to Catholic social doctrine—and provide a model plan for its introduction.

Collective bargaining over the Living Wage has also taken place at the single-employer level. Thus, following the rejection by employers of a bid to have the Living Wage adopted in English and Welsh local government, the GMB, UNISON, and UNITE launched a campaign to have the standard adopted by individual local authorities in 2013 (Prowse et al. 2017). Two years later the GMB was reporting that 175 councils had done so (Prowse and Fells 2016b). At about the same time, PCS launched an attempt to secure the Living Wage for gallery attendants, cleaning, and retail staff in the heritage sector, which resulted in negotiations but not always collective agreements, at the National Gallery, Tate Galleries, the Wallace Collection, the V&A, National Museums Liverpool, and Kew Gardens. BECTU, the media and entertainment union, also developed a push to establish the Living Wage for front-of-house and support staff in theatres, cinemas, and concert halls, securing agreements with the National Theatre, the Royal Shakespeare Company, the Royal Opera House, and the Curzon cinema chain. A prolonged dispute at the Ritzy Cinema in Brixton failed to secure the Living Wage but did result in an increase in pay. More recently, the GMB has attempted to secure the Living Wage for outsourced cleaning and catering employees at NHS Trusts in the South East, PCS has organized strikes to win the Living Wage for outsourced portering, security, and receptionist staff in Whitehall, UNISON has won the Living Wage for outsourced school meals, cleaning, and social care employees employed by arm's length businesses set up by local authorities, and UNITE has negotiated the Living Wage for attendants at privatized leisure centres in London.

One of the most novel attempts to obtain a commitment to the Living Wage from individual employers was developed by construction union UCATT (now part of UNITE). The targets in this case were property development companies, businesses which did not employ UCATT members and which had no history of dealing with the union. Despite the absence of recognition, first LandSec and then other property companies agreed protocols with UCATT that committed them to ensuring the Living Wage was paid to employees of contractors on major development sites in London. Protocols of this kind fall short of full collective bargaining but form part of a broader attempt by unions to use the power of companies located at the apex of value chains to raise employment standards within supplier businesses (Wright and Brown 2013).

What was notable about these episodes of collective bargaining, whether at multi-employer or single-employer level, was the limited part played by the Living Wage campaign. Some of the union officials interviewed had played a part in Citizens UK and in the wider Living Wage campaign—one was a member of the supporters' group pressing for the adoption of the Living Wage at Manchester City—but this activity was described as separate from their involvement in bargaining to secure the Living Wage. Others had made use of campaign resources—taking business case arguments from the Foundation website, telephoning campaign workers to find out more about the standard, or checking with academics about how the Living Wage was calculated—but, again, this action was described as marginal to the main thrust of union activity. Asked about how their unions had come to include the Living Wage in collective bargaining, most union interviewees referred to established processes of union decision-making; to conference policies, proposals from activists within union committees, and the support of national leaders. Those from UNISON referenced the union's long tradition of prioritizing action on low pay. Outside pressure or encouragement from the Living Wage campaign were not identified as key triggers for action (see also Prowse et al. 2017). 'I've never had occasion to speak to the Living Wage Foundation', was how one union official summarized the relationship, 'They just publish a number, and we use it'.

In progressing the Living Wage through collective bargaining, unions have largely relied upon their traditional repertoire. In some cases, this has involved launching disputes and making use of strike activity to obtain the Living Wage. Thus, BECTU's dispute at the Ritzy Cinema became a labour movement *cause célèbre*, featuring repeated strikes, a social media campaign, a consumer boycott, and visits to the picket-line by celebrities, like Eric Cantona. Although it was unsuccessful, the dispute had an important demonstration effect, persuading other employers in the industry to negotiate on the Living Wage. Other Living Wage strikes have been called by the GMB at Topshop distribution, by UNITE at Luton Airport and the Woolwich Ferry, and by PCS at BEIS and HMRC. Unions have also exerted pressure on employers in other ways, using the kinds of action employed by Citizens UK. The protocols negotiated by UCATT with property development companies originated in a demonstration outside the LandSec Head Office in central London, PCS organized a picket at the opening of the new Museum of Liverpool to embarrass the employer into paying the Living Wage, and UNISON organized a night-time deputation to Camden Council to win the Living Wage for outsourced school meals staff. Another way in which the Living Wage has been woven into the dispute activity of unions is by providing a solution to conflicts that began over other issues. A long and bitter dispute between PCS and the National Gallery over the outsourcing of gallery attendants was eventually resolved when the Gallery agreed to fund the Living Wage on its service contracts, while in Wales a national pay strike in the NHS was averted when the Welsh Government agreed to subsidize payment of the Living Wage to several thousand support staff.

Another classic element of the union repertoire that has featured in the appropriation of the Living Wage is the linking of the standard to other issues, with unions sometimes making concessions to secure employer agreement. At a national arts facility in London, for example, the introduction of the Living Wage was conditional on union acceptance of flexible working, such that employees could be redeployed between catering and front-of-house roles. At a local authority in Scotland, the main concession took the form of reduced rates for overtime and restrictions on overtime working for largely male full-time workers to fund the Living Wage for mainly female part-timers. This change was reinforced through a change in recognition arrangements that increased the representation of female-dominated groups of employees on the council's joint negotiating body. A third example of this kind of trade-off was provided by PCS, which reported that progress on introducing the Living Wage in the heritage sector had sometimes required concessions on weekend allowances: 'In the context of austerity, unfortunately we have to make concessions: negotiations are about giving and taking' [PCS lay representative]. Trade-offs of this kind were not reported by all the union representatives we spoke to, but they have seemingly been a common feature of the union appropriation of the Living Wage. When unions have raised the Living Wage through established channels of negotiation, employers have often responded in bargaining mode, seeking concessions that can offset the cost of higher wages.

While union bargaining has often been successful in winning the Living Wage, collective agreements have often fallen short of full implementation of the standard. The main way in which this has happened is by confining the Living Wage to direct employees, without provision for extending the rate to employees of contractors. This limitation is a feature of all the industry agreements listed above and has also been characteristic of many single-employer agreements. At the Royal Shakespeare Company, for example, BECTU negotiated the Living Wage for directly employed catering, retail, and nursery staff, but action to extend the rate to employees of contractors was taken unilaterally by the employer, outwith the agreement. In recent years there has been a shift from this position, with several unions making concerted efforts to extend the Living Wage to contract employees. Examples involving GMB, PCS, UNISON, and UNITE are given above and, as we will see, the new indie unions have been particularly associated with moves of this kind. It remains though that the prime union effort has been directed at obtaining the Living Wage for direct workers: workers who are covered by union recognition agreements with employers and who are themselves union members.

Because collective agreements do not implement all components of the Living Wage standard, they have often not led to employer accreditation. They have spread the Living Wage hourly rate, but in a way that reinforces separation between union initiatives and the Living Wage campaign proper. In our interviews with trade union representatives, we tried to ascertain whether they believed this separation was desirable and if they had attempted to secure accreditation when raising the Living Wage with employers. In some cases, union officials reported that they had raised the issue of accreditation, though not always with success. The main reason given was that accreditation could cement the Living Wage in place, committing the employer to maintaining the standard over time: 'We also encourage employers to become accredited Living Wage employers because that locks it in and it's good for them because they get to have the badge' [UNISON national organizer]. It is worth noting in this respect that several union representatives reported that they had secured the introduction of the Living Wage through negotiation but, in the absence of accreditation, employers had withdrawn from this commitment in a relatively short period of time.

Not all of those interviewed voiced support for accreditation, however, and the contrary view was also expressed that unions should seek to obtain the Living Wage without involving the Foundation. One reason for adopting this position stemmed from the perception of institutional rivalry identified above. A BECTU official, for example, argued that accreditation of employers through the Foundation could reduce demand for representation through trade unions: 'If you've got an independent organization setting your wage rate, what's the point of joining a trade union?'. The same official also argued that accreditation could impose a cap on wage increases for the low-paid when the union's objective was to reach beyond, negotiating the Living Wage in the first instance but then securing a higher rate in the future. Trade unionists from other unions also expressed this view and Living Wage campaigners reported that they had encountered this argument and had sought to reassure unions that the Living Wage was a minimum, acceptable rate, not a wage-ceiling. A third, more qualified argument against accreditation was made by a representative from UNITE. He said he was in favour of accreditation and reported that the union had urged employers to take this step, but only after the Living Wage had been adopted through negotiation: 'We don't want this paternalism where we've just got to wait for somebody to decide—the Living Wage Foundation and our Director have a nice cup of tea together—and decide it's a jolly good idea to give us the Living Wage'. On this view, accreditation was only valuable if it was fought for by those who were directly affected.

Inclusion of the Living Wage in collective bargaining is the main way in which the standard has been appropriated by trade unions, but it is important to recognize that there have been limits to this process. Interviews with union officials representing social care, retail, and hospitality workers suggested that although there was a formal union policy of pursuing the Living Wage, this had not impinged greatly on negotiations with employers. This absence was partly due to limited pressure on negotiators from union members. As one USDAW official put it, 'I don't have a line of members banging on my door asking for the Living Wage'. It was also due to resistance by employers and the scale of the breakthrough that would be required to secure the Living Wage in low-wage industries. The same USDAW official observed that:

> There's a reality-check ... if you are dealing with somebody who is on seven quid an hour, eight pound twenty-five pence an hour is a massive amount, isn't it; to try and uplift something one pound twenty-five pence an hour. Yeah. It's a massive amount. So, it's not realistically achievable.

A confirming view was provided by an employers' representative in retail, who said that while the unions had been successful in raising pay for the lower paid over time, there had been little pressure to concede on the Living Wage. The objectives of union negotiators, he said, were to increase the gap between existing wage rates and the statutory minimum wage and to match the median percentage increase in the sector. Securing these objectives was achievable below the Living Wage rate. These observations were made in 2016, and it may be that union horizons have broadened since, because of the high profits of major food retailers during the pandemic and public support for key workers. In early 2021, USDAW negotiated the introduction of a £10.00 minimum hourly rate at Morrison's supermarket chain, exceeding the UK but not the London Living Wage; albeit at the price of scrapping the company's annual bonus scheme. It remains to be seen whether this agreement represents a breakthrough, loosening the limitations to collective bargaining on the Living Wage in retail and other low-wage industries.

Campaigning

A second way in which trade unions have appropriated the Living Wage is by including the standard in their campaigning activity. Unions have identified the Living Wage as a desirable objective, have publicized it, featured it in member recruitment, and urged its adoption by employers and public authorities. Frequently in this work, the Living Wage has been coupled with other desirable employment and business standards to form a code or charter, a piece of soft regulation often tailored to the requirements of a particular industry, occupation, or place. UNITE's Hospitality Charter, for example, calls for restaurant workers to be paid the Living Wage, alongside paid rest breaks, guaranteed minimum hours, payment for trial shifts, paid transport home after 12.00am, payment of all tips to staff, a sexual harassment policy, and trade union access to the workplace. The prime goal of campaigning around charters of this kind has been to secure their implementation through collective bargaining. Union campaigning has not always been directed at joint regulation through bargaining, however, and unions have sometimes relied upon other methods, trying to persuade employers to sign up voluntarily to charters that incorporate the Living Wage. In doing so they have effectively reproduced the method of civil regulation used by the Living Wage Foundation.

One way in which unions have promoted the Living Wage to employers is by supporting charters authored by other labour market institutions. In Brighton, UNISON has backed and helped fund the Brighton Living Wage, a local campaign run by the Chamber of Commerce, which seeks to persuade Brighton employers to pay the Living Wage to direct employees and operates its own system of business accreditation, separate from that of the Living Wage Foundation. In Greater Manchester, UNISON and TUC North-West were involved in the development of the Mayor's Good Employment Charter, which incorporates the Living Wage as one of its elements, though it does not require businesses to become accredited by the Living Wage Foundation. At a national scale, the TUC has lent its support to the Good Business Charter, the brainchild of entrepreneur Julian Richer, which was launched in 2020 and which includes paying the Living Wage to both direct and contract employees and which does require business supporters to become accredited.

In addition to supporting codes developed by other labour market institutions, trade unions have formulated their own. The most successful example of a code of this kind is the Ethical Care Charter, developed by UNISON to raise employment and care standards in domiciliary care. The Charter was launched in 2012 and is targeted principally at local authorities, seeking to use the commissioning function of local government to leverage improvements for the home-care workforce employed by private providers (Johnson et al. 2021). Like UCATT's initiative described above, the Charter attempts to raise employment standards by enlisting the support of those at the 'top of the supply chain' [UNISON national organizer]. The Charter itself lists a set of desirable employment and care standards, including the Living Wage, which signatory local authorities undertake to incorporate into their contracts with suppliers. Other standards include payment of workers for travelling time, phasing out of zero-hours contracts, provision of occupational sick pay, an end to fifteen-minute service-visits, and continuity of care to allow carers to form supportive relationships with clients. Given their cost implications, councils can implement these standards through a phased, three-stage process.

Although the Ethical Care Charter incorporates the Living Wage, the Foundation was not involved in its development, which was a separate initiative by UNISON. The Living Wage was included in the Charter because it was available, 'easily understandable', and had gained currency in the labour market. The Charter is promoted to councils through the union, sometimes with local authority branches taking the initiative and in other cases through Regional Organizers making use of their contacts with local politicians. In 2021, however, the Living Wage Foundation included a recommendation that local authorities adopt the Ethical Care Charter in its toolkit for social care (Living Wage Foundation 2021b). By 2020, forty-two local authorities across England, Scotland, and Wales had become signatories to the Ethical Care Charter, as had four independent care providers. UNISON also reported that elements of the Charter had been incorporated into care contracts by other councils, the kind of 'shadow' effect generated by the wider Living Wage campaign. The Ethical Care Charter is another example of the appropriation of the Living Wage by trade unions, in this case not through its inclusion in collective bargaining, but through its adoption by a union campaign. The Charter relies upon similar methods to the Living Wage campaign, seeking to persuade local councils to become signatories and apply its elements within their operations, but until recently it has been an independent initiative, separate and distinct from the Living Wage campaign.

Organizing

Trade unions have also made use of the Living Wage in their attempts to recruit and organize workers. As we have seen, it was organizing which led UNISON North-West to develop its alliance with Greater Manchester Citizens, and campaign tools which feature the Living Wage, such as the Ethical Care Charter or UNITE's Hospitality Charter, have formed the basis of organizing activity. Perhaps the clearest and most single-minded attempt to use the Living Wage to organize workers is that developed by the new 'indie unions', IWGB and UVW. These unions emerged initially in London, though they have since spread to other parts of the UK. They describe themselves as 'member-led' to differentiate themselves from the mainstream trade union movement and have used militant tactics to build membership amongst groups of low-paid employees in precarious forms of employment, which include many migrants and members of ethnic minorities (Alberti and Però 2018; Però 2019; Shenker 2019). Over the past ten years these indie unions have built a membership of several thousand and have become a new, disruptive force within the British trade union movement. Central to their strategy has been a demand that low-wage workers should be paid the Living Wage.

One of the main groups that indie unions have tried to organize are workers providing outsourced services to public service organizations, such as universities, hospitals, and local authorities. IWGB has launched a Justice for Outsourced Workers campaign, and cleaners, security guards, catering staff, and porters are prominent among the membership of these unions. Like their mainstream counterparts, indie unions have coupled the demand for the Living Wage to other issues. The IWGB has often campaigned for the '3 Cosas' for outsourced workers, a demand for the London Living Wage plus improvements in pensions, sick pay, and paid holidays, such that they match provision for directly employed workers. UVW also lists the London Living Wage as one of its core objectives, along with paid sick pay, and treatment of workers that enshrines the principles of 'dignity, equality, and respect'. More recently, these demands have been extended to include a return to direct employment. Both IWGB and UVW have sought to have outsourced cleaning, catering, and security services returned in-house, often in the wake of a successful attempt to win the Living Wage. In several cases these insourcing campaigns have been directed at accredited Living Wage Employers and have included the employees of accredited service providers.

Central to the efforts of indie unions to win the Living Wage is the organizing of low-wage workers. These unions are led by charismatic organizers (Shenker 2019), have developed activists from among the contract workforce, and have built pockets of membership across a range of low-wage industries and occupations with new groups of members being added over time. During the pandemic, UVW added care workers to its roster of members and organized strikes at Sage Nursing Home in Golders Green in early 2021 for higher pay and conditions equivalent to those in the NHS. Reflecting this organizing mission, members actively participate in campaigns to win the Living Wage. IWGB and UVW rely heavily on strike action by their members, who take part in picketing, demonstrations, and sometimes workplace occupations, typically with a strong performative element including music, dancing, and elements of street theatre. Union members have also been involved directly in meetings with employers, which can resemble mass meetings rather than conventional negotiation sessions (Shenker 2019). Indie unions have arguably been more successful and more consistent in mobilizing low-wage workers in campaigns for the Living Wage than has Citizens UK, which as we have seen has made extensive use of worker testimony but largely in the context of campaigns that rely principally upon community groups beyond the workplace. Contrary to what has been suggested by some (Tapia 2013), it is unions—or at least this new disruptive element within the trade union movement—that have proved most effective at mobilizing the low-paid within Living Wage campaigns.

Another feature of indie unions which differentiates them from the broader Living Wage campaign is their pronounced militancy. IWGB and UVW are strongly adversarial both in the way they describe and relate to employers and in the methods they use. They completely eschew reliance on the 'business case' for higher labour standards espoused by the Living Wage Foundation. Strike action has been the primary method indie unions have used to win the Living Wage, and although they have sometimes attempted to win recognition from employers, there is a reluctance to engage in traditional collective bargaining, with its trade-offs and search for compromise. Their behaviour towards employers approximates to Crouch's (1982) notion of 'contestation', in which the legitimacy of the employer is not accepted and there is reliance on repeated bouts of conflict to extract gains without making concessions in return (Però 2019). Nowhere is this orientation more visible, and the difference with the Living Wage campaign more apparent, than in indie unions' orientation towards outsourcing. Outsourcing and outsourcing companies are not accepted as legitimate and have been the target of strikes, legal action, and hostile social media coverage. The fight for the Living Wage has been repeatedly coupled either with a demand for parity of employment terms with direct workers or the insourcing of contracted services. This approach contrasts markedly with that adopted by the Living Wage Foundation, with its emphasis on regulating rather than reversing outsourcing and its attempt to enlist contract businesses in the campaign for the Living Wage through the service provider accreditation (Heery et al. 2022).

Given the difference in approach, it is not surprising that contact between indie unions and the main Living Wage campaign has been limited. Activists from indie unions attended meetings of the Living Wage Foundation's leadership network, alongside representatives of mainstream unions, but this was wound up in 2016 and there has been an absence of formal contact since. Indeed, in 2019

IWGB picketed the Foundation's annual awards ceremony, although the target of the demonstration was Sadiq Kahn and his refusal to exempt minicabs from the London congestion charge, rather than the Foundation as such. Across the trade union movement, the new indie unions have been amongst the strongest and most persistent advocates of the Living Wage, but they have developed this position independently, while having minimal contact with the Foundation. In this regard, as we have seen, indie unions resemble their mainstream counterparts and indeed both IWGB and UVW have worked jointly with PCS and RMT in the campaign against outsourcing. Elements of a common agenda have emerged that includes the Living Wage and has provided the basis for joint work, but this collaboration between different elements in the trade union movement has not been brokered by nor involved Living Wage campaigners.

How sustainable the efforts of indie unions prove to be remains to be seen, but both IWGB and UVW have registered notable successes in winning the Living Wage for low-wage employees. IWGB has secured the Living Wage for workers on outsourcing contracts at the University of London, the London School of Economics, the School for Oriental and African Studies, and the elite members' club frequented by Conservative politicians, 5 Hertford Street. UVW has registered successes at the University of Greenwich, La Retraite Roman Catholic Girls School, Ark Globe Academy, the Daily Mail Group, the Royal Parks, Sotheby's, the Royal Borough of Kensington and Chelsea, and London office blocks 100 Wood Street and the Adelphi Building. In some of these cases the union campaign has led to the employer becoming accredited by the Living Wage Foundation. Notwithstanding this outcome, however, the relationship between indie unions and the Foundation has been characterized by appropriation rather than alliance. The Living Wage standard has been used in the organizing drives of indie unions, but in other respects their activity has been distinct from the Living Wage campaign. Indeed, as the emphasis on winning support from employers has come more to the fore within the latter, so the distance from the indie unions, with their very different approach to campaigning, has become more apparent.

Conclusion

The evidence presented above shows that there has been no single, union response to the Living Wage. Even within individual unions, representatives have reacted to the campaign in different ways, offering firm support in some cases while remaining sceptical in others. Each of the three union responses to civil regulation identified in earlier research—cooperation, conflict, and indifference—have been seen in the reaction to the Living Wage campaign. Unions have cooperated with the campaign by occupying positions within governance arrangements, becoming accredited employers, affiliating to local chapters of Citizens UK, and contributing to efforts to secure a Living Wage commitment from individual employers. Balancing cooperation of this kind, however, has been a widespread critique of the Living Wage movement and elements of conflict between unions and campaigners. Critique has focused on the Living Wage standard, Citizens UK, and the methods employed by the Living Wage Foundation and has led to refusals to support the Living Wage campaign and to unions developing the alternative £10.00 living wage. Indifference is apparent in the trade union appropriation of the Living Wage: the adoption of the Living Wage standard without engaging in joint work with Living Wage campaigners. Unions have pursued their own initiatives to promote the Living Wage, often relying upon traditional union methods of interest representation. Thus, the Living Wage has been included within collective bargaining at both multi-employer and single-employer levels and has on occasion been the cause of disputes with employers. Unions have also campaigned for business and government to adopt the Living Wage standard, either by backing good employment charters created by other labour market actors or by formulating their own. In some cases, such as UNISON's Ethical Care Charter, unions have developed their own systems of civil regulation that include the Living Wage standard. Finally, unions have made use of the Living Wage as an organizing issue, recruiting workers and activists from amongst the low-paid through militant campaigns designed to obtain the Living Wage from resistant employers. The actions of the new indie unions IWGB and UVW have been particularly noteworthy in this regard.

How does this complex of findings relate to the wider debates about union revitalization and the relationship between trade unions and civil society organizations? A central argument of the literature on union revitalization is that unions need to abandon old methods rooted in workplace organization or incremental collective bargaining with employers and recreate themselves as social movement organizations or 'community unions' (Holgate 2015b; Luce 2014). Cooperation with civil society organizations is one means through which renewal of this kind might be achieved. 'Coalitional unionism', based on alliances with other social movement organizations, has been identified as one of the main paths to revitalization, while it has also been suggested that unions can gain by importing activists, skills, and techniques from campaigning civil society organizations (Gumbrell-McCormick and Hyman 2013; Holgate 2015a; Voss and Sherman 2000). If this course is followed, it is suggested, unions can gain new resources and rebuild their power and will be positioned to develop new groups of members amongst the hitherto marginalized workforce (Frege et al. 2004; Milkman and Ott 2014).

The experiences of UNISON North-West are broadly consistent with this line of argument. The regional union has actively cooperated with Citizens UK and has entered a formal alliance through affiliation to Greater Manchester Citizens. It has also recruited community organizers, trained its officials and activists in community organizing, and made use of community organizing techniques.

Cooperation of this kind has yielded benefits for the union, giving it access to the soft power of its community allies and allowing it to build up membership amongst care workers. It remains, however, that the experiences of UNISON North-West are unusual and are not currently being reproduced elsewhere within the trade union movement: they are an outlier rather than the norm. Moreover, even when other parts of the trade union movement have cooperated with the Living Wage campaign, such cooperation has not followed the course outlined by theorists of revitalization. Unions have backed the Living Wage, often in the manner of supporting a good cause with little implication for their activities as representative institutions. Furthermore, union involvement in Living Wage campaigns directed at individual employers has frequently been an expression of solidarity with unorganized low-paid workers working for contractors; again, without any implication for the internal reconfiguration of union practice. The evidence provides some support for the union revitalization thesis, therefore, but the latter captures only one, minority facet of union experience.

The obverse of the revitalization thesis is the claim that the emergence of civil society actors and of civil regulation poses a threat to unions. It has been suggested that over time CSOs may displace unions as institutions of worker representation (Heckscher and McCarthy 2014; Piore and Safford 2006) and that the growth of civil regulation can forestall unionization and crowd out more traditional means of regulating the employment relationship (Compa 2001). We believe that concerns of this kind are exaggerated when considering the Living Wage campaign. We encountered no cases of the Living Wage displacing union-led bargaining on pay and conditions but did identify numerous situations where the Living Wage standard had been included within union-based industrial relations. Nevertheless, it is the case that many in the trade union movement have perceived the Living Wage campaign as threatening and have opposed it as a result. Partly this response may arise from the culture of British trade unionism and the strong commitment to maintaining the single channel of worker representation through trade unions. Others who have researched union opposition to the Living Wage have attributed it to similar factors: the conservatism of UK unions, ignorance of community organizing, and attachment to 'hierarchical structures' that make it difficult for unions to work with more decentralized, member-led community organizations (Holgate 2009: 71; see also Wills 2009). While these factors are important, we feel it is also necessary to note the institutional rivalry between unions and civil society that has been engendered by the Living Wage campaign. The latter seeks influence over the pay policies of employers and does so by forging a direct relationship through accreditation. In organizations where unions are recognized, trade union representatives are also trying to shape employer policy on pay through the medium of collective bargaining. These shared concerns can provide the basis for joint working between trade unions and Living Wage campaigners, but they can also lead to tension. While cultural and ideological factors might underlie union opposition to the Living Wage campaign, there are deeper, structural factors at play which have drawn the two sides towards conflict.

The most striking and most significant feature of the union response to the Living Wage is their appropriation of the Living Wage standard. Unions have bargained and campaigned for and organized with the Living Wage without becoming involved in the wider campaign or drawing upon the support of non-union, Living Wage campaigners. Unions have helped diffuse the Living Wage, particularly through their bargaining activity, but while doing so have maintained their separation from—their 'indifference' to—civil society. Trade unions have incorporated the Living Wage in their traditional repertoire and through campaigning, bargaining, and organizing have secured pay increases for many thousands of low-wage workers. The union response to the Living Wage campaign may have generally fallen short of the radical embrace of civil society and community organizing, which advocates of union revitalization have wished to see. It has nonetheless been significant and has created a shadow Living Wage that is substantial in coverage and extends well beyond the ranks of accredited employers.

6
Public Authorities and the Real Living Wage

Introduction

This chapter considers the relationship between the Living Wage and public authority. Although the Living Wage is a form of private regulation, campaigners, as we have seen, have sought to enlist the support of public authorities in spreading the Living Wage standard. In what follows, we examine to what degree and in what ways different parts of the UK state have acted to promote the Living Wage and assess the significance and impact of these measures. Two questions are paramount. In the first place, we examine the extent and pattern of Living Wage accreditation amongst public service employers. One central conclusion here is that Living Wage accreditation is disproportionately high amongst public sector employers, and we believe that this is evidence of a continuing 'good employer' commitment in much of UK public service that has survived, despite the challenge of austerity. In addition, however, public sector accreditation is skewed towards the devolved nations and is particularly prominent in local and regional government. It is in the more outlying institutions of UK government that support for the Living Wage is strongest, a pattern that is the reverse of earlier phases of public sector innovation in employment practice which often have been led by central government. Our second question concerns the methods that public authorities have used to promote the Living Wage in their areas of jurisdiction. Much of our evidence here comes from the devolved nations and from local and regional government, and reveals that a broad range of policy levers has been used to help spread the Living Wage, including but not restricted to new procurement initiatives. Our evidence also indicates that this effort has been impactful and that local authorities that have made the most extensive effort, including those designated Living Wage Cities, have registered a significantly higher take-up of the Living Wage by other employers.

Living Wage Accreditation in Public Services

In the UK and in other countries, public sector employment has often been identified as distinctive, reflecting a commitment on the part of the state and its agencies to act as a 'good employer' (Winchester and Bach 1995). One element of this good employer commitment is greater acceptance of trade union representation and collective bargaining, with the consequence that in many countries, union-based

The Real Living Wage. Edmund Heery, Deborah Hann and David Nash, Oxford University Press.
© Edmund Heery, Deborah Hann and David Nash (2023). DOI: 10.1093/oso/9780198835264.003.0006

employment relations are now concentrated in public services (Bach and Kessler 2012). There are other elements, however, including stronger attachment on the part of public sector organizations to equality and diversity, greater preparedness to respect both the letter and spirit of employment law and to rely on formal procedures to resolve employment disputes, and more widespread adoption of developmental forms of human resource management (Beaumont 1992; Bewley 2006; Bryson and Green 2018). Another distinction of public sector employment is that employers have often offered relatively good terms of employment to those who are lower paid, including relatively high wages (Rubery 2014). Moreover, not only have public sector organizations traditionally aspired to act as good employers, in many cases they have aspired also to be 'model employers', adopting exemplary practices that can be followed by other organizations, including their own contractors (Beaumont 1992).

While there is substantial evidence that public sector employers are distinctive, there is an equally substantial critique of the notion that they are good employers, which has been voiced more strongly in recent years. A phalanx of critical scholars has argued that the adoption of the new public management in public services from the 1980s onwards has led to work intensification and casualization for many public sector workers and has pushed public sector employment towards private sector practice, reversing the earlier direction of influence (Gill-McLure and Seifert 2008; Mather and Seifert 2013; Mooney and Law 2007). Wills (2009) includes public service hospitals, museums, and universities in a list of institutions implicated in the emergence of what she calls 'subcontracted capitalism'; by outsourcing cleaning and other support functions, large public service organizations have pushed down wages and other employment conditions, thereby generating need for a living wage. Others have highlighted the role of austerity in the period since the global financial crisis in undermining the traditional pattern of public sector employment relations. For Bach and Bordogna (2013), reviewing developments across Europe, a key feature of the post-crisis period has been reduced employer commitment to trade unionism and collective bargaining, hitherto core features of public service employment.

A third strand in the literature on public sector employment relations has focused on sources of variation. For example, Bach and Kessler (2012) have identified a centre-local pattern in public service employment relations. Using the spread of performance-related pay in the 1980s and 1990s as an indicator, they note that take-up was much greater at the centre of the UK state, in the civil service, with the government 'mandating departments and agencies to introduce such schemes'. In health and local government, in contrast, where the government's influence is less direct, 'the take-up was much lower'. A rather different interpretation of centre-local patterns can be found in the literature on political devolution. Here, it is suggested that the new constitutional settlement has led to differentiation in public policy affecting employment relations, as national governments in Scotland

and in Wales have pursued a course distinct from that of Westminster. According to Samuel and Bacon (2015), writing particularly about Scotland, devolved government has attempted to develop a broadly social democratic policy, emphasizing social partnership, which accords with the collectivist component of the good employer tradition in public services and which contrasts sharply with the anti-collectivist stance adopted at UK level.

Another potential source of variation in public sector employment relations is the 'political contingency'. Long ago, in studies of state-owned firms, it was noted that businesses of this type were subject to intervention by politicians that directly shaped employment relations in a manner that was not experienced by their private sector counterparts, which primarily faced market and technological contingencies (Batstone et al. 1984; Ferner 1988). What this argument suggests is that public service employment relations will be shaped by the choices of politicians and that variation in practice will in part be determined by political ideology. Political parties, like the SNP in Scotland, will favour certain types of intervention in the field of employment relations, leading to a situation in which important features of management practice follow the contours of political control.

In what follows, we use the case of Living Wage accreditation in the public sector to examine these arguments about the good employer tradition. It seems to us that the Living Wage is an appropriate indicator of the persistence of the latter. The standard is actively marketed to employers as a badge of good employment practice, it involves going beyond the legal minimum, and the main beneficiaries are holders of low-wage jobs who are often women and members of minority groups. Moreover, while adoption of the Living Wage does not require the reversal of outsourcing, it does seek to protect low-wage workers from the negative effects of 'subcontracted capitalism'. Finally, although the Living Wage standard itself has no requirement for trade union involvement, in public services, as we have seen, it has often been subject to negotiation and joint consultation and its adoption can reinforce the collectivist element in the good employer commitment. In the remainder of this section, we first establish whether the incidence of Living Wage adoption is higher in the public sector than in other parts of the economy, as one would expect if the good employer tradition remains viable. We also consider how austerity has shaped both the level and form of Living Wage adoption in the public sector. We then go on to examine the pattern of Living Wage accreditation within the public sector to test arguments about variation in good employment practice. Specifically, we explore whether the Living Wage is found particularly in central or more peripheral state institutions, in areas of devolved government, and—in local government—in councils that are led by left or centre-left governing parties. Although the Living Wage campaign is formally apolitical, we want to test whether local authorities of a social democratic stamp (i.e. more sympathetic to state intervention and likely to espouse redistributive policies) are more receptive to the campaign's message and therefore more likely to become accredited Living Wage Employers.

Level of Living Wage Accreditation

Central to the good employer argument is a claim about the *relative* behaviour of employers in the public sector; that they are more likely than other employers to adopt benign employment practices that provide decent work for their employees. It is this claim that is tested here. We examine whether public sector employers are more likely to adopt the Living Wage than employers in the private and not-for-profit sectors, as one would expect if the good employer commitment continues to operate.

In the eleven years to May 2022, 418 public sector organizations were accredited as Living Wage Employers, 5.5 per cent of the total number of public sector organizations in the economy. In the same period, 8,080 private businesses and 3,708 not-for-profit organizations joined the scheme, while the rates of accreditation across the private and not-for-profit sectors were 0.6 and 6.8 per cent, respectively. The pattern of Living Wage accreditation therefore provides evidence of a continuing good employer commitment in the public sector when the point of comparison is the private sector. Public sector employers have been much more likely than their private sector counterparts to adopt the Living Wage. They have been marginally less likely to adopt the standard than their counterparts in the not-for-profit sector, however, and the evidence suggests that the key dividing line is between the private sector and the other two main branches of the economy. As far as the Living Wage is concerned, both public sector and not-for-profit employers exhibit a good employer commitment.

Accreditation of Living Wage Employers began in 2011, shortly after the global financial crisis, and for most of this period public sector organizations have been faced with austerity, real cuts to budgets as central government pursued a policy of reducing the deficit. Adoption of the Living Wage has occurred in the public sector notwithstanding these pressures and attests both to the strength of the good employer commitment and its survival through the period of austerity. However, austerity has undoubtedly made adopting the Living Wage a challenging decision for many public sector organizations. When Cardiff Council became accredited in October 2015, over 2,000 workers received a pay increase and the city's wage bill increased by £1M at a time when other expenditure was being reined back, 'a big political commitment' [local authority manager].

While austerity has not prevented the spread of the Living Wage in the public sector, it has affected both the level and pattern of take-up. For some, the cost has proved prohibitive, and at a time of cuts the priority has been to maintain service at as high a level as possible rather than to protect wages. A representative of a regional employers' organization in local government, explaining why few of her member employers had become accredited, questioned 'Whether that's [the Living Wage] the best way to help people in general', and went on to say 'People forget as well that with local authorities, their whole *raison d'etre* is to deliver services to vulnerable people, a lot of them'. It was also noticeable that in some parts of the public sector, Living Wage accreditation was concentrated in smaller organizations with relatively few low-paid employees, whilst larger organizations likely to experience a significant increase in labour costs had remained aloof. Thus, in the police service the offices of twelve police and crime commissioners have become accredited in England and Wales but only ten police forces have done so. Another common form of adaptation in the public sector has been to introduce the Living Wage for direct employees but to stop short of including contractors and seeking accreditation. Living Wage campaigners in Dundee reported that while their local health board paid the Living Wage to its own employees, it had declined the invitation to become accredited because to do so would increase the cost of contracted services at a time when it was struggling with a 'huge deficit'. As we will see below, this kind of partial adoption of the Living Wage has also been a significant feature in local government. Even when public sector organizations have become accredited, they have often delayed the extension of the Living Wage to contract workers to spread out the increased cost over several years. Lewisham Council was one of the first London Boroughs to adopt the Living Wage, becoming accredited in 2012, but it was only in 2019 that the scheme was fully extended to social care workers, providing services under contract (see also Johnson 2017). Austerity has not prevented the good employer commitment from leading public sector organizations to adopt the Living Wage, but it has reduced its spread, induced caution in larger organizations where costs are likely to be significant, and led to partial and phased adoption.

Industry Differences within the Public Sector

Public sector organizations are more likely than their private sector counterparts to adopt the Living Wage, but what about variation within the public sector? Table 6.1 shows the pattern of accreditation across the main branches of the public sector: central government, local government, health, and police and fire. The table indicates that local government has seen the largest concentration of Living Wage accreditation, with a quarter of principal authorities signing up. In addition, fifty town and parish councils (not included in the table) have become accredited Living Wage Employers, four in Wales and the remainder in England. Several functional bodies, established by or accountable to local authorities, have also become accredited, including Transport for London and Transport for the North.

Table 6.1 Living Wage accreditation across the main branches of the public sector, Great Britain

	Central government[1]			Local government[2]			Health[3]			Police and Fire[4]		
	N	% LWEs[5]	% in category	N	% LWEs	% in category	N	% LWEs	% in category	N	% LWEs	% in category
UK/England	20	22	5	72	74	21	25	76	7	23	79	18
Scotland	57	64	58	23	23	72	7	21	30	2	7	100
Wales	13	14	30	3	3	14	1	3	6	4	14	40
All	90	100	17	98	100	25	33	100	8	29	100	21

1. Central Government comprises the legislatures, ministries, agencies, corporations, and other bodies that form the UK state and devolved governments of Scotland and Wales. There are 517 central government employers, 375 at UK level, ninety-nine in Scotland, and forty-three in Wales.
2. Local government comprises the principal regional and local authorities of England, Scotland, and Wales, including county councils, shire districts, metropolitan boroughs, London boroughs, unitary authorities, and combined regional authorities (N = 397).
3. Health comprises the organizations which make up NHS England, NHS Scotland, and NHS Wales (N = 412). In England, these organizations include NHS Trusts of various types and Clinical Commissioning Groups. In the devolved nations, they include regional health boards and specialist NHS services.
4. In England and Wales these services consist of regional police and fire and rescue forces and the offices of elected police and crime commissioners. In Scotland, Police Scotland and the Scottish Fire and Rescue Service cover the entire country (Total N = 140).
5. All accredited Living Wage Employers that have joined the scheme since its inception in 2011; i.e. the figures include employers that are no longer part of the scheme.

The pre-eminence of local government indicates that adoption of the Living Wage has not followed a centre-local pattern but rather that change has been concentrated amongst the more peripheral institutions of government. The evidence for central government further reinforces this view. Central government employers that have adopted the Living Wage are concentrated in Scotland and Wales, where both governments, other state institutions, and public corporations have become accredited. In England, in contrast, only one ministry has become accredited, the now-defunct Department of Energy and Climate Change, which joined the scheme under the Coalition Government when the Liberal politician, Ed Davey, was energy minister. Other UK government organizations that have signed up are non-departmental bodies that discharge activities at arm's length from ministers and possess considerable operational autonomy. They include a cluster of cultural organizations—the Arts Council for England, British Council, British Library, National Gallery, and National Portrait Gallery—as well as the Crown Estate and the National Lottery Community Fund. These institutions also occupy peripheral positions within the UK state-system, and it is this relative distance from government that has allowed them to adopt the Living Wage.

Another finding displayed in Table 6.1 is the existence of distinct national patterns of Living Wage accreditation in the three countries of Great Britain. In England the pattern is one of minimal support for the Living Wage in central government, balanced by stronger-take-up in local government and in regional police and fire services. This weak centre/stronger-periphery pattern flows from the opposition of the Conservative Government to Living Wage accreditation in the public sector, probably because endorsing the standard would be an admission that the statutory National Living Wage is not sufficient to support a decent standard of living. There have been repeated attempts to persuade government ministries to adopt the Living Wage for cleaners and other outsourced support staff from both Living Wage campaigners and trade unions, but to date these have not been successful. Faced with obduracy at the centre, the campaign has concentrated on more peripheral government institutions, bringing a substantial number of these within the Living Wage fold.

In Wales, the pattern is the reverse of that seen in England. There has been quite strong adoption of the Living Wage amongst the core institutions of the Welsh Government, but in health and local government take-up has been less extensive. In Welsh local government only two authorities, Cardiff and Bridgend, are currently accredited Living Wage Employers (Caerphilly was also accredited for a short period of time but is no longer), and in NHS Wales, Cardiff and Vale University Health Board is the only major employer to have joined the scheme, though several general practitioners have done so. Until recently there was also only a single Welsh police organization accredited—the South Wales Police and Crime Commissioner—but in late 2021 and early 2022 South Wales Police Force, North Wales Police, and Heddlu Dyfed-Powys also joined. In the Welsh public sector, Living Wage accreditation has assumed a strong-centre/weak-periphery pattern.

In Scotland, a third pattern is visible characterized by both strong central and strong peripheral support for the Living Wage. More than half of Scottish central government employers are accredited, and there is also majority support in local government. The entire Scottish police and fire services are covered by the Living Wage, and while there is lower support in the National Health Service, four regional health boards have joined the scheme. Given that both Scottish and Welsh Governments have sought to promote the Living Wage, why is it that the standard has spread further within the Scottish public sector? One likely explanation is administrative: the Scottish Government took action to promote the Living Wage earlier than its Welsh counterparts and has put in place stronger operational supports, including subsidizing the Living Wage campaign itself and funding payment of the rate in local authority-provided care services (Cunningham et al. 2018). Another likely explanation is party-political. At a local authority in Scotland, we were told that the council was accredited as a Living Wage Employer because 'It's an SNP city'. The SNP has identified strongly with the Living Wage at all levels of government in a way that is not apparent within the Welsh Labour Party. The SNP has served as an integrating force across Scottish public services, pushing for Living Wage accreditation, essentially as part of its mission to position itself as party of the centre-left.

A final pattern visible in Table 6.1 is that the highest rates of Living Wage accreditation are found in parts of the public sector where there is an elected leadership and where politicians can most directly shape employment practice. All four main legislative bodies in Great Britain are Living Wage Employers: the House of Commons, the House of Lords, the Scottish Parliament, and Y Senedd Cymru. As we have seen, regional and local government and the central governments of the devolved nations have relatively high rates of accreditation and are subject to elected political control. This pattern is also true of the police service, where the largest group of accredited organizations are those controlled by elected police and crime commissioners. In other parts of the police service, in fire, and in health, where political control is more attenuated, there has been lower take-up of the Living Wage. This pattern suggests that the 'political contingency' continues to hold sway within public sector employment and that elected politicians continue to exert influence over management practice. It is to a fuller analysis of the political contingency in the specific sphere of local government that we now turn.

Political Contingency

The Living Wage campaign is apolitical and has sought support from across the political spectrum. This backing has been forthcoming from most mainstream political parties. One indicator of this backing is that several political parties have themselves become accredited as Living Wage Employers, part of a broader trend for representative institutions to provide support for the campaign. The Co-operative Party, the Green Party, the Labour Party, the Liberal Democrats and Scottish Liberal Democrats, Plaid Cymru, and the Scottish National Party (SNP) are all accredited Living Wage Employers. The Conservative Party is absent from this list and has not adopted a formal position of support for the Living Wage. However, individual Conservative politicians have provided backing; Boris Johnson was a strong advocate whilst London Mayor and several Conservative politicians have given support to the Living Wage in Social Care campaign. This broad range of support suggests that adoption of the Living Wage in the public sector will occur in a range of political contexts, with political leaders from across the spectrum adopting the standard. An alternative view, however, has been expressed by Bacon and Samuel (2017), who have noted that political devolution has provided an opportunity for parties of the centre-left to develop alternative employment policies to those pursued by the Conservative Government at UK-level. They note the adoption of distinctive social democratic policies in Scotland and Wales, which over time could lead to growing divergence in employment practice across the separate nations of the UK. This divergence, they make clear, emerges from different political ideologies, and reflects differences in party control of elected governments. If this contrary view is accepted, then one would expect the Living Wage to be adopted by public sector organizations where political control is invested in parties of the left.

Our evidence so far has provided support for the second of these two propositions, in that SNP-led Scotland and Labour-led Wales have been more receptive to the Living Wage than the Conservative-controlled UK government. In this section we consider further evidence, drawn from local government across Great Britain (i.e. Northern Ireland is not included), to examine if this relationship between Living Wage accreditation and political control continues to apply at a lower level of elected government. The evidence itself is drawn from the dataset of local authorities. The dataset contains information on all 397 regional and local councils in England, Scotland, and Wales, including information on both their policy on the Living Wage and their political composition. Policy on the Living Wage comprises three types of response. The first is to become accredited as a Living Wage Employer and to pay the Living Wage to all direct employees and to employees of contractors located on council premises. This first response, of accreditation, has been adopted by ninety-seven regional and local authorities (twenty-four per cent).

The second response has been to adopt a policy of paying the Living Wage but not to become accredited, which has been adopted by 145 authorities (thirty-seven per cent). In cases of this kind, the positive commitment is usually recorded in the annual Pay Policy Statement that all local authorities are obliged to complete, and which includes a description of pay arrangements for the 'lowest-paid employee'. In most of these authorities the rate has not been extended to outsourced workers, but this is not always the case. Several local authorities that have not been accredited as Living Wage Employers, such as Nottingham, Knowsley, and Cumbria, have signed up to UNISON's Ethical Care Charter, which requires extending the Living Wage to those delivering home care. The rationale for adopting the Living Wage in these authorities is shared with many of their accredited counterparts and accords directly with the good employer tradition. In explaining their decision, authorities have often declared that they are committed to acting as both good and model employers:

> The Council prides itself on being a good employer. Work should pay and introducing this policy will help our lowest paid workers. [West Lancashire]

> The Council is a major employer in the area and, as such, must have regard to its role in improving the economic well-being of the people of Anglesey. The availability of good quality employment on reasonable terms and conditions and fair rates of pay has a beneficial impact on the quality of life in the community as well as on the local economy. The Council also has a role in setting a benchmark example on pay and conditions to other employers in the area for the same reasons. [Anglesey/Ynys Môn]

> The Council is committed to being a good employer and as part of this pays our lowest earners at the highest affordable hourly rate. [Bolton]

The final response has been to not adopt the Living Wage as council policy either in its accredited or in its non-accredited form. Local authorities in this category have often paid a proportion of their direct employees below the Living Wage rate and have not considered or have deliberately rejected the extension of the standard to contract employees. In some cases, though, direct employees have been paid above the Living Wage rate, possibly because the council is located in an area with a high prevailing wage and has experienced market pressure to pay higher rates. In at least some years, moreover, many councils in this category will have paid the Living Wage to direct employees because the lowest collectively bargained rate has been set at this level. It remains though that these non-adopting councils have given no formal undertaking to commit to the Living Wage standard. This third response of non-adoption of the Living Wage was found in 155 local authorities (thirty-nine per cent), indicating that the strength of commitment to the 'good employer' tradition in local government is variable.

Table 6.2 shows the pattern of Living Wage accreditation and adoption in local government broken down by the political control of authorities and provides support for both possibilities outlined above. The first, that there will be take-up across the political spectrum, is supported in that councils led by all the main political parties and by independents have both become accredited Living Wage Employers and have adopted a policy of paying the Living Wage. The apolitical nature

Table 6.2 Support for the Living Wage in local and regional government by political control

	Political control[1]				
	Conservative N = 174	Labour N = 139	Liberal N = 44	Nationalist[2] N = 18	Other[3] N = 22
No LW policy	67.2	12.9	29.5	0.0	31.8
Policy to pay LW but not accredited	27.6	42.4	50.0	38.9	40.9
LW accredited	5.2	44.6	20.5	61.1	27.3
Total	100	100	100	100	100

1. Political control combines cases where political parties have formed both majority and minority administrations; data on political control are taken from 2020.
2. Nationalist councils include those in which either the Scottish National Party or Plaid Cymru are in control
3. Other councils comprise 21 councils led by independents and Lewes council, in which the Green Party is in minority control in alliance with Liberals, Labour, and independents

of the Living Wage campaign and the fact that it has won cross-party backing is evidenced in the table.

There is also evidence for the second position, however, that parties of the left will be most receptive. Labour and the nationalist parties in Wales and Scotland emerge from the table as the strongest backers, with well over eighty per cent of councils controlled by these parties either adopting the Living Wage or becoming accredited. The association between Living Wage adoption and social democracy, suggested by Bacon and Samuel, is apparent in the data. It is also notable though that there has been a positive response to the campaign from the Liberals and from authorities controlled by independents, with about seventy per cent of councils controlled by these two groups providing tangible support for the Living Wage. The sharpest division recorded in the table, indeed, is that between the response of all other parties and that of the Conservatives. Conservative-led councils have clearly provided least backing, with a majority failing to adopt a position in favour of paying the Living Wage. The table attests to the fact that political choices matter and shape management practice in the public sector; that the 'political contingency' continues to operate and underpins the degree of commitment to the good employer tradition. Amongst councils led by political parties which have declared support for the Living Wage by themselves becoming accredited, eighty-four per cent have adopted the Living Wage. Amongst councils led by parties or politicians which have not declared support in this way, the figure drops to thirty-seven per cent.

Further evidence of party politics influencing take-up of the Living Wage was collected through our analysis of local authority websites. The latter yielded cases of party division over Living Wage adoption, with incumbent and opposition parties articulating different positions. Much of this evidence showed a conventional left-right split, with Labour supporting the Living Wage and Conservatives opposing. In Bromsgrove District Council, for example, a Labour motion calling for 'at least the living wage' to be paid to all employees of 'contractors, agencies, and organizations doing work' for the council was voted down by the leading Conservative group in 2020, while a year earlier the Labour group within Oxfordshire County Council attempted to persuade the Conservative leadership to adopt the Living Wage with an identical lack of success. The website analysis also identified cases of local authorities changing their policy on the Living Wage when there was a change of political control, which also followed this left-right pattern. When Labour lost control of Derbyshire County Council to the Conservatives in 2017, the Living Wage ceased to be guaranteed to the lowest earning employees in the county's schools, but when Labour gained control of Scarborough Borough Council from the Conservatives in 2019, it was announced that the authority would seek Living Wage accreditation (see also Prowse and Fells 2016b).

However, not all political division over the Living Wage has followed this left-right pattern. In the London Borough of Sutton, the Liberal-controlled council introduced the London Living Wage for direct employees under combined pressure from Labour and Conservatives, while Liberal Bath and North-East Somerset has been urged by the Labour opposition to extend the Living Wage to employees of contractors, while Conservatives have called for the council to introduce a higher Living Wage for its own staff. Calls for a higher, local Living Wage to reflect the high cost of accommodation have also been made in Cambridge but this time by the Liberals, targeting a Labour-controlled council. What these cases suggest is that the Living Wage has become the subject of competition between parties, with politicians calling variously for its introduction, extension, or for more generous local variants as part of their ongoing interaction with rivals. The dominant pattern is for support for the Living Wage to be distributed on a left-right axis, but this distribution is by no means fixed, and politicians from a range of parties have provided backing for the Living Wage, reflecting local circumstances and in order to secure local political advantage.

A final piece of evidence demonstrating the importance of the political contingency for the spread of the Living Wage is the very high take-up of the standard in authorities with a directly elected mayor. Directly elected mayors are a relatively recent phenomenon in British local government and are confined to only a small number of regional and local authorities. Of the twenty-four authorities which do elect mayors, twenty-three are either accredited Living Wage Employers or are committed to paying the Living Wage. The majority of elected mayors from these authorities are from the Labour Party, including London's Sadiq Kahn, Greater Manchester's Andy Burnham, and Sheffield City-Region's Oliver Coppard, plus the Labour mayors of Bristol, Liverpool, and Newham. Other elected mayors that have backed the Living Wage, however, come from other parties, such as Andy Street, the Conservative Mayor of the West Midlands City-Region, the Liberal mayors of Bedford and Watford, and Lutfur Rahman, the Aspire mayor of Tower Hamlets. In most of these cases, mayors have strongly endorsed the Living Wage and have promoted it within their areas of jurisdiction; for several it has been a signature policy. The high take-up of the Living Wage by directly elected mayors, and indeed by directly elected police and crime commissioners referred to above, suggests that it has been espoused because it is an issue that resonates with voters. On a global scale since the 1990s, minimum and living wages have proved popular with electorates and have been advocated by politicians in a wide range of jurisdictions (Cominetti 2019; Manning 2014). The support for the Living Wage of directly elected mayors in the UK is a small, local example of this wider trend.

Living Wage Promotion by Public Sector Organizations

In this section we turn from the adoption of the Living Wage by public sector organization to their attempts to promote the standard to other employers. Public authorities can shape employment practice in their areas of jurisdiction in a variety of ways. They are often major employers in their own right, but they can also use their economic power as funders and as purchasers to shape the employment practices of other organizations, fiscal instruments can be used to incentivize use of particular management techniques, and as legislators and regulators public authorities can require employers to adopt desirable labour standards (Hyman 2008). In addition, public authorities have the power to influence by promoting, endorsing, publicizing, and recognizing the kinds of employment practice they want to see. As we will see, what is striking about the actions of public authorities to promote the Living Wage is the broad range of methods that have been used.

In what follows, we present information on the activities of the devolved governments of Scotland and Wales and of regional and local government to encourage employers to adopt the Living Wage. A range of documentary and interview sources are drawn upon for this analysis, and for regional and local government we also make use of the local authority dataset. The latter is used to measure the extent and nature of local government efforts to promote the Living Wage and to gauge the effectiveness of this activity in spreading the standard. Living Wage campaigners have often regarded public authorities as 'anchor institutions' whose support is vital in spreading the Living Wage, and our purpose is to gauge the validity of this description in the case of regional and local government (Hull 2019). Before entering an examination of specific policies, however, it is important to provide some context and describe the broader commitment to 'fair work', of which attempts to promote the Living Wage form a part.

Fair Work

Support for the Living Wage among public authorities has typically emerged from a more general determination to improve the quality of jobs and reverse the trend towards precarious and low-paid employment, which is commonly said to define the labour market in the period since the financial crisis (Sisson 2020). This determination has found expression at UK level in the government's commissioning of the Taylor Review of Modern Working Practices (Taylor et al. 2017). Preparedness to take action has been stronger at other levels of government, however, with the Scottish and Welsh devolved governments and combined regional authorities in England being particularly keen to advance a fair work agenda.

The Scottish Government has established a Fair Work Convention to formulate advice and conduct research to support the Government's intention of making fair work a defining feature of the Scottish economy by 2025. The first task performed by the Convention was the formulation of a Fair Work Framework, comprising a set of five principles, the application of which are believed to underpin good quality employment. These five principles are effective voice, opportunity, security, fulfilment, and respect. In elaborating these principles, the Convention declared that an important guarantee of security is 'paying the Living Wage (as established by the Living Wage Foundation)' (Fair Work Convention 2016: 15). The Convention continues to function as a standing body formulating advice on specific issues or for specific industries, such as social care (Fair Work Convention 2019). In addition, the Fair Work Framework, together with its attendant commitment to the Living Wage, has been incorporated into other areas of Scottish Government policy, including the Government's labour market strategy and its guidance on public sector procurement (Scottish Government 2016b; 2018a). The percentage of Scottish employees being paid at or above the Living Wage is one of Scotland's National Indicators within the National Performance Framework (Scottish Government 2018a).

In Wales, developments have followed a broadly similar path. In 2017, the then First Minister, Carwyn Jones, declared to the Welsh Labour Party conference that 'I want to make Wales a Fair Work Nation', and this declaration was followed first by the creation of a tripartite Fair Work Board and then by the establishment of an independent Fair Work Commission. The Commission reported in March 2019 and produced both a definition of fair work and a long series of policy recommendations. The definition stated that 'the Welsh Living Wage (equating to the Real Living Wage) [should provide] the *minimum* wage floor for all working hours', while policy recommendations included the adoption of the Living

Wage by the Agricultural Advisory Panel, which sets minimum wage rates in Welsh agriculture, and tracking the percentage of the Welsh workforce receiving the Living Wage over time (Fair Work Commission 2019).The Welsh Government fully accepted the Commission's report and has subsequently created a Social Partnership and Fair Work Directorate within the Office of the First Minister to oversee the implementation of recommendations.

Within England, similar initiatives have been launched at regional level. The Greater London Authority (GLA) has developed a Good Work Standard for London employers, a 'set of best employment practices' covering 'fair pay and conditions', 'workplace wellbeing', 'skills and progression', and 'diversity and recruitment'. Payment of the London Living Wage, including its payment to interns and apprentices, is one of these best employment practices. The Greater Manchester Combined Authority (GMCA) has developed an equivalent 'good employment' initiative, which embraces secure employment, flexible employment, employee engagement and voice, recruitment, and well-being. Payment of the Living Wage is again part of this list of desirable practices. A notable feature of developments in London and Manchester, and indeed of those in Scotland and Wales, is that fair or good work is promoted as economically beneficial, with the rationale for policy referencing the UK's poor productivity record as well as a decline in job quality. Public authorities have promoted fair work, including the Living Wage, with reference to a 'business case' in precisely the same manner as the Living Wage Foundation has done.

Promoting Fair Work

In the USA the living wage has often been introduced through local ordinances, citywide laws that require public contractors to pay the rate (Luce 2017). In the UK, legislative action of this kind is not possible. Employment law is a matter reserved to the UK Government, and even the devolved parliaments of Scotland and Wales have no power to legislate on the Living Wage, outside the specific sphere of agriculture where there is a devolved power to establish wage-setting machinery. In seeking to promote the Living Wage therefore the Scottish and Welsh Governments, English regional councils, and local authorities have had to rely upon alternative levers, making use of soft regulation, economic incentives, subsidy, and other forms of influence to encourage employers to adopt the standard. In what follows, we identify the range of methods that have been used across these different levels of government, mapping the full range of non-legislative actions that public authorities can take to intervene in the employment relationship and shape employer behaviour.

Employment Charters. One way in which public authorities have sought to promote the Living Wage is by including it alongside other employment standards in a charter which employers can adopt voluntarily. Initiatives of this kind exemplify a broad trend on the part of both states and intergovernmental bodies to rely upon soft regulation (Deakin et al. 2012; Kinderman 2016). They also give tangible form to the commitments to promote 'fair' or 'good' work noted above. The governments of Scotland and Wales have both gone down this route. The Scottish Business Pledge was launched by First Minister Nicola Sturgeon at Tynecastle Stadium, the home of Hearts football club, in May 2015. The Pledge consists of ten actions to which participating businesses are asked to commit. Three of these commitments are required of all who participate, while member businesses must give an undertaking to make progress on five of the remaining issues. The three 'core Pledge elements' are payment of the Real Living Wage, no inappropriate use of zero-hour contracts, and action to address the gender pay gap. The other elements include action to promote employee engagement and development, as well as non-employment items, such as action to support local communities or to reduce environmental impact. The Welsh equivalent of the Pledge is the Code of Practice on Ethical Employment in Supply Chains, released by the Welsh Government in 2017. Unlike the Scottish Business Pledge, the Welsh Code is targeted primarily at public sector organizations, all of which are expected to adopt the Code while other employers are encouraged to apply it. The Code itself emerged from the Government's policy on Modern Slavery (Welsh Government 2017a) and deals with several employment issues, including modern slavery and human rights abuses, blacklisting, false self-employment, and unfair use of umbrella schemes and zero-hours contracts. It also encourages signatories to 'consider paying all staff the Living Wage Foundation's Living Wage as a minimum and [to] encourage ... suppliers to do the same'. The Code does not require but asks employers to consider Living Wage accreditation. The GLA and GMCA have also issued charters, which in both cases have different levels of compliance, allowing businesses to adopt basic, core standards before proceeding onwards to adopt the full set of defined best practices. In each charter the Living Wage is a component, with encouragement to seek accreditation by the Living Wage Foundation. Other public authorities which have developed employment charters that incorporate the Living Wage include the Liverpool City Region Combined Authority, North of Tyne Combined Authority, the London Borough of Croydon, and Salford City Council.

Procurement. A second way in which public authorities have attempted to promote the Living Wage is through their procurement policies; by factoring payment of the Living Wage into purchasing decisions they have sought to provide an economic incentive to suppliers to adopt the standard. There are limits to the capacity of public authorities to act in this way under competition law, and payment of the Living Wage cannot be mandatory for public contractors. The law has become more accommodating towards the inclusion of social value considerations in public procurement, however, and it is legitimate for public authorities both to inquire of suppliers whether they pay the Living Wage and to take this information into account when awarding contracts (Barnard 2017). Reflecting this changed legal context, both the Scottish and Welsh Governments have not only incorporated the Living Wage into their own procurement policies, but have encouraged other public authorities to do so. Through the Procurement Reform (Scotland) Act 2014, the Scottish Government has required all public authorities engaged in procurement to develop a formal strategy and has imposed a 'sustainable procurement duty', which obliges them to embed fair work in their procurement activity (Scottish Government 2016a). These steps have been echoed in Wales, and in 2019 the Welsh Government proposed legislation that would require designated public bodies to adopt a procurement strategy that embraces the pursuit of fair work (Welsh Government 2019). A Social Partnership and Public Procurement (Wales) Bill was subsequently published in June 2022. Both devolved governments have also issued specific guidance to public sector organizations on how to incorporate the Living Wage within public procurement (Scottish Government 2018a; Welsh Government 2017b). In regional and local government, the Living Wage has been identified as a factor to be taken into account in awarding contracts by a growing number of authorities. Cardiff Council's Socially Responsible Procurement Policy, for example, states that the council's procurement strategy is increasingly focused on delivering 'community benefits' through 'the promotion of fair working practices, including payment of the Living Wage'. In some cases, procurement policies of this kind are linked explicitly to employment charters, with adherence to charter standards being considered in procurement decisions. At GMCA, it was explained that 'charter membership would increase the chances of success in procurement for suppliers' [employer interview 2019].

Funding. Public authorities cannot just exert economic influence through procurement; they are also funders of economic activity, disbursing grants and providing investment to a broad range of private and not-for-profit organizations. Funding of this kind has also been used as a lever to promote the Living Wage. In 2019 the Scottish Government adopted a new Fair Work First policy which seeks to use the Government's 'financial power to make fair work the norm'. The aim of the policy is to extend fair work criteria 'to every type of grant, funding stream, and business support budget', using the funds allocated to business through Scottish Enterprise and other agencies to leverage fair work (Scottish Government 2021). The latter includes payment of the Living Wage. The Welsh Government has followed a similar course, though to date its policy is less advanced. An important element of this policy is the Economic Contract, a new framework to govern Welsh Government's relationship with business, which strives to link financial support to responsible business activity, including fair work. It has been suggested that an obligation to pay the Living Wage should become a specific component of the Economic Contract, with grants from the government's Economic Futures Fund being conditional on businesses adopting the standard. The Welsh Government has also used its funding of specific industries to encourage Living Wage accreditation. Reform of the funding regime for Welsh higher education has been tied to adoption of the Living Wage, for example, with the consequence that all of Wales's eight universities are now accredited Living Wage Employers. In local government the most visible way in which authorities have sought to use their funding power to promote the Living Wage is through individual councils becoming accredited Living Wage Funders (See Chapter 2). Councils that have taken this step include Birmingham City Council, the City of London Corporation, and the London boroughs of Brent, Croydon, Islington, Lambeth, and Southwark, all of which have committed to funding the Living Wage in grants given to charities.

Subsidy. Another way in which public authorities can use their economic power to promote the Living Wage is by providing subsidies to Living Wage Employers. Cardiff Council, for example, has introduced a scheme under which it covers the cost of accreditation for small and medium-sized enterprises in the city when they adopt the Living Wage. Other local authorities, including Sheffield, Brent, Ealing, Lambeth, and Lewisham, have introduced business rate relief for accredited Living Wage Employers. The most ambitious subsidy, however, has been introduced by the Scottish Government. In 2016 the Scottish Government announced that it would underwrite payment of the Living Wage to all front-line workers delivering adult social care on publicly funded contracts. The commitment to fund the Living Wage in adult social care 'has led to sums of public money being transferred to external providers through re-negotiation of contract prices, fees (including fees agreed under the National Home Care Contract) and hourly rates for paid service delivery' (Cunningham et al. 2018: 8). This transfer of public money has gone from central government to local health and social care partnerships and thence to Scotland's thirty-two local authorities, which have incorporated the subsidy in their contracts with both private and not-for-profit care providers. More recently, the Scottish Government has established a similar scheme to subsidize payment of the Living Wage in publicly funded childcare. The precedent set by Scotland has provided leverage for Living Wage campaigners, who have sought to extend the social care subsidy to other parts of the UK. The most notable success of this campaign has been the formal commitment of the Welsh Government to establish a scheme to fund payment of the Living Wage to care workers over the course of the 2021–2026 Senedd (Welsh Government 2021). Attempts to persuade the UK Government to make an equivalent commitment for England are ongoing.

Ethical Care Charter. The Scottish Government's subsidy is directed specifically at social care. Another initiative targeted at this industry, which local authorities have used to promote the Living Wage, is the Ethical Care Charter (ECC). Like the general employment charters described above, the ECC contains different levels, and at the third and highest level signatory councils are expected to ensure the Living Wage is paid to all employees delivering home care, including those working on outsourced contracts (UNISON 2013). More than forty local authorities have signed up to the charter, along with several arm's length and not-for-profit commissioners of social care. There is no requirement for local authorities committing to the charter to become accredited Living Wage Employers or to require their suppliers to do so, but most signatory councils are accredited, and many have been active in encouraging other employers to sign up. It should also be noted that the ECC is a clear example of public authorities linking the issue of combatting low pay to another central component of the good employer model, a commitment to acting jointly with trade unions.

Living Wage Places. Another way in which public authorities have tried to promote the Living Wage is through the development of local Living Wage schemes, a line of action that exemplifies their potential to serve as anchor institutions. Local authorities have been at the heart of all initiatives under the Foundation's Living Wage Places scheme (see Chapter 2). Councils in Bristol, Cardiff, Dundee, Salford, and Southwark have taken the lead role in seeking Living Wage City accreditation and in formulating plans to spread the Living Wage amongst local employers (Living Wage Foundation 2019b). In Cardiff, for example, the Leader of the council chairs the Living Wage City Action Group, council officers have worked to implement the Action Plan, and the latter has targeted the city's 'southern arc' of wards characterized by social deprivation, which are the focus of the council's economic development strategy.

Several local authorities have also launched local Living Wage schemes outside the Foundation's programme. Some of these initiatives, indeed, pre-date the emergence of a national Living Wage standard and reflect the localized nature of the early Living Wage campaign. Councils which have their own Living Wage schemes, with their own systems of accreditation for employers, include Brighton and Hove, Cheshire West and Chester, Glasgow, Lincoln, and Oxford. Brighton and Hove's scheme is the product of a Living Wage Commission, set up by the council in 2011, and is operated by Brighton Chamber of Commerce: by mid-2020, 626 local employers had signed up. In some cases, as in Brighton, the council is itself a Living Wage Employer, but this is not always so and neither is there a requirement on the part of employers joining these schemes to seek accreditation. The Brighton Living Wage, for example, only obliges businesses to pay the Living Wage to their direct employees and so falls short of the Foundation's stipulation that employees of contractors must also be covered. In most of these schemes the local Living Wage is the same as the Foundation's Living Wage, though with a different label and logo, but this is not always the case: the Oxford Living Wage is higher than the Foundation's UK rate, reflecting the high cost of living in Oxford.

In certain respects, the Living Wage in Scotland resembles these local schemes. It is described as the Scottish Living Wage, and accreditation is handled by Living Wage Scotland, at arm's length from the campaign in the rest of the UK. The distinct nature of the Scottish campaign has allowed it to be infused with a patriotic register. Many quintessential Scottish companies, brands, and products have joined the scheme, including Scottish corporates, such as RBS and SSE, manufacturers of oat cakes and porridge oats, whisky distillers, and golf courses. A.G. Barr, the maker of Irn Bru, is an accredited Living Wage Employer. Active promotion of the Living Wage as a distinctively Scottish labour market standard reinforces the social democratic nationalism espoused by the SNP, which fuses the politics of redistribution with those of Scottish nationalism (Bacon and Samuel 2017; Jackson 2020). The Scottish Government's strong support for the Living Wage both flows from and seeks to reinforce this distinctive political project.

Campaign Support. A final way in which public authorities have promoted the Living Wage is by providing financial, operational, and moral support to the campaign itself. Again, the Scottish Government stands out in this regard. The main action the Scottish Government has taken to support the campaign has been to provide funding to the Poverty Alliance to host Living Wage Scotland, allowing the programme to recruit seven campaign workers by 2020. Funding has been accompanied by target-setting, and the Scottish Government has in certain respects provided direction to the Scottish Living Wage campaign. Early objectives were to secure initially 150, then 500, then 1,000 accredited Living Wage Employers in Scotland. Subsequently, targets have focused on the redistributive impact of the Living Wage. In the period 2017–2020, Living Wage Scotland was asked to increase the number of workers receiving a Living Wage pay increase by 25,000, to expand accreditation in low-wage sectors such as hospitality and tourism, and to launch a scheme for citywide Living Wage schemes (Scottish Government 2018b). As well as providing financial support, the Scottish Government has given operational assistance to the Living Wage campaign. Ministers and civil servants have facilitated contact directly with employers and with other government agencies that can assist with employer recruitment. A civil servant explained to us that she had contacted 'our enterprise agencies, Scottish Enterprise, Skills Development Scotland, the Funding Council, and asked them to encourage the organizations they support to think about becoming accredited Living Wage employers ... A lot of the work I do is trying to make introductions and looking for other networks to put Poverty Alliance in touch with when we've seen the gap'. Further support has taken the form of political backing. In Living Wage Week in 2018, for example, the First Minister publicly announced the new Living Wage rate and Scottish Government Ministers visited thirteen Living Wage Employers to recognize their commitment.

Similar political support has been forthcoming in Wales, and in 2022 the Welsh Government agreed to fund the employment of a Living Wage campaign worker by Cynnal Cymru. At lower levels of government, public authorities have also provided campaign support. It is common for local authorities to host and participate in campaign events during Living Wage Week, to provide information and web-links to the campaign, and, in some cases, to provide staffing: Cambridge, Dundee, and other councils have funded or appointed organizers to boost

Living Wage take-up in their localities. Integral to this effort has been the exertion of 'soft power' by political leaders. In Greater Manchester, for instance, it was explained that the Mayor brought together different interests to 'coproduce' the region's Good Employment Charter, with its Living Wage commitment, and had intervened personally to persuade key employers to sign up to the standard. His support was also vital for the accreditation of Greater Manchester as the first Living Wage City-Region in 2021. Other politicians have acted in the same way, serving as champions to promote the Living Wage in their communities. Boris Johnson's active role in promoting the Living Wage when he was Mayor of London was reported to us on several occasions. His activities included writing to all Premier League clubs in London to ask them to back the Living Wage, as well as direct contact with City firms and institutions. Another Conservative politician approvingly reported that Johnson had 'just rock and rolled up' at the offices of leading companies to pressure them to sign up.

Effects of Living Wage Promotion

Evidence presented above (see Table 6.1) indicates that the efforts of the Scottish Government to promote the Living Wage have been effective, spreading accreditation across much of the Scottish public sector. The evidence for Wales is less striking, but it is clear also that the promotion efforts of the Welsh Government have boosted Living Wage accreditation in central government and higher education. The dataset of local authorities allows us to examine whether the efforts of English regional authorities and local councils across England, Scotland, and Wales have generated equivalent effects.

To perform this examination, we first created a scale measuring the range of steps regional and local authorities have taken to promote the Living Wage. This scale was derived from ten dummy variables as follows: (1) A stated intention to promote the Living Wage to other employers; (2) A charter or set of employment standards that includes the Living Wage; (3) A Fairness Commission or equivalent inquiry that has recommended the Living Wage as a means of combatting in-work poverty in the local area (Bunyan and Diamond 2014; Lyall 2015); (4) A procurement or social value policy which mentions the Living Wage; (5) Living Wage Funder accreditation or other evidence of supporting the Living Wage through grant giving and investment; (6) Rate relief or a similar incentive for employers to adopt the Living Wage; (7) Living Wage Places accreditation or an equivalent plan to spread the Living Wage across the authority's employers; (8) An authority-specific Living Wage scheme, like that at Brighton and Hove; (9) Commitment to UNISON's Ethical Care Charter; (10) Other action to support the Living Wage campaign, such as hosting events in Living Wage Week or appointing officers to promote the Living Wage.

Table 6.3 Effects of attempts to promote the Living Wage by regional and local authorities

Promotion policies	Percentage of authorities (N = 397)	Percentage of LWEs (N = 20,487)[1]	Median LWEs per authority	Mean rate of accreditation[2]
0	63.7	26.3	12	14.94
1–2	15.4	13.2	21	24.27
3–4	13.9	22.0	46	43.94
5+	7.1	38.5	126	65.41
All	100	100	18	23.95

1. The number of LWEs from which these percentages are calculated is high because of double-counting, arising from the tiered nature of local and regional government in England; for example, the number of LWEs in the ten boroughs of Greater Manchester will also appear in the estimate for the Greater Manchester Combined Authority. Similarly, LWEs based in the shire districts of Surrey will also appear in the count for Surrey County Council.
2. The number of accredited Living Wage Employers and Service Providers with ten or more employees per thousand employers with at least ten employees registered in the authority area; differences in average rates of accreditation shown in the table are statistically significant at the 0.000 level.

Development of the scale indicated that promotion of the Living Wage is a minority preoccupation in local government. Of 397 elected authorities, only 144 (36.3 per cent) had taken steps to promote the Living Wage, and of these thirty-two had taken only a single step and sixty-one no more than two (see Table 6.3). There are local authorities which have been very active in promoting the Living Wage: Croydon has a promotion score of eight, while Birmingham, Islington, and Lewisham have scores of seven. These active promoters form only a small fraction of the totality of authorities, however, indicating that while some councils have acted as 'anchor institutions', most have not.

Another striking feature of the scale is that authorities with high promotion scores tend to be accredited Living Wage Employers themselves. There are some active promoters that are not accredited, including Glasgow, Leeds, and Luton, but those councils that have been most active in trying to spread the Living Wage have identified formally with the Living Wage movement. Accreditation, on this evidence, influences the response of employers to the Living Wage, drawing them into the campaign and encouraging them to act as anchors within their local communities. Other characteristics of active promoters are that they tend to be larger authorities, to be located in cities, in areas with a Citizens UK chapter, and to have a large percentage of councillors from left-of-centre parties. They are also significantly more likely to be London boroughs or Scottish unitary authorities and to have a directly elected mayor. The characteristics of local authorities that have encouraged them to adopt the Living Wage are also associated with active promotion of the standard.

Table 6.3 indicates that promotion policies may have been effective in boosting Living Wage accreditation. More than half of accredited employers are found in areas where the council has adopted three or more promotion policies, and the median number of accreditees per authority tracks the number of policies adopted. The key evidence in the table though is that showing the rate of accreditation, which shows that a stronger effort to promote the Living Wage is associated with higher take-up when controlling for the scale of the local economy. The table suggests that regional and local authorities which have promoted the Living Wage have acted as anchor institutions, serving to spread the standard within their local economies. It is important to note, however, that the table demonstrates that efforts to promote the Living Wage have been *relatively* effective. The *absolute* impact of these policies in many cases remains relatively modest, with less than ten per cent of employers signing up to the Living Wage in most authorities where it has been actively promoted. Efforts to promote the Living Wage have generated substantial effects, but they are yet to transform local labour markets, which continue to hold a substantial pool of low-wage employment even where public authorities have been most active in trying to push wages upwards.

Conclusion

This chapter has examined the response of public authorities to the Living Wage, following two lines of investigation. On the one hand we have examined the adoption of the Living Wage by public sector organizations, while on the other we have explored the attempts by public authorities to promote the standard to other employers. In short, we have used the issue of the Living Wage to establish whether public authorities in the UK continue to act as good employers and whether they have added to this traditional role that of anchor institution, seeking to shape employment practice within their supply chain and beyond. Our answer to both questions is affirmative.

With regard to the good employer commitment, public sector employers have a stronger propensity than their private sector equivalents to adopt the Living Wage and have introduced the standard often at substantial cost during a period of austerity. What also emerges from the analysis, however, is that not-for-profit organizations are even more likely to adopt the Living Wage than their public sector counterparts and also display the attributes of the good employer. The behavioural dividing line, on this evidence, runs between the private sector and the two wings of the non-private economy, not between the public sector and the rest.

The analysis of public sector employers also identified which types of organization are likely to adopt the Living Wage, using the latter to test several arguments in the literature on public sector employment relations. A central finding to emerge from this analysis is that the Living Wage has been adopted more readily in the outlying institutions of the British state, by the devolved governments of Scotland and Wales, regional authorities in England, and by local government: the diffusion of the standard has failed to follow a conventional centre-to-periphery pattern. The prominent part played by devolved national and regional authorities in adopting (and promoting) the standard points to the importance of recent constitutional change within the UK in shaping the pattern of employment relations and creating new spatial differences (Bacon and Samuel 2017). There has been a global 'unbundling' of the nation state in recent decades, with regional authorities being created or strengthened, and even the highly centralized UK has been a participant in this trend (Ayres et al. 2018). The changed structure of the state, in turn, has shaped diffusion of the Living Wage.

A second finding to emerge from the analysis of which public sector organizations have adopted the Living Wage is that politics matters. Adoption is more common amongst organizations with an elected leadership, and leaders of the political left, whether from the Labour Party or the SNP, are more likely to commit to the Living Wage. Politicians of other parties have adopted the standard on occasion, but the primary finding is that the good employer commitment is strongest when social democratic politicians hold office. This is an important finding, we feel, because in theories of the neo-liberal state, which are predominant in the field of employment relations, there is a tendency to downplay political explanations: all mainstream parties are presented as implicated in neo-liberal restructuring (Baccaro and Howell 2017). The evidence on the Living Wage suggests, in contrast, that social democratic parties remain committed to a politics of redistribution.

With regard to the question of promoting the Living Wage, our evidence shows that the Scottish and Welsh governments, English combined authorities, and a small but active minority of local authorities have encouraged others to adopt the Living Wage. None of these political authorities have the power to legislate directly on the Living Wage, and instead they have relied upon soft regulation and a range of economic and reputational incentives. There is growing interest in the use of public procurement to promote good labour standards, and public authorities have tried to use the power of purchase to encourage employers to implement the Living Wage (Barnard 2017). Indeed, the Scottish Government has placed a legal obligation on public sector employers to consider the Living Wage in procurement decisions, and the Welsh Government is planning to do something similar. What emerges from the research, however, is the broad range of other, non-legislative methods that have been used. Sub-national parts of government have intervened actively to promote the Living Wage, and this activism has encompassed a broad range of policy instruments.

In Chapter 1 it was stated that the literature on private regulation tends to view the role of the state in one of two ways. On the one hand, private regulation is often regarded as a functional equivalent to regulation through the state, emerging where states are weak or absent, while on the other there is a belief that private and state regulation can complement one another in some kind of 'smart mix'. The evidence on public authorities and the Living Wage supports this second position. The standard has been adopted and actively promoted by public authorities, and state action has boosted private regulation. A range of public authorities from across the UK have sponsored both the Living Wage campaign and Living Wage campaigners, helping to spread the standard across their areas of jurisdiction. The Scottish Government is the prime example of this kind of sponsorship, but it has also been seen in Wales, English regional authorities, local councils, and other public sector bodies. In all these cases public authorities have served as anchor institutions, helping to embed civil regulation, in the form of the Living Wage, in their local economies.

7

The Impact of the Real Living Wage

Introduction

In this final substantive chapter we present evidence on the effects of the Living Wage, considering three types of impact in turn. First, we examine the impact of the Living Wage on workers, seeking to assess the scale of its redistributive effect. To this end, we consider the number and characteristics of workers receiving a Living Wage pay increase, the value of the money transferred to these workers, and where they are found in the economy. We also consider whether the Living Wage has a downside for workers, through job loss or the reduction of other terms and conditions of employment, as employers seek to claw back the cost of higher wages. While advocates of the Living Wage have argued it is an effective means of lifting workers out of in-work poverty, particularly workers performing outsourced jobs in public services (Wills and Linneker 2013), others have questioned the effectiveness of private regulation and are deeply sceptical about its redistributive potential (LeBaron et al. 2022). In reviewing the evidence on the impact of the Living Wage on workers, we evaluate these competing claims.

Second, we examine the impact of the Living Wage on employers, using our survey and interview data to establish whether there is a business case for civil regulation. This evidence is used to identify the nature and scale of the positive impact on business and is also used to gauge whether there are significant negative effects, such as higher labour and outsourcing costs and disruption to internal pay structures from tying the wages of the lowest paid to an external standard. In carrying out this review, we have regard to the three positions on the impact of civil regulation on business outlined in our introduction: that external regulation can stimulate significant improvements in business functioning and operations; that regulation imposes an unsustainable burden on business; and that regulation is performance-neutral, generating effects that are often benign in themselves but which have few implications for the fundamentals of business performance. Once again, our evidence is marshalled to choose between these competing positions.

Third and last, we consider the wider effects of the Living Wage beyond the bounds of the employment relationship. Campaigners have promoted the Living Wage on the grounds that it can generate a broad set of positive economic and social impacts, including fostering greater family integration and improved health and well-being, facilitating community participation through reducing long working hours, and boosting social mobility (Naik et al. 2020; Searle and

The Real Living Wage. Edmund Heery, Deborah Hann and David Nash, Oxford University Press.
© Edmund Heery, Deborah Hann and David Nash (2023). DOI: 10.1093/oso/9780198835264.003.0007

McWha-Hermann 2021; Werner 2016). Critics of civil regulation, however, often express a very different viewpoint. Schemes like the Living Wage, it is argued, furnish the trappings of 'woke capitalism' and serve to legitimate a neo-liberal political and economic order (Rhodes 2022). It has also been argued, as we have seen, that civil regulation can forestall more effective ways of regulating the employment relationship, with business interests or conservative politicians promoting soft, private regulation as an alternative to hard regulation through law (Kinderman 2012, 2016). Industrial relations commentators have similarly expressed concern that voluntary standards, like the Living Wage, can act as a barrier to collective bargaining and reduce demand for union representation amongst employees (Elliot and Freeman 2005; Kuruvilla 2021). Our ability to use evidence to choose between these competing assessments of the wider effects of the Living Wage is limited, partly because they are intrinsically difficult questions to answer and partly because of the limits of the data we have been able to assemble. Nevertheless, we use what evidence we have to evaluate these broad claims, focusing particularly on the argument that civil regulation forestalls other, more effective forms of regulation where our evidence-base is strongest.

Impact on Employees

In this section we test competing arguments about the impact of the Living Wage on employees. The central claim of supporters of the Living Wage is that it is redistributive, an effective means of addressing the problem of in-work poverty and of raising the earnings of low-waged employees. Supporters have further argued that the Living Wage can exert an especially beneficial effect on low-paying industries, such as social care or industries providing outsourced services to the public sector and to large corporates (Wills 2009). In addition, they have argued that the campaign has been particularly effective in raising the earnings of those groups within the workforce who are found disproportionately in low-waged employment, such as women, part-time employees, migrant and ethnic minority workers, and young people (Living Wage Foundation 2017b).

The contrary argument is that voluntary regulation, like the Living Wage, is likely to be ineffective or generate only modest positive effects (Johnson et al. 2019). The primary basis for this claim is the belief that a voluntary scheme will mainly attract employers who are already largely compliant with the standard and who can accredit at minimal cost (Hoque 2003). If this belief is correct, then one would expect the aggregate impact of the Living Wage to be modest, most accrediting employers to report few or any employee beneficiaries, and for the pay uplift received by these employees to be limited. The pattern of impact one would anticipate if this argument is correct is one in which a limited number of low-wage workers, employed in high-wage locations, industries, and businesses, receive a modest pay increase. It might also be anticipated that those experiencing labour market disadvantage, such as women and minorities, will secure only modest gains from the Living Wage, while many employers will try to claw back the cost of higher wages through work intensification and cuts to jobs and working hours.

In choosing between these arguments, we draw upon our database of Living Wage Employers and our 2021 survey of accredited organizations. The former contains information on the number and types of employees who received a pay increase at the point at which their employer became accredited, and also contains information on the lowest rate of pay for each type of benefitting employee (part-time, full-time, direct, contract, UK and London-based) prior to accreditation. This last set of data allows us to produce estimates of the money value of the Living Wage to employees. These data are not perfect—they capture the number of employees and the value of the Living Wage at the point of entry to the scheme and not for subsequent years—but they provide a unique, quantitative source for assessing the impact of civil regulation. The survey data also contain useful information, of two main types. On the one hand, they contain information on the occupational and demographic characteristics of workers receiving a pay increase, allowing us to further explore which types of employee benefit from the Living Wage. On the other hand, they include employer reports of changes associated with Living Wage accreditation, such as workforce reduction, work intensification, and the withdrawal of other elements of remuneration, allowing us to test whether civil regulation generates perverse effects for those employees it is meant to benefit.

Measures of Redistribution

Our evidence allows us to measure the redistributive impact of the Living Wage at three separate levels. At an aggregate level we can assess the overall impact of the campaign since the launch of the accreditation scheme in 2011, by estimating both the number of workers who have received a Living Wage pay increase and the total wage transfer to these workers. At the level of the employer, we can assess the relative impact of accreditation by expressing the number of direct and indirect employees who have received a pay increase as a percentage of direct headcount at the point of accreditation. Finally, at the level of the individual employee we can calculate the percentage increase in hourly rate of pay for those receiving a Living Wage pay increase, again at the point of accreditation, averaged across different types of employees (i.e. full-time and part-time, direct and indirect, UK and London). For each of these three types of measure, moreover, we can produce breakdowns by organizational size, sector, and other contextual factors.

In the eleven years from May 2011 to May 2022, 12,168 accredited employers provided information on the number of employees who had received a pay increase, reporting in aggregate that 319,686 employees had done so. A further 560 employers failed to submit this information, but it is possible to estimate impact in these cases from data received from equivalent organizations that did provide a return. If these estimates are added, then the total number of benefitting employees rises to 337,602. Our cautious estimate of the wage transfer to these employees since the scheme began is just over £1.9bn.[1] These findings indicate that the Living Wage campaign has had a substantial redistributive effect, delivering a pay increase to many thousands of low-wage workers. This effect is particularly impressive given the modest resources of the Living Wage Foundation and its partners, consisting of a few dozen campaigners.

While the campaign has had a positive impact, it is important to set this against the scale of the problem of low pay in the UK economy. According to the Resolution Foundation (Cominetti et al. 2022), 4.5m jobs (seventeen per cent) were paid below the Living Wage in April 2021. The total number of workers receiving a Living Wage pay increase is just 7.4 per cent of this figure, suggesting that while a voluntary campaign can ameliorate the problem of low pay it cannot of its own provide a solution. Another way of assessing the impact of the scheme is to compare its reach with that of other methods for dealing with low pay. The Low Pay Commission (2020) estimates that in 2019, before the coronavirus pandemic, 1.89m employees in the UK aged 18 and over gained directly from the statutory minimum wage, the vast majority of whom (1.6m) received the National Living Wage. The number of workers benefitting from the Living Wage is eighteen per cent of this figure, proof of the greater reach of statutory regulation. What this suggests is that the Living Wage is best regarded as a supplement, and not an alternative, to hard regulation by the state.

Our second measure of redistribution captures the impact of the Living Wage at the level of the employer. It is calculated by dividing the number of workers reported to have received a Living Wage pay increase by workforce size at the point of accreditation. The distribution of this figure, showing the number and percentage of employers that have experienced low and high levels of impact, is presented in Table 7.1. The most striking finding in the table is the fact that in more than 4,500 cases there is no reported impact, with employers declaring that all workers were paid at or above the level of the Living Wage at the point they joined the scheme. In some cases, this may be because wage rates were increased ahead of accreditation. As reported in Chapter 4, some employers have adopted the Living Wage well before taking the final step of becoming accredited. In other cases, impact might be experienced after initial accreditation. The Living Wage Foundation has recently encouraged accredited employers to report impact on an annual basis, and while only a small proportion do so, nearly half (forty-two per cent) of those reporting no impact at the point of accreditation record employees benefitting in subsequent years. It remains though that the large number of zero-impact employers amongst the ranks of accredited organizations provides grist to the mill of those who are sceptical about the value of civil regulation. Clearly the Living Wage standard has

Table 7.1 Distribution of impact within Living Wage Employers

Recipients of Living Wage as a percentage of headcount	Living Wage Employers	
	Number	Per cent
Zero	4,651	36.6
Above zero to 10%	2,592	20.4
Above 10% to 25%	1,711	13.5
Above 25% to 50%	1,351	10.6
Above 50% to 75%	733	5.8
Above 75%	1,658	13.1

Source: Employer database, including lapsed employers N = 12,696; the distribution of the underlying continuous variable is positively skewed (skewness = 72.4). Overall median uplift is six per cent of headcount.

been adopted by many organizations that can easily afford to do so, and while the motivation for joining might often have been to support the campaign rather than a cynical exercise in badge-collecting, the direct, redistributive effect within these employers has been minimal.

Amongst organizations that do report impact there is a rough split between those where a relatively small percentage of the workforce have benefitted and those where more than a quarter have done so. In nearly twenty per cent of accredited organizations it is reported that a majority of the workforce received a Living Wage pay increase at the point of accreditation and a substantial number of employers report that more workers have benefitted than are directly employed. An impact 'score' of more than 100 per cent of this kind can arise when employers make extensive use of contract, agency, or casual labour to supplement their core workforce. A Premier League football club, for instance, reported that 198 per cent of its workforce had benefitted from the Living Wage because of its indirect employment of match-day attendants and catering assistants. The evidence from the table is therefore mixed. While the measure of employer-level impact is skewed towards zero or lower levels, a large number of employers nevertheless report a substantial redistributive effect, with 3,742 declaring that more than a quarter of the workforce have received a pay increase. Amongst employers that report impact, the median for the proportion of workers benefitting from the Living Wage is twenty-two per cent. On this second measure of redistributive impact, as with the first, there is evidence of civil regulation generating a positive effect within the labour market.

Table 7.2 shows the distribution of the average pay increase received by employees at the point their employer became accredited. Across the population of employers providing information the median increase in pay was 9.4 per cent, attesting once again to the redistributive impact of the scheme. As the table

Table 7.2 Distribution of impact for employees receiving a wage increase at the point of accreditation

Weighted average wage increase (%)	Living Wage Employers	
	Number	Per cent
Zero–4.99%	1353	23.9
5–9.99%	1641	29.0
10–14.99%	1116	19.7
15–19.99%	569	10.1
20–24.99%	458	8.1
25–29.99%	159	2.8
30% +	364	6.4

Source: Employer database, including lapsed employers N = 5,660 (forty-five per cent of the total dataset who provided wage uplift data). The median percentage pay increase reported by employers providing data was 9.4 per cent, while the mean was 12.1 per cent.

indicates, however, this global figure masks considerable variation. In just under a quarter of accredited organizations the average increase in pay has been modest, at less than five per cent. In more than half of accredited organizations, however, the average value of the increase in pay to employees was ten per cent or higher, and in a fifth of cases the uplift in hourly pay was twenty per cent or more. In many organizations, the adoption of the Living Wage has led to a substantial increase in pay for low-wage workers, well above the annual cost of living awards through which pay is usually adjusted. An increase of pay by twenty per cent or more is clearly significant; it can change living standards and push back the material constraints that many on low wages experience.

Distribution of Impact

Table 7.3 presents evidence on the distribution of Living Wage impact, showing in which parts of the economy the redistributive effect of the scheme has been strongest. The first thing to note from the table is that the impact of the Living Wage is concentrated in large employing organizations: the latter make up six per cent of accredited organizations but are responsible for nearly seventy per cent of impact. It is also clear from the table, however, that the bite of the Living Wage decreases with size, with large employers tending to report that only a small percentage of the employed workforce have received a pay increase. Bite is highest in smaller businesses, where paying the Living Wage to a cleaner or an office junior can result in an impact score of greater than ten per cent. The average pay increase per Living Wage recipient, however, trends in the opposite direction, with employees in larger organizations receiving higher pay increases. This pattern probably reflects the

Table 7.3 Estimates of redistributive impact by contextual factors

	Living Wage Employers N = 12,721	Living Wage Recipients N = 337,602	Recipients per Employer Median %	Pay Increase per Recipient Median %
All	100	100	5.78	9.41
Organization size				
Below 10 employees	35.1	2.8	0[1]	9.03
10–49	38.9	9.8	7.69	9.07
50–249	16.7	12.9	5.36	9.82
250–499	3.4	6.7	4.72	11.03
500+ employees	5.9	67.8	3.64	13.28
Sector				
Private sector	66.7	53.3	5.26	9.33
Not-for-profit sector	30.0	21.3	7.14	10.00
Public sector	3.3	25.5	6.64	11.25
Central government	36.5	3.6	2.52	16.27
Local government	38.9	78.0	9.40	16.12
NHS	13.1	17.3	3.64	9.22
Police and Fire	11.5	1.2	0	8.26
Industry clusters				
Low-paid industries[2]	14.3	15.8	43.75	8.94
Social care[3]	5.7	10.8	55.56	7.22
Outsourcing industries[4]	11.4	17.3	32.00	6.71
Low and high paid industries[5]				
<£10.00	11.2	7.2	50.00	8.94
£10.00–£11.99	14.6	26.3	27.27	8.42
£12.00–£14.04	21.9	8.4	8.16	9.74
£14.05–£16.99	26.2	33.2	4.00	9.93
£17.00–£20.00	16.3	8.1	2.16	10.38
£20.00 +	9.9	16.6	0.67	9.62
Low and high paying districts[6]				
<£12.00	4.6	5.7	19.44	8.30
£12.00–£14.04	37.3	30.1	8.33	9.08
£14.05–£16.99	38.1	38.5	5.00	9.41
£17.00–£19.99	5.5	4.8	6.06	10.99
£20.00–£22.99	10.9	11.6	3.57	13.13
£23.00 +	3.6	9.2	2.02	14.38

Continued

Table 7.3 *Continued*

	Living Wage Employers N = 12,721	Living Wage Recipients N = 337,602	Recipients per Employer Median %	Pay Increase per Recipient Median %
COVID-19				
Accredited during pandemic[7]	24.3	16.5	5.83	6.77
Key industries[8]	31.0	58.9	22.22	8.94
COVID-affected industries[9]	12.6	16.5	33.33	9.70

Source: Employer database, including lapsed employers
Notes:
1. Zero is recorded for the median percentage of recipients for micro-businesses because of the large proportion of employers reporting no recipients for this category. If one examines the mean percentage of beneficiaries, however, then micro-businesses report the highest proportion of employees receiving a Living Wage pay increase, 40.77 per cent.
2. Retail, residential care, hospitality, and cleaning.
3. Residential care, domiciliary care, and childcare.
4. Cleaning, residential care, domiciliary care, catering, security, landscaping, and combined facilities and office services.
5. Median hourly pay, excluding overtime, using 4-digit SIC codes taken from the 2021 Annual Survey of Hours and Earnings. The median hourly rate for all employees was £14.05.
6. Median hourly pay, excluding overtime, by local authority area taken from the 2021 Annual Survey of Hours and Earnings. The median hourly rate for all employees was £14.05.
7. Employers accredited between March 2020 and September 2021, during the peak of the COVID pandemic.
8. Those industries identified by government as providing key services during the pandemic: (1) health and social care; (2) education and childcare; (3) essential public services; (4) local and national government; (5) public safety and national security; (6) passenger and freight transport; (7) financial services; (8) energy and utilities; (9) food production, manufacture, and distribution. Figures are for employers accredited between March 2020 and September 2021.
9. Industries which were particularly adversely affected by the pandemic through lockdowns and other disruptions to business: (1) non-food retail; (2) passenger transport and travel; (3) hospitality and conferences; (4) cinema and music production; (5) arts and entertainment; (6) personal services, such as hairdressing. Figures are for employers accredited between March 2020 and September 2021.

characteristics of workers employed by larger organizations: they are more likely to have young people amongst the workforce on a low statutory minimum rate of pay and to employ contract workers and workers entitled to receive the London Living Wage. Workers in all these categories are likely to have received a relatively large boost to their pay through the Living Wage.

The table also shows that impact is concentrated disproportionately in the public sector, reinforcing the evidence presented in Chapter 6. Public sector organizations account for fewer than five per cent of accredited organizations but are responsible for more than twenty-five per cent of impact. The bite of the Living Wage and the average pay increase received by workers are also relatively high in the public sector, pointing to the continuing significance and material effect of the 'good employer' commitment within public service organizations. Within the public sector, local government accounts for the bulk of impact; it also has the highest proportion of employees benefitting from the Living Wage and the second highest average pay increase. Central government, including Scottish and Welsh national government, the NHS, and police, fire, and rescue services have contributed much less to impact and tend to report that only a small proportion of employees have benefitted. In the wider public services sector, universities are another major contributor to impact, reporting that 18,349 employees have received a Living Wage pay increase with a median 'bite' of nine per cent. The evidence indicates that in parts of the public services the commitment to the Living Wage is meaningful and associated with significant costs.

Much of the remainder of Table 7.3 focuses on the pattern of impact across low-paying and high-paying parts of the economy. It was stated above that the Living Wage has been advocated as a means of addressing the problems of low-paying, outsourcing industries, and there is evidence that this is the case. There are disproportionately high percentages of employees receiving a Living Wage pay increase in social care and in outsourcing industries, and in these and other low-paid industries the proportion of recipients per employer is high. The bite of the Living Wage is particularly noteworthy in social care where more than half the workforce tends to receive a pay increase when an employer accredits. It is also notable, though, that in social care and other low-paid industries the average pay increase for those receiving the Living Wage is relatively modest. It seems that employers have accredited in these low-wage industries when prior rates of pay were relatively close to the Living Wage and the cost implications of moving a high proportion of the workforce onto the rate were therefore limited.

The table also contains a breakdown of impact figures by low- and high-paying industries and low- and high-paying local authority districts. Both sets of figures show the same broad pattern, with accreditation and impact tilted towards high-paying parts of the economy, where median hourly pay is above the national figure. Thus, fifty-two per cent of accredited employers are found in industries with hourly median pay of £14.05 or more, and these employers account for fifty-eight per cent of employees receiving a pay increase. Local authority districts with median pay above the national figure contain fifty-eight per cent of accredited employers and account for sixty-four per cent of impact. Living Wage accreditation is therefore biased towards parts of the economy where it can most readily be afforded, as critics have suggested, but this does not mean it is without redistributive effect. The evidence indicates that many thousands of low-wage workers in high-paying industries have benefitted from the scheme, and the same is true of employees working for employers based in high-wage parts of the country. The average wage increase delivered to workers through Living Wage accreditation is also relatively high in these parts of the economy. While many low-wage workers have benefitted in the high-wage economy, however, it remains that the redistributive impact of the scheme *within* employing organizations in these areas has been limited. In high-wage industries and high-wage locations, the 'bite' of the Living Wage tends to drop below five per cent.

Although accreditation is concentrated in high-paying parts of the economy, it is also found in low-wage industries and low-paying districts. More than a quarter of accredited employers are based in industries where median hourly pay is below £12.00 an hour, and there is also a cluster of accredited organizations in those districts with median pay below this level. Employers in these areas of low-wage employment unsurprisingly report a disproportionately high number of benefitting workers. The bite of the Living Wage is also more pronounced in these areas, with more workers benefitting per employer. This effect is particularly pronounced within the lowest-paying industries, where half the workforce tends to benefit directly from the adoption of the Living Wage. The campaign has been successful in extending the Living Wage to parts of the economy where low pay is prevalent, and it is here that the scheme has been most impactful, though it should be noted that the average pay increase per worker in low-paid parts of the economy tends to be lower. The inverse relationship between 'bite' and the size of individual pay increases, visible in the table, suggests that when relatively few workers benefit directly from the Living Wage employers can be more generous, extending the scheme to those paid statutory minimum rates of pay.

The final evidence in Table 7.3 deals with the impact of COVID-19. It shows, firstly, that the campaign continued to be impactful during the pandemic, notwithstanding the severe disruption to economic activity. More than a fifth of all Living Wage Employers joined the scheme in the eighteen months following the outbreak of the pandemic in March 2020, though these organizations employ only fifteen per cent of workers receiving a pay increase. The table also shows that the bite of the Living Wage dropped slightly during the pandemic, as did the value of the median pay award to individual employees. It has been suggested that employers have used COVID-19 to escape from commitments to employees and further erode employment standards, but this is not borne out by the experience of the Living Wage campaign (Herman et al. 2021).

The table also shows that there was substantial recruitment to the Living Wage scheme amongst employers in 'key-industries', those industries identified by government as providing essential goods and services to help the population through the crisis. As we saw in Chapter 3, campaigners have targeted these industries because of strong public support for low-paid 'key-workers'. The evidence suggests that these campaign efforts have borne fruit, as employers in key industries make up nearly a third of those recruited during the pandemic and account for more than half of impact. The bite of the Living Wage has also been pronounced in key-industries, and workers have on average received a pay increase of just below nine per cent, when their employers have joined the scheme.

Another set of industries on which evidence is provided in Table 7.3 are those that were particularly adversely affected by COVID-19, such as hospitality, tourism, and the arts. The evidence indicates that, notwithstanding difficult circumstances, employers from these industries continued to adopt the Living Wage, and indeed there was net-growth, with the number of employers joining exceeding those that dropped out. The evidence also shows that 9,195 employees in these COVID-affected industries gained from the Living Wage in the peak months of the pandemic and that at the level of the individual employer the scheme was particularly impactful. This latter pattern reflects the fact that there are low-wage industries, such as hospitality, within the COVID-affected group. It is also the case that many of these industries have been affected by labour shortages, and this is a likely explanation of why many bars, cafés, hotels, caterers, and other hospitality and entertainment businesses have become accredited since the outbreak of the pandemic. There has been a business imperative to raise pay which has pushed these organizations towards adopting the Living Wage.

Distribution by Employment Status

Table 7.4 presents a breakdown of impact by employment status and whether benefitting employees have been paid the London or the UK Living Wage. The table indicates, firstly, that the Living Wage has been successful in raising the pay of indirect workers on outsourcing contracts. Just over 2,500 employers (twenty-one per cent) report increasing the pay of indirect workers at the point of accreditation, with nearly a third of benefitting workers having this employment status. These workers, on average, have also received a relatively large Living Wage pay increase. Outsourced workers benefitting from the Living Wage tend to work for large employers and for public sector organizations, based in London and other core cities and in high-wage parts of the economy. More than a third have been recipients of the London Living Wage. One of the objectives of the campaign from the outset has been to pressure large corporates and public sector organizations to assume responsibility for the pay of indirect employees, many of whom occupy jobs where conditions have been degraded through successive waves of

Table 7.4 Employment status of Living Wage recipients

	Number	Per cent	Median pay increase %
All employees	319,686	100.0	9.41
Direct employees	217,495	68.0	9.05
Contract employees	100,886	31.6	11.75
Part-time employees	167,953	52.5	9.85
Full-time employees	148,960	46.6	9.03
UK Living Wage	241,040	75.8	8.95
London Living Wage	74,682	23.3	15.31

Source: Employer database. Base all accredited Living Wage Employers and Service Providers which provided information on the characteristics of workers who had benefitted from the Living Wage (N = 11,982–12,137).

outsourcing (Grimshaw et al. 2019; Wills 2009). This objective has been met in large degree, and many thousands of these employees have benefitted from the Living Wage.

Another group who has benefitted are part-time workers. More than 5,400 organizations reported that part-time employees have received a Living Wage increase, and these employees amount to more than half of those gaining from the scheme. The table also shows that the average value of the Living Wage is higher for part-time workers than for full-timers. Part-time employment in the UK tends to be poorly paid and continues to be performed mainly by women, although there has been some narrowing of the gap between women and men since the 1990s (Cominetti et al. 2021; Devine et al. 2021). The high percentage of part-timers amongst those benefitting from the Living Wage further underscores the redistributive effect of the Living Wage and provides *prima facie* evidence that working women have been primary beneficiaries.

The final evidence in Table 7.4 shows that just under a quarter of those receiving the Living Wage have been paid the higher London rate. This figure may appear surprisingly low given the large number of accredited organizations in London, but it arises from the fact that many of the latter have UK-wide operations that extend beyond the capital. Most large corporates that have signed up to the Living Wage are headquartered in London, but their operations, and their low-paid employees, are found in multiple locations. The average value of the Living Wage is greatest for employees receiving the London Living Wage, reflecting the wider gap between the London rate and the NLW.

Distribution by Occupation

Data on the occupations held by Living Wage recipients were gathered through our 2021 survey of Living Wage Employers. Employers completing the survey were asked whether members of thirty-four low-wage occupations had received or were scheduled to receive a Living Wage pay increase in the current year and were asked also whether members of these occupations were directly or indirectly employed. Their responses generated a total of 2,238 reports of occupations gaining from the Living Wage. These data provide information on the occupational spread of the Living Wage, allowing us to identify which occupations have most frequently benefitted from the scheme. It is important to recognize, however, that they do not allow us to estimate the number of recipients within each occupation: for example, if an employer has one cleaner, two receptionists, and five telesales employees who benefit from the Living Wage, the data simply report that members of these three occupational groups are covered. Asking for more detailed information was not judged feasible.

All thirty-four occupational categories on which information was sought were reported to have gained from the Living Wage, underlining a point made several times above about the broad spread of the standard across the UK economy. Nevertheless, some occupational categories were particularly likely to have benefitted. Across the entire sample the ten most frequently reported benefitting occupations were: (1) clerical or administrative assistant; (2) office or domestic cleaner; (3) receptionist; (4) warehouse operative; (5) care worker or home carer; (6) kitchen or catering assistant; (7) machine or process operative; (8) security guard or attendant; (9) sales assistant or shelf-filler; and (10) call- or contact-centre operative. Amongst indirect employees a narrower range of recipient occupations was identified, with five accounting for forty per cent of coverage: office cleaner, security guard, industrial or window cleaner, receptionist, and administrative assistant. All of these are jobs that are commonly outsourced.

To further examine occupational coverage by the Living Wage, the thirty-four jobs were placed in larger groupings with common characteristics. The results of this exercise are shown in Table 7.5, which shows both the frequency with

Table 7.5 Occupational groups benefitting from the Living Wage

Occupational Group	Per cent of employer reports N = 2,238	Per cent of low-paid jobs reported by ASHE, 2019
Administrative jobs[1]	28.5	10.0
Building service jobs[2]	26.3	13.5
Hospitality and leisure[3]	8.7	14.3
Retail and customer services jobs[4]	6.9	18.5
Transport and storage[5]	5.9	11.9
Manufacturing[6]	5.4	5.7
Care and personal services[7]	4.5	12.0
Construction[8]	2.2	1.0
Education[9]	1.9	12.0
Refuse[10]	0.8	0.4
Farming[11]	0.4	0.5

Source: Survey of Living Wage Employers, 2021; Annual Survey of Hours and Employment, 2019.
1. Administrative: clerical or administrative assistant, receptionist, library assistant, secretary, typist, or keyboard operator.
2. Building service: office or domestic cleaner, security guard or attendant, industrial or window cleaner, housekeeper, porter, postal or mailroom worker, caretaker, gardener or grounds-person.
3. Hospitality and leisure: bar worker, waiter or waitress, kitchen or catering assistant, sport or leisure attendant.
4. Retail and customer service: telesales, call- or contact-centre operative, sales assistant or shelf-filler, cashier or checkout operator.
5. Transport and storage: warehouse operative, van, taxi, or mini-bus driver.
6. Manufacturing: packer or assembly operative, machine or process operative.
7. Care and personal services: care worker or home carer, hairdresser or beautician, launderer, dry-cleaner, or presser.
8. Construction: building labourer.
9. Education: teaching or educational support assistant, school breakfast or midday supervisor or crossing patrol, nursery nurse, assistant, or playworker.
10. Refuse: street cleaner, refuse and salvage collector or sorter.
11. Farming: farm labourer.

which these clusters were reported to have benefitted from the Living Wage and their relative contribution to low-wage employment across the UK economy. Two groups of jobs are shown particularly to have gained from the Living Wage—administrative and building service jobs—and to have done so to an extent that exceeds their share of low-wage employment. What distinguishes these two groups of jobs is their quality of ubiquity: cleaners, office assistants, receptionists, security guards, porters, and caretakers are found in multiple industries, spread across the economy. They are also low-wage jobs which are found in high-wage industries.

Several of the other job clusters in the table, such as hospitality and leisure, retail and customer service, and care and personal services, are shown to have low Living Wage coverage, relative to their scale. Many of these jobs, such as care assistant, checkout operative, hairdresser, sport or leisure attendant, waiter or waitress, and bar worker, are concentrated in particular industries that are characterized by low-wage employment; for example, social care, retail, personal services, leisure, and hospitality. The table shows that those performing jobs of this kind have benefitted from the Living Wage, reflecting the latter's penetration of low-wage industries. But it also shows that the campaign has found it harder to impact these types of jobs. The pattern of impact described above, with its tilt towards high-wage industries and parts of the economy, is echoed in the pattern of occupational coverage with its bias towards ubiquitous low-wage jobs and away from jobs concentrated in low-wage parts of the economy.

Distribution by Demographic Characteristics

Advocates of the Living Wage have argued that it can be of especial benefit to women and members of minorities (Living Wage Foundation 2017b). It has been claimed that the Living Wage can help close gender and ethnic pay gaps and prove of particular value to young workers who are not entitled to the National Living Wage, the highest level of statutory minimum. Unfortunately it has not proved possible to collect accurate data on the demographic characteristics of those paid the Living Wage, and so these questions can only be approached indirectly. We have two sources of evidence. Employers responding to our 2021 survey reported on what percentages of employees benefitting from the Living Wage were women, young people aged under twenty-five, or members of ethnic minorities. Separate estimates were requested for those directly employed and those employed by contractors. In addition, our database of accredited employers allows us to examine the extent and pattern of Living Wage impact in industries with a majority female workforce and industries in which ethnic minorities and young workers form a relatively high percentage.

Our survey results are shown in Table 7.6. The table indicates that amongst direct workers, female employees have benefitted from the Living Wage in at least

Table 7.6 Percentage of those receiving the Living Wage who are women, from BAME communities, or who are aged below 25

	0–10%	11–25%	26–50%	51–75%	76–90%	91–100%
Percentage of *direct* employees receiving a pay increase who are women	24.7	7.4	15.0	15.1	11.4	26.4
Percentage of *contract* employees receiving a pay increase who are women	65.6	3.4	3.4	5.2	3.6	19.1
Percentage of *direct* employees receiving a pay increase who are BAME	72.3	10.2	6.9	2.8	1.5	6.3
Percentage of *contract* employees receiving a pay increase who are BAME	80.9	3.2	3.5	3.0	0.8	8.6
Percentage of *direct* employees receiving a pay increase who are aged below 25	51.8	18.1	11.3	4.9	2.4	11.6
Percentage of *contract* employees receiving a pay increase who are aged below 25	86.4	4.9	2.7	1.1	0.0	4.9

Source: Survey of Living Wage Employers, 2021; estimates for direct employment are based on 738–801 cases, those for indirect employment on 371–390 cases. For all items there are a substantial number of missing values.

three-quarters of organizations and in just over a half form the majority of those gaining a pay increase. The proportions of ethnic minority and young workers benefitting are notably smaller, but it is still the case that in a substantial minority of organizations they are part of the direct workforce that have gained from the Living Wage, and in some cases they constitute an absolute majority. Amongst direct workers, the table indicates, women, young workers, and those from BAME communities have often gained from the Living Wage in the manner intended by campaigners, though it is not possible to conclude on this evidence that they have benefitted disproportionately to their presence in the employed workforce. Amongst indirect workers the pattern is different, and women and young workers in particular are poorly represented amongst contract employees receiving a Living Wage pay increase. Men aged 25 and over, perhaps working as security guards, ground-staff, and industrial cleaners, feature strongly within this group.

Our evidence from the employer database is presented in Table 7.7. The table shows the percentages of UK employment and workers receiving a Living Wage pay increase, together with estimates of impact at the levels of the individual employer and employee, for industries with relatively high numbers of women, ethnic minorities, and young people. For women and young workers, the data reveal a similar pattern. In each case substantial numbers of workers have benefitted from the Living Wage, but the percentages are low relative to the volume of employment. Both clusters contain low-wage industries—hospitality is common to both—and the pattern reflects the fact that it is harder to spread the Living Wage in industries of this kind, where cost implications for employers are more severe. For ethnic minorities, the situation shown in the table is rather more positive in that the percentage of impact is directly proportionate to the share of the workforce located in industries with a large proportion of ethnic minority workers. The table also shows that when the Living Wage is adopted in industries with a relatively high percentage of women, young, and ethnic minority workers, a relatively large percentage of the workforce benefits.

Table 7.7 Living Wage impact in industries with high levels of women's, ethnic minority, and young workers' employment

Industries	**UK employment[1]** %	**Living Wage impact[2]** %	**Median impact per employer[3]** %	**Median impact per worker[4]** %
Women's employment[5]	48.6	42.3	11.8	9.4
Young workers' employment[6]	20.4	14.6	29.1	9.4
Ethnic minority employment[7]	24.9	24.9	22.2	8.6
All	100	100	6.0	9.4

Sources: Employer database, including lapsed employers; Annual Survey of Hours and Earnings 2018.
1. Percentage share of total UK employment. Data for women's employment are based on 4-digit SIC codes; data for young workers' and ethnic minority employment are based on principal industry divisions (ASHE 2018).
2. Percentage share of employees reported to have received a Living Wage pay increase at the point of accreditation.
3. The median number of beneficiaries (direct and contract) per employer at the point of accreditation, expressed as a percentage of the direct workforce.
4. The weighted average of the increase in pay for those employees receiving a pay increase at the point of Living Wage adoption.
5. Industries in which women make up at least fifty per cent of the employed workforce.
6. Industry divisions in which young workers (16–25) make up at least twenty per cent of the employed workforce.
7. Industry divisions in which ethnic minorities make up at least fifteen per cent of the employed workforce.

The final point of note in the table is that the average uplift for workers in industries with relatively large proportions of women and young workers is identical to that for the population as a whole; at 9.4 per cent. If one focuses on industries with the highest proportions of women and young workers, however, this figure drops, to 7.84 per cent where women make up more than three-quarters of the workforce and to 9.33 per cent where young workers are more than thirty per cent. Industries with a large proportion of ethnic minority workers also have an average uplift below the national figure: 8.57 per cent. This pattern of low average uplift in industries with the highest proportions of women, young people, and ethnic minorities probably reflects the facts that these industries are low-paying. The pattern echoes the wider trend for uplift to be smaller in low-paid industries, identified above.

It is important to note that the data in Table 7.7 do not show conclusively that women or young workers are under-represented amongst employees benefitting from the Living Wage. Many women, for example, work in male-dominated industries as cleaners, office-staff, and in catering and are not included in the estimates shown in the table. What the table does show is that there are structural barriers to spreading the Living Wage in industries with a disproportionately female or young workforce, which arise from the fact that they are characterized by low pay. When the Living Wage is adopted in these industries, however, it tends to be impactful, serving to reduce inequality by uplifting wages for a relatively large percentage of the workforce.

Adverse Effects for Workers

Conservative critics of employment regulation often claim that the latter generates perverse effects, rebounding against the very groups it is meant to protect (Heery 2011). If regulation raises pay, the conservative critique asserts, then the end result will be lower levels of employment as businesses substitute workers for technology or relocate operations elsewhere. A similar line of argument can be found in critical comment on private regulation. Employer motives for signing up to the latter, it is asserted, are largely cynical, resulting in surface-level compliance which masks continuing exploitative treatment of workers (LeBaron et al. 2022). Extrapolating from either of these positions to the case of the Living Wage would lead one to anticipate that adoption of the standard would have adverse consequences for low-paid workers, as employers claw back the costs of higher pay through workforce reduction and work intensification. For both conservative and critical sceptics, employees are likely to pay a cost for receiving the Living Wage.

Table 7.8 presents survey responses to items designed to measure if claw back of this kind is significant. It shows the percentage of accredited employers who report that introducing the Living Wage has been accompanied by measures designed to

Table 7.8 Negative effects of Living Wage accreditation for employees

Changes to pay and benefits	**Yes**	
	N	%
Removed or reduced the value of some employee benefits to help fund payment of the Living Wage; e.g. withdrawal of paid breaks or meals	24	1.6
Reduced pay growth for other groups in the organisation to help pay for the Living Wage	77	5.2
Reducing the hours of employees paid the Living Wage to help fund the higher rate of pay	20	1.3
Reducing the number of employees in the organisation to help fund the Living Wage	15	1.0
Reducing overtime working to help fund the Living Wage	22	1.5
Asking employees paid the Living Wage to take on more work	40	2.7
Changing work organisation amongst employees paid the Living Wage to raise productivity; e.g. introducing more flexible ways of working	240	16.1
Changing the jobs of workers paid the Living Wage so that they have more responsibilities	88	5.9
Absorbing the cost of the Living Wage without making significant changes to working practices	1,174	77.9

Source: Survey of Living Wage Employers, 2021 (N = 1492–1507).

reduce labour costs, such as the withdrawal of other elements of remuneration or changes to working time. Caution must be exercised in interpreting this evidence, as it comes from employers rather than from employees themselves. Nevertheless, the results are striking and point overwhelmingly to an absence of negative side-effects for workers being paid the Living Wage. Thus, only one per cent of employers have reduced hours or reduced the size of the workforce, while only two or three per cent report that they have withdrawn benefits, reduced overtime, or asked employees to take on more work. Higher percentages of employers report making other compensating changes, such as restraining pay growth for other groups, making changes to work organization, or changing low-wage jobs to increase levels of responsibility. These changes are still confined to a small minority, however, and either do not ask the low-paid to bear the costs themselves or carry potential benefits, such as job enrichment.

In our qualitative research we did encounter employers who had made changes to other conditions to help fund the Living Wage. A number of these examples are described in Chapter 5 and are notable because of the involvement of trade unions. When trade unions have sought the Living Wage through collective bargaining, it seems that employers have responded by seeking concessions, such as a reduction of overtime or the relaxation of demarcation rules. Table 7.8, however, suggests that in most cases, where unions are not present, this kind of trade-off has not been sought. On the contrary, the vast majority of employers appear to have absorbed the cost of the Living Wage, 'without making significant changes to working practices'.

This finding of relatively few adverse consequences for low-paid workers echoes that of an earlier study, which examined the response of employers to the introduction of the statutory National Living Wage in 2016 (Davies and D'Arcy 2016). This research found that many employers planned simply to absorb the costs of the new, higher rate, with only small percentages reporting that they would reduce overtime, bonuses, working time, or the size of the workforce. What this study, together with our own, suggests is that conservative claims about the perverse effects of regulation and critical claims about its cynical manipulation are both exaggerated. Employers have generally adopted the Living Wage without expecting low-paid employees to incur a penalty in return for their higher rate of pay.

Impact on Employers

Living Wage campaigners have argued consistently that redistributing income to low-wage workers can also work to the benefit of their employers (e.g. Institute of Workplace and Facilities Management 2021). Arguments of this kind are part of a long tradition that has made the case for the regulation of the employment relationship on the grounds of mutual gains. Progressive regulation, it is held, can broaden the scope of shared interests in the employment relationship, protecting the interests of employees while pushing employers towards more cooperative, sustainable approaches to workforce management (Heery 2016). Applied to the case of the Living Wage, these arguments suggest that adopting the standard will help stabilize and motivate the workforce, while also yielding other benefits, such as enhancing corporate reputation and attracting clients, customers, and investors (Werner 2021b; Wills et al. 2009; Wills and Linneker 2012).

In what follows, we use a mix of survey and interview evidence to test these claims. We also use this evidence to test competing arguments, which deny that regulation produces positive effects for business. One such argument comes from conservatives and claims that regulation can jeopardize other desirable states, harming the performance of organizations either by directly raising costs or by impeding management decision-making and ability to respond to market signals (Heery 2011). For commentators in this tradition, adoption of the Living Wage is likely to be seen as damaging to business, disrupting payment structures and relations with suppliers, and needlessly adding to the cost of hiring both direct and contract labour (Lamman 2014; Shackleton 2012). The second argument can be found in empirical work that has examined other bodies of progressive regulation, such as equal opportunities policy (Riley et al. 2013). The essential claim of this work is that while regulation may benefit employees, its beneficial consequences for employers have often been exaggerated. On this second view, adherence to good labour standards, such as payment of the Living Wage, is desirable on moral grounds but is likely to be performance-neutral, without substantial positive or negative impact.

Positive and Negative Effects

Figure 7.1 shows the response of employers to survey questions about the positive and negative effects of Living Wage accreditation on their organizations. Employers were presented with a list of twenty-eight possible effects and were asked to rank the degree to which they were visible using a four-point scale, ranging from 'no noticeable effect' to an impact of 'major significance'. In the figure, the twenty-two positive and six negative effects are ranked in terms of average score, with those identified as being of most significance at the top. The first thing to note about the pattern of evidence in the table is that all twenty-eight effects are identified by at least some employers: the Living Wage has had both positive and negative effects on organizations that have adopted it. The second thing to note from the table, however, is that positive effects are reported more frequently and are rated as more impactful. Thus, ninety-four per cent of surveyed employers identified positive effects from adopting the Living Wage, compared with seventy-four per cent who identified negative effects; and the average impact 'score' for the top six positive effects listed is 2.35, while that for the six negative items is 1.51. The balance of effects is clearly positive, providing support for the claim that there is a business case for progressive labour standards.

Two types of benefit stand out from the figure as being reported most frequently. The first are reputational effects, with majorities of surveyed employers reporting that accreditation has boosted corporate reputation and their reputation as an employer and permitted the organization to differentiate itself from competitors. Our qualitative research reinforced these findings, with employers attesting to the positive reputational effect of the Living Wage. The director of a small charity in Wales described Living Wage accreditation as 'great PR' and emphasized the value of being listed alongside other, larger, and more prominent organizations in campaign publicity. An HR manager at an English university stressed the value of being 'the first in the City to accredit' and reported that accreditation had reinforced the university's position as an 'employer of choice'. In a third organization, a waste collection and recycling business, a manager simply declared: 'Since getting accreditation through the Living Wage Movement our business has had a positive reputation across the region. Many thanks!'

The second type of widely reported benefit were improvements to human resource management. Clear majorities of employers reported that Living Wage accreditation had improved recruitment and retention, the quality of job applicants and workplace relations, led to positive changes in work organization,

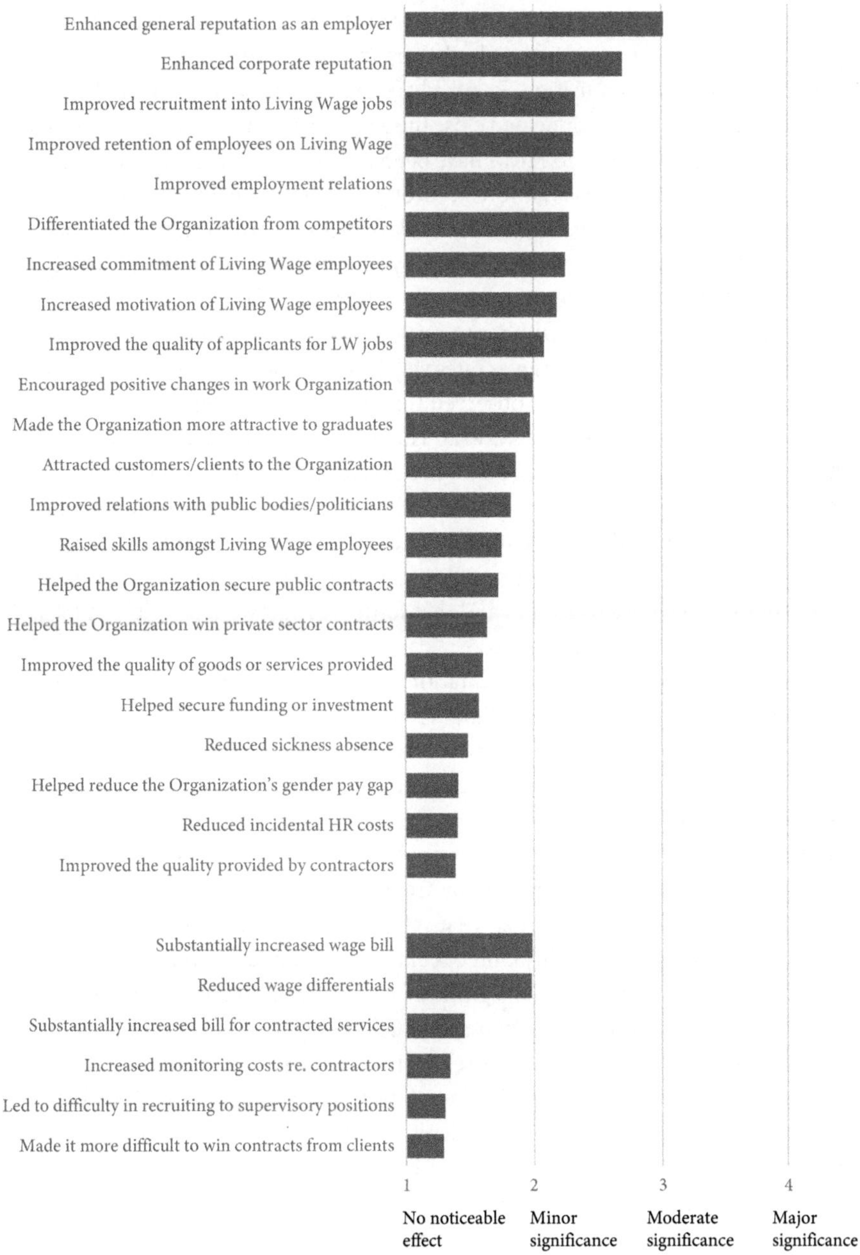

Figure 7.1 Impact of Living Wage accreditation

Source: 2021 Survey of Living Wage Employers (N = 1471–1499).

and raised employee commitment and motivation. Substantial minorities also reported that the scheme had made the organization more attractive to graduates and helped skill acquisition. Relatively few reported that the Living Wage had reduced sickness absence or helped close the gender pay gap, but it is clear from the survey that improvements to HRM have been one of the main gains from accreditation. This impression was reinforced through qualitative evidence, with a range of employers citing positive effects, particularly with regard to employee resourcing. The HR manager of a theatre company said that the Living Wage 'has been positive in that we feel able to attract and select the best candidates', while her counterpart in an educational charity said that 'retention is good' and reported that the scheme had led to turnover rates well below those expected for low-paying employment. Other employers observed that paying the Living Wage had helped them retain key workers during COVID. The manager of a homecare provider said that 'We feel it was a contributing factor to our stability during the pandemic', while an operator of residential care homes in Greater Manchester, which employed 600 care workers, reported in 2021 that 'We just don't have a recruitment problem anymore'. This employer further stated that paying the Living Wage had reduced expenditure on costly agency fees and that future savings were anticipated in staff recruitment and induction training.

Other beneficial effects of accreditation were reported by only a minority of employers and tended to have low 'impact' scores. Items in this category comprise improvements to business performance beyond the employment relationship, such as attracting customers, winning contracts or funding, and improving both the quality of the organization's own goods and services and those provided by suppliers. For some accredited employers benefits of this kind were significant: a visual arts organization supported by Creative Scotland reported that 'Being a Living Wage Employer means that we meet the criteria when applying for certain funding'. For most, though, this kind of commercial pay-off from the Living Wage was either absent or of minimal significance. The business case for labour standards has often emphasized commercial benefits, with the attraction of consumers featuring particularly in the literature on international civil regulation. Benefits of this type, however, lagged behind reputational and HR gains and possessed a rather niche quality, reported by particular segments within the survey population, such as those providing services to larger organizations keen to encourage the Living Wage through procurement.

While positive effects outweighed the negative consequences of accreditation, it is clear from Figure 7.1 that the latter have been experienced by a substantial number of employers. The most frequent complaint was that the Living Wage had increased costs, with nearly sixty per cent of employers reporting that the scheme had substantially increased their wage bill and twenty per cent reporting that it had increased the cost of contracted services. Several reported that difficult trading conditions arising from the pandemic had exacerbated these problems, while others complained that tight public sector contracts made it difficult to continue paying the rate. Reports of this kind attest both to the substantial commitment that some employers have made in implementing the Living Wage and to the difficulty for individual firms in low-wage industries adopting a wage standard when their competitors do not. The other main problem identified by the survey was disruption to internal pay structures. More than half of those responding reported that introducing the Living Wage had reduced pay differentials, and about a fifth said that this had led to difficulty in recruiting to team leader positions. In interviews with managers, some explained that problems of this kind had not proved as severe as they feared, and in many cases employers have awarded compensating increases for higher-graded staff to preserve differentials. It remains, though, that pegging wage rates to an external standard has disrupted internal pay relativities.

Performance Neutrality

The responses shown in Figure 7.1 support the view that there is a business case for the Living Wage, but this assessment needs to be qualified in two ways. First, it is notable that several of the most widely reported benefits are rather intangible, enhancing corporate reputation and employer brand rather than securing new contracts or winning new customers. Reputation and branding matter to many organizations, but it is notable that the reported effects of the scheme tend to cluster at the softer end of the range of possibilities. Second, while the frequency of positive reports is often high, the intensity of reported effects is generally low. For only one item—enhancing the organization's reputation as an employer—do more than twenty per cent of respondents report that the change was of 'major significance', and in most cases positive (and negative) changes flowing from accreditation are said to be of 'moderate' or 'limited significance'. Written comments on questionnaires reinforced this impression of non-radical change:

> We have found that being a Living Wage Employer has made little difference to whether or not we win contracts—even when those contracts are being offered by some of the most vocal LWF champions they seem quite happy to use non-LWE suppliers instead. Similarly, we have found that it makes little difference to our ability to attract and retain staff. We stick with it because I believe in the concept of fair pay and action to reduce social inequalities, but I can honestly say we've seen little, if any, business benefit. [Utility meter reading company]

> As a relatively new organization adopting RLW early it is hard to evidence the positive impact of RLW. It is not evident that it has impacted absence, turnover, or quality of applications as this can't be easily disaggregated from other factors, such as policy developments and changes in management personnel. Our driver for being a RLW employer is that it is the right thing to do and if you can't pay RLW then you don't have a viable business model. It should not be an option. [Social enterprise providing building maintenance services]

> As a small employer that has always paid above the Living Wage, even before being accredited, we have seen very little influence using the Living Wage logo to our recruitment of new staff or public acceptance. [Domestic cleaning company]

> We believe the Living Wage accreditation is important, but it has little tangible effect on a small organisation like ours which mostly already met the Real Living Wage. We wanted the accreditation to show we think it is important and set an example rather than to transform our own organization necessarily. [Community foundation]

> We are proud to be a Living Wage Employer and will continue to do so, but we are unsure how much this accreditation really enhances our ability to attract, recruit, and retain quality staff. It is certainly part of the 'jigsaw', but we also offer a host of other benefits and development opportunities alongside the Living Wage with an aim to become an 'employer of choice' within our business sector and geographic location. [Home care provider]

These statements do not just attest to the limits to the impact of the Living Wage, but also identify reasons. The Living Wage, they suggest, has not produced major effects because businesses were already compliant, few if any workers benefitted materially, and other progressive policies were in place whose effects were difficult to disentangle from the Living Wage. The statements also indicate that many organizations remain committed to accreditation despite limited practical outcomes: their motivation for joining the scheme was to show support and not to boost performance. Indeed, one respondent objected to our survey, even asking about positive business benefits when the purpose of the scheme was 'to do the right thing'.

Our research findings do not show that the Living Wage has been performance-neutral in a strong sense of the term. Nearly all employers report positive impact, and a high percentage also identify negative effects. There is evidence though for a qualified version of the performance-neutrality argument. The survey results indicate that the Living Wage brings modest benefits to most employers; it emerges from the data as a benign rather than transformative influence. Regulation of the employment relationship is often proposed on the grounds that it can be transformative, shocking employers onto a new line of development which not only improves employment terms for workers but also raises performance. In most organizations that have adopted it, the Living Wage does not seem to have generated a shock effect of this kind. Rather, it has stimulated modest improvements to business reputation and operations in line with a model of incremental, not transformative change.

Mutual Gains

Living Wage campaigners have repeatedly made the case that the standard can benefit multiple stakeholders, including both employees and their employers. In academic literature it is also often argued that effective regulation can generate 'mutual gains', working to the benefit of both employers and employees (Kochan and Osterman 1994). Claims of this kind, indeed, are a defining feature of contemporary pluralist scholarship within the field of employment relations (Heery 2016). For pluralists, well-designed regulation can eliminate opportunistic and adversarial behaviour by employers and so widen the scope for common interests and cooperation within the employment relationship. To conclude our assessment of the impact of the Living Wage on employers, we want to test this argument and see whether employer reports of positive consequences from accreditation are associated with positive gains for employees in the same organization.

To examine this question, we first created a scale measuring the extent to which employers reported positive effects from Living Wage accreditation. The scale was produced by summing the replies to the twenty-two positive items listed in Figure 7.1 and then expressing this total as a percentage of the maximum score available, i.e. sixty-six. It was possible to complete this process for 1,514 respondents to the survey, the vast majority of whom (ninety-four per cent) reported at least some positive effects from accreditation (i.e. scored more than zero). Just under half (forty-eight per cent) of survey respondents reported an impact score of twenty-five per cent or more, and this group of 720 employers are those that have gained most from the scheme.

Our measure of positive effects for employees was the number of workers reported to have received a pay increase at the point of accreditation, expressed as a percentage of the organization's headcount. Across the 1,514 employers with an impact score, 1,004 (sixty-six per cent) reported that workers had had their pay increased, with 467 (thirty-one per cent) reporting that twenty-five per cent or more of the workforce had received an uplift. It is important to emphasize that while both measures of positive effects were provided by employers, they were gathered through separate processes, at different times, and in many cases were supplied by different individuals. The data are therefore free of common method bias.

From these two measures it is possible to identify four groups amongst the survey population: employers who report no gains from the Living Wage either for themselves or for the workforce; employers who report that workers have benefitted but that there are no business benefits; employers who identify gains for themselves but do not record any workers receiving a pay increase; and employers who report mutual gains, encompassing both business benefits and uplift for employees. The relative sizes of these four groups within the survey sample are shown in Figure 7.2. It is clear from the figure that most employers report mutual gains, where both parties to the employment relationship have benefitted from the Living Wage. A total of 902 employers (sixty-three per cent) report mutual gains, and within this group a smaller number of 270 (eighteen per cent) report strong mutual gains, in which twenty-five per cent or more of the

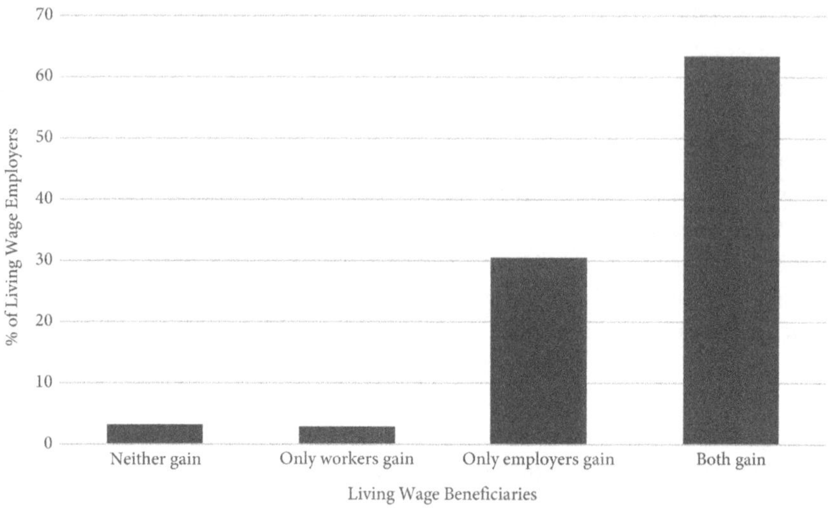

Figure 7.2 Mutual gains from Living Wage accreditation

Sources: Employer database and 2021 Survey of Living Wage Employers (N = 1514). Note that employer responses to survey questions on the beneficial impacts of the Living Wage have been recoded for this figure, with the response of 'no noticeable effect' given a score of zero and the remaining responses running from 1–3.

workforce received a pay increase and the employer registered a positive impact score of twenty-five or higher.

Although the evidence is broadly supportive of the Living Wage generating mutual gains, the evidence in Figure 7.2 warrants an important qualification. The figure shows a substantial minority of employers who report that they have gained from accreditation without reporting gains for their employees. Critical writers have sometimes claimed that this kind of asymmetry is a defining characteristic of private regulation, which may generate reputational benefits for employers while producing few or any positive outcomes for employees (LeBaron et al. 2022). Our evidence does not support so definitive a judgement, but it does suggest that gains from the Living Wage scheme have favoured employers. In most organizations both parties to the employment relationship have benefited from the scheme, but there is a sizeable group of employers who have gained without any seeming benefit for their employees. The Living Wage has produced mutual gains, in the manner anticipated by pluralist analysis, but this pattern has not been universal across the population of accredited organizations.

Societal Impact

Discussion of the societal effects of the Living Wage, and of civil regulation more generally, has tended to follow two courses. On the one hand, the issue has been examined through a 'person-centric lens' where the emphasis has been on teasing out the impact of higher pay on individual health and well-being, family-life, and community participation (Searle and McWha-Hermann 2021). Much of this work has been informed by Sen's notion of capability and has focused on the extent to which receiving the Living Wage pushes back the constraints of low income, allowing greater self-determination and the ability to live a fuller, less restricted life (Carr et al. 2016; Werner 2016). On the other hand, the question of wider impact has been examined from an institutional perspective, in which the abiding concern is the extent to which the Living Wage cuts across and undermines other, desirable institutions, such as employment law and collective bargaining. From this macro, institutional perspective, the focus is on the relationship between civil regulation and other forms of labour market governance, with some claiming that the former can reinforce the latter and others arguing that they are incompatible (Kinderman 2016; Kuruvilla 2021).

Impact on Individuals

An absence from our research, and from other research on the Living Wage in the UK, is a detailed assessment of how it has impacted individual workers. We have information on how many workers have benefitted economically from the Living Wage but have not collected original data on how it has affected their feelings, health, relationships, and patterns of non-work behaviour. There is a secondary source, however, that can provide insight into these questions: the testimony of workers receiving the Living Wage which is delivered through campaign videos, quoted in reports and on websites, and which has been spoken at many of the campaign meetings we have attended. This evidence is not ideal: it has been selected to convey a campaign message and may have been scripted to a degree by community organizers. Non-supporting voices, denying that the Living Wage has had a marked positive effect, one can assume have been screened out. Nevertheless, worker testimony is quite widely available, has been voluntarily given, and in the absence of an alternative provides our only source of information on the qualitative impact of the Living Wage.

A theme that leaps out from testimony is the pushing back of financial constraints, such that people experience less anxiety over their finances and are more able to afford things. A care worker, for instance, stated that 'I feel like I don't have to scrimp and save. I can put petrol in the car without thinking twice about it'. A museum attendant made a similar point, saying that on the statutory minimum 'You have to worry about what you are spending all the time' but that with the Living Wage the 'pressure is off', and she has been able to have more of a social life. In a third example, a young man working as a lifeguard said that before his employer introduced the Living Wage 'I could not do interesting things because I had no money'. Since, he has moved out of shared accommodation, goes out twice a month, and has bought a guitar. A final case is that of a detection dog-handler who described the change in her circumstances as follows:

> Before being paid a Living Wage, life was difficult financially for me. I had no social life, and constantly had to tell family and friends that I was unable to meet them for a meal, drinks. However, since being given the Living Wage, my life has improved for the better. I can now afford to go out for the day with my son, and go out with friends and family, as well as not having to constantly think about whether I will have enough food for the rest of the month until my next payday.

Another way in which the Living Wage was reported to have released constraint was by allowing people to reduce their working time. Lynne, a cleaner at Aviva who features in campaign videos, reported that she had given up a second, part-time job to spend more time with her granddaughter, who lived with her. Ralph, a store-worker for IKEA, made the same point, saying that the Living Wage had allowed him to see more of his children and have a better work-life balance. Another man reported that he had stopped working long hours and taken on a share of childcare, allowing his wife to work part-time: 'It absolutely made an amazing difference to our lives'. Not everyone giving testimony reported this kind of change—one woman commented approvingly that her twelve-hour shifts were much more remunerative with the Living Wage—but for some, being paid more has enabled a reduction of working time in the manner hoped for by campaigners.

Release from financial constraint has meant a greater ability to spend on leisure, on family, or to save. Many of the resulting changes reported in testimony are small, minor improvements to the quality of life, which nevertheless were significant for those who experienced them. One man reported that 'On Monday night I can eat something nutritious, not beans on toast', a woman said that she and her husband could now afford occasionally to go out to dinner, the museum-attendant quoted above had taken up ice-skating, while another man, whose hobby was keeping tropical fish, said he could afford to buy more fish! In some cases, however, changes were more significant, with higher earnings allowing people to alter their life circumstances. A young barista, for instance, said she was now able to save for the deposit for a flat and was planning to move out of her parents' house, while a young man said that he was able to remain living in London and no longer felt the need to move somewhere cheaper.

Much of the additional expenditure enabled through the Living Wage was directed at children and grandchildren. In testimony, people described using their extra earnings to pay for things for children that they could not previously afford. These included school trips, weekly visits to the swimming pool, days out, and going on holiday. In several cases it also involved investing directly in the personal development of children and grandchildren. Lynne from Aviva had bought a laptop for her granddaughter to help with homework, another man had bought a computer for his daughter who was starting university, while Ralph from IKEA had bought his adult son a Fender amp to support his emerging career as a professional musician. Saving for, investing in, and treating children are the most frequently mentioned benefits of the Living Wage across the whole set of testimony.

A final theme to emerge from the testimony is that of the symbolic quality of the Living Wage for those receiving it. Lynne said that 'it makes me feel quite emotional to think about it' and reported that being paid the Living Wage had raised her self-esteem and made her feel more confident. Ralph similarly said that he felt 'respected', while Oliver, a delivery driver, declared that 'I feel valued in a way that no other flexible work has provided'. One consequence of these feelings of recognition and respect was that those giving testimony frequently stated that they had become more committed to their employer and planned to remain in their jobs. Quite apart from beneficial consequences for their employers, however, is the direct contribution to personal well-being which appears to flow from higher pay: those receiving the Living Wage did not just feel better about their employer, they felt better about themselves.

There are some absences in the testimony of those being paid the Living Wage. Thus, we could find no reports of reduced working time leading to greater community involvement or active citizenship. The benefits people reported were exclusively privatized, confined to a domestic setting, and to their personal lives. Moreover, no firm conclusions can be drawn from the testimony that the Living Wage is promoting social mobility, improving the health of low-wage workers, or making their communities more resilient. The evidence is congruent with wider, putative developments of this kind but falls well short of definitive proof. What it does indicate, however, is that the Living Wage can enhance the capabilities of those who receive it in the manner suggested by those advocates influenced by Amartya Sen. The testimony of employees who have been paid the Living Wage shows that it has pushed back the constraints on their lives, reduced anxiety and promoted well-being, and allowed greater self-determination. In Chapter 2 it was stated that the Living Wage is a form of payment for need, designed to promote the greater inclusion of low-wage employees in society. The testimony of those who have received it indicates that it has met these goals, improving life-quality and allowing those who are low-paid to enjoy some of the quotidian pleasures that the better-off take for granted.

Impact on Trade Unionism

A common criticism of private regulation is that it can erode or forestall the emergence of other, more effective regulatory institutions, such as trade unionism and collective bargaining (Dundon et al. 2020; Kuruvilla 2021). We have already touched on this question and used cross-sectional evidence to show that while the Living Wage is concentrated in the non-union economy, it is also found where unions are present. The pattern of accreditation, described in Chapter 4, indicates that the two types of labour market institution can coexist. Below, we further examine the relationship between trade unions and the Living Wage using additional information. First, we use longitudinal evidence to ascertain whether the spread of the Living Wage over the past twenty years has been accompanied by the retreat of trade unionism and collective bargaining. Second, we use our qualitative research to probe whether Living Wage accreditation has been used deliberately by employers to block or weaken trade union representation.

If civil regulation is inimical to trade unionism, then one would expect its flourishing to be accompanied by a diminishing union presence. At first sight, this seems to be the case. Since 2001, when the Living Wage campaign was launched, trade union density in the UK has dropped from 29.3 per cent to 23.7 per cent, while collective bargaining coverage has shrunk from 35.5 to 25.6 per cent. However, the period before the launch of the campaign witnessed even sharper decline. The two decades from 1980 to 1999 saw a drop in union density from 54.5 to 29.4 per cent and a fall in coverage by collective bargaining from seventy-five to below forty per cent (Brown et al. 2003; Waddington 2003). It is also the case that the period since 2011, when the Living Wage has spread most broadly, has been one of relatively modest union decline. Membership density dropped by less than two percentage points, while bargaining coverage fell by six points between 2011 and 2020. These trends suggest that the spread of civil regulation in the form of the Living Wage has not been a major factor eroding trade unionism and collective bargaining and that other causal forces have been much more significant. They also suggest that the direction of influence in the relationship between trade union decline and the Living Wage points in the opposite direction to that suggested by critics. In the Nordic countries, where union membership and collective bargaining remain high, an independent living wage movement of the kind seen in Britain has not emerged (Alsos et al. 2019). It is likely that a condition for the emergence of the latter has been union retreat from much of the UK labour market, which has left a vacant institutional space that civil regulation can occupy.

The other set of evidence on the impact of the Living Wage on trade unionism comes from the interviews with employers and union officials. It was apparent that some of the former had a strong preference to operate without trade unions. The owner-manager of a medium-sized construction firm, for instance, told us that he would consider that he had failed as an employer if his workforce decided they needed a union. In this and other cases, the Living Wage formed part of a bundle of paternalist employment practices that probably served to ensure non-union status. It was not the case, however, that the Living Wage had been adopted by companies of this kind as part of an explicit policy of union substitution. The decision stemmed from other motives, and the prospect of unionization was, in any case, remote. In none of the employer interviews was it reported that the Living Wage had been adopted in response to an attempt to unionize workers or to erode the position of an existing union. A very similar impression was gained from the interviews with union representatives. As we have seen, many of the latter were suspicious of the Living Wage campaign and perceived in it a potential threat, a perception which has led unions both to appropriate the standard while standing aloof from the campaign and develop their own, alternative £10.00 living wage. Despite this suspicion, however, we gathered no accounts from union representatives of employers using the Living Wage deliberately against unions, either to frustrate organizing initiatives or to supplant collective bargaining. It may be that in some cases the Living Wage has been used in this way, but it is likely that situations of this kind are uncommon and that most employers have not viewed the Living Wage as an instrument of anti-unionism.

Impact on Employment Law

The relationship between civil regulation and employment law has tended to be viewed in two ways. As with collective bargaining, it is suggested that civil regulation can forestall regulation through law, forming a barrier that inhibits the introduction of more effective statutory regulation (Bartley 2018; Kinderman 2012). In addition, it has been suggested that private regulation of international supply chains can serve as a functional replacement for absent or ineffective statutory regulation, both at an international scale and in the host countries of supplier firms (Kuruvilla 2021; Vogel 2010b). Neither of these arguments accurately describe the relationship between the Living Wage and employment law in the UK, at least in their simplest and strongest forms.

Civil regulation has been used by public policy makers as an alternative to regulating through law in the UK. In the early 1990s, the Conservative Government encouraged Business in the Community to launch an Opportunity 2000 initiative to encourage businesses to adopt equal opportunities policy as an alternative to strengthening sex discrimination law (Richards 2001). This pattern has not been reproduced in the case of the Living Wage. The campaign for the latter emerged after the UK introduced its statutory minimum wage in 1998, and the two forms of regulation have coexisted since. Moreover, in the period since 2011 when accreditation of Living Wage Employers began, there has been a strengthening, not a weakening, of the National Minimum Wage. In 2016, the Government introduced a higher National Living Wage for those aged 25 and over and has since declared its intention to reduce the qualifying age to 21. In addition, the Government has adopted a policy of increasing the 'bite' of the National Living Wage, with a target level of two-thirds of median hourly pay by 2024. The success of the Living Wage campaign is arguably one of the factors that has led to this shift in policy, not least in the Government appropriating the 'living wage' term for its own standard. Two other factors, though, have also been significant. One is a determination on the part of the Conservative Party to compete for working class votes by ending its earlier opposition to minimum wage law. The Conservative breakthrough in 'red wall' constituencies in the 2019 General Election indicates the success of this electoral repositioning. Second, support for a higher statutory minimum wage has formed part of the Government's austerity programme, with its determination to reduce transfer payments for those on low incomes. Cuts to low-wage incomes through the introduction of universal credit and other measures have been accompanied by a higher minimum wage, effectively transferring the burden for maintaining low incomes from the state to employers. Living Wage accreditation has grown therefore not in a period when statutory regulation of pay has been weakened, but at a time when the state has reduced its own commitment to supporting those on low incomes.

Since the launch of the campaign, the Living Wage has operated alongside statutory regulation of pay in precisely the same way it has operated alongside collective bargaining. It has functioned neither as a barrier nor as an alternative to statutory regulation of the labour market. This coincidence of civil and statutory regulation has led to some mutual influence between the two forms. As we have noted, the success of the Living Wage campaign is one of the factors that led the Government to strengthen statutory regulation of low pay, while campaigners in turn have developed their policy of diversification, through the launch of Living Hours and other new standards, in response to the higher statutory rate. Perhaps the best way to think of the relationship between employment law and the Living Wage is in terms of the former providing a platform on top of which the higher, voluntary standard sits. Collective bargaining has often operated through this kind of relationship to employment law, with joint regulation leading to higher employment standards that go beyond statutory minima (Brown et al. 2000). This is precisely how the Living Wage operates, offering an additional tier of regulation that stands upon and does not replace employment law.

Woke Capitalism

'Woke capitalism' refers to the appropriation of progressive social movements by private corporations, which declare themselves advocates and defenders of social and environmental justice. In a recent critique of this trend, Rhodes (2022) argues that this development has overwhelmingly negative consequences and represents the unwarranted extension of private, corporate power over social and economic life. Rhodes' critique of woke capitalism contains several arguments, all of which conform to a long tradition of critical evaluation of purportedly progressive management (Heery 2016). Thus, corporate advocacy of progressive causes is identified as cynical, stemming from a desire to protect business interests rather than from genuine commitment. The embrace of such causes is also depicted as a surface-phenomenon that leaves the essential, and exploitative, functioning of capitalist enterprise unchanged. And the intrusion of business into progressive movements inhibits or precludes more democratic and more effective means of dealing with social and environmental problems. Finally, Rhodes argues that woke capitalism is functional, both for individual corporations and for the wider formation of neo-liberal capitalism of which they form a part. It serves to legitimate business and defuse attacks from social justice and environmental campaigners.

Rhodes makes no mention of business support for living wage movements, but his critique of woke capitalism might readily be extended to developments of this kind. In our view, however, they have only limited validity when applied to employer support for the Living Wage in the UK. We have identified examples of instrumental adoption of the Living Wage, but in the majority of cases employer support for the standard has not been cynical and has often grown from a wider anti-poverty or social justice commitment, which in turn reflects the support for the Living Wage of many not-for-profit and public service organizations. We have shown that for many employers adopting the Living Wage has not been highly disruptive and has led to only a limited increase in costs. This is not always the case, however, and amongst employers reporting impact the median percentage of workers receiving a pay increase is about twenty per cent: in more than a hundred organizations, 500 or more employees received an increase in pay at the point of accreditation. We have further shown that civil regulation through the Living Wage is compatible with other forms of regulation, such as collective bargaining and employment law, and that voluntary adoption of labour standards by employers does not preclude their pursuit through other means. Different forms of regulation can reinforce one another in a 'smart mix'. Finally, we have shown that a primary benefit of the Living Wage for employers is that it enhances reputation: it contributes to the legitimacy of employing organizations that adopt it. This legitimacy is bought for a price, however, which includes ceding an element of external control of reward policy to external institutions and, in many cases, increased labour costs. There is evidence of mutual gains, with reported benefits for employers, in most organizations, accruing alongside pay increases for workers. Employers have gained legitimacy from the Living Wage, but tens of thousands of low-paid workers have gained a pay increase.

This latter combination of features is important and, again, in some ways is analogous to the experience of collective bargaining. The emergence of the latter in the early twentieth century was accompanied by a critique from the left on the grounds that, in the absence of a revolutionary party, it served only to incorporate the organized working class and stabilize capitalist societies, an argument that continues to animate contemporary Trotskyism today (Kelly 2018). The response of pluralist defenders of trade unionism to this critique has been to argue that non-revolutionary trade unionism may have helped stabilize capitalist societies, but it also transformed them through the cumulative concessions secured through collective bargaining (Flanders 1975). The Living Wage is a single-issue campaign, and the impact of civil regulation is not equivalent in significance to the enduring regulatory effect of the labour movement, but an essentially similar exchange lies at the heart of both, in which enhanced legitimacy for employers has been secured through material concessions to employees. It is this exchange, we believe, which diminishes the force of the critique of woke capitalism developed by Rhodes and reduces its applicability to the Living Wage campaign.

Conclusion

In this chapter we have examined the impact of the Living Wage from three perspectives. From the perspective of employees, we have reviewed evidence of the redistributive effect of the Living Wage, looking at how many and which types of workers have benefitted and to what degree, and we have also considered whether workers have paid a price for the Living Wage in the form of work intensification and loss of other benefits. From the perspective of employers, we have considered whether there is a business case for the Living Wage, using our survey of employers to identify the extent and nature of reported benefits that flow from accreditation. Finally, from the perspective of the wider society, we have looked at the degree to which quantitative redistribution has generated qualitative improvements for low-wage workers and their communities, and whether the use of civil regulation has carried an institutional cost, eroding other, more effective means of regulating employment based on collective bargaining and law.

Our examination of the redistributive effects of the Living Wage provides some support for the critical position on private regulation, which is sceptical about its capacity to generate sizeable and sustained benefits for employees. Thus, a large proportion of employers report no employee beneficiaries at the point of accreditation, accredited employers tend to be found in parts of the economy with higher pay, and our survey evidence suggests that economic benefits have not been particularly targeted at women, the young, or ethnic minorities. However, despite these weaknesses in the scheme there is still evidence of a very substantial redistributive effect. Many thousands of low-wage workers have gained from the Living Wage, and in organizations where there are reported beneficiaries they typically form a substantial percentage of the workforce. These workers have also on average received a pay increase of more than twelve per cent and are employed disproportionately in part-time and outsourced jobs. There is virtually no evidence that they have been penalized by employers seeking to claw back the cost of the Living Wage. Many of these recipients of the Living Wage work in high-wage industries, performing the ubiquitous building-service jobs that are found throughout the economy. However, although accreditation is skewed towards high-paying parts of the economy, this is not universally the case, and there is substantial and growing impact in low-wage industries, such as social care, where the Living Wage has been particularly impactful. The evidence on employee impact provides a degree of support for those who are critical of civil regulation, but the bulk of evidence is supportive of the contrary view, that private regulation can have a positive, redistributive effect.

The evidence for the impact on business was also used to test competing arguments: that the Living Wage imposes a burden on business and generates largely negative effects; that its impact has been overwhelmingly positive, stimulating a broad set of improvements in business performance; and that the scheme has been performance-neutral, generating positive effects for workers without any significant pay-off for employers. Our findings provide least support for the first of these positions. Employers report that signing up to the Living Wage can be challenging, leading to increased labour costs and disruption to internal pay structures. For some employers, these challenges have led to withdrawal from accreditation. In the main, however, these effects are reported to be modest and in most cases are outweighed by reported benefits. There is much more support for the second argument, that there is a business case for the Living Wage, with most employers reporting a range of positive consequences that embrace enhanced reputation, differentiation from competitors, improvements to recruitment, retention, and other aspects of human resource management, and success in winning contracts and funding. There are important qualifications to this positive record, however. Reputational benefits are reported more frequently than are more tangible gains from the Living Wage, such as winning new business, and for many the reported positive effects are modest. The Living Wage emerges from the research as a benign force, producing a range of outcomes that support business activity, but not as transformative. In most cases it has not produced a regulatory shock, jolting accredited employers onto a new, higher trajectory of performance. The modest impact of the Living Wage on many employers provides a degree of support for the third argument, that civil regulation is performance-neutral. A strong version of this claim is not supported by the evidence, but clearly many employers have joined the scheme and maintained membership without experiencing a sharp upturn in performance. The pattern of findings for employer impact are similar to that for worker impact, in that they are intermediate between two claims. Most employers stand between the poles of a transformative positive effect and an absence of performance gains, reporting worthwhile but modest impact.

An additional, significant finding from the research is that there is clear evidence of mutual gains, of employers and employees jointly benefitting from the Living Wage in the same organization. Most employers that report positive organizational effects also report that employees have gained from the scheme. This pattern is not seen in all accredited organizations: there is a sizeable minority where only employers have benefitted, and much smaller proportions where only workers or neither party has gained. The dominant pattern, though, is one of mutual gains. Living Wage campaigners have argued that both parties to the employment relationship can benefit from civil regulation, and this is largely borne out by the evidence.

Our examination of the social impact of the Living Wage pursued two divergent paths. In the first place, we followed a 'person-centric' course using employee testimony to see if the Living Wage has led to qualitative improvements for individuals, families, and communities. Much of this evidence indicates that the campaign has increased the 'capabilities' of low-wage workers, freeing them from debt and anxiety and enabling them to make choices and invest, particularly in the life-quality of children. Wider putative benefits, such as greater community participation, remain unproven, however, and the main impact of the Living Wage seems to have been to enhance the privatized personal and family lives of those on low incomes.

Along the other course, we have examined the impact of the Living Wage on other, more established methods for regulating low pay. With regard to collective bargaining, the evidence suggests that the decline of joint regulation provided an opportunity for the Living Wage campaign to emerge and flourish. It does not suggest, however, that the campaign has further eroded collective bargaining and the standard has been adopted in both unionized and non-union parts of the UK economy. Our study indicates that civil regulation in the form of the Living Wage is compatible with joint regulation through collective bargaining and is not actively curtailing or forestalling the latter. The evidence also suggests that the Living Wage is compatible with legal regulation of low pay. The campaign has been almost coterminous with the UK's adoption of a statutory wage-floor, and both have thrived in tandem, the Living Wage continuing to attract employers while the bite of the minimum wage has increased. The relationship conforms to the notion of a regulatory mix, in which statutory regulation provides a foundation and civil regulation builds above, offering additional protection to employees.

In the final part of the chapter, we considered whether the Living Wage is vulnerable to the critique of 'woke capitalism'. For a variety of reasons, we do not believe this to be the case. The Living Wage has not been adopted for cynical reasons by many employers, it is not a surface-level phenomenon but has generated a substantial redistributive effect, and it has not displaced but operates alongside other methods for regulating the employment relationship, such as collective bargaining and employment law, that are subject to democratic forces. Central to the critique of woke capitalism is a functionalist argument that the espousal of progressive causes by business legitimates the prevailing economic order. Our evidence shows that employers value the reputational effects of Living Wage accreditation, but for many this legitimacy has been secured through increases in pay and labour costs. Like collective bargaining, the Living Wage has reinforced the legitimate authority of employers but at the price of redistribution.

Notes

1. To estimate the value of the wage transfer to employees following accreditation a multi-stage process was adopted. In the approximately half of cases where the Living Wage Foundation was able to provide information on the lowest prevailing rate of pay prior to accreditation, the hourly uplift is easily identified by subtracting this figure from the relevant Living Wage rate. In cases where wage data are not provided, we estimated wage levels using median wage rates by industry, obtained from ASHE. To model the counterfactual wage growth over time we used ASHE time-series data for the lowest decile of employees. Thus, we were able to calculate separate hourly uplift figures for each year of accreditation, and separately for the UK and London Living Wage. Annualized figures were calculated using data on average hours worked by industry, again derived from ASHE. Finally, all figures were converted to 2021 levels to account for inflation.

8
The Significance of the Real Living Wage

Announcing the Living Wage, 2021

Five years after the event announcing the 2016 Real Living Wage at the British Library, described in Chapter 1, the 2021 rates of £9.90 for the UK and £11.05 for London were announced at a similar event in Cardiff. The Cardiff launch was virtual, reflecting the ongoing impact of COVID-19, but in many respects it followed the same format as its British Library predecessor. Like the latter, it was one of a cluster of campaign events to announce the new rates, spread across the country, which included launches in Scotland, Birmingham, Manchester, and Newham in East London. These events exemplify many of the campaign features and the responses of employers, unions, and public authorities that we have analysed in the preceding chapters. In microcosm, they capture the defining features of the Living Wage campaign.

All these events originated within civil society and form part of a concerted attempt to develop and diffuse civil regulation. Thus, the Cardiff announcement was organized by Cynnal Cymru, the accreditation body for the Living Wage in Wales, and was hosted by two leaders from the Citizens Cymru-Wales network. The events also embodied the methods of the Living Wage campaign. The event in Wales reported on campaign success in achieving strategic targets, using numerical indicators, and there was a research presentation of results from our 2021 survey, which demonstrated the business case for the Living Wage. The success of the campaign in building membership in low-wage industries, such as hospitality and social care, was reported, as was the spread of accreditation beyond Cardiff, Wales's core city, to other parts of the country. Two recent developments in campaign strategy were especially prominent. First, there was a focus on social care with testimony from a care recipient, a care worker, a community organizer specializing in care, a faith leader, and a recently accredited employer, all of whom made the case for adopting the Living Wage in Welsh social care and appealed to Welsh Government for support. Second, the leader of Cardiff Council reported on the Cardiff Living Wage City campaign, which had exceeded the targets set out in its initial action plan and successfully accredited the first two Living Wage Buildings in Wales. This theme of place-based campaigning was echoed elsewhere: Birmingham and Edinburgh were recognized as Living Wage Cities, and at the Manchester event an ambitious plan was announced to create the UK's first Living Wage City-Region.

The Real Living Wage. Edmund Heery, Deborah Hann and David Nash, Oxford University Press.
© Edmund Heery, Deborah Hann and David Nash (2023). DOI: 10.1093/oso/9780198835264.003.0008

Like its British Library predecessor, the Cardiff launch was 'business-friendly'. Welsh employers were thanked for their adoption of the Living Wage, and a series of speakers made the case that paying the Living Wage was good for employers as well as employees. A series of 'actions' targeting Welsh local authorities that have not yet adopted the Living Wage were announced at the event, but these were to include handing out Living Wage cupcakes, following the rather whimsical, non-adversarial approach to campaigning favoured by Citizens UK. Three recently accredited Welsh employers took part in the event, who illustrated different aspects of the employer response to the Living Wage. Home Instead Wrexham and East Flintshire is a provider of home-care services to the elderly and part of the Home Instead franchise. Its managing-owner spoke at the launch and made a strong social justice case for paying the Living Wage. Care work, he said, is demanding, skilled, responsible, and appallingly under-valued, and a desire to recognize the contribution of staff was the motive for becoming accredited. He also made the point, however, that the business catered to private clients and was not reliant upon local authority contracts and was therefore able to afford the Living Wage. The Welsh Millennium Centre, the arts and theatre complex in Cardiff Bay, had also recently accredited, though it reported it had been paying the Living Wage since 2019. A primary motive in this case was to secure reputational benefits—'to support our brand in local communities'—but the HR director who spoke also said that there were tangible HR gains from paying the Living Wage, reporting that the centre had been able to recruit to vacancies ahead of reopening in October 2021 because it paid a premium rate. The final newly accredited employer was Heddlu Dyfed-Powys, the police force for mid and west Wales. Here a desire to act as a regional leader was significant, championing the Living Wage and encouraging both contractors and other 'anchor institutions' in this part of Wales to become accredited.

There was no trade union involvement in the launch at Cardiff and the ambivalent response of trade unions to the Living Wage was visible across the set of events. In Manchester, care worker members of UNISON North-West gave testimony, and trade unions are part of the action group put together to create the Living Wage City-Region. The response of the TUC to the announcement of new rates for the UK and London Living Wage, however, was to note the large number of workers still paid below the rate and call for an immediate increase in the statutory minimum wage to £10.00 an hour as well as the abolition of zero-hours contracts and new rights for unions to organize low-wage workers. Unions are embedded in the Living Wage campaign in some parts of the country, but elsewhere they have maintained a distance and have increasingly focused on other mechanisms to deal with the problem of low pay.

Like the British Library event, the more recent announcements all involved politicians. Labour First Minister Mark Drakeford announced the new Living Wage rates in Cardiff and declared that Living Wage Week was now 'an important annual event in the political calendar'. In Scotland, his role was filled by Richard Lochhead, SNP Minister for Fair Work. Other politicians involved in the launch events included Labour councillors from Birmingham, Cardiff, and Newham, and the Labour mayors of Greater London and Greater Manchester, Sadiq Kahn and Andy Burnham. At the Welsh event, Plaid Cymru were also represented through Dafydd Llywelyn, the elected Police and Crime Commissioner for Dyfed-Powys. Politicians taking part in the meetings, therefore, came from parties of the centre-left that generally have been more receptive to the Living Wage campaign. Both Drakeford and Llywelyn were re-elected in 2021 on pledges to promote the Living Wage.

The involvement of politicians in the launch events also highlighted some of the ways in which public authorities have promoted the Living Wage. Mark Drakeford reported that he had written to all Welsh public bodies when he first assumed office in 2019, urging them to adopt the Living Wage, and was about to do so again to mark the twentieth anniversary of the campaign. He also reported that Welsh Government was acting to implement its manifesto commitment to ensure all care workers in Wales would be paid the Living Wage. A representative Social Care Forum had been asked to formulate proposals, and Welsh Government has developed a plan to implement these over the course of the Senedd. Funds to subsidize payment of the Living Wage were allocated in the government's December 2021 budget. Another way in which public authorities taking part in the events had promoted the Living Wage was by backing place-based campaigns. Birmingham City Council has been the prime mover behind the Birmingham Living Wage City campaign, and Andy Burnham's office has played this role in Greater Manchester. In Edinburgh, the SNP-led City of Edinburgh Council has taken the initiative. The launch events demonstrate how embedded is the Living Wage campaign in the political process and how public authorities below the level of the UK state have been a vital source of impetus and support.

Summary of Findings

Observation of events like the Cardiff announcement is just one of several methods that we have used to develop our case study of the Living Wage. Other methods comprise surveys of employers, interviews with campaigners, employers, and trade unionists, analysis of documents and websites, and the creation of a novel dataset of Living Wage Employers, drawn from information collected by the Living Wage Foundation supplemented with official statistics and other data. We have used this mix of research methods to try and produce a rounded account of the Living Wage campaign that explores its different facets. We have also used the research to reflect upon the debates over civil and other forms of private regulation that have emerged in the academic literature. It is to a summary of the main findings and of their implications for these debates that we now turn.

The Living Wage. Our first set of findings presents an analysis of the Living Wage standard as a body of civil regulation. Among the main pieces of evidence are the following: (1) The Living Wage embodies the principle of payment for need and prioritizes payment on this basis for low-paid workers above other principles of pay determination that privilege paying the person, the job, for performance, or according to labour market context. Employee need is conceived broadly in terms of a decent, not subsistence, level of income and is measured using the MIS methodology, with hourly rates of pay for London and the rest of the UK calculated annually from estimates of the minimum income needs of different types of low-wage family. Employers conforming to the standard agree to pay these rates to all direct and indirect employees aged 18 and over and to implement new rates within six months of their announcement each November; (2) The Living Wage is an example of civil regulation; that is, private regulation of the employment relationship formulated and promoted by CSOs. It is also a voluntary form of regulation that is not inscribed in law or enforced by the state, a feature of the Living Wage in the UK which differentiates it from its American counterpart. Because the standard is voluntary it is supported by reputational and other incentives, reinforced by campaigning pressure that 'names and shames' non-conforming employers. Civil regulation is a form of unilateral regulation, such that employment rules are formulated, promoted, and administered by civil society organizations. As the campaign has developed, however, this unilateral character has softened and been overlain with a stakeholder system of governance. The latter is exemplified by the Living Wage Commission, created in 2016, which includes representatives from a range of institutions, and which has oversight of the campaign and formally approves the new rates each year; (3) The Living Wage standard requires accredited employers to exceed legal minima but in other respects is a relatively soft form of regulation. It fails several tests of robustness for private regulation that have been identified in the literature, such as the requirement to involve representatives of employees and operate an independent system of monitoring. The standard also falls short of the 'capability approach' to enforcing voluntary regulation, in which regulators help businesses to upgrade their operations so that improved labour practices can be more readily afforded. Despite the relative absence of both deterrence-based and capability approaches to enforcement, evidence of non-compliance by employers is limited. The voluntary nature of the scheme, the fact that employers often absorb costs for contractors, and the simplicity of the standard and the ease with which many can implement it have allowed it to function effectively without intrusive monitoring; (4) In the manner of other bodies of private regulation, the Living Wage has evolved to become more elaborate over time. New supplementary standards have been introduced which seek to help spread the Living Wage; the Service-Provider, Living Wage Funder, and

Living Wage Places schemes. More recently, the Living Hours scheme has been developed, and other substantive standards, such as Living Pensions, may appear in the future. Although this logic of evolution is shared with other bodies of private regulation, the causal mechanism differs from that identified in the literature. In studies of international private regulation, it is the repeated exposure of failings by external campaigners and attendant threat to consumer brands which drives evolution. This dynamic is missing from the Living Wage, with development of supplementary standards and the diversification into other substantive standards emerging from the campaign itself. It is the entrepreneurial quality of the campaign and the desire of campaigners to maintain momentum that have driven evolution.

The Living Wage campaign. The second set of evidence describes the nature of the Living Wage campaign and the organizations behind it. The main findings are as follows: (1) The CSO which has orchestrated the Living Wage campaign since its inception is Citizens UK, the British arm of the American community organizing movement. In 2011, Citizens UK set up the Living Wage Foundation as an arm's length subsidiary with the dedicated task of accrediting employers that agree to adopt the standard. These two linked organizations are rather different. Citizens UK employs community organizers to develop and support a network of faith, educational, and community groups, organized into local chapters which campaign on a variety of issues, including the Living Wage. The Living Wage Foundation, in contrast, is a professional movement organization, which employs communications and business development specialists who focus specifically on accrediting employers. Although there are differences, there are also commonalities, and the workforce of both is like that of other social justice organizations: young, educated, diverse, and highly engaged; (2) The campaign for the Living Wage possesses several notable features, which are shared with other attempts to promote civil regulation. These include 'scaling up', such that a single standard is promoted across the UK through an integrated national campaign: relying upon the 'politics of expertise' (Hilton et al. 2013), most notably by basing the Living Wage rate on research into the income needs of low wage families; formal targeting of priority industries, localities, and types of employer, with an increasing focus since the onset of COVID-19 on recruiting employers in key industries characterized by low pay, such as social care; and diversification, with additional schemes of accreditation, such as Living Wage Places and Living Hours, being added to the core standard over time; (3) The methods used to promote the Living Wage differ between Citizens UK and the Living Wage Foundation. Citizens UK relies upon the classic repertoire of American community organizing, including listening campaigns, power analysis, actions, and testimony, while the Living Wage Foundation employs methods that have become standard within campaigns to encourage responsible business. The latter include developing a business case, accreditation of member-employers, reliance upon business champions, and reinforcing membership through award schemes. These different methods can reinforce one another, and campaigners often refer to them as the 'stick and the carrot'. There can also be a degree of tension, however, and most employers are recruited through the 'business-friendly' methods of the Foundation, without involving Citizens UK; (4) In developing the Living Wage campaign, Citizens UK and the Living Wage Foundation have forged relationships with a range of other labour market institutions. Particularly important are relations with other CSOs, including the Poverty Alliance and Cynnal Cymru who promote the scheme to employers in Scotland and Wales. Campaigners have also cultivated political support, with Citizens UK making effective use of accountability assemblies to win the backing of politicians from across the political spectrum. Trade unions have been another important ally and have featured prominently in the campaign in some parts of the country and in certain industries though, overall, union involvement has been patchy.

This set of findings has three main implications for the literature on civil regulation. The employment relations contribution to the latter has often focused on the analysis of union-community coalitions (Heery 2019). The case confirms some of the benefits that CSOs can derive from joint work with unions identified in this literature, including gaining access to workers in unionized workplaces, relying upon unions to monitor and enforce employer commitment to voluntary standards, and securing legitimacy for civil regulation through union-backing. Despite these tangible benefits, however, the campaign has not relied extensively on union involvement. Campaigners have worked with other coalition partners, including other CSOs, employer champions, and political supporters, to a greater degree than they have trade unions. This feature of the campaign—seeking support from labour market institutions other than unions—is perhaps a function of union decline and the emergence of an extensive non-union economy since the 1970s. It is also characteristic of other CSOs that seek to influence employment relations (Heery, Abbott, and Williams 2012).

A second theme in the literature has also been developed within employment relations and stresses the distinctiveness of the methods used by CSOs, in comparison with those of trade unions. CSOs have variously been said to be more effective at mobilizing support for campaigns, more reliant upon informal, unstructured forms of protest, and better able to deploy consumer opinion against employers. Our case did not provide strong support for any of these claims. While the Living Wage campaign has effectively mobilized public opinion, it has not relied heavily upon worker mobilization, and the participation of low-wage employees in campaigning has often been confined to providing testimony. The indie unions, UVW and IWGB, have seemingly been more single-minded and more effective in mobilizing low-wage workers in Living Wage campaigns than has Citizens UK (Alberti and Però 2018; Shenker 2019). Neither has the Living Wage campaign relied upon consumer mobilization or informal, unstructured protest. Community organizing is a formal, planned, and strategic approach to exerting pressure on business and government, which eschews the kind of 'swarming' behaviour celebrated by theorists of new social movements (Heckscher and McCarthy 2014), and while there has been an attempt to develop a Living Wage consumer brand this is neither a core element of the campaign nor associated with the use of consumer activism to pressure employers. The leverage that campaigners have used to encourage employers to adopt the Living Wage has generally come not from low-wage workers themselves or from consumers, but from investors, public authorities, grant-making organizations, client businesses located at the top of supply chains, and anchor institutions within local communities.

The final theme in the literature emphasizes the switch in method of many CSOs from 'naming and shaming' poorly behaving businesses to seeking to garner business support (Vogel 2010a). The case study provides strong support for this account, as a 'business-friendly' approach has come to dominate the campaign, particularly since the creation of the Living Wage Foundation in 2011 (Bunyan 2016). The campaign for the Living Wage relies upon many of the same methods used by other CSOs seeking to promote responsible business. This conformity to the CSR norm is limited, however, in that Citizens UK continues to use community organizing methods to promote the Living Wage and to pressure resistant employers. 'Naming and shaming', albeit always with the aim of opening dialogue, has not been abandoned but continues to be applied when business is recalcitrant. The case study indicates that CSOs, like other labour market institutions, use a variety of methods to pursue their objectives, depending on circumstance and the reaction of employers they are trying to influence.

Employer responses. The third element in the case study explored employer responses to the campaign, gathering information on how many and which types of employers had adopted the Living Wage and the motives that underpinned this decision. By May 2022 more than 12,500 employers had joined the Living Wage scheme, and our analysis revealed that they possessed the following characteristics: (1) Accredited organizations are spread across the size-distribution of UK employers, though most accredited employers are small organizations. Many large employers, including FTSE-listed corporations, have joined the scheme, but the retail, clothing, and electronics brands that feature in international systems of private regulation are largely absent; (2) Employers from all main sectors have adopted the Living Wage, though support for the scheme has been strongest in the not-for-profit sector, with faith, anti-poverty, and social justice organizations prominent amongst the ranks of accredited organizations; (3) Employers from all the main industry divisions have also adopted the Living Wage. Most employers are found in relatively high-paying parts of the economy, however, where the cost of implementing the standard can more readily be afforded; (4) Although the distribution is tilted towards high-paying industries, many employers in low wage industries have joined the scheme. Employer membership is especially strong in social care and in outsourcing industries such as cleaning, catering, and security; (5) The Living Wage is a national standard, and accredited employers are found in all nations and regions of the UK. London and Scotland stand out, however, as the main centres of employer support, with Wales also recording a high rate of accreditation; (6) The Living Wage emerges from the data as a primarily urban phenomenon, with most accredited employers concentrated in the UK's core cities. It is also found disproportionately in remain-voting parts of the country. Employer support for the Living Wage is strongest in progressive cities, as it is in the USA (Swarts and Vasi 2011), while support for the standard is at its lowest in the rural districts and post-industrial small towns that voted to leave the EU; (7) Most Living Wage Employers are located in parts of the economy with a low union presence, though a significant proportion are found where membership is high, indicating that the two types of labour market institution can coexist; (8) Other institutional forces are more strongly linked with the pattern of employer support than are unions, and accreditation occurs disproportionately where there is an active campaign to promote the Living Wage and where local authorities are controlled by the centre-left.

It is possible to infer employer motives for supporting the Living Wage from the characteristics of those that sign up, but we also explored this question directly through our employer survey. The main findings are as follows: (1) Expressive motives are cited most frequently by accredited employers, reporting that they adopted the Living Wage as an expression of organizational values or mission or to lend support to the campaign; (2) Instrumental motives are also significant, with reputational benefits being the most frequently cited anticipated gain, followed by HR benefits and more general commercial benefits; (3) Defensive motives for adopting the Living Wage, such as a desire to avoid reputational harm, are an important consideration for some employers, but a rationale of this kind appears to be less important than expressive motivation or a desire to secure positive gains; 4) Institutional motives, such as the need to respond to pressure from external campaigners, politicians, or trade unions, are the least frequently cited. A partial exception to this pattern, however, is a desire to respond to a local initiative to promote the Living Wage in a specific town, city, or region, which was identified as an important motive by a substantial minority. The evidence suggests employers are receptive to place-based campaigning.

The final set of evidence on employer responses dealt with resistance to the Living Wage. We cannot estimate how many employers consciously reject the Living Wage, but employer resistance is integral to the campaign and stems from a variety of motives. These include unwillingness to cede influence over reward policy to an external institution, concern about increases to labour costs, refusal to accept responsibility for the employment conditions of contract staff, and a belief that some low-wage employees do not warrant the Living Wage. In many cases, though, resistance is not absolute, and it seems to be common for employers to pay the Living Wage while declining to become accredited. Our qualitative research identified a continuum of employer responses to the Living Wage, ranging from absolute rejection at one extreme to exceeding the requirements of the standard at the other. This continuum suggests that employer responses to regulation are not reducible to an overriding impulse to 'unruliness'.

The literature on employer responses to civil regulation accords priority to instrumental motives. Amongst supporters of standards like the Living Wage, it tends to be argued that employer support flows from a belief that tangible business benefits can be secured, such as improvements to labour supply and performance (Bhattarchaya et al. 2008). More critical voices, in contrast, tend to emphasize less reputable motives, such as a desire to forestall legislation, influence public perceptions of business activity in the manner of green-washing, or minimize risk (Schuessler et al. 2019). Our research provides evidence in support of both these interpretations of employer responses to civil regulation. The most striking finding, however, is that instrumental motives of whatever type seem to play second fiddle to expressive motives in explaining why employers sign up to the Living Wage. This finding is echoed by case studies of Living Wage employers, which observe that a wish to 'do the right thing' was central to the decision to accredit (Carson 2022; Prowse and Dobbins 2022). The normative or ideological springs of employer behaviour tend to be discounted in the field of employment relations, with researchers regarding declarations of mission or values as a cynical cover for underlying, instrumental motives (Rhodes 2022). Cynicism can readily be identified in the corporate world, but we are minded to give credence to local entrepreneurs saying they adopted the Living Wage to give something back to their communities, charities saying they have implemented it because it reflects their basic purpose, and local politicians saying it complements a broader strategy to promote inclusive growth. Having regard to the normative basis of employer behaviour and the changing ideologies that underpin it, we believe can enrich analysis.

Union responses. The fourth purpose of the case study was to examine how trade unions, for long the default institution of worker voice, have reacted to the Living Wage campaign and to the attempts by Citizens UK and the Living Wage Foundation to shape employer behaviour. The primary evidence collected was as follows: (1) Unions have reacted favourably to the Living Wage campaign and have lent their support in several ways. They have participated in the campaign governance structure created by the Living Wage Foundation, become accredited as Living Wage Employers, taken part in campaigns to win the Living Wage for outsourced workers at unionized workplaces, and become affiliates to Citizens UK chapters; (2) The most notable example of affiliation is that of UNISON North-West within Greater Manchester Citizens. Here, an extended and fruitful link has been forged between UNISON and the Living Wage campaign, and involvement in the latter has helped the union organize and secure improvements for low-wage workers, particularly within social care; (3) Although there has been a favourable response to the campaign, this has existed alongside considerable tension and the relationship between unions and the Living Wage campaign has also been characterized by conflict (Holgate 2009). Manifestations of the latter include a widespread critique within trade unions of both the Living Wage standard and Citizens UK, the refusal of unions to become involved in Living Wage campaigning, and the development of an alternative union-specific living wage standard of £10.00 per hour; (4) The union response to the Living Wage campaign has also been characterized by 'indifference'; that is, unions pursuing their own attempts to improve the condition of low-wage workers separately from that of the Living Wage campaign. Unions have 'appropriated' the Living Wage standard, including it within their bargaining and campaigning activities, often with minimal reference to or contact with Citizens UK or the Living Wage Foundation. A feature of this appropriation of the Living Wage has been union reliance upon a traditional repertoire to spread the standard amongst employers, including collective bargaining, industrial disputes, and political influence exerted through the Labour Party. Unions have helped create a shadow Living Wage, beyond the ranks of accredited employers, and in doing so have made use of their established methods.

Much of the literature on unions and civil regulation has been concerned with whether growth of the latter will either erode or strengthen trade unionism; what might be described as the replacement and reinforcement theses. Our research yielded cases of union anxiety about the Living Wage and resentment at campaigners 'trespassing' within their domain. The shared interest of both unions and campaigners in improving the conditions of low-wage workers through direct interaction with employers had led to a degree of tension. We did not encounter cases of employers using the Living Wage to obstruct or displace unions, however, and in many parts of the economy the Living Wage has been adopted alongside trade unions without producing notable adverse effects for the latter. Our case study did not provide strong support for the replacement thesis. Neither did it provide strong support for the reinforcement thesis. To be sure, the experiences of UNISON North-West in promoting the Living Wage within Greater Manchester Citizens does fit this interpretation. The union gained from its coalition with community organizers, gaining access to workers, supplementing its campaigning power, and gaining legitimacy through joint work with community and faith organizations (Frege et al. 2004). As we have seen, Greater Manchester Citizens also benefitted from this relationship. The research did not encounter other examples of this kind of 'deep coalition', however, and the more typical relationship was conducted at arm's length, with unions appropriating the Living Wage standard and incorporating it within their established repertoire. Unions have made use of the Living Wage, therefore, but the campaign has not 'reinforced' unions in the manner identified in the literature, through the development of an extensive and enduring coalition with civil society.

Response of public authorities. The case study explored two aspects of the response of public authorities to the Living Wage: the adoption of the Living Wage by public sector organizations and the efforts taken by devolved, regional, and local government to spread the standard amongst other employers. Our inquiry into the adoption of the Living Wage revealed the following: (1) Public sector employers have a relatively high level of Living Wage accreditation, indicative of the continuing influence of the 'good employer' commitment despite the impact of austerity; (2) Unlike other innovations in employment practice, which have flown outwards from the centre of the UK state, the Living Wage has been adopted most frequently on the periphery, with local government having the highest level of accreditation; (3) The pattern of accreditation has also been shaped by constitutional devolution, and public bodies in Scotland and Wales have been strong supporters, as have English regional combined authorities; 4) The Scottish and Welsh Governments are controlled by the centre-left, and their determination to use the Living Wage to promote 'inclusive growth' has led to its take-up across much of the devolved public sector. The influence of the political contingency can also be seen in local government, where administrations with a centre-left leadership are more likely to have implemented the standard; (5) Local and regional authorities with an elected mayor and other public bodies with elected leaders have been notable adopters of the Living Wage, reflecting the popularity of policies on low pay amongst the electorate.

Public authorities have also often acted as 'model' employers, encouraging other employers to adopt the Living Wage. They have acted as 'anchor institutions'. Our findings on this activity to spread the Living Wage were as follows: (1) Promoting the Living Wage has frequently formed part of a broader attempt to encourage 'fair work' or 'good work', and both the Scottish and Welsh Governments and several regional and local authorities have produced charters setting out a list of desirable employment standards that they wish to see adopted. These charters invariably include the Living Wage; (2) A major lever that public authorities have used to spread the Living Wage is procurement, with many adopting statements that adherence to the standard will be considered when awarding contracts; (3) Other economic levers have also been used, including linking the Living Wage to the awarding of grants and funding and to tax concessions. Several local authorities have been accredited as Living Wage Funders; (4) A particularly notable measure taken by the Scottish and Welsh Governments has been to subsidize payment of the Living Wage by private employers in social care; (5) Public authorities have also played an important part in the Living Wage campaign, using their influencing power to publicize the standard and encourage its adoption. In some cases, this has led to regional and local authorities taking a lead role in Living Wage Places campaigns; (6) There is evidence that attempts to promote the Living Wage have proved effective, and the rate of accreditation amongst employers is higher where local authorities have adopted policies to promote the standard.

How do these findings relate to the literature on civil regulation and the state? One core conclusion is that the Living Wage has not served as a functional alternative to an absent or failing state in the way that international civil regulation is often reported to do (Vogel 2010a). On the contrary, the campaign has sought to win support from public authorities, and that support, when it has been forthcoming, has made an important contribution to campaign success. Public authorities have adopted the Living Wage for their own employees and provided incentives and offered encouragement to other employers to take the same step, indicating that state action can reinforce civil regulation. The methods that public authorities have used to reinforce the Living Wage in this way, however, fall short of the legislative or regulatory steps identified in the literature. The devolved governments of Scotland and Wales, English metro mayors, and local authorities do not have the power to legislate on employment matters, which is confined to the UK Government. In the absence of this power, they have acted as model employers and used procurement, grant-making, funding, and subsidy to promote the Living Wage. They have also used their convening and influencing powers, articulating an appeal to civic or national sentiment as a means of persuading employers to become accredited. The two events to announce the Living Wage, with which we have opened and ended this book, illustrate the kinds of appeal that have been made to spread the Living Wage.

Living Wage impact. The final purpose of the case study was to estimate the impact of the Living Wage campaign. We gathered evidence on the redistributive effects of the scheme, examining its impact on workers, on the degree to which the Living Wage has also benefitted employers, testing the 'business case', and on its wider societal impact beyond the workplace.

Our main findings on the redistributive effect of the campaign are as follows: (1) At an aggregate level, the Living Wage has directly benefitted nearly 340,000 workers since the launch of the accreditation scheme in 2011, with a total wage transfer of about £1.9bn. This is a substantial redistributive achievement, but benefitting workers form only a small percentage of the 4.5 million earning less than the Living Wage in 2021; (2) The scheme has also registered a redistributive effect at the level of individual enterprises. While there is a substantial minority of employers who report no benefitting employees at the point of accreditation, in most cases workers have received a pay increase, and in more than a quarter of accredited organizations a quarter or more of the workforce have gained; (3) The value of the pay increase received is also substantial in the majority of cases, with workers on average obtaining an uplift in hourly pay of about twelve per cent; (4) The distribution of impact across the economy varies, depending on the indicator used. The number of workers benefitting is highest in large organizations, high-paying industries, such as finance, local authority districts with relatively high pay, and in key industries that operated through the COVID-19 pandemic, including health and social care. The bite of the Living Wage (the percentage gaining within an individual employer), in contrast, is higher in smaller organizations, low-paying industries, districts with relatively low pay, and industries adversely affected by

COVID-19, such as hospitality and leisure. The size of the pay increase received by individual employees is inversely related to the 'bite' of the scheme. Thus, it is higher in large organizations, in the public sector, and in high-paying parts of the economy and lower in small firms, in social care and outsourcing industries, and other low-paying parts of the economy. The highest uplift for individuals tends to be found where a small proportion of the workforce is affected by the scheme and generous pay increases can be more readily afforded; (5) One of the objectives of the campaign was to raise the pay of outsourced workers, and this has been achieved: contract workers make up about a third of those who have received a pay increase and include many London-based employees working for large corporates and public service organizations. There is also evidence that the Recognized Service Provider accreditation has spread the Living Wage to a growing number of workers on outsourcing contracts; (6) Part-time employees are another group who have benefitted and make up more than half of the directly benefitting workforce. Part-time work is largely performed by women, and women likely make up a substantial majority of those part-time workers who have gained from the scheme; (7) Our survey demonstrated that those gaining from the Living Wage are drawn from a broad range of low-paid occupations. Nevertheless, there is a concentration of impact amongst administrative and business service jobs, such as receptionists, cleaners, and security guards; occupations that are characterized by ubiquity and are found across the economy. The evidence suggests that the most frequent gainers from the scheme have been low-paid employees working in high-wage industries; (8) The survey also indicated that women, young people, and members of ethnic minorities have frequently benefitted from the Living Wage. Amongst direct employees receiving a pay increase, women form the majority, though this is not true of contract workers; (9) There is little evidence of gains for workers being undermined by employers clawing back costs through job losses or reductions in hours or benefits. Claims of both critical and conservative commentators that measures like the Living Wage generate perverse effects for employees are not supported.

Our findings on the effects of the Living Wage on employing organizations were as follows: (1) Virtually all accredited employers report some benefits to their business from signing up to the Living Wage, with reputational gains being the most frequently reported, followed by HR gains and commercial and financial benefits, such as success in winning contracts; (2) While business benefits are widespread, they are also reported by most employers to be fairly modest in scope; worthwhile rather than radical improvements; (3) Many employers report some disadvantages of accreditation, including an increase in labour costs and disruption to internal pay structure, but in the main these are not believed to outweigh the benefits of accreditation; (4) There is evidence for the Living Wage producing 'mutual gains' for employers and employees in the same organization: the majority of employers reporting benefits from adopting the Living Wage also report that employees received a pay increase. However, although the dominant outcome-pattern is one of mutual gains, there is a substantial minority of cases where employers have benefitted but not workers, and a small minority where the obverse is seen, and workers have gained but not their employer.

The third and most speculative set of findings on Living Wage impact dealt with effects beyond the workplace. There were four principal findings: (1) Testimony from workers receiving a Living Wage pay increase suggest that it has enhanced 'capability' in the manner suggested by campaigners. Recipients spoke of experiencing fewer money troubles, reducing working hours, and spending more on themselves and their families. Often these changes were not dramatic, but they had enhanced the quality of people's lives; (2) There is little evidence that the Living Wage has eroded the institutional position of trade unions in the UK economy. On the contrary, it is probable that union decline has provided an opportunity for the campaign to emerge and thrive; (3) There is also little evidence that the Living Wage has eroded legal regulation of the labour market. If anything, the reverse is true, with the period of the campaign coinciding with the launch of the National Living Wage and the government adopting a policy of setting the latter at two-thirds of median hourly earnings; (4) The Living Wage campaign represents a more significant and impactful intervention in the labour market than is suggested by the concept of 'woke capitalism'.

Debate on the effects of civil regulation has tended to pursue two courses. The first has focused on the business case for voluntary standards and whether employers can secure benefits if they adhere to voluntary regulation. Our research provides empirical support for this frequently repeated claim: most Living Wage Employers report that accreditation has benefitted their organization. There is an important qualification to this conclusion, however. The gains that most employers report are benign rather than transformative, representing an incremental but not a radical step forward. There is a business case for adherence to good labour standards, the Living Wage indicates, but its strength should not be exaggerated.

The second line of inquiry has focused on the redistributive effects of private regulation, with many commentators pointing to limited positive impact (Kuruvilla 2021; Lebaron et al. 2022; Locke 2013). Our research contradicts this dominant view and provides evidence that the Living Wage campaign has secured a substantial wage transfer for low-wage workers. Campaigning for social justice through voluntary regulation can be successful. Again, however, a qualification is warranted. While many thousands of workers have benefitted from the Living Wage, they form only a small percentage of those on low pay or experiencing in-work poverty. Moreover, other forms of regulation, such as the statutory minimum wage, have broader reach, uplifting pay for a larger number of people than have gained from the Living Wage. A policy conclusion can be drawn from this pattern of findings. The Living Wage, we believe, should be regarded as a supplemental method for addressing the UK's problem of low pay, which can contribute to but not replace other policy instruments. Decisive action to address low pay will continue to require legislation, not just to raise pay rates but to address the problems of short and unpredictable hours that contribute to low earnings. The law should also be used to strengthen the rights of unions to recruit and organize low-wage workers and to establish industry forums through which wages and other conditions of employment can be collectively bargained in low-wage industries. Civil regulation through the Living Wage, we believe, can supplement other measures of this kind, in a regulatory 'smart mix' to bear down on low pay.

Much of the literature that we have used to frame the case study of the Living Wage deals with international civil regulation and attempts to promote voluntary standards within global supply chains. A final conclusion is that the account of civil regulation in a domestic setting that we have offered differs in certain important respects from the account of international private regulation found in this literature (Bartley 2018; Donaghey et al. 2014; Kuruvilla 2021). Common features emerge from both, but there are also striking differences, which include the following: (1) The place occupied by retail chains, clothing, and electronics manufacturers within international private regulation is occupied by professional service businesses and outsourcing firms in the Living Wage campaign; (2) The commercial relationships that have driven the spread of the Living Wage amongst business are those between outsourcing firms and their clients, not pressure from individual consumers as has been the case for regulation of global supply chains; (3) The role of public authorities looms large in the spread of the Living Wage, while in international private regulation public governance is often minimal or absent; (4) The panoply of auditing, monitoring, and enforcement mechanisms that support international regulation have not been reproduced in the case of the Living Wage; (5) Despite this absence, evidence for civil regulation generating substantive, redistributive change is stronger for the Living Wage than is the case for its international equivalent.

This pattern of difference suggests two things. The first is simply that domestic economies may offer a more conducive environment for civil regulation than do supply chains that circle the globe. In the UK, supportive public authorities, a degree of trade union backing, and a network of allies within civil society have provided a supportive context and allowed the Living Wage campaign to flourish. In the Global South, all these reinforcing conditions may be lacking. The second is that the dynamic driving regulation appears to differ. The mobilization of consumers has been less important in promoting the Living Wage than is the case with international regulation, while the roles of public service anchor institutions and large corporate clients have been more important. The claim that the global spread of private regulation has been driven by forces emanating from the realm of consumption (Donaghey et al. 2014) appears to have less validity for civil regulation within domestic economies.

Significance of the Real Living Wage

Our study is a contribution to the long tradition of case study research within the field of employment relations. Classic contributions to this tradition have focused on workplaces, organizations and their employment strategies, trade unions, collective agreements, and strikes (e.g. Batstone et al. 1977; Beynon 1984; Brown 1973; Delbridge 1998; Flanders 1964; Hartley et al. 1983; Hyman 1972; Pollert 1981; Roche and Geary 2006; Scott 1994). Our case study, however, has adopted a different unit of analysis, focusing on a social justice campaign. In the pages above, we have offered an employment relations case study, focusing on the institutions, processes, and outcomes of regulation, but in a novel setting. We now want to conclude the study by drawing out the significance of the case study for the wider field of employment relations. We do this by examining firstly what the study tells us about the significance of new actors in employment relations, such as civil society organizations, and secondly what it has to say about the changing behaviour of traditional employment actors, trade unions, employers, and the state. We finish this review by highlighting the emergence of a multiform system of regulation in UK industrial relations, in which civil regulation sits alongside and interacts with other methods for regulating the employment relationship.

New Actors

The Living Wage campaign is the work of new actors in employment relations, civil society organizations that developed the standard and have spread it across the labour market. A useful framework for assessing the contribution of new actors to employment relations and gauging its significance has been developed by Bellemare (2000; see also Heery, Abbott, and Williams 2012; Legault and Bellemare 2008). Bellemare argues that non-traditional institutions can legitimately be deemed employment actors, worthy of attention by the field, if they satisfy four tests. These tests are: (1) continuity—an ongoing concern with the employment relationship and institutional presence within the system of employment relations; (2) ubiquity—understood as activity that encompasses different levels of the employment system, such as the workplace, enterprise, industry, nation, and the international sphere; (3) relationships—substantial contact with the population of other, more established employment actors, trade unions, employers and their organizations, and the state; and (4) impact—conceived both in terms of substantive change in employment relations and procedural change, including the creation of new labour market institutions. In what follows, we assess whether the Living Wage campaign and the CSOs behind it, Citizens UK and the Living Wage Foundation, satisfy these four tests.

Continuity. Like many CSOs (Heery, Abbot, and Williams 2012), Citizens UK is not concerned solely with the workaday selves of the people it represents. Recent issues that it has prioritized in its community organizing activity include housing and homelessness, voter registration, making misogyny a hate crime, and welcoming refugees. For most of its history, however, the Living Wage has been a major focus of concern. Citizens UK has been running the Living Wage campaign for twenty years, and the system of accrediting employers through the Living Wage Foundation has been operational since 2011. There is no prospect at present of the campaign ending. Citizens UK has also broadened its workplace focus, adding Living Hours and likely other standards and launching other work-focused campaigns through its local chapters. In Cardiff Bay, Citizens Cymru-Wales has developed a Community Jobs Compact, through which local employers not only commit to pay the Living Wage but use anonymized recruitment and other measures to facilitate the employment of ethnic minorities. The other CSOs involved in the Living Wage campaign have a similar profile, focusing on employment problems within a broader portfolio that encompasses additional anti-poverty, social justice, and environmental issues. Cynnal Cymru, the Poverty Alliance, and ShareAction range across a broad agenda but have made a substantial and open-ended commitment to the Living Wage campaign.

Ubiquity. The Living Wage campaign also passes Bellemare's test of ubiquity. The campaign targets individual employers, seeking their voluntary commitment to the Living Wage standard, but in doing so it has operated at a variety of scales and within multiple institutional domains. Branches of the campaign have focused on specific sectors, industries, and types of employers, including charities, social care providers, local authorities, and members of the FTSE100. Campaign initiatives have also been developed at a variety of geographical scales, including towns, cities, city-regions, and the constituent nations of the UK. The campaign has a UK-wide presence and in recent years has become international in scope, exporting elements of the Living Wage standard, and partnering with campaigns in other countries. A notable feature of this multi-scalar activity is that it has involved exploiting opportunities presented through political devolution. Like other CSOs (Heery, Abbott, and Williams 2012), Citizens UK, the Living Wage Foundation, and their partners have been active in the devolved nations and regions of the UK, winning political support for the Living Wage at these levels, while above the UK state has been more obdurate.

Relationships. Another feature that Citizens UK shares with other CSOs (Heery, Abbott, and Williams 2012) is its propensity to cooperate with other not-for-profit and campaigning organizations. Citizens UK is itself a network, comprised of faith, community, and educational organizations, and in the Living Wage campaign it has worked closely with other CSOs that have provided funding, research, and campaigning expertise. The campaign has been marked by collaboration across an extensive network of social justice organizations. Amongst traditional employment actors, the Living Wage campaign has prioritized building a direct relationship with employers, and Citizens UK created the Living Wage Foundation specifically for this purpose. The Foundation, and its Welsh and Scottish counterparts, have proved highly effective in accrediting employers which have adopted the Living Wage. In addition, and again like other employment-focused CSOs (Williams et al. 2011), they have developed a closer relationship with individual employer partners, leading businesses and public service organizations that have championed the Living Wage in their industries and localities. This partnering has also encompassed employers' organizations. Local chambers of commerce, business improvement districts, employers' associations, trade bodies, and specialist organizations catering to cooperatives, social enterprises, and to specific issues such as corporate responsibility and social inclusion, have offered support to the Living Wage Foundation. Trade unions have occupied a less central position in the campaign but have played a part. Unions have a presence in the Citizens UK network and have participated in the formal governance of the Living Wage campaign. They have also been influenced indirectly by the campaign, including the Living Wage within collective bargaining and, more recently, developing their own alternative £10.00 and £15.00 standards. Finally, the campaign has successfully forged relationships with public authorities, with Citizens UK using accountability assemblies to secure political support for the Living Wage, while the Foundation has drawn local and regional political leaders into the campaign through the Living Wage Places initiative. Much of the relationship between the campaign and public authorities has hinged on the latter acting as 'anchor institutions', using their purchasing, funding, convening, and influencing powers to promote the Living Wage in their areas of jurisdiction.

Impact. The central claim of Freeman's (2005) influential critique of living wage and associated campaigns in the USA is that they lack scale. Compared to the historical success of the labour movement in raising wages and compressing inequality, the efforts of American living wage campaigners are deemed modest. To what extent is this judgement valid also for the Living Wage campaign in the UK? As we saw in the previous chapter, many more employees have benefitted directly from the statutory minimum wage than have gained from the Living Wage, and it is likely that joint regulation through collective bargaining also has a greater effect (Metcalf 2005). The *relative* contribution of civil regulation in responding to low pay is therefore less than that of more established forms of labour market regulation, but this does not mean that the *absolute* contribution of the campaign to redistribution is trivial or unworthy of consideration. Thousands of employers have joined the Living Wage scheme, employing millions of workers, tens of thousands of whom have benefitted directly. The campaign has also generated further impact, influencing the behaviour of non-accredited employers and the content of collective agreements. Other recent attempts to combat low pay, such as the TUC's £10.00 an hour campaign or the efforts of indie unions to extract higher pay and other concessions from employers, have, to date, benefitted many fewer low-wage workers. The activities of Citizens UK and its allies in spreading the Living Wage have raised pay for only a minority of low-paid employees, and have not reached the scale of influence exerted by more established methods of regulation, but they have nevertheless crossed a threshold of substantive effect that justifies continued research on organizations of this kind.

The Living Wage campaign has also created new labour market institutions. The latter do not take the form of traditional institutions, such as wages councils or industry-level collective bargaining, but rather are comprised of the body of civil regulation described in Chapter 2. The labour market institutions created by Citizens UK are the Living Wage standard and system of accreditation, the supplementary standards and the Living Hours scheme with their additional systems of accreditation, and the stakeholder-based forms of governance that stretch from the Living Wage Commission, through bodies overseeing the campaign in Scotland and Wales, to the steering groups guiding Living Wage City campaigns. It is this complex of institutional arrangements that has sustained the campaign and allowed it to record its substantive redistributive effect.

A final effect of the campaign, which it also shares with other CSO activity, has been its ability to shape a wider policy agenda (Heery, Abbott, and Williams 2012; Johnson et al. 2019). The efforts of Citizens UK are one of the factors that have led to the recent strengthening of statutory regulation and the launch of the National Living Wage. As we have seen, they have also shaped the activities of trade unions and stimulated an interest in policy to combat low pay across a range of political interests and at different levels of the political system. As Mark Drakeford remarked, Living Wage Week has become a feature of the political calendar. One striking example of this agenda-setting effect has been the inclusion of the Living Wage standard in a broad set of policy initiatives from other employment actors. These include UNISON's Ethical Care Charter (Johnson et al. 2021), the Scottish Government's Scottish Business Pledge and the Code of Practice on Ethical Employment of the Welsh Government, the codes and charters on fair or good employment promoted by English regional authorities, the procurement codes and social value initiatives of many local authorities, and the Good Business Charter, launched in 2020 by the Good Business Foundation with CBI and TUC backing, which requires signatory businesses to become accredited Living Wage Employers. Other actors, both new and traditional, have been influenced by the Living Wage campaign and the desirability of promoting a living wage has been accepted by a broad range of institutions.

In our assessment, Citizens UK and the Living Wage Foundation pass Bellemare's four tests of 'actor' status. They have a continuing focus on the employment relationship, are active at different levels of the employment system, have forged relationships with other employment actors, and have generated significant impacts of both a substantive and procedural kind. This record warrants their inclusion in the core subject matter of employment relations, and, indeed, civil society actors of this type have featured increasingly in employment relations literature. The latter encompasses not just research studies of CSOs, but also their inclusion in handbooks surveying the current state of the field and in student textbooks and syllabi (Cooke and Wood 2014; Dundon et al. 2020; Heery and Williams 2020; Williams 2020). The case study of the Living Wage campaign, we believe, provides further justification for this extension of the field.

Neo-Paternalism

It was noted in Chapter 4 that the Living Wage has been adopted by what might be thought of as archetypal paternalist businesses, family-owned firms, rooted in a particular locality, and with a long tradition of offering secure and relatively benign employment. As well as attracting paternalist businesses, however, it can be argued that the Living Wage standard and the campaign to promote it themselves display elements of paternalism. The standard requires employers to assume responsibility for ensuring both direct and indirect employees are paid a living wage, and discharging this responsibility takes precedence over other potential functions of payment, such as rewarding performance or responding to labour market pressures. For many employers, adopting the Living Wage has led to an appreciable increase in labour costs. In addition, the campaign has operated principally through persuasion, encouraging employers voluntarily to adopt the Living Wage without external pressure from campaigners being applied in most cases. The significance of the case study for research on employers, we believe, lies in the discovery of these elements of paternalism. The Living Wage campaign is a manifestation of a fresh wave of paternalism in employer behaviour, which possesses distinctive features when compared to the classic form of paternalism that flourished in company towns in the nineteenth and early twentieth centuries. Paternalism has often been pronounced dead in British employment relations or dismissed as an empty ideology espoused by employers whose actual practice follows a different course (Dore 1973; Lane and Roberts 1971). The case study of the Living Wage suggests that judgements of this kind are too definitive and that elements of a neo-paternalism are present and indeed expanding within the employment system.

Studies of classic paternalism in cotton, chemical, and railway towns and engineering and mining districts have identified a series of common characteristics (Abercrombie and Hill 1976; Ackers 1998; Ackers and Black 1991; Greene 2001; Joyce 1980). In what follows, we identify several of these characteristics and record how the Living Wage campaign differs in important respects from these classic manifestations of paternalism:

Motivation. Classic paternalism was often motivated by the religious convictions of Victorian entrepreneurs, with Quaker employers often at the forefront. As we have seen, the Living Wage campaign has also originated from a largely faith-based movement, and religious organizations are found disproportionately amongst the ranks of accredited employers. But the Living Wage has not been promoted to the generality of employers in religious terms and most have not adopted it because of religious motivation. Accredited employers view the Living Wage primarily as a secular phenomenon, and to the extent that adoption is motivated by a particular set of beliefs these emphasize the obligations of corporate citizens and the need for dutiful employers to be responsive to the needs of multiple stakeholders, including low-paid employees. Neo-paternalism is born of a secular age and, in the main, does not arise from religious motivation.

Origins. Writing about the employment practices of large Japanese firms, Hill (1981) refers to 'bureaucratic paternalism', the listing of the reciprocal obligations of employees and employees in detailed work rules, personnel, and welfare policies. While maybe not as elaborate as the Japanese version, the classic paternalism of early industrialists in Britain assumed a similar form, with the commitments of the employer and the requirements of the employee expressed in written codes and rulebooks. An essential feature of this paternalist bureaucracy was that it was home-grown, developed in some cases by the first professional personnel officers in British business (Clegg 1979). The neo-paternalism of which the Living Wage forms a part, however, often does not have this home-grown quality. Rather, it is set out in externally authored standards, codes, and charters, developed by CSOs, multistakeholder organizations, or state agencies. It is for this reason that accreditation is so important to neo-paternalism. It is through accreditation that employers demonstrate that they are compliant with a set of bureaucratic regulations that enshrine their commitments to employees.

Focus. The offer of good employment at the heart of classic paternalism was addressed typically to the core, directly employed workforce. The latter, whether engineers, train drivers, coalminers, or cotton spinners, were male breadwinners, and there was typically a patriarchal thrust to classic paternalism, with wage, benefit, and welfare policies designed to reinforce traditional gender relations within working class families. What is notable about the Living Wage, in contrast, is that the policy is directed largely at workers in secondary labour market positions, low-paid employees often performing ancillary tasks and, in many cases, working for contractors. This feature is seen in other examples of standards-based HRM, which are directed at women workers, members of ethnic minorities, LGBT+ employees, the disabled, and ex-offenders (Demougin et al. 2021; Heery, Abbott and Williams 2012). At an international scale, codes of good employment practice seek to regulate supply chains rather than conditions for core employees. There is a switch in focus in neo-paternalism, therefore, with employers assuming obligations for those in secondary labour market positions and in supply chains, located beyond the formal bounds of the employing organization.

Scope. The paternalism of Victorian and Edwardian entrepreneurs was broad in scope, encompassing all aspects of the employment relationship and extending beyond work to include the provision of housing, education, and leisure activities. There was a totalizing aspect to the relationship, in which the employer catered to the multiple needs of employees, often in an intrusive and controlling manner. Neo-paternalism tends to be much narrower in scope. The Living Wage campaign is focused on a single labour standard, and other similar campaigns often deal with a discrete aspect of the employment relationship, such as the need for flexible hours for those with caring responsibilities. Even when employers sign up to good employment charters, such as those promoted by the devolved governments or English regional authorities, these deal with only a limited selection of employment issues. An objective of the Living Wage campaign is to improve the quality of family life by reducing the need for low-wage workers to work excessive hours or hold multiple jobs, but action to secure this end stops short at paying higher wages, and there is no attempt to regulate the personal lives of Living Wage recipients. Compared to its classic counterpart, neo-paternalism tends to be focused solely on the employment relationship and to be narrower in the set of issues with which it is concerned.

Scale. Classic paternalism flourished in company towns, such as Bourneville, Crewe, Glossop, Port Sunlight, and Saltaire. It operated at a local scale, and the owners of paternalist businesses were also pillars of the local community, dominating political, religious, and cultural life. The Living Wage campaign contains an echo of this localism in the Living Wage Places scheme, which has been successful in attracting employers wishing to enhance their local communities. The anchor institutions, which are pivotal to attempts to build up accreditation in towns and cities, are large organizations rooted in place. Neo-paternalism is therefore associated with a revival of place-based activism by employers, but it remains that schemes like the Living Wage operate at national level and form part of an international movement to raise labour standards. Compared to classic paternalism, with its basis in company towns and industrial districts, neo-paternalism operates at a broader scale. The voluntary standards, codes, and charters which lie at its heart are applied across the constituent regions and nations and the entirety of the UK, as well as along global supply chains.

Deference. Classic paternalism flourished not just in highly unequal societies, but also in a culture with pronounced status differences. Within such a context, benevolence, expressed through the provision of good employment and welfare benefits, was expected to elicit loyalty and deference from employees. The expression of deference might have been largely performative and accompanied by resentment and class hostility, but the visible subordination of employees to 'masters' was integral to this pattern of relationships. In the Living Wage campaign, as we have seen, there has again been an echo of this pattern in the public thanking of employers for paying the Living Wage by low-wage workers. Despite this, neo-paternalism is largely free of the performative subordination of employees that characterized the classic form. There is often an assumption that employees have an entitlement or right to the standards set out in private regulation and that their adoption does not impose an obligation or, even less, require deference. Those introducing these provisions, moreover, may often identify or empathize with those they are designed to help, rather than viewing them as recipients of charity.

Reciprocity. Studies of classic paternalism stress the reciprocal nature of the relationship between employers and employees that lay at its heart. Employees received from the employer good wages and extensive benefits, but in return were subject to a demanding work regime (Huberman 1987). The economic function of the paternalist employment package it has been argued, moreover, was to attract and stabilize an industrial workforce and inculcate work discipline. The reciprocal relationship which the system was designed to cultivate and reinforce was that between the employer and the core, direct workforce. Neo-paternalism is also accompanied by a strong economic rationale, and the Living Wage is advocated through a business case, which emphasizes the scope to improve labour supply and labour performance. Arguably, however, the reciprocal relationship between employer and employees is less central to neo-paternalism. The economic purpose in adopting standards like the Living Wage is often not to elicit higher performance from employees, but to strengthen corporate reputation, develop a consumer brand, cultivate closer relations with client businesses or investors, or secure political support. There is less focus on the employer-employee dyad, and the purpose of raising employment standards is often to signal to other actors beyond the organization about the nature of the enterprise and its adherence to good practice. There is reciprocity in neo-paternalism, therefore, but it is not confined to eliciting improved work attitudes or behaviour from employees.

Conflict. While the purpose of classic paternalism was to generate reciprocity and cooperation, it also generated a specific form of conflict. The hallmark of the latter was often an attempt by workers to contest their subordination by developing independent institutions beyond the control of paternalist masters. In the workplace this challenge to subordination led to the development of independent trade union organizations, whilst in the wider community it could take the form of affiliation to the Liberal Party and later to Labour, involvement in non-conformist congregations beyond the reach of Anglican employers, and the development of consumer cooperatives, friendly societies, and independent schools. This quest for independence from a seemingly benign but also controlling employer finds an echo today in the concerns of some trade unionists about the Living Wage and the limited part played by employees themselves in its diffusion. The primary conflict surrounding the Living Wage and other experiments with neo-paternalism, however, assumes a different form. Often those engaging in conflict are not workers, but social justice campaigners from outside the organization who exert pressure on employers to adopt good labour standards, in the way that members of the Citizens UK network engage in actions to persuade local employers to adopt the Living Wage. The purpose of this conflict, moreover, is not to break with an established paternalist relationship, but to put one in place. Protest, campaigning, and the mobilization of communities and consumers are designed to pressure employers to adopt externally validated employment standards. Repeated episodes of conflict, moreover, may be used to prevent backsliding and to widen the range of commitments to which employers enter. Conflict, originating from beyond the employing organization, is a force that drives neo-paternalism rather than challenging it.

Neo-paternalism shares with its classic forebear the voluntary provision of relatively good employment conditions to employees, which go beyond legal or market requirements and which are invested with moral purpose, a desire to act in a way that is virtuous, benevolent, or just. Despite this common root, the paternalism exhibited by the Living Wage campaign differs from that of Victorian and Edwardian entrepreneurs. Today's neo-paternalism is secular, inscribed in standards and codes external to the employing enterprise, targeted at those in secondary labour market positions and along supply chains, and is narrower in scope but broader in scale. It does not require the performance of deference by those who benefit from enhanced employment conditions, and its primary economic function is often not to motivate employees but to signal to customers, clients, investors, and public authorities that the employer adheres to good practice. The social conflict to which it gives rise is often directed at extending, rather than subverting, paternalist relationships. All these features are seen in the Living Wage campaign, but it is important to recognize that they are also visible elsewhere. Other bodies of private regulation within the UK economy share many of the same characteristics (Bowkett et al. 2017; Demougin et al. 2021), and the same is true of international codes of good employment practice that seek to regulate employment conditions within supply chains in the Global South (Kuruvilla 2021). Moreover, there are other developments in the contemporary employment scene that are congruent with the paternalist features of the Living Wage campaign. These include a switch in HRM towards emphasizing standards of good practice, an associated growth in attempts to promote well-being or 'wellness' at work, and increasing interest in non-traditional forms of enterprise, such as mutuals, cooperatives, and social enterprises, whose governance arrangements make them more receptive to the interests of employees. There have also been calls for a more responsible form of capitalism, exemplified by the British Academy's Future of the Corporation Programme (British Academy 2021; Mayer 2018). Arguably, we are witnessing a fresh paternalist turn within contemporary employment relations.

The significance of the Living Wage campaign for the study of employers, we believe, lies in the fact that it identifies and provides an analysis of this important development. It is also significant because it provides a corrective to the dominant accounts of employer behaviour which highlight the commodification of labour and the spread of precarious forms of employment (Dundon et al. 2020). In contemporary critical analysis of employment relations, there is a strong immiseration narrative in which a powerful impulse towards less secure, more contingent forms of employment is identified (Heery 2016). The value of our study, we believe, is that it questions the universality of this kind of development. Many employers have pushed workers into less favourable, more precarious forms of employment in recent years, but this is not the whole story. There are cross currents and counter trends, and one of these is the emergence of neo-paternalism.

Union Resilience

A major current in recent writing about trade unions has dealt with the question of renewal or revitalization, seeking to identify the changes that unions must undergo if they are to reverse their long-term decline. A central proposition at the heart of this literature is that unions must adopt new methods and assume a new form if they are to renew themselves. It has been variously suggested that unions should withdraw from member servicing through grievance-handling and collective bargaining and invest in organizing, switch their main locus of activity from the workplace to the external labour market or the local community, or reinvent themselves as social movements (Heery 2015; Holgate 2015b, 2021; Luce 2014; Milkman 2013, 2020). In all formulations of this renewal argument, it is assumed that unions must first reform their processes if they are to secure radically improved substantive outcomes. Another version of the renewal argument, as we have seen, is that unions should forge coalitions with other social movements, importing the methods of community organizing into their repertoire (Tattersall 2018). Our research on the union response to the Living Wage campaign identified some attempts to renew trade unions in this manner. Most notably, UNISON North-West has forged a coalition with Citizens UK and made use of community organizing methods in its campaign on social care. Developments of this kind are a minority trend, however, and our case study of the Living Wage emphatically did not provide widespread evidence of attempts to refashion trade unionism in line with the prescriptions of union renewal.

What the case did reveal, however, was an attempt to promote the Living Wage using the existing repertoire of union representation. Unions have bargained and campaigned for the Living Wage and used their established relations with the Labour Party to promote it within local, regional, and devolved national government (Prowse and Fells 2016a; Prowse et al. 2017). More recently, the same traditional methods have been used to promote the union's own £10.00 and £15.00 living wage standards. A useful way of interpreting these developments can be found in recent work by Moore and colleagues (Moore et al. 2019). In a study of developments in collective bargaining, they note two key features. The first is that union-led bargaining continues to have a redistributive effect, raising pay and improving employment terms for unionized workers in comparison to those who are not covered by collective agreements. The second is the continuing evolution of the content of bargaining as new issues are introduced to agreements to deal with current problems employees face. Their research highlights new agreements across a range of industries and sectors dealing with precarious work, the two-tier workforce, working time, low pay, apprenticeships, and career structures. In two of the ten collective agreements they studied, negotiation had led to the introduction of the Living Wage. These developments, Moore et al. suggest, are indicative of collective bargaining 'resilience', the continuing capacity of unions to serve as effective institutions of representation, advancing worker interests through their traditional repertoire.

Our case study of the Living Wage provides further evidence for this interpretation of trade unionism. The main union response to the Living Wage campaign has been to appropriate the standard, while relying on largely traditional methods to promote its spread across the unionized segment of the economy. This effort has been successful, generating a 'shadow' Living Wage beyond the ranks of accredited employers and possessing the essential characteristics of 'resilience' identified by Moore et al.: substantive innovation, coupled with continuity of method. This combination can also be seen in other recent developments in British trade unionism, including the growth of collective bargaining over equality, family-friendly practices, and sustainability (Gregory and Milner 2009; Hampton 2018; Heery 2006) and the creation of new representative roles, such as disability champions, green, and equality reps, which seek to reinvigorate the long-tradition of workplace trade unionism (Bacon and Hoque 2012; 2015; Hampton 2018). Another aspect of the union response to the Living Wage which fits with reliance on traditional methods is the lack of enthusiasm and occasional hostility towards working with Citizens UK. There is a conservatism to union resilience, which finds expression in a strong preference for working through the single channel of trade union recognition and collective bargaining. This conservatism is visible in the union response to the Living Wage campaign but has also been seen in other fields, such as the limited engagement of unions with statutory forms of consultation emanating from the European Union (Hall and Purcell 2012).

In our view, Moore et al.'s definition of union resilience can be expanded to comprise the following four elements: (1) a continuing redistributive effect, seen in the union mark-up and higher employee benefits and job security for unionized workers; (2) incremental adjustment to the bargaining agenda, such that new topics and new interests continue to be addressed through negotiations with employers; (3) reliance on an established repertoire of interest representation, comprising advocacy, collective bargaining, and the exercise of political influence through the Labour Party; (4) imperviousness to new forms of unionism and reluctance to work with other social movements, particularly when to do so compromises reliance on the single channel of union representation. Our case study, we believe, highlights these four linked characteristics of contemporary trade unionism. British trade unions have displayed resilience, rather than undergoing revitalization, and their response to the Living Wage campaign conforms to this dominant characteristic.

Inclusive Growth

Our case research has several implications for the study of state intervention in the employment relationship. One that we wish to highlight is the fact that adoption of the Living Wage by public authorities has often emerged from a wider shift in economic strategy and attempts to promote 'inclusive growth'. The latter denotes the prioritizing of redistribution in policies of economic development, to ensure that those who have been excluded from the benefits of growth in the past gain from new investments and that attempts to stimulate economic activity focus explicitly on reducing poverty and inequality. According to Lee (2018: 424), inclusive growth has come to provide a 'new mantra for urban and regional policy'. At an international scale, the OECD launched an Inclusive Growth in Cities programme in 2016 and looked to recruit 'champion mayors' to drive the programme forwards (OECD 2018). In the UK, promotion of inclusive growth has been espoused by think tanks and research centres. The RSA established an Inclusive Growth Commission, which reported in 2017 (Inclusive Growth Commission 2017), the Joseph Rowntree Foundation has provided advice on how to develop a strategy for pursuing inclusive growth for public authorities (Beatty et al. 2016), and at Manchester University the Inclusive Growth Analysis Unit has been established to provide research support and advice.

Public sector organizations have responded to these initiatives and have sought to incorporate inclusive growth in their policy making. The economic policies of both the Scottish and Welsh Governments declare that pursuit of inclusive growth is a central objective, and regional authorities in England, such as Greater Manchester, Liverpool City Region, North of Tyne, and West Midlands, have embedded inclusive growth in their strategic planning (Lupton et al. 2019). Individual local authorities have also sought to pursue inclusive growth, particularly the metropolitan borough councils in the big cities. Leeds, Salford, and Manchester have developed strategies for inclusive growth, and many other councils have drawn upon the concept and used it to frame their activities. Perhaps the most notable experiment is that of Preston City Council. In Preston, the council has embraced the objective of inclusive growth as the centrepiece of the 'Preston

Model' of economic development, and its ambitious attempts to revive its local economy have been presented as an exemplar of progressive policy for the political left (Centre for Local Economic Strategies 2019).

Developments in Preston and elsewhere have also been influenced by the related concept of 'community wealth building' (Guinan and O'Neill 2020). This is an approach to economic development that emphasizes the need to extend local, democratic control of the economy by expanding not-for-profit and worker and community-owned forms of organization, returning outsourced services to public ownership, and relying on local procurement within shortened supply-chains. Another associated concept, which has been particularly influential in Wales, is that of the 'foundational economy'. Here, the emphasis is on redirecting the focus of policy attention and investment towards sectors such as social care, retail, hospitality, and utilities that furnish the necessaries of life, but which are often neglected in economic policy (Morgan 2019). Again, in the foundational economy literature there is an emphasis on experimenting with new forms of organization and on the need to upgrade conditions of employment as a prerequisite for raising service quality in foundational industries (Foundational Economy Collective 2018). A third related policy concept is that of 'social value', the requirement to have regard to the social effects of commissioning and procurement decisions, which has become obligatory for public sector organizations in the UK since the passage of the Public Services (Social Value) Act 2012 (Lupton et al. 2019).

Most of the organizations that have adopted policies of inclusive growth are accredited Living Wage Employers, and the promotion of the Living Wage to other employers is a common way in which public authorities have tried to operationalize their commitment to inclusive growth. The percentage of employees earning below the Living Wage in a city or region has often been used as an indicator of the need for inclusive growth, the Living Wage has been linked explicitly to public procurement, and charters of good employment practice have been developed for local business which include payment of the Living Wage as a core component. Advocates of related policy concepts, such as community wealth building and the foundational economy, have also called on public authorities to promote the Living Wage (Foundational Economy Collective 2018; Guinan and O'Neill 2020), and it is common for local authorities to refer to the Living Wage in policy statements on social value. The promotion of the Living Wage has become tied, therefore, to a range of new policy frameworks that have won support from UK public authorities, and which seek to direct local economic activity along a more inclusive course.

Across these policy frameworks five main types of recommendation have emerged, all of which represent a significant break with hitherto dominant approaches to economic development. These five recommendations are as follows:

Fair work. Central to the promotion of 'inclusive growth' are attempts to promote good quality employment, illustrated by the charters of good work or fair work, which incorporate the Living Wage, that have been adopted by national, regional, and local governments (Lupton et al. 2019). Embrace of this agenda represents the revival of the 'good' and 'model' employer traditions within public service. There is an emphasis in initiatives of this kind on redistribution, by ensuring new jobs are well-paid and secure, and on reversing the deleterious effects of previous phases of economic growth, by taking action to reduce zero-hours contracts and other forms of precarious employment. The effort to raise employment standards, moreover, has often been directed at foundational industries, with the actions of the Scottish and Welsh Governments to spread the Living Wage in social care exemplifying this concern. According to advocates of inclusive growth, the object of economic development in the past has been to increase the volume of employment, with scant regard paid to the quality of jobs created. The result has been the spread of minimum wage and often insecure employment in the distribution, leisure, and hospitality industries that now dominate many British cities. Policies of inclusive growth are intended to reverse this direction of travel.

Social partnership. Integral to attempts to promote fair work has been action to revive worker representation through trade unions, restoring another core element of the good employer tradition. Action of this kind is typically presented using the language of 'social partnership' and encompasses two types of measure. The first is creating consultative machinery within government, through which unions and employers can shape economic and social policy (Bacon and Samuel 2017; Samuel and Bacon 2015). The Scottish Fair Work Convention, which has urged Scottish Government to promote the Living Wage alongside other elements of good employment standards, and the Welsh Social Care Forum, which recommended that the Welsh Government fund the Living Wage in adult social care, are examples of social partnership bodies of this kind. The second type of measure involves encouraging other employers to accept and negotiate with unions through the inclusion of 'worker voice' in the list of commitments contained within charters of good employment practice. This latter provision is weak, reflecting the fact that employment law is not devolved, and its effect uncertain, but it is indicative of a return to the explicit encouragement of trade unionism and collective bargaining by public authorities which was the dominant position in public policy before the 1980s. For much of the past four decades this policy has been in abeyance, with Conservative Governments at UK level excluding unions from policy making and introducing successive waves of legislation to restrict their activities. The Welsh and Scottish Governments, and many regional and local authorities, explicitly reject this anti-union position and hold that worker representation through unions is not only compatible with but is a precondition for inclusive growth.

Social licencing. The main lever that advocates of inclusive growth want to use to spread fair work is a form of 'social licencing' (Foundational Economy Collective 2018), in which the operation of private sector businesses becomes conditional on accepting a series of social obligations. In practical terms, this has meant making the award of contracts, grants, and funding to businesses dependent on them adhering to good employment standards, an approach that is exemplified by the Scottish Government's Fair Work First initiative (Scottish Government 2021). Payment of the Living Wage invariably is one of these good employment standards. This element of conditionality represents a change in the state's orientation to business, which hitherto has focused largely on the offer of incentives to encourage business to invest. Tax concessions, grants, deregulation, and the provision of infrastructure and skills have been the conditions-free means through which public authorities have attempted to stimulate economic development. These incentives, moreover, have been accompanied by institutional changes that have allocated a central place to business in economic policy-making, epitomized by the Local Enterprise Partnerships responsible for promoting economic growth in England. Advocates of inclusive growth want public authorities to continue to work in partnership with business, but to do so in a context in which business is more responsible and more accountable for its actions.

New forms of enterprise. Another pronounced theme in inclusive growth is encouragement of non-traditional forms of enterprise, such as mutuals, cooperatives, social enterprises, and not-for-profit businesses owned by public authorities (Lupton et al. 2019). Channelling investment through organizations of this kind is believed to have several advantages over relying on conventional, profit-seeking businesses. Their core purpose is to generate social value, their governance arrangements can make them accountable to employee and community interests, and they are more likely to be rooted in a particular place. They are also more likely to be receptive to the development of fair work and, as we have seen, not-for-profit enterprises, such as credit unions, have been especially receptive to the Living Wage. This focus on new forms of enterprise, including the renewal of public ownership, amounts to a further break with the dominant approach to economic development, which has accorded priority to the activities of private business. Under the new approach, the private sector is no longer fetishized as the sole source of innovation and dynamism.

Localism. The final element of inclusive growth is a pronounced localism, a desire to revive city and regional economies using local resources and to retain the fruits of economic growth within the local area (Lee 2018). The localism of inclusive growth assumes several forms. There is an emphasis on the role of 'anchor institutions', including public authorities themselves, using their purchasing and investing power to stimulate local economic activity and spread good employment. An important component of this effort is the shortening of supply chains, such that more local firms and more local employees are drawn into supply networks. Another component has been the articulation by political leaders of a kind of civic patriotism, encouraging employers to identify with their locale, channel investment, and upgrade employment conditions as part of a concerted effort to strengthen local economies in an inclusive way. Living Wage City initiatives exemplify this approach. The localism of inclusive growth contrasts with the emphasis on forging connections to the global economy in the dominant approach to stimulating economic activity. The emphasis in the latter has been on attracting property developers and large corporations from outside the locality to make investments in a particular city or region. Inclusive growth represents a partial break with this approach, seeking to nurture local economic resources that will have a long-term commitment to their home base and reinvest in the local area. There is an element of civic mercantilism about inclusive growth; it is an approach to economic development perhaps suited to the more inward-facing economy that has emerged since Brexit.

How significant the espousal of inclusive growth proves to be is uncertain (Lee 2018). Public authorities below the level of the UK state may lack the economic heft or legislative and regulatory powers to make truly decisive changes to their local economies. Moreover, the embrace of 'robust unionism' in the Conservative Party may clip the wings of devolved administrations at the forefront of experimenting with inclusive growth. It remains, though, that the emergence of inclusive growth represents a departure from the dominant approach to economic development and indicates the emergence of a more activist state. Arguably, it contains a new, emerging paradigm for state policy towards the labour market. The value of the case study is that it reveals this shift and demonstrates its significance for employment relations. The case shows that public authorities at national, regional, and local level have promoted the Living Wage as part of a broader concern to promote fair work, using elements of social licencing and through an appeal to civic patriotism, with the ultimate purpose of stimulating inclusive growth. Other elements of this policy package include the revival of social partnership and promotion of non-traditional forms of enterprise. The case suggests that researchers should look beyond the employment relationship to policies of economic development to generate a full account of contemporary change. It also suggests that employment relations scholars should engage with the adjacent fields of political studies, social geography, and regional economics. Employment relations has often been enriched by incorporating theories, concepts, and findings from other disciplines, and today this infusion can come from the study of city and regional governments and their attempts to redevelop local economies.

Multiform Employment Relations

Our final set of conclusions concern the impact of the Living Wage campaign on the configuration of the UK's employment system. The prime effect of the Living Wage and other similar developments has been to make the system more complex and multiform, in two senses. On the one hand there has been an increase in the institutions of worker representation or voice, with a growing number of civil society organizations seeking to advance employee interests within the employment system. Citizens UK, the Living Wage Foundation, and their various partners are representative of this trend, performing a function that in the past was largely confined to trade unions. On the other hand, there has been an increase in forms of regulation, with civil regulation of the kind developed by the Living Wage campaign operating alongside other forms of private regulation, legal regulation emanating from the state, and joint regulation emerging from collective bargaining between trade unions and employers. Different types of regulation, developed by different types of employment actor, now sit alongside one another, providing a complex web of rules that shapes the employment relationship (cf. Wright et al. 2019).

A major concern of our case study has been to examine the interaction of these multiform institutions. We have traced the sometimes supportive and sometimes difficult relationship between trade unions and the Living Wage campaign and the way in which civil regulation has stimulated both legal regulation and collective bargaining over low pay. Other researchers have explored similar topics, investigating the relationship between new and old institutions of worker representation and long-established and more recently created methods of regulation (Holgate 2015a; Kinderman 2012). In our view, further work in this vein would be beneficial. Over time, the system of employment relations has become more complex, with new institutions emerging alongside those that date back to the system's origins. Exploring how these multiform elements relate to one another and whether they reinforce or contradict one another should repay further inquiry.

To conclude, we believe that the significance of the Living Wage campaign for the wider field of employment relations lies in the following: (1) It provides further evidence that CSOs have become important employment actors that warrant further research; (2) It points to the emergence of a neo-paternalism amongst a substantial body of employers, one of the hallmarks of which is the voluntary adoption of employment standards promoted by CSOs; (3) It indicates that unions are resilient and have adapted to the changing world of work by pursuing new substantive issues using their established repertoire of methods; (4) The case points to the emergence of a more activist state, more prepared to intervene in the employment relationship, that is visible in the efforts of devolved, regional, and local government to promote inclusive growth; (5) And the case records the emergence of a multiform system of employment relations in which new and old institutions of worker voice and new and old forms of regulation rub along together, generating both conflict and mutual reinforcement in the process.

Bibliography

Abbott, B. and Williams, S. (2014). 'Widening the 'representation gap'? The implications of the 'lobbying act' for worker representation in the UK', *Industrial Relations Journal*, 45/6: 507–523.

Abercrombie, N. and Hill, S. (1976). 'Paternalism and patronage', *British Journal of Sociology*, 27/4: 413–429.

Ackers, P. (1998). 'On paternalism: seven observations on the use and abuse of the concept in industrial relations, past and present', *Historical Studies in Industrial Relations*, 5: 173–193.

Ackers, P. and Black, J. (1991). 'Paternalist capitalism: an organization culture in transition', in M. Cross and G. Payne (eds), *Work and the Enterprise Culture*. Falmer: British Sociological Association, 30–56.

Alberti, G., Holgate, J., and Tapia, M. (2013). 'Organizing migrant as workers or as migrant workers? Intersectionality, trade unions, and precarious work', *International Journal of Human Resource Management*, 24/22: 4132–4148.

Alberti, G. and Però, D. (2018). 'Migrating industrial relations: migrant workers' initiatives within and outside trade unions', *British Journal of Industrial Relations*, 56/4: 693–715.

Alinsky, S. (1972). *Rules for Radicals: A Pragmatic Primer for Realistic Radicals*. New York: Vintage Books.

Alsos, K., Nergaard, K., and Van Den Heuval, A. (2019). 'Collective bargaining as a tool to ensure a living wage: experiences from the Nordic countries', *Transfer*, 25/3: 351–365.

Anker, R. (2011). *Estimating a Living Wage: A Methodological Review*, Conditions of Work and Employment Series No. 29. Geneva: International Labour Organization.

Anner, M. (2019). 'Predatory purchasing practices in global apparel supply chains and the employment relations squeeze in the Indian garment export industry', *International Labour Relations Review*, 158/4: 705–727.

Arrowsmith, J., Parker, J., Young-Hauser, A., Hodgetts, D., Haar, J., Carr, S., and Alefaio-Tugia, S. (2022). 'Employer and employee perspectives on the living wage in New Zealand', in T. Dobbins and P. Prowse (eds), *The Living Wage: Advancing a Global Movement*. London: Routledge, 178–190.

Ayres, S., Flinders, M., and Sandford, M. (2018). 'Territory, power and statecraft: understanding English devolution', *Regional Studies*, 52/6: 853–864.

Baccaro, L. and Howell, C. (2017). *Trajectories of Neoliberal Transformation*. Cambridge: Cambridge University Press.

Bach, S. and Bordogna, L. (2013). 'Reframing public service employment relations: the impact of the economic crisis and of the new EU economic governance', *European Journal of Industrial Relations*, 19/4: 279–294.

Bach, S. and Kessler, I. (2012). *The Modernization of the Public Services and Employee Relations*. Basingstoke: Palgrave MacMillan.

Bacon, N. and Hoque, K. (2015). 'The influence of trade union disability champions on employer disability policy and practice', *Human Resource Management Journal*, 25/2: 233–249.

Bacon, N. and Hoque, K. (2012). 'The role and impact of trade union equality representatives in Britain', *British Journal of Industrial Relations*, 50/2: 239–262.

Bacon, N. and Samuel, P. (2017). 'Social partnership and political devolution in the National Health Service: emergence, operation, and outcomes', *Work, Employment and Society*, 31/1: 123–141.

Bangham, G. (2019). *Happy Now? Lessons for Economic Policy Makers from a Focus on Subjective Well-being*. London: The Resolution Foundation.

Barford, A., Gilbert, R., Beales, A., Zorilla, M., and Nelson, J. (2022). *The Case for Living Wages: How Paying Living Wages Improves Business Performance and Tackles Poverty*. Cambridge: Business Fights Poverty and University of Cambridge Institute for Sustainability Leadership.

Barnard, C. (2017), 'To boldly go: social clauses in public procurement', *Industrial Law Journal*, 46/2: 208–244.

Barrientos, S., Bianchi, L., and Berman, C. (2019). 'Gender and governance of global value chains: promoting the rights of women workers', *International Labour Relations Review*, 158/4: 729–752.

Bartley, T. (2018). *Rules Without Rights: Land, Labor, and Private Authority in the Global Economy*. Oxford: Oxford University Press.

Batstone, E., Boraston, I., and Ferner, A. (1984). *Consent and Efficiency: Labour Relations and Management Strategy in the State Enterprise*. Oxford: Basil Blackwell.

Batstone, E., Boraston, I., and Frenkel, S. (1977). *Shop Stewards in Action*. Oxford: Basil Blackwell.

Beatty, C., Crisp, R., and Gore, T. (2016). *An Inclusive Growth Monitor for Measuring the Relationship between Poverty and Growth*. York: Joseph Rowntree Foundation.

Beatty, K. and Fothergill, S. (2018). 'Welfare reform in the United Kingdom 2010–2016: expectations, outcomes and local impacts', *Social Policy and Administration*, 52/5: 950–968.

Beaumont, P.B. (1992). *Public Sector Industrial Relations*. London and New York: Routledge.

Bellemare, G. (2000). 'End users: actors in the industrial relations system', *British Journal of Industrial Relations*, 38/3: 383–405.

Benassi, C. and Kornelakis, A. (2021). 'How do employers choose between types of contingent work? Costs, control, and institutional toying', *Industrial and Labor Relations Review*, 74/3: 715–738.

Berkowitz, H. and Dumez, H. (2016). 'The concept of meta-organization: issues for management studies', *European Management Review*, 13/2: 149–156.

Bewley, H. (2006). 'Raising the standard? The regulation of employment and public sector employment policy', *British Journal of Industrial Relations*, 44/2: 351–372.

Beynon, H. (1984). *Working for Ford*. Second edition. Harmondsworth: Penguin Books.

Bhattarcharya, C.B., Sen, S., and Korschun, D. (2008). 'Using corporate social responsibility to win the war for talent', *MIT Sloan Management Review*, 49/2: 36–44.

Bird, Y., Short, J.L., and Toffel, M.W. (2019). 'Coupling labor codes and supplier labor practices: the role of internal structural conditions', *Organization Science*, 30/4: 647–667.

Bloodworth, J. (2018). *Hired: Six Months Undercover in Low Wage Britain*. London: Atlantic Books.

Blyton, P. and Jenkins, J. (2012). 'Life after Burberry: shifting experiences of work and non-work life following redundancy', *Work, Employment and Society*, 26/1: 26–41.

Bowkett, C., Hauptmeier, M., and Heery, E. (2017). 'Exploring the role of employer forums—the case of Business in the Community Wales', *Employee Relations*, 39/7: 986–1000.

British Academy (2021). 'Policy and Practice for Purposeful Business. Final Report of the Future of the Corporation Programme'. London: British Academy.

Brown, W. (2017). 'The toxic politicising of the National Minimum Wage', *Employee Relations*, 39/6: 785–789.

Brown, W. (1973). *Piecework Bargaining*. London: Heinemann Educational Books.

Brown, W., Deakin, S., Nash, D., and Oxenbridge, S. (2000) 'The employment contract: from collective procedures to individual rights', *British Journal of Industrial Relations*, 38/4: 611–629.

Brown, W., Marginson, P., and Walsh, J. (2003). 'The management of pay as the influence of collective bargaining diminishes', in P. Edwards (ed.), *Industrial Relations: Theory and Practice*. Oxford: Blackwell Publishing, 189–213.

Brown, W. and Wright, C.F. (2018). 'Policies for decent labour standards in Britain', *The Political Quarterly*, 89/3: 482–489.

Brown, W. and Wright, M. (1994). 'The empirical tradition in workplace bargaining research', *British Journal of Industrial Relations*, 32/2: 153–164.

Bryson, A. and Forth, J. (2011). 'Trade unions', in P. Gregg and J. Wadsworth (eds), *The Labour Market in Winter: The State of Working Britain*. Oxford: Oxford University Press, 255–271.

Bryson, A. and Green, F. (2018). 'Do private schools manage better?', *National Institute Economic Review*, 243/1: 17–26.

Bunyan, P. (2016). 'The role of civil society in reducing poverty and inequality: a case study of the living wage campaign in the UK', *Local Economy*, 31/4: 489–501.

Bunyan, P. and Diamond, J. (2014). *Agency in Austerity: A Study of Fairness Commissions as an Approach to Reducing Poverty and Inequality in the UK*. London: The Webb Memorial Trust.

Carr, S.C., Parker, J., Arrowsmith, J., Watters, P., and Jones, H. (2016). 'Can a 'living wage' spring human capability? An exploratory study from New Zealand', *Labour & Industry*, 26/1: 24–39.

Carson, C. (2022). 'Employer experiences of the living wage in higher education, hospitality, and the construction sectors', in T. Dobbins and P. Prowse (eds), *The Living Wage: Advancing a Global Movement*. London: Routledge, 52–65.

Casey, C., Delaney, H., and Fiedler, A. (2021). 'Recalling the moral dimension: transnational labour interests and corporate social responsibilities', *Industrial Relations Journal*, 52/5: 389–405.

Centre for Local Economic Strategies (2019). *How We Built Community Wealth in Preston: Achievements and Lessons*. Manchester: Centre for Local Economic Strategies/Preston City Council.

Centre for Towns (2017). 'Launch Briefing', available at https://www.centrefortowns.org/reports/launch-briefing.

Clark, I. and Colling, T. (2018). 'Work in Britain's informal economy: learning from roadside hand car washes', *British Journal of Industrial Relations*, 56/2: 32–341.

Clarke, H.C., Goodwin, M., and Whiteley, P. (2017). *Brexit: Why Britain Voted to Leave the European Union*. Cambridge: Cambridge University Press.

Clegg, H.A. (1979). *The Changing System of Industrial Relations in Great Britain*. Oxford: Basil Blackwell.

Cominetti, N. (2020). *Calculating the Real Living Wage for London and the Rest of the UK: 2020–21*. London: The Resolution Foundation.

Cominetti, N. (2019). *Ain't No Minimum High Enough: Minimum Wage Policy in the 2019 Election*. London: The Resolution Foundation.

Cominetti, N., Costa, R., Datta, N., and Odamtten, F. (2022). *Low Pay Britain 2022: Low Pay and Insecurity in the UK Labour Market.* London: The Resolution Foundation.

Cominetti, N., Henehan, K., and Clarke, S. (2019). *Low Pay Britain 2019.* London: The Resolution Foundation.

Cominetti, N., McCurdy, C., and Slaughter, H. (2021). *Low Pay in Britain 2021.* London: The Resolution Foundation.

Compa, L. (2001). 'Wary allies', *The American Prospect*, 12/12, available at https//prospect.org/features/wary-allies/

Cooke, F.L. and Wood, G. (2014). 'New actors in employment relations', in A. Wilkinson, G. Wood, and R. Deeg (eds), *The Oxford Handbook of Employment Relations.* Oxford: Oxford University Press, 683–700.

Coulson, A.B. and Bonner, J. (2015). *Living Wage Employers: Evidence of UK Business Cases.* London: Living Wage Foundation.

Crouch, C. (2019). 'Post-democracy and populism', *The Political Quarterly*, 90/1: 124–137.

Crouch, C. (1982). *Trade Unions: The Logic of Collective Action.* Glasgow: Fontana.

Cunningham, I., Baluch, A., Cullen, A-M., and James, P. (2018), *Implementing the Scottish Living Wage in Social Care.* Glasgow: Coalition of Care and Support Providers Scotland and University of Strathclyde.

D'Arcy, C. (2018). *Low Pay Britain 2018.* London: The Resolution Foundation.

D'Arcy, C. (2017). *Low Pay Britain 2017.* London: The Resolution Foundation.

D'Arcy, C. and Finch, D. (2017). *The Great Escape? Low Pay and Progression in the UK's Labour Market.* London: Social Mobility Commission.

D'Arcy, C. and Finch, D. (2019). 'The calculation of a living wage: the UK's experience', *Transfer*, 25/3: 301–317.

Dauvergne, P. and Lebaron, G. (2014). *Protest Inc: The Corporatization of Activism.* Cambridge: Polity Press.

Davies, G. and D'Arcy, C. (2016). *Weighing up the Wage Floor: Employer Responses to the National Living Wage.* London: Chartered Institute of Personnel and Development.

Davis, A., Hirsch, D., Padley, M., and Shepherd, C (2020). *A Minimum Income Standard for the UK in 2020.* York: Joseph Rowntree Foundation.

Deakin, S., McLaughlin, C., and Chai, D. (2012). 'Gender inequality and reflexive law: the potential of different regulatory mechanisms', in L. Dickens (ed.), *Making Employment Rights Effective: Issues of Enforcement and Compliance.* Oxford and Portland Oregon: Hart Publishing, 115–138.

Delbridge, R. (1998). *Life on the Line in Contemporary Manufacturing.* Oxford: Oxford University Press.

Demougin, P., Gooberman, L., Hauptmeier, M., and Heery, E. (2021). 'Revisiting voluntarism: private voluntary regulation by employer forums in the United Kingdom', *Journal of Industrial Relations*, 63/5: 684–705.

Devine, B.F., Foley, N., and Ward, M. (2021). *Women and the Economy.* Briefing Paper CBP06838. London: House of Commons Library.

Dickens, L. (1994). 'The business case for women's equality: is the carrot better than the stick?', *Employee Relations*, 16/8: 5–18.

Dineen, B.R. and Allen, D.G. (2016). 'Third party employment branding: human capital inflows and outflows following Best Places to Work certifications', *Academy of Management Journal*, 59/1: 90–112.

Distelhorst, G., Hainmueller, J., and Locke, R.M. (2017). 'Does lean improve labor standards? Management and social performance in Nike's supply chain', *Management Science*, 63/3: 707–728.

Doellgast, V., Bidwell, M., and Colvin, A.J.S. (2021). 'New directions in employment relations theory: understanding fragmentation, identity, and legitimacy', *Industrial and Labor Relations Review*, 74/3: 555–579.

Doellgast, V., Wright, C.F., Cooke, F.L., and Bamber, G.J. (2021). 'Conclusions: Globalization, Crises, and Institutional Responses', in G.J. Bamber, F.L. Cooke, Doellgast, V., and Wright, C.F. (eds), *International and Comparative Employment Relations: Global Crises and Institutional Responses*, Seventh Edition, New York: Sage, 363–388.

Donaghey, J. and Reinecke, J. (2018). 'When industrial democracy meets corporate social responsibility—a comparison of the Bangladesh Accord and Alliance as responses to the Rana Plaza disaster', *British Journal of Industrial Relations*, 56/1: 14–42.

Donaghey, J., Reinecke, J., Niforou, C., and Lawson, B. (2014). 'From employment relations to consumption relations: balancing labor governance in global supply chains', *Human Resource Management*, 53/2: 229–252.

Dore, R. (1973). *British Factory, Japanese Factory: The Origins of National Diversity in Industrial Relations*. London: George Allen and Unwin Limited.

Dundon, T., Martinéz Lucio, M., Hughes, E., Howcroft, D., Keizer, A., and Walden, R. (2020). *Power, Politics and Influence at Work*. Manchester: Manchester University Press.

Elliot, K.A. and Freeman, R.B. (2005). 'White hats or Don Quixotes? Human rights vigilantes in the global economy', in R.B. Freeman, J. Hirsch, and L. Mishel (eds), *Emerging Labor Market Institutions in the Twenty-first Century*. Chicago and London: University of Chicago Press, 47–97.

Ewing, K., Hendy, J., and Jones, C. (eds) (2018). *Rolling Out the Manifesto for Labour Law*. Liverpool: Institute of Employment Rights.

Fair Work Commission (2019). *Fair Work Wales: Report of the Fair Work Commission*. Cardiff: Welsh Government.

Fair Work Convention (2019). *Fair Work in Scotland's Social Care Sector*. Glasgow: Fair Work Convention.

Fair Work Convention (2016). *Fair Work Framework*. Glasgow: Fair Work Convention.

Ferner, A. (1988). *Governments, Managers and Industrial Relations: Public Enterprises and their Political Environment*. Oxford and New York: Basil Blackwell.

Figart, D.M., Mutari, E., and Power, M. (2002). *Living Wages, Equal Wages: Gender and Labor Market Policies in the United States*. London and New York: Routledge.

Flanders, A. (1975). *Management and Unions: The Theory and Reform of Industrial Relations*. London: Faber and Faber.

Flanders, A. (1964). *The Fawley Productivity Agreements*. London: Faber and Faber.

Forth, J. and Rincon-Aznar, A. (2008). *Equal Opportunities, Employee Attitudes and Workplace Performance: Evidence from WERS 1998*. Employment Relations Research Series No. 38, London: Department of Business, Enterprise, and Regulatory Reform.

Foundational Economy Collective (2018). *Foundational Economy*. Manchester: Manchester University Press.

Freeman, R. (2005). 'Fighting for other folks' wages: the logic and illogic of Living Wage campaigns', *Industrial Relations*, 44/1: 14–31.

Frege, C., Heery, E., and Turner, L. (2004). 'The new solidarity? Trade union coalition-building in five countries', in C. Frege and J. Kelly (eds), *Varieties of Unionism: Strategies for Union Revitalization in a Globalizing Economy*. Oxford: Oxford University Press, 137–158.

Frenkel, S. and Kim, S. (2004). 'Corporate codes of practice and employment relations in sports shoe contractor factories in South Korea', *Asia-Pacific Journal of Human Resources*, 42/1: 6–31.

Fuller, S. and Prince Cooke, L. (2018). 'Workplace variation in fatherhood wage premiums: do formalization and performance pay matter?', *Work, Employment and Society*, 32/4: 768–788.

Gardiner, L. and Hussein, S. (2015). *As If We Cared: The Costs and Benefits of a Living Wage for Care Workers.* London: Resolution Foundation.

Gill-McLure, W. and Seifert, R. (2008). 'Degrading the labourer: the reform of local government manual work', *Capital and Class*, 94: 1–30.

Gooberman, L., Hauptmeier, M., and Heery, E. (2018). 'Contemporary employer interest representation in the United Kingdom', *Work, Employment and Society*, 32/1: 114–132.

Gooberman, L., Hauptmeier, M., and Heery, E. (2020). 'A typology of employers' organizations in the United Kingdom', *Economic and Industrial Democracy*, 41/1: 229–248.

Goodwin, M. J. and Heath, O. (2016). 'The 2016 Referendum, Brexit and the left behind: an aggregate-level analysis of the result', *The Political Quarterly*, 87/3: 324–332.

Green, F., Felstead, A., and Gallie, D. (2015). 'The inequality of job quality', in A. Felstead, D. Gallie, and F. Green (eds), *Unequal Britain at Work*, Oxford: Oxford University Press, 1–21.

Greene, A-M. (2001). *Voices from the Shopfloor: Dramas of the Employment Relationship.* Aldershot: Ashgate.

Gregory, A. and Milner, S. (2009). 'Trade unions and work-life balance: changing times in France and the UK?', *British Journal of Industrial Relations*, 47/1: 122–146.

Gregory-Smith, I. (2018). 'Positive action towards gender equality: evidence from the Athena SWAN charter in medical schools', *British Journal of Industrial Relations*, 56/3: 463–483.

Grimshaw, D., Cartwright, J., Keizer, A., and Rubery, J. (2019). 'Market exposure and the labour process: the contradictory dynamics in managing contracted services work', *Work, Employment and Society*, 33/1: 76–95.

Grimshaw, D., Lloyd, C., and Warhurst, C. (2008). 'Low-wage work in the United Kingdom: employment practices, institutional effects, and policy responses', in C. Lloyd, G. Mason, and K. Mayhew (eds), *Low-Wage Work in the United Kingdom.* New York: The Russell Sage Foundation, 284–326.

Guinan, J. and O'Neill, M. (2020). *The Case for Community Wealth Building.* Cambridge: Polity Press.

Gumbrell-McCormick, R. and Hyman, R. (2013). *Trade Unions in Western Europe: Hard Times, Hard Choices.* Oxford: Oxford University Press.

Hall, M. and Purcell, J. (2012). *Consultation at Work: Regulation and Practice.* Oxford: Oxford University Press.

Hampton, P. (2018). 'Trade unions and climate politics: prisoners of neoliberalism or swords of climate justice?, *Globalizations*, 15/4: 470–486.

Hartley, J., Kelly, J., and Nicholson, N. (1983). *Steel Strike: A Case Study in Industrial Relations.* London: Batsford.

Harvey, G., Hodder, A., and Brammer, S. (2017). 'Trade union participation in CSR deliberation: an evaluation', *Industrial Relations Journal*, 48/1: 42–44.

Hauptmeier, M. and Turner, L. (2007). 'Political insiders and social activists: coalition-building in New York and Los Angeles', in L. Turner and D.B. Cornfield (eds), *Labor in the New Urban Battlegrounds: Local Solidarity in a Global Economy.* Ithaca and London: ILR Press, 129–143.

Heckscher, C. and McCarthy, J. (2014). 'Transient solidarities: commitment and collective action in postindustrial societies', *British Journal of Industrial Relations*, 52/4: 627–657.

Heery, E. (2006). 'Equality bargaining: where, who, why?' *Gender, Work, and Organization*, 13/6: 522–542.

Heery, E. (2010). *Amnesty International and Trade Unions in Britain: Thirty Years of Solidarity for Human Rights*. London: Amnesty International UK.

Heery, E. (2011). 'Debating employment law: responses to juridification', in P. Blyton, E. Heery, and P. Turnbull (eds). *Reassessing the Employment Relationship*. Basingstoke: MacMillan, 71–96.

Heery, E. (2015). 'Unions and the organizing turn: reflections after 20 years of Organizing Works', *The Economic and Labour Relations Review*, 26/4: 545–560.

Heery, E. (2016). *Framing Work: Unitary, Pluralist, and Critical Perspectives in the Twenty-first Century*. Oxford: Oxford University Press.

Heery, E. (2019). 'Fusion or replacement? Labour and the new social movements', *Economic and Industrial Democracy*, 39/4: 661–680.

Heery, E., Abbott, B., and Williams, S. (2012). 'The involvement of civil society organizations in British industrial relations: extent, origins, significance', *British Journal of Industrial Relations*, 50/1: 47–72.

Heery, E., Gooberman, L. and Hauptmeier, M. (2017). 'The Petroleum Driver Passport Scheme: a case study in reregulation', *Industrial Relations Journal*, 48/3: 274–291.

Heery, E., Hann, D., and Nash, D. (2022). 'Outsourcing and the Real Living Wage: evidence from the United Kingdom', in T. Dobbins and P. Prowse (eds), *The Living Wage: Advancing a Global Movement*. London: Routledge, 39–51.

Heery, E., Hann, D., and Nash, D. (2020). 'Political devolution and employment relations in Great Britain: the case of the Living Wage', *Industrial Relations Journal*, 51/5: 391–409.

Heery, E., Hann, D., and Nash, D. (2018). 'Trade unions and the real Living Wage: survey evidence from the UK', *Industrial Relations Journal*, 49/4: 319–335.

Heery, E., Nash, D., and Hann, D. (2017). *The Living Wage: Employer Experience*. Cardiff: Cardiff Business School.

Heery, E., and Williams, S. (2020). 'The expression of worker voice through civil society organizations', in A. Wilkinson, J. Donaghey, T. Dundon, and R.B. Freeman (eds), *Handbook of Research on Employee Voice*. Second Edition. Cheltenham: Edward Elgar, 202–221.

Heery, E., Williams, S., and Abbott, B. (2012). 'Civil society organizations and trade unions: cooperation, conflict, indifference', *Work, Employment and Society*, 26/1: 145–160.

Herman, E., Rubery, J., and Hebson, G. (2021). 'A case of employers never letting a good crisis go to waste? An investigation of how work becomes even more precarious for hourly paid workers under COVID', *Industrial Relations Journal*, 52/5: 442–457.

Hill, S. (1981). *Competition and Control at Work*. London: Heinemann Educational Books.

Hilton, M., McKay, J., Crowson, N., and Mohout, J-F. (2013). *The Politics of Expertise: How NGOs Changed Modern Britain*. Oxford: Oxford University Press.

Hirsch, D. (2017). 'Contemporary UK wage floors and the calculation of a living wage', *Employee Relations*, 39/6: 815–824.

Hirsch, D. and Valadez-Martinez, L. (2017). *The Living Wage*. Newcastle: Agenda Publishing.

HM Government (2022). *Levelling Up the United Kingdom*. London: HM Government.

HM Treasury (2020). *Budget 2020*. London: HM Treasury.

Holgate, J. (2021). *Arise: Power, Strategy, and Union Resurgence*. London: Pluto Press.

Holgate, J. (2015a). 'An international study of trade union involvement in community organizing: same model, different outcomes', *British Journal of Industrial Relations*, 53/2: 460–483.

Holgate, J. (2015b). 'Community organizing in the UK: a "new" approach for trade unions?', *Economic and Industrial Democracy*, 36/3: 431–455.

Holgate, J. (2009). 'Contested terrain: London's living wage campaign and the tension between community and union organising', in J. McBride and I. Greenwood (eds), *The Complexity of Community Unionism: A Comparative Analysis of Concepts and Contexts.* Basingstoke: Palgrave, 49–74.

Holgate, J. and Wills, J. (2007). 'Organizing labor in London: lessons from the campaign for a Living Wage', in L. Turner and D.B. Cornfield (eds), *Labor in the New Urban Battlegrounds: Local Solidarity in a Global Economy.* Ithaca and London: ILR Press, 211–223.

Hoque, K. (2003). 'All in all it's just a plaque on the wall: the incidence and impact of the Investors in People Standard', *Journal of Management Studies*, 40/2: 543–571.

Hoque, K., Bacon, N., and Parr, D. (2014). 'Employer disability practice in Britain: assessing the impact of the Positive About Disabled People 'Two Ticks' symbol', *Work, Employment and Society*, 28/3: 430–451.

Howard, D. (2022). 'The Living Wage Foundation's 'Real Living Wage' campaign', in T. Dobbins and P. Prowse (eds), *The Living Wage: Advancing a Global Movement.* London: Routledge, 13–24.

Huberman, M. (1987). 'The economic origins of paternalism: Lancashire cotton spinning in the first half of the nineteenth century', *Social History*, 12/2: 177–192.

Hughes, C., Kenway, P., Kelly, P., and Barry-Born, T. (2016). *Enlightened Self-Interest? The Role of Private Sector Employers in Reducing Poverty.* Glasgow: The Poverty Alliance/New Policy Institute.

Hughes, E. and Dundon, T. (2018). 'Wage councils could address endemic pay inequality in the UK', *The Conversation*, https://theconversation.com/wage-councils-could-address-endemic-pay-inequality-in-the-uk-economy-102682.

Hull, A. (2019). *Becoming a Living Wage Employer: A Toolkit for Local Authorities.* London: Living Wage Foundation.

Hyman, R. (1972). *Disputes Procedure in Action.* London: Heinemann.

Hyman, R. (2008). 'The state in industrial relations', in P. Blyton, N. Bacon, J. Fiorito, and E. Heery (eds), *The Sage Handbook of Industrial Relations*, Los Angeles CA: Sage, 258–283.

Inclusive Growth Commission (2017). *Making Our Economy Work for Everyone.* London: Royal Society for the Encouragement of Arts, Manufactures, and Commerce.

Institute of Workplace and Facilities Management (2021). *The Living Wage: Why Pay It and What Does It Mean for Our Profession? London*: Institute of Workplace and Facilities Management.

Jackson, B. (2020). *The Case for Scottish Independence: A History of Nationalist Political Thought in Modern Scotland.* Cambridge: Cambridge University Press.

Jackson, G., Doellgast, V., and Baccaro, L. (2018). 'Corporate social responsibility and labour standards: bridging business management and employment relations perspectives', *British Journal of Industrial Relations*, 56/1: 3–13.

Jamoul, L. and Wills, J. (2008). 'Faith in politics', *Urban Studies*, 45/10: 2035–2056.

Jensen, N. and Wills, J. (2013). *The Prevalence and Impact of the Living Wage in the UK: A Survey of Organizations Accredited by the Living Wage Foundation.* London: Centre for Public Engagement, Queen Mary University of London.

Johnson, M. (2017). 'Implementing the Living Wage in UK local government', *Employee Relations*, 39/6: 840–849.

Johnson, M., Koukiadaki, A., and Grimshaw, D. (2019). 'The Living Wage in the UK: testing the limits of soft regulation?', *Transfer*, 25/3: 319–333.

Johnson, M., Rubery, J., and Egan, M. (2021). 'Raising the bar? The impact of the UNISON ethical care campaign in UK domiciliary care', *Transfer*, 27/3: 367–382.

Joint Ethical Trading Initiatives (2015). *Living Wages in Global Supply Chains: A New Agenda for Business*. Copenhagen, JETIs.

Joseph Rowntree Foundation. (2021). *UK Poverty 2020/21*. York: Joseph Rowntree Foundation.

Joseph Rowntree Foundation. (2020). *UK Poverty 2019/20*. York: Joseph Rowntree Foundation.

Joyce, P. (1980). *Work, Society, and Politics: The Culture of the Factory in Later Victorian England*. Brighton: Methuen.

Kelly, J. (2018). *Contemporary Trotskyism: Parties, Sects, and Social Movements in Britain*. London: Routledge.

Kinderman, D. (2012). 'Free us up so we can be responsible! The co-evolution of neoliberalism and corporate social responsibility in the United Kingdom, 1977–2010', *Socio-Economic Review*, 10: 29–57.

Kinderman, D. (2016). 'Time for a reality check: is business willing to support a smart mix of complementary regulation in private governance?', *Policy and Society*, 35/1: 29–42.

Kochan, T.A. and Osterman, P. (1994). *The Mutual Gains Enterprise: Forging a Winning Partnership among Labor, Management, and Government*. Boston MA.: Harvard Business School Press.

KPMG (2015). *The Living Wage: An Economic Impact Assessment*. London: KPMG.

Kuruvilla, S. (2021). *Private Regulation of Labor Standards in Global Supply Chains*. Ithaca and London: ILR Press.

Lamman, C. (2014). *The Economic Effects of Living Wage Laws*. Vancouver: The Fraser Institute.

Land, H. (1980). 'The family wage', *Feminist Review*, 6: 55–77.

Lane, T. and Roberts, K. (1971). *Strike at Pilkingtons*. London: Fontana

Lawler III, E.E. (1990). *Strategic Pay: Aligning Organizational Strategies and Pay Systems*. San Francisco and Oxford: Jossey Bass.

LeBaron, G., Edwards, R., Hunt, T., Sempéré, C., and Kyritsis, P. (2022). 'The ineffectiveness of CSR: understanding garment company commitments to living wages in global supply chains', *New Political Economy*, 27/1: 99–115.

Lee, E. (1994). 'The Declaration of Philadelphia: retrospect and prospect', *International Labour Review*, 133/4: 467–484.

Lee, N. (2018). 'Inclusive Growth in cities: a sympathetic critique', *Regional Studies*, 53/3: 424–434.

Legault, M.-J. and Bellemare, G. (2008). 'Theoretical issues with new actors and emergent models of labour regulation', *Relations Industrielles/Industrial Relations*, 63/4: 742–768.

Levi-Faur, D. (2009). 'Regulatory capitalism and the reassertion of the public interest', *Politics and Society*, 27/3: 181–191.

Levin-Waldman, O.M. (2005). *The Political Economy of the Living Wage: A Study of Four Cities*. London and New York: Routledge.

Littman, D., Donne, M., and Wakefield, B. (2010). *Unfinished Business: The Quest for a Living Wage*. London: Fair Pay Network.

Living Wage Foundation (2021a). *Lessons from Our Global Living Wage Network*. London: Living Wage Foundation.

Living Wage Foundation (2021b). *The Living Wage in Social Care: A Toolkit for Social Care Providers and Local Authorities Commissioning Care*. London: Living Wage Foundation.

Living Wage Foundation (2020). *Investing in the Living Wage: A Toolkit for Responsible Investors*. London: Living Wage Foundation.

Living Wage Foundation (2019a). *Living Hours: Providing Security of Hours alongside a Real Living Wage*. London: Living Wage Foundation

Living Wage Foundation (2019b). *Living Wage Places: A Toolkit on Tackling Low Pay by Celebrating Local Action*. London: Living Wage Foundation.

Living Wage Foundation (2018). *Life on Low Pay*. London: Living Wage Foundation.

Living Wage Foundation (2017a). *Low Pay in the Charity Sector*. London: Living Wage Foundation.

Living Wage Foundation (2017b). *The Sustainable Development Goals and the Living Wage*. London: Living Wage Foundation.

Living Wage Foundation (2015). *The Living Wage: Core Principles and Global Perspectives*. London: Living Wage Foundation/Association of Chartered Certified Accountants.

Locke, R.M. (2013). *The Promise and Limits of Private Power: Promoting Labor Standards in a Global Economy*. Cambridge: Cambridge University Press.

Locke, R.M., Qin, F., and Brause, A. (2007). 'Does monitoring improve labor standards? Lessons from Nike', *Industrial and Labor Relations Review*, 61/1: 3–31.

Locke, R.M., Rissing, B.A., and Pal, T. (2013). 'Complements or substitutes? Private codes, state regulation and the enforcement of labour standards in global supply chains', *British Journal of Industrial Relations*, 51/3: 519–552.

Lopes, A. and Hall, T. (2015). 'Organizing migrant workers: the living wage campaign at the University of East London', *Industrial Relations Journal*, 46/3: 208–221.

Low Pay Commission (2020). 'National Minimum Wage: Low Pay Commission Report 2020'. London: Low Pay Commission.

Luce, S. (2017). 'Living Wages—a US perspective', *Employee Relations*, 39/6: 863–874.

Luce, S. (2014). *Labor Movements: Global Perspectives*. Cambridge: Polity Press.

Lupton, R., Hughes, C., MacDougall, A., Goldwyn-Simpkins, H., and Hjelmskog, A. (2019). *Inclusive Growth in Greater Manchester: 2020 and Beyond*. Manchester: University of Manchester.

Lyall, S. (2015). *Fairness Commissions: Understanding How Local Authorities Can Have Impact on Poverty and Inequality*. London: New Economics Foundation.

Manning, A. (2014). 'Minimum wages: the economics and the politics', *Centrepiece*, 19/1: 8–10.

Marinetto, M. (1999). 'The historical development of business philanthropy: social responsibility in the new corporate economy', *Business History*, 41/4: 1–20.

Marmot, M., Allen, J., Boyce, T., Goldblatt, P., and Morrison, J. (2020). *Health Equity in England: The Marmot Review 10 Years On*. London: Institute of Health Equity.

Martinelli, L. (2017). *Assessing the Case for a Universal Basic Income in the UK*. Bath: Institute for Policy Research, University of Bath.

Mather, K. and Seifert, R. (2013). 'The close supervision of further education lecturers: "You have been weighed, measured, and found wanting"', *Work, Employment and Society*, 28/1: 95–111.

Mayer, B. (2009). *Blue-Green Coalitions: Fighting for Safe Workplaces and Healthy Communities*. Ithaca and London: ILR Press.

Mayer, C. (2018). *Prosperity: Better Business Makes the Greater Good*. Oxford: Oxford University Press.

McAlevey, J.F. (2016). *No Shortcuts: Organizing for Power*. New York NY: Oxford University Press.

McCarthy, J.D. and Zald, M.N. (1973). *The Trend of Social Movements in America: Professionalism and Resource Mobilization*. Morristown NJ: General Learning Press.

Meister, J.C. and Willayerd, K. (2010). *The 2020 Workplace: How Innovative Companies Attract, Develop, and Keep Tomorrow's Employees Today*. New York, NY: Harper Business.

Metcalf, D. (1999). 'The British National Minimum Wage', *British Journal of Industrial Relations*, 37/2: 171–201.

Metcalf, D. (2005). 'Trade unions: resurgence or perdition?', in S. Fernie and D. Metcalf (eds), *Trade Unions: Resurgence or Demise?*, London: Routledge, 83–117.

Metcalf, D., Hansen, K., and Charlwood, A. (2001). 'Unions and the sword of justice: unions and pay systems, pay inequality, pay discrimination, and low pay', *National Institute Economic Review*, 176: 61–75.

Milkman, R. (2013). 'Back to the future? US labour in the new gilded age', *British Journal of Industrial Relations*, 51/4: 645–665.

Milkman, R. (2020). *Immigrant Labour and the New Precariat*. Cambridge: Polity.

Milkman, R. and Ott, E. (eds) (2014). *New Labor in New York: Precarious Workers and the Future of the Labor Movement*. Ithaca and London: ILR Press.

Mooney, G. and Law, A. (eds) (2007). *New Labour/Hard Labour: Restructuring and Resistance inside the Welfare Industry*. Bristol: The Policy Press.

Moore, S., Onaran, O., Guschanski, A., Antunes, B., and Symon, G. (2019). 'The resilience of collective bargaining—a renewed logic for collective regulation?', *Employee Relations*, 41/2: 279–925.

Morgan, K. (2019). 'The future of place-based innovation policy (As if 'lagging regions' really mattered)', in M. Barzotto, C. Corradini, F.M. Fai, S. Labory, and P.R. Tomlinson (eds), *Revitalizing Lagging Regions: Smart Specialization and Industry 4.0*. London: Routledge, 79–90.

Morris, P. (2000). 'UNISON and low pay policy', in M. Terry (ed.), *Redefining Public Sector Unionism: UNISON and the Future of Trade Unions*. London: Routledge, 15–166.

Naik, Y, Abbs, I., Elwell-Sutton, T., Bibby, J., Spencelayh E., Shafique, A., Burbidge, I., Antink, B., Alanko, L., and Anttila, J. (2020). *Using Economic Development to Improve Health and Reduce Health Inequalities*. London: The Health Foundation.

Newell, P. (2008). 'Civil society, corporate accountability and the politics of climate change', *Global Environmental Politics*, 8/3: 122–153.

O'Rourke, D. (2006). 'Multi-stakeholder regulation: privatizing or socializing global labor standards?', *World Development*, 34: 889–918.

OECD (2018). *Opportunities for all: OECD framework for policy action on inclusive growth*. Paris: Organization for Economic Cooperation and Development.

ONS (2015). 'Estimates of employee jobs paid less than the living wage in London and other parts of the UK', *Office for National Statistics*, available at https://www.ons.gov.uk/employmentandlabourmarket/peopleinwork/earningsandworkinghours/articles/londonanalysis/2015-10-12.

Osterman, P. (2006). 'Community organizing and employee representation', *British Journal of Industrial Relations*, 44/4: 629–650.

Peró, D. (2019). 'Indie unions, organizing and labour renewal: learning from precarious migrant workers', *Work, Employment and Society*, 34/5: 900–918.

Piore, M. and Safford, S. (2006). 'Changing regimes of workplace governance, shifting axes of social mobilization and the challenge to industrial relations theory', *Industrial Relations*, 45/3: 299–325.

Pollert, A. (1981). *Girls, Wives, Factory Lives.* London and Basingstoke: The MacMillan Press.

Prowse, P. and Dobbins, T. (2022). 'The real living wage and 'the good employer' in UK football clubs', in T. Dobbins and P. Prowse (eds), *The Living Wage: Advancing a Global Movement.* London: Routledge, 25–38.

Prowse, P. and Fells, R. (2016a). 'The Living Wage in the UK—an analysis of the GMB campaign in local government', *Labour and Industry*, 26/1: 58–73.

Prowse, P. and Fells, R. (2016b). 'The Living Wage: policy and practice', *Industrial Relations Journal*, 47/2: 144–162.

Prowse, P., Lopes, A., and Fells, R. (2017). 'Community and union-led living wage campaigns', *Employee Relations*, 39/6: 825–839.

Rhodes, C. (2022). *Woke Capitalism: How Corporate Morality Is Sabotaging Democracy.* Bristol: Bristol University Press.

Richards, W. (2001). 'Evaluating equal opportunities initiatives: the case for a 'transformative' agenda', in M. Noon and E. Ogbonna (eds), *Equality, Diversity, and Disadvantage in Employment*, Basingstoke: Palgrave, 15–31.

Richardson, J. (2022). *The Living Hours Index.* London: Living Wage Foundation.

Richardson, J. (2021). *The Insecurity Complex: Low Paid Workers and the Growth of Insecure Work.* London: Living Wage Foundation.

Riley, R., Metcalf, H., and Forth, J. (2013). 'The business case for equal opportunities', *Industrial Relations Journal*, 44/3: 216–239.

Roche, B. and Geary, K. (2006). *Partnership at Work: The Quest for Radical Organizational Change.* London: Routledge.

Rocket Science (2017). *Feasibility and Features of a Living Wage Place Accreditation Scheme: Final Report.* Glasgow: The Poverty Alliance.

Rooks, D. (2004). 'Sticking it out or packing it in? Organizer retention in the new labor movement', in R. Milkman and K. Voss (eds), *Rebuilding Labor: Organizing and Organisers*, Ithaca NY: ILR Press, 195–224.

Rose, F. (2000). *Coalitions across the Class Divide: Lessons from the Labor, Peace and Environmental Movements.* Ithaca and London: ILR Books.

Rubery, J. (2014). 'From "women and recession" to "women and austerity"', in M. Karamessini and J. Rubery (eds), *Women and Austerity: The Economic Crisis and the Future of Gender Equality.* London and New York: Routledge, 17–36.

Samuel, P. and Bacon, N. (2015). 'Social partnership in devolved nations: Scotland and Wales', in S. Johnstone and P. Ackers (eds), *Finding a Voice at Work? New Perspectives on Employment Relations.* Oxford: Oxford University Press, 177–192.

Schuessler, E., Frenkel, S., and Wright, C. (2019). 'Governance of labor standards in Australian and German garment supply chains: the impact of Rana Plaza', *Industrial and Labor Relations Review*, 72/3: 552–579.

Scott, A. (1994). *Willing Slaves? British Workers under Human Resource Management.* Cambridge: Cambridge University Press.

Scottish Government (2021). *Fair Work First Guidance: Supporting the Implementation of Fair Work First in Scottish Workplaces.* Edinburgh: Scottish Government.

Scottish Government (2018a). *Best Practice Guidance on Addressing Fair Work Practices, Including the Living Wage, in Procurement.* Edinburgh: Scottish Government.

Scottish Government (2018b). *Fairer Scotland Action Plan: Progress Report.* Edinburgh: Scottish Government.

Scottish Government (2016a). *Guidance under the Procurement Reform (Scotland) Act 2014.* Edinburgh: Scottish Government.

Scottish Government (2016b). *Scotland's Labour Market Strategy*. Edinburgh: Scottish Government.

SCRIG (2018). *Inclusive Growth Outcomes Framework*. Edinburgh: Scotland's Centre for Regional Inclusive Growth.

Searle, R.H. and McWha-Hermann, L. (2021). 'Money's too tight (to mention): a review and psychological synthesis of living wage research', *European Journal of Work and Organizational Psychology*, 30/3: 428–443.

Shackleton, L. (2012). 'Living Wage likely to destroy jobs and increase poverty', *Institute of Economic Affairs Blog*, http://www.iea.org.uk/blog/living-wage-likely-to-destroy-jobs-and-increase-poverty

Shenker, J. (2019). *Now We Have Your Attention: The New Politics of the People*. London: The Bodley Head.

Shildrick, T., MacDonald, R., Webster, C., and Garthwaite, K. (2010). *The Low Pay, No Pay Cycle: Understanding Recurrent Poverty*. York: Joseph Rowntree Foundation.

Simms, M., Holgate, J. and Heery, E. (2013). *Union Voices: Tactics and Tensions in Union Organizing*. Ithaca NY: ILR Press.

Sisson, K. (2020). 'Making Britain the best place in the world to work: how to protect and enhance workers' rights after Brexit...and coronavirus', *Warwick Papers in Industrial Relations*, Number 111.

Smith, A. and McBride, J. (2021). '"Working to live, not living to work"': low-paid multiple work and work-life articulation', *Work, Employment and Society*, 35/2: 256–276.

Sobolewska, M. and Ford, R. (2020). *Brexitland*. Cambridge: Cambridge University Press.

Social Mobility Commission (2019). *The Adult Skills Gap: Is Falling Investment in UK Adults Stalling Social Mobility?* London: Social Mobility Commission.

Stewart, M.B. (1999). 'Low pay in Britain', in P. Gregg and J. Wadsworth (eds), *The State of Working Britain*, Manchester: Manchester University Press, 225–248.

Streeck, W. (2009). *Re-forming Capitalism: Institutional Change in the German Political Economy*. Oxford: Oxford University Press.

Sutherland, I. (2016). 'Inequalities in the distribution of training in Britain', *Economic and Industrial Democracy*, 37/3: 469–491.

Swarts, H. and Vasi, I.B. (2011). 'Which US cities adopt living wage ordinances? Predictors of adoption of a new labor tactic', *Urban Affairs Review*, 47/6: 743–774.

Tapia, M. (2013). 'Marching to different tunes: commitment and culture as mobilizing mechanisms of trade unions and community organizations', *British Journal of Industrial Relations*, 51/4: 666–688.

Tarrow, S. (1998). *Power in Movement: Social Movements and Contentious Politics*, Cambridge: Cambridge University Press.

Tattersall, A. (2018). 'How do we build power in coalition? Rethinking union-community coalition types 12 years on', *Labour and Industry*, 28/1: 68–81.

Taylor, M., Marsh, G., Nichol, D., and Broadbrent, P. (2017). *Good Work: The Taylor Review of Modern Working Practices*. London: Department of Business, Energy, and Industrial Strategy.

Tomlinson, D. (2018). *Irregular Payments: Assessing the Breadth and Depth of Month to Month Earnings Volatility*, London: The Resolution Foundation.

Toynbee, P. (2003). *Hard Work: Life in Low-Pay Britain*. London: Bloomsbury.

Tsogas, G. (2001). *Labor Regulation in a Global Economy*. Armonk NY and London: M.E Sharpe.

UNISON (2013). *UNISON's Ethical Care Charter*. London: UNISON.

Vogel, D. (2010a). 'Taming globalization? Civil regulation and corporate capitalism', in D. Coen, W. Grant, and G. Wilson (eds), *The Oxford Handbook of Business and Government*. Oxford: Oxford University Press, 472–494.

Vogel, D. (2010b). 'The private regulation of global corporate conduct: achievements and limitations', *Business and Society*, 49/1: 68–87.

Voss, K., and Sherman, R. (2000). 'Breaking the iron-law of oligarchy: union revitalization in the American labor movement', *American Journal of Sociology*, 106: 303–349.

Waddington, J. (2003). 'Trade union organization', in P. Edwards (ed.), *Industrial Relations: Theory and Practice*. Oxford: Blackwell Publishing, 214–256.

Walls, D. (2015). *Community Organizing*. Cambridge: Polity Press.

Welsh Government (2021). *Programme for Government*. Cardiff: Welsh Government.

Welsh Government (2019). *A More Equal Wales: Strengthening Social Partnership*. Cardiff: Welsh Government.

Welsh Government (2017a). *Code of Practice: Ethical Employment in Supply Chains*. Cardiff: Welsh Government.

Welsh Government (2017b). *Code of Practice: Guide to Implementing the Living Wage through Procurement*. Cardiff: Welsh Government.

Werner, A. (2016). 'The ethics of the living wage: a review and a research agenda', *Journal of Business Ethics*, 137/3: 433–447.

Werner, A. (2021a). *Living Wage Implementation in Adult Social Care: Challenges, Solutions, and Benefits*. London: Middlesex University.

Werner, A. (2021b). 'Why do managers of small and medium-sized businesses seek voluntary Living Wage accreditation? An exploration of choice rationales', *European Journal of Work and Organizational Psychology*, 30/6: 778–789.

Werner, A. (2022). 'Making the living wage work in SMEs: evidence from accredited employers in the UK hospitality sector', in T. Dobbins and P. Prowse (eds), *The Living Wage: Advancing a Global Movement*. London: Routledge, 79–90.

Werner, A. and Lim, M. (2016). *Putting the Living Wage to Work: Strategies and Practices in Small and Medium Sized Enterprises*. London: The Barrow Cadbury Trust.

Werner, A. and Lim, M. (2017). 'A new living contract: cases in the implementation of the Living Wage by British SME retailers', *Employee Relations*, 39/6: 850–862.

Williams, M., Zhou, Y., and Zou, M. (2020). *Mapping Good Work: The Quality of Working Life Across the Occupational Structure*. Bristol: Bristol University Press.

Williams, S. (2020). *Introducing Employment Relations: A Critical Approach*. Fifth edition. Oxford: Oxford University Press.

Williams, S., Heery, E. and Abbott, B. (2011). 'The emerging regime of civil regulation in work and employment relations', *Human Relations*, 64/7: 951–970.

Wills, J. (2009). 'Subcontracted employment and its challenge to labor', *Labor Studies Journal*, 34/4: 441–460.

Wills, J. (2012). 'The geography of community and political organization in London today', *Political Geography*, 31: 114–126.

Wills, J. (2016). *Locating Localism: Statecraft, Citizenship, and Democracy*. Bristol: Policy Press.

Wills, J., Datta, K., Evans, Y., Herbert, J., May, J., and McIlwaine, C. (2009). 'Religion at work: the role of faith-based organizations in the London living wage campaign', *Cambridge Journal of Regions, Economy and Society*, 2/3: 443–461.

Wills, J., Kakpo, N., and Begum, R., (2009). *The Business Case for the Living Wage: The Story of the Cleaning Service at Queen Mary, University of London*. London: Queen Mary, University of London.

Wills, J. and Linneker, B. (2013). 'In-work poverty and the living wage in the United Kingdom: a geographical perspective', *Transactions of the Institute of British Geographers*, 39: 182–194.

Wills, J. and Linneker, B. (2012). *The Costs and Benefits of the London Living Wage*. London: Trust for London.

Winchester, D. and Bach, S. (1995). 'The state: the public sector', in P. Edwards (ed.), *Industrial Relations: Theory and Practice in Britain*. Oxford, Blackwell, 304–344.

Wright, C.F. and Brown, W. (2013). 'The effectiveness of socially sustainable sourcing mechanisms: assessing the prospects of a new form of joint regulation', *Industrial Relations Journal*, 44/1: 20–37.

Wright, C.F. and Kaine, S. (2015). 'Supply chains, production networks and the employment relationship', *Journal of Industrial Relations*, 44/1: 30–37.

Wright, C.F., Wood, A.J., Trevor, J., McLaughlin, C., Huang, W., Harney, B., Geelan, T., Colfer, B., Cheng, C., and Brown, W. (2019). 'Towards a new web of rules: an international review of institutional experimentation to strengthen employment protection', *Employee Relations*, 41/2: 313–330.

Zielonka, J. (2018). *Counter-Revolution: Liberal Europe in Retreat*. Oxford: Oxford University Press.

Zimmer, R. (2019). 'Living wage in international and European law', *Transfer*, 25/3: 285–299.

Index

For the benefit of digital users, indexed terms that span two pages (e.g., 52–53) may, on occasion, appear on only one of those pages.

Note: The following abbreviations are used - 't' after a page reference denotes a table, 'f' denotes figures and 'n' denotes a footnote.

Q

R

T